Y0-BWV-281

MAY 0 9 1988

DATE DUE

FOR LIBRARY USE ONLY

BRC A. C. BILBREW 323

R016.2096 Ofori, P. E.
            Christianity in
         tropical Africa. 1977.

REF
AAC   LACo   1
        L 323

A C Bilbrew Library
150 East El Segundo Blvd.
Los Angeles, Ca. 90061

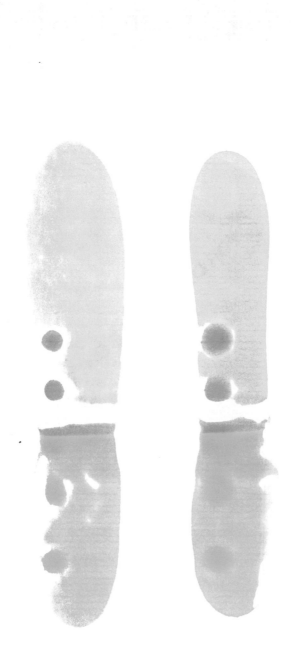

CHRISTIANITY IN TROPICAL AFRICA

K 142
20

CHRISTIANITY IN TROPICAL AFRICA

K 142
20

CHRISTIANITY IN TROPICAL AFRICA
A selective annotated bibliography

Patrick E. Ofori
University of Cape Coast

1977
KTO PRESS
Nendeln

LACo 1
L 323

© COPYRIGHT PATRICK E. OFORI, 1977

ISBN 3-262-00002-7

Printed in the Netherlands

TO MY PARENTS
AKUA BADU AND KWADWO NSIA

CONTENTS

ACKNOWLEDGEMENTS

Many people and institutions contributed in various ways to make the completion of this volume a reality. These are too numerous to mention by name individually, however, I cannot fail to mention a few names. My travels and researches on this work were generously supported by grants from the Research and Conferences Committee of the University of Cape Coast and the Board of Trustees of the Authorship Development Fund. I am grateful to these institutions for their support.

My personal indebtedness goes to the following persons: Mr. David Bentil of the Science Library, University of Cape Coast, for reading through parts of the manuscript and pointing out numerous errors; Dr. S.Y. Boadi Siaw and Dr. S.H. Afrifah of the Department of History, University of Cape Coast, for their invaluable suggestions and advice on the history of the Christian religion in Africa; Mr. E. K. Koranteng, University Librarian, University of Cape Coast, and my wife, Nana Amma for their encouragement.

Finally, my thanks go to Mr. E.O. Kissi of the University Library for typing this manuscript.

P.E.O.

University Library,
Cape Coast.

July, 1976.

INTRODUCTION

This bibliography is the second in the series of subject
bibliographies intended by the compiler to cover various aspects of
religion in Africa, south of the Sahara. The first volume in the
series is entitled Black African traditional religions and philosophy.
The present volume is designed to embrace the available literature
relating to the Christian religion in tropical Africa. It will be
followed by a third volume which will be devoted to the literature
of the Islamic religion in Africa.

Essentially, Christianity is an alien religion to the African.
Notwithstanding the fact that the Christian religion has been in
existence on the African continent for more than five centuries now,
it is yet to be accepted as an authentic African religion.

Africa north of the Sahara fell under the influence of Christianity at a very early date, and christianity spread into the kingdom
of Axum (Ethiopia) by the year 333 A.D. However, following the Arab
conquest of the Maghreb in the 7th century, Islam practically wiped
out the early traces of Christianity in northern Africa and extended
its influence to the western Sudan as a result of the Almoravid
conquest in the eleventh century. Thus, even though Christianity
had existed in the northern sector of Africa from as early as the
third century, it was not until the 15th century, when under the
leadership of Prince Henry the Navigator, the Portuguese set out to
discover Africa, that the Christian religion began to be planted in
tropical Africa.

As early as in 1489, the King of the Congo (Manikongo) sent an
ambassador to Lisbon. In response to this mission, Portuguese missionaries and artisans arrived in the Congo in 1490. The Manikongo
was baptised in 1491, and this was followed by progressive Christianization of some African peoples along the coastline of Africa.
Even though the coastline of Africa was fairly well known by the end

of the 15th century, it was not until the 19th century that the
explorers and missionaries ventured into the interior of Africa.

By 1795 Mungo Park, the West African explorer, had followed the
course of the Gambia River as far as the Niger. Timbuktu (Mali) was
discovered by Rene Caillie in 1828, and Barth, a German geographer
and scientist, travelled through the Western Sudan from Cameroon to
Mali between 1850 and 1856. David Livingstone of the London Missionary
Society explored the Zambezi basin and founded a mission station on
the banks of Lake Nyansa between 1854 and 1864. By 1877, Africa's
four great rivers, the Niger, the Zambezi, the Nile and the Congo had
been put on the map.

Following the successful exploratory voyages of the early explorers and missionaries, European governments began to show economic
and political interests in Africa. At this juncture, the main aim of
the explorers and missionaries was to secure for their country the
right to occupy the newly discovered lands in Africa. By the middle
of the nineteenth century, missionary stations had been opened all
along the West African coast from Guinea to Angola and up the east
coast from Mozambique to Mombasa.

Ram Desai[1] has pointed out that in the process of evengelizing
the African the Cross always preceeded the flag. Western observers
would have us believe that the early missionaries were inspired by
purely humanitarian motives in their evangelization crusade. However,
there is no doubt at all that their inspiration emanated from economic
interest for themselves and their various countries. For example, the
London Missionary Society, under whose auspices many of the missionaries came to Africa, was generously supported by government and
business circles in England. The Christian Church supported, to some
extent, the inhuman traffic in slaves, finding their justification for
so doing from St. Paul's ruling that "Slaves must obey their masters".

---

[1] Ram Desai. Christianity in Africa as seen by Africans. Denver, 1962.

(Ephesians, 6: 5-7).

In 1819, Dr. Philip, superintendent of the London Missionary Society, is known to have made the following statement after a visit to South Africa:

> Missionary stations are the most efficient
> agents which can be employed to promote the
> internal strength of our colonies, and the
> cheapest and best military posts a govern-
> ment can employ[2]

The motive of the early missionaries therefore was not solely to proselytise the African. In their over-enthusiasm to carry on with their 'civilizing mission' to Africa, the early missionaries arrived with preconceived ideas, despising the African and his way of life. They erroneously assumed that Africans were without any acceptable religion, education or culture, and that the continent provided a fertile ground where they could sow the seeds of western Christian culture.

The reaction of many educated Africans to the Christian presence in Africa can best be summed up in the words of Mosipho Makeje, a native South African:

> The missionary came here and said 'Let us pray;
> and we closed our eyes, and when we responded
> 'Amen' at the end of the prayer, we found the
> Bible in our hands, but lo and behold, our land
> had gone into the hands of the missionaries.[3]

From these two quotations above, it would not be too far-fetched to infer that Christianity in Africa has been associated with the domination and the exploitation of the African.

---

[2] J. Philip, Researches in South Africa. London, 1828. v. 22. p. 227.

[3] Op. cit. p.7.

Despite its foreign origin and practices, however, and the contempt of some of its missionaries for African traditions and cultures, Christianity has nevertheless made an impact on the African continent. Though Christianity in Africa is associated with the white-man and his way of life, statistically its impact on the African continent seems impressive. Out of a total population of 280 million, there are 68 million Christians, that is, nearly 25% of the population subscribe to it. Taking into account the fact that the majority of the 83 million who are muslims live north of the Sahara, the proportion of Christians living South of the Sahara must be higher than 25%[4].

The Christian impact of Africa has been quite substantial. The Christian missionaries reduced many of the African languages into writing and translated the Bible into a large number of African languages. Christian missionaries had an almost complete monopoly over education throughout sub-Saharan Africa. Most of the contemporary African leaders and professionals were trained in mission schools. Another area where missionaries have made positive contribution in Africa is in the introduction of modern medical science. The training in nutrition, sanitation and hygiene has helped to reduce the incidence of diseases and the mortality rate, thereby helping to raise the life expectancy of the population. The nationalist agitation in many African countries which culminated in total independence for Black Africa was partly the result of the awakening of the educational and political consciousness of the African in the mission schools.

In spite of these impressive contributions however, Christianity cannot be said to have made any profound impact on the African. Most African Christians live in two worlds. They are members of a western Christian Church and its civilization, but at the same time, they are deeply embedded in their own traditional religious beliefs and customs. The coexistence of two kinds of religion and the dilemma in which many Africans find themselves have led to the rapid growth of spiritual

---

[4]E.G. Parrinder, Religion in Africa, New York, Praeger, 1969. p.167.

churches which try to blend Christian forms of worship with aspects of African tradition.

Perhaps these separatist or independent church movements remain the only hope that one day there will be an authentic African Christianity. These syncretic churches have tried to indigenise the Christian religion by bringing in traditional elements like drumming, dancing, healing and, to some extent, divination. Whereas many Africans profess the Christian faith in theory and in practice, the actual impact of the religion on most of the adherents has been superficial. This is because the Christian religion has failed to convert the cultural substratum of traditional African society. Its main contribution to Africa has been in the area of progress and modernization of the continent. Christianity is yet to reach the heart and the soul of the African.[5]

One may perhaps understand the mistakes and failures of the agents of mission Christianity in Africa. The early missionaries were mainly foreigners who regarded African traditions and customs as pagan and primitive. It is therefore hoped that now that Africans themselves are at the helm of affairs, some of the past mistakes can be corrected in an attempt to reach the heart and the soul of the African people. In order to achieve this goal, it is necessary to introduce certain indigenous practices which can reflect the African way of life. One way of realising this objective is that African Christian leaders must shake off their colonial past and try to introduce elements of African culture into the Christian religion in an effort to establish an authentic African Christianity.[6]

To achieve this noble objective, it is essential that research be conducted into the history, doctrine, practices and the lives of the

---

[5]P.G. Neefjees, "The impact of Christianity in Ghana". Ghana Bulletin of Theology, v.4, No.7. 1974. p.45.

[6]Ibid.

early Christian missions and missionaries in Africa. Sociological research must be conducted into various African societies to enable the necessary adaptations to be introduced so that Christianity will no longer be regarded as foreign to the African. Research, however, cannot be easily undertaken without the relevant bibliographic guides.

It is for this reason that this modest bibliography has been compiled in an attempt to provide a basic guide to the literature of the Christian religion in Africa. Much of the relevant literature on the subject has already been documented in some of the general bibliographies listed in items nos. 1 - 42 of this bibliography. Many of the relevant bibliographic sources are scattered in various journals which are not easy to trace and therefore likely to elude even the serious research worker. R.C. Mitchell and H.W. Turner's A comprehensive bibliography of modern African religious movements (no.32) provides the widest selection on the subject. It is, however, limited in scope to only the literature of syncretic religious movements and cults of Africa. The present bibliography is an attempt to amalgamate materials from the numerous scattered sources from 1841-1974, so as to bring into a single volume a comprehensive selection of materials relevant to the study of Christianity in Africa.

The material in this volume, though highly selective, is comprehensive in the sense that unlike the previous volume, it is not limited to English language sources. Books and other documents of German, French, Finnish, Italian, Portuguese, Afrikaans and Spanish origin have been included, and where appropriate the relevant English translation supplied. Materials listed in this bibliography include books, periodical articles, pamphlets, theses and unpublished mimeographed monographs. Microfilm materials, however, have been excluded. Annotations have only been provided where copies of the relevant materials had been examined personally by the compiler. In a few instances the annotated information was extracted from review articles and abstracts.

This bibliography has been arranged under broad regional divisions of Western, Central, Eastern and Southern Africa. Each broad regional division is subdivided by an alphabetical listing of the countries forming each region. Under each country dubdivision, the names of the authors and titles of books and articles, in case of anonymous works, have been arranged in one alphabetical sequence.

Titles of published works have been underlined, theses and other unpublished monographs are in quotation marks. Periodical articles are put in quotation marks with the title of the journal underlined. The bibliographical details provided in the entries include authors' names, titles of books or articles, edition statement, place of publication, publisher's name, date of publication, series, illustrative material and the inclusion of bibliographical references. The items have been numbered consecutively with an author index. Each index entry refers to the item number.

Ghanaian sources alone have been used in compiling this volume, hence the greater proportion of the materials listed in this volume relate to West African Countries. As research for this work was undertaken mainly in Ghanaian libraries and archives, it is likely that many omissions and errors exist in this bibliography. It is hoped that librarians, bibliographers and scholars who use this work will draw the compiler's attention to any omissions and errors.

P.E. OFORI
1976.

Library,
University of Cape Coast,
Ghana.

REFERENCE AND BIBLIOGRAPHIC WORKS

1. AGUOLU, C.C. Ghana in the humanities and social sciences, 1900-
   1971; a bibliography. Metuchen, Scarecrow, 1973. xi, 469p.
   The most up to date bibliography on Ghana devoted exclusively
   to the humanities and social sciences. It supersedes the
   works of A.W. Cardinall and A.F. Johnson. Materials relating
   to Christianity can be traced under the heading 'Religion and
   Philosophy' in pages 370-388. Contains 4309 entries on various topics.

2. AGUOLU, C.C. Nigeria: a comprehensive bibliography in the humanities and social sciences. Boston, G.K. Hall, 1973. iv,620p.
   A companion volume to the above, containing over six thousand
   entries.

3. AJAYI, William Olaseinde. Checklist of C.M.S. missionaries in the
   Yoruba mission, 1845-1880. Nsukka. Department of Religion,
   University of Nigeria, 1965. (Materials for the study of
   Nigerian Church History, No.2) (Mimeograph).

4. AMEDEKEY, E.Y. The culture of Ghana: a bibliography. Accra,
   Ghana Universities Press, 1970. 215p.
   A comprehensive bibliography on the culture of Ghana. This
   work contains 1670 entries, arranged under the following
   headings: general culture, Social Institutions, Government
   and law, Traditional religion and ceremonial, impact of
   religions, music, language and literature, biographies. Its
   aim is to be a guide to the interpretation of responses in
   thought and feeling to changes in Ghanaian Society.

5. ATLAS, Hierarchicus. A geographical and statistical atlas of the
   (Roman) Catholic Church throughout the world. Compiled with
   the sanction of the Holy Apostolic See, by C. Streit, S.V.D.
   Atlas. London, Herder, 1914.

8

6. BEACH, Harlan Page. A geography and atlas of Protestant missions;
    methods, problems, results and prospects at the opening of the
    twentieth century. New York, Student Volunteer Movement for
    Foreign Missions, 1901-06. 2 vols.

7. BEACH, Harlan Page and FAHS, Charles H. ,eds. World missionary
    atlas, containing a directory of missionary societies,
    classified summaries of statistics, maps showing the location
    of mission stations throughout the world, a descriptive acco-
    unt of the principal mission lands, and comprehensive indices.
    New York, Institute of Social and Religious Research, 1925.
    251p.

8. BROWNLEE; M. The lives and work of South African missionaries:
    a bibliography. Cape Town, School of Librarianship, Univer-
    sity of Cape Town, 1952. vi, 33p.

9. CARTE partielle des missions de l'Afrique equatoriale, dressée
    par   Le R.P.F. Charmetant. missionnaire apostoloque d'Alger,
    1879. Lyon, Missions Catholiques, 1879.

10. CARTES des missions Catholiques du sud africain. (Ste. Helene.
    Supplement au journal Les missions catholiques, 1902: 1722)
    Paris. 1902.

11. CASE, S.J. and others. A bibliographical guide to the history of
    Christianity. Chicago, University of Chicago. 1931, xi,
    265p. (Publications in religious education. Handbook of
    ethics and religion).

12. CHICAGO. Center for Research Libraries. Church Missionary Soc-
    iety archives relating to Africa and Palestine, 1799-1923;
    index to records on microfilm at the Centre for Research

Libraries. Chicago, 1968.

13. COLLINS,R. and DUIGNAN, P. Americans in Africa: a preliminary guide to American missionary archives and library manuscript collections on Africa. The Hague, 1965. 96p.

14. DARGITZ, Robert E. A selected bibliography of books and articles in the disciplines of Christ Research Library in Mbandaka, Democratic Republic of the Congo and the Department of Africa and Jamaica of the United Missionary Society in Indianapolis, Indiana. Indianapolis, United Christian Missionary Society, 1968. 431p.

15. DUIGNAN, Peter and others. Africa south of the Sahara: a bibliography for undergraduate libraries. Williamsport, Pa; Bro-Dart Publishing Co., 1971. (Foreign Area Materials Center. University of the State of New York, occasional publications series, no. 12).

16. ECA, Filipe Grastao de Mbura. Subsidios para uma bibliografia missionaria mocambicana (Catolica). Prefacio do padre Moreira das Neves. Lisboa, Depositaria Petrony. 1969. 157p.

17. EPELLE, E.M.T. "The collection of Church historical materials in south-eastern Nigeria". Bulletin of the Society of African Church History. v.2, No.3, 1967: p276-280. Description of manuscript materials relating to local church history collected from the Niger Delta area between March 1965 and February 1966 which are deposited in the University of Nigeria, Nsukka.

18. FROST, Pamela J. A bibliography of missions and missionaries in Natal. Cape Town, University, 1969. vi 29p. (School of Librarianship. Bibliographical series. 74a).

19. HAIR, P.E.H. "Material on religion in Sierra Leone before 1780." Sierra Leone Studies. New series, No. 21. July 1967: p80-86.
A study of published and unpublished records of Christian missions in Sierra Leone which throw light on five centuries of traditional, Islamic and Christian religions in the area.

20. HAIR, P.E.H. "Guides to the records of early West African missions." Journal of Religion in Africa. v.1. 1968: p129-137.
A guide to the manuscript materials preserved in Western Europe which relate to the history of West Africa, especially useful to the African Church historian.

21. HENIGE, D.P. "White fathers materials in the London area: African Research and Documentation. (Birmingham), v.2., 1973, p18-20.

22. HEYSE, T. Associations religieuses au Congo Belge et au Ruanda - Urundi: legislation generale - cessions et concessions, bibliographie. Bruxelles, Institut Royal Colonial Belge, 1948. 157p.

23. INTERNATIONAL AFRICAN INSTITUTE. Select annotated bibliography of Tropical Africa. Compiled under the direction of Daryll Forde. New York, Kraus Reprint, 1969. (Twentieth Century Fund. Survey of Tropical Africa).
"The aim of this bibliography is to provide reliable sources of information on all the more important aspects of African studies... Designed to meet the needs of the general enquirer, it does not attempt to provide in itself an exhaustive guide

for speclialists."

24. JOHNSON, A.F. A bibliography of Ghana 1930-1961. London,
    Published for the Ghana Library Board by Longmans, 1964.
    210p.
    A comprehensive bibliography which lists 2,608 items on
    various topics relating to Ghana within the period covered.
    The sections on 'Education', 'Missions and Churches',
    pages 25-39, include literature on the Christian religion
    in Ghana. It is a sequel to A.W. Cardinal's Bibliography
    of the Gold Coast. Accra. Govt. Printer, 1931.

25. KAFE, Joseph Kofi. Ghana: an annotated bibliography of academic
    theses, 1920-1970 in the Commonwealth, the Republic of
    Ireland and the United States of America. Boston, Mass;
    G.K. Hall, 1973. 219p.

26. KAMPALA. Uganda. Makerere University College. Dept. of Reli-
    gious Studies.
    Bibliography of African Church history. Intended for use in
    connection with the University of East Africa Diploma in
    theology. Kampala, 1967. 25p.

27. LEOPARD, Donald D. "African-related materials in European
    missionary archives". African Studies Bulletin, v.10, No.2,
    September 1967: p1-5.
    The intention of this brief article is to indicate the
    location, facilities and the holdings of the archives of four
    Missionary Societies in Europe: The London Missionary Society,
    The United Society for the Propagation of the Gospel, Friends
    Foreign Missionary Society and La Société des Missions
    Evangéliques.

28. HAIR, Paul Edward Hedley. "Christianity in medieval Nubia and the Sudan: a bibliographical note". Bulletin of the Society for African Church History. v.1. No. 3/4, 1964: p67-73.

29. MASSON, J. Bibliographie missionnaire moderne, choix classe de 1400 titres et notes d'histoire. Paris Casterman, 1945. 184p.

30. McINTOSH, Brian G. "Archival resources of the University College, Nairobi, relating to missionary work and independent churches in Kenya". Bulletin of the Society for African Church History, v.2, No.4, 1968: p350-351.
    A record of oral testimony and documents on some independent churches available in the Department of History.

31. MEINARDUS, Otto F.A. "Ecclesiastica Aethiopia in Aegypto". Journal of Ethiopian Studies, v.3, No.1, January 1965: p23-35.
    A study based on Ethiopian Church archival materials in various museums and churches in Egypt.

32. MITCHELL, Robert Cameron and TURNER, H.W. A comprehensive bibliography of modern African religious movements. Evanston, Northwestern University Press, 1966. 132p. Contains 1313 items dealing with the literature of non-Islamic modern African religious movements, i.e. the syncretic and independent church movements in Africa. Attempts to include every available reference in any language that has been published and achieved more than local circulation.

33. NASRI, Abdel Rahman El   A bibliography of the Sudan, 1938-1958.
    London, Published on behalf of the University of Khartoum
    by the Oxford University Press, 1962. 171p.
    A comprehensive bibliography containing 2763 entries on
    various aspects of life in the Sudan. The section on
    religions is divided into Islam and Christianity with only
    12 entries on Islamic and 26 entries on the Christian
    religion. No annotations are provided.

34. TASIE, Godwin O.M. "Instrumenta studiorum at the Scottish
    Institute of Missionary Studies relating to Ibo studies."
    West African Religion, v.15, 1974. p32-35.

35. TASIE, Godwin O.M. A register of registers: church historical
    documents at Crowther Building. Nsukka, Dept. of Religion,
    University of Nigeria, 1966: 14p. (mimeo).
    A guide to the collection of books and other records of
    Eastern Nigerian churches held by the Dept. of Religion,
    University of Nsukka.

36. TURNER, H.W. ed. "Bibliography of modern African religious
    movements, supplements." Journal of Religions in Africa,
    v.1, No.3, 1968: p173-211. v.3, 1970: p161-208.
    Supplements to a Comprehensive bibliography of modern
    African religious movements, byR.C. Mitchell and H.W.Turner.

37. WALLS, Andrew Finlay ed. "Bibliography of the Society for
    African church history". Journal of Religion in Africa,
    v.1, No.1, 1967: p46-94.
    Contains 425 items devoted exclusively to the history of the
    Church in Africa. Arrangement is alphabetical by the name

14

of the countries. Very useful source for the study of
African Church history.

38. WATSON, Charles R. The sorrow and hope of the Egyptian Sudan:
     a survey of missionary conditions and methods of work in
     the Egyptian Sudan. Philadelphia, Board of Foreign
     Missions of the United Presbyterian Church of North America.
     1913.

39. WEBSTER, John B   and MOHOME, P. A bibliography on Swaziland.
     Syracuse, New York. Programme of Eastern African Studies.
     Syracuse University, 1968. 32p.

40. WEBSTER, James Bertin. "Source material for the study of the
     African Churches". Bulletin for theSociety of African
     Church History, v.1. No.2, 1963: p41-49.
     A short bibliographical essay.

41. WILLIAMS, Ethel L   and BROWN, Clifton. Afro-American biblio-
     graphy with locations in American libraries. Metuchen, N.J.
     Scarecrow Press, 1972.

42. WORK, Monroe N. "A bibliography of the Negro in Africa and
     America." New York, Octagon Books, 1965. 698p.
     A comprehensive and monumental work on the negro (the black
     race) relating to all phases of life, the conditions
     affecting his life and his anthropological and historical
     background. Chapter xv contains materials on Christian
     missions in Africa up to 1928.

GENERAL WORKS

43. AKINYELE, Isaac Babalola. "The place of divine healing in the church. Ibadan, Government Printer, 1962. 7p.

44. ALLEGRET, Elie. "The missionary question in the French colonies". International Review of Missions, April, 1923: p161-181.

45. ALLIER, Raoul. Psychologie de la conversion chez les peuples non-civilisés. Paris, Payot, 1925.

46. AMISSAH, Monseigneur. "Religion catholique et cultures indigenes: influences et interactions". In Colloque sur les religions, Abidjan, 5-12 Avril 1961. Paris, Presence Africaine, 1962: p199-208.

47. ANSON, Peter. Bishops at large. London. Faber, 1964. 503p. illus.

48. AUSTIN, M. "Good news deserves a telling". African Ecclesiastical Review, v.11. No.1, January 1969: p66-72.

49. BASTIDE, R. "Religious adaptations in changing societies" les metamorphoses du sacre dans les societes en transition". Civilizations, v.9, No.4, 1959: p432-441.

50. BATES, Miner S. and PAUCK, Wilhelm. The prospects of Christianity throughout the world. New York, Scribner, 1964. 286p. A series of essays dedicated to Henry Pitney Van Dusen.

51. BEAVER, Robert Pierce. Envoys of peace; the peace witness in the Christian world mission. Grand Rapids, Michigan, Eerdmans, 1964. 133p.

16

Concerned with the present reaction against Christian missionary work by the emerging peoples of Africa, Asia and Latin America.

52. BEAVER, Robert Pierce. "Nationalism and missions." Church History, v.21, 1957: p22-42.

53. BEAVER, Robert Pierce. "Recent literature on overseas missionary movements." Journal of World History. v.1. 1953: p316-325.

54. BERTSCHE, James. "What are independent churches saying to traditional Christianity?" In. Messages and Reports of the African Mennonite Fellowship, Bulawayo. 1965. p26-30.

55. BEYERHAUS, Peter. "What is our answer to sects?" Ministry, v.1, No.4, July 1961: p4-13.
A theological evaluation of independent church movements in Africa.

56. BEYERHAUS, Peter and LEFEVER, Henry. The responsible church and the foreign mission. London, World Dominion Press, 1964. 199p. bibliog.
Revised and condensed version of Die Selbstandigkeit der jungen kirchen als missionarisches Problem.

57. BOUQUET, A.C. The Christian faith and non-Christian religions. London, 1958.

58. BIRNIE, Ian H. The church in the Third World. London, Arnold, 1971, 64p. illus. (Focus on christianity).

59. BUTHELEZI, Manas. "Change in the church." Pro Veritate,
    v.12, No.5, 1973: p4-7.

60. BUTHELEZI, Manas. "Polygyny in the light of the New Testament."
    African Theological Journal. No.2, February 1969: p58-70.

61. CHAULEUR, Pierre. "Comment s' est operee la decolonisation
    dans le domaine religieux" Compte-Rendus Mensuels de
    l'Academie de Sciences d'outre-mer, v.30, No.5, Mai - Juin,
    1970: p223-242.

62. COKER, S.A. Three sermons of the Christian ministry. London,
    Unwin, 1904. 32p.

63. CONES, J.H. Black theology and black power. New York, Friend-
    ship Press, 1969.

64. COOK, Harold R. Highlights of Christian missions: a history
    and survey. Chicago, Moody, 1967. 256p. bibliog.

65. CRAIG, Robert. Politics and religion: a Christian view:
    a public lecture given at the University of Rhodesia.
    Salisbury, University of Rhodesia, 1972. 23p.

66. CROSSLAND, C. "Sigh of the cross". Sudan Notes and Records.
    v.1. 1918: p216.

67. CUMING, G.J. The mission of the Church and the propagation of
    the faith. New York, Cambridge University Press, 1970:
    192p.

68. CUST, R.N. Essay on the prevailing methods of the evangeliza-
    tion of the Non-Christian world. London, 1894.

69. DANIELOU, Rev. P. "Catholicisme et personalité culturelle des
    peuples." In Colloque sur les religions, Abidjan, 5-12
    Avril 1961: Paris, Presence Africaine, 1962: p215-218.
    Contributions of Catholicism to the development of the
    cultural personality of the African.

70. DANKER, William J. Profit for the Lord: economic activities
    in Moravian missions and the Basel Mission Trading Company.
    Grand Rapids, Eerdmans, 1971. 183p. bibliog. (Christian
    world Mission books).
    The author's concern is to provide some basic information
    to the English-speaking world on two major German attempts
    at missionary commercial enterprises. Half of the book is
    devoted to Moravian trading activities, the other to the
    Basel Mission Trading Company.

71. DAVY, Yvonne. African adventure unlimited: a collection of
    stories. New York, Greenwich Book Publishers, 1958. 111p.

72. DE MOOR, Vincent. Leur combat: essais de missiologie. Paris,
    Beauchesne, 1937.

73. DELAVIGNETTE, Robert. Christianity and Colonialism. New York,
    Hawthorn Books, 1964. 172p. bibliog.
    Relevant to the study especially in the area of missionary
    coopting by the colonial administration.

74. DESROCHES, Henri. "Les messianismes et la categorie de
    l'echec." Cahiers Internationaux de Sociologie, New Series,
    v.35, July-December 1963: p161-184.

75. LIND, Marie. Missionary stories for church programs: 39
    incidents relating to missionaries and their work.
    Grand Rapids, Michigan, Baker Books, 1969. 109p. illus.

76. DE WAAL MALEFIJT, Annemarie. Religion and culture: an
    introduction to anthropology of religion. New York,
    Macmillan, 1968. 407p. illus.
    Introductory textbook on primitive religion for the social
    science student.

77. DOUGALL, James W.C. "The case for and against mission schools."
    Journal of the African Society, v.38, 1939: p91-110.

78. DOUGALL, J.W.C. "Religious education". International Review
    of Missions, v.3. 1926: p493-505.

79. DUNSTONE, A.S. and KERR, J.F. "The objectives of theological
    education in developing countries." Learning for Living:
    a journal of religion in education. v.13, No.5, May 1974:
    p193-197.
    An enquiry carried out into theological education in some
    developing countries concerning their socio-political
    objectives, devotional objectives, basic skills, attitudes
    to people and attitudes to study. Data based on questionn-
    aires.

80. EBY, Omar. The sons of Adam. Scottdale, Pa., Herald Press, 1970. 176p.
Brief account of Americans in Africa and their experiences of Muslim - Christian and Afro-American encounter.

81. EKWA, M. "Catholic education in the mind of the church". In Catholic education in the service of Africa: report of the Pan-African Catholic Education Conference, Leopoldville, 16-23 August 1965: p149-172.

82. EXLEY, Richard and EXLEY, Helen. The missionary myth: an agnostic view of contemporary missionaries. Guilford, Lutterworth Press, 1973. 190p. (Hodder Christian paperbacks).

83. FINDLAY, G.C. and HOLDSWORTH, W.W. The history of the Wesleyan Methodist Missionary Society. London, 1922 xix, 519p. maps.

84. FIRTH, R. "Problem and assumption in an anthropological study of religion". Journal of the Royal Anthropological Institute, v.89, No.2, 1959.

85. FLEMING, Daniel. What would you do when Christian ethics conflict with standards of non-Christian cultures. New York, Friendship Press, 1949: 183p.

86. FORMAN, Charles W. ed. Christianity in the non-western world. London, Prentice Hall International, 1966. 146p.

87. FORMAN, Charles W. The nation and the kingdom; Christian mission in the new nations. New York, Friendship Press. 1964. 174p. Bibliography.

88. FULLER, W. Run while the sun is hot. New York, Sudan Interior
    Mission, 1966. 256p.

89. GARAUDY, R. "L'église, le colonialisme et les mouvements d'
    independance nationale." Cahiers du Communisme, v.11, 1959.

90. GENSICHEN, Hans-Werner. "Der syncretismus als Frage an die
    Christenheit heute." Evangelische Missions-Zeitschrift
    (Stuttgart) N.F. 23, 1966: p58-69.

91. GOODALL, Norman. A history of the London Missionary Society,
    1895-1945. London, Oxford University Press, 1954. 640p.
    illus.

92. GOODALL, Norman. "Principles and characteristics of missionary
    policy during the last fifty years, as illustrated by the
    history of the London Missionary Society." D. Phill. Thesis,
    Oxford University, 1950.

93. GREEGAN, Charles Cole and GOODNOW, J. Great missionaries of the
    church. With an introduction by Francis E. Clark. Freeport,
    N.Y.,Books for Libraries Press, 1972. xvl. 404p. (Essay
    index reprint series).

94. GRIFFIN, J.H. The Church and the black man. Dayton, Ohio,
    Pflaum Press, 1969. vii, 132p.

95. HASTINGS, Adrian. Mission and ministry. London, Sheed & Ward,
    1971. ix, 214p. (Sheed & Ward stagbooks).

96. HENNIG, H. "The role of charisma in the Seventh Day Adventist denomination, 1844-1915." M.A. Thesis, Columbia University, 1940. 46p.
Analyses the role of charisma in the church from the point of view of Max Weber's conception of the charismatic as distinguished from the rational leader.

97. HENNING, E.F. History of the African Mission of the Protestant Episcopal Church in the United States. New York, Stanford and Swords, 1850. 300p.

98. HINCHLIFE, Peter Bingham. "Indegenizing" church history. Bulletin of the Society for African Church History, v.1. No.2, 1963: p29-34.

99. HORTON, Robin. "A definition of religion and its uses." Journal of the Royal Anthropological Institute, v.90, 1960: p201-226.

100. IDOHOU, Pascal. "Musique indigene et sacree." Revue du Clergé Africain , v.3, No.3, May 1948: p207-213.

101. "The IMPACT of Christianity." In The African Experience, vol.2. Syllabus, by John N. Paden and Edward W. Soja. Evanston, Northwestern University Press, 1970: p193-197.
Historical summary of the impact of Christianity on Africa.

102. IMRAY, Elizabeth. "Christianity and native education". Race Relations, v.12, No.2, 1945: p46-49.

103. "The INFLUENCE of religion on language." In Proceedings of the

First International Congress of Africanists, Accra, 1962. London, 1964; p115-123.

104. ISSUES in theological education 1964-1965. Asia, Africa, Latin America: a report of the Theological Education Fund. New York, Theological Education Fund, (1968) v, 65p.

105. JAMES, E.O. "The Christianization of native rites". In W.G. de Lora Wilson (ed) Christianity and native rites, London, 1950: p41-51.

106. JASPER, Gerhard. "Polygyny in the Old Testament." African Theological Journal, No.2, February 1969: p27-57.

107. JOHNSON, Howard A. Global Odyssey; an Episcopalian's encounter with the Anglican Communion in eighty countries. Photos by the Author. New York, Harper & Row, 1963. 448p. illus.

108. JOHNSON, Joseph A. "The need for a black Christian theology". The Journal of the Interdenominational Theological Center, v.2, No.1, Fall 1974: p19-29.

109. JONES, Elizabeth Brown. All the children of the world: missionary stories from almost everywhere for boys and girls. Anderson, Ind., Warner Press, 1958. 63p.

110. JONES, William R. "Is God a white racist? a preamble to Black theology. Garden City, Doubleday, 1973.

111. JUNOD, Henri-Philippe. "Anthropology and missionary education." International Review of Missions, April 1935: p213-228.

112. KANE, J. Herbert. Winds of change in the christian mission. Chicago, Moody Press, 1973. 160p.

113. KELLY, J. "A hundred fruitful years." African Ecclesiastical Review, v.10, No.4, October 1968: p367-371.

114. KOBBEN, A.J.F. "Prophetic movements as an expression of social protest." International Archives of Ethnography. v.49, 1960: p138-163.
Groups prophetic movements into five categories (1) syncretic, (2) ecstatic, (3) iconoclastic, (4) sickness and (5) separatist with detailed discussion and examples.

115. KRAEMER, Hendrik. The Christian message in a non-Christian world. London, The Edinburgh House Press, 1938.

116. LANGEVIN, Albert. "Pagan customs and Christianity." African Ecclesiastical Review, v5, No.4, October 1963: p320-325.

117. LANTERNARI, Vittorio. Les mouvements religieux de liberté et de salut des peuples opprimés. Traduit de 1' Italien par Robert Paris. Paris, Maspero, 1962. 399p. (Les textes a' 1' appui bibliotheque de culture sociale).

118. LANTERNARI, Vittorio. The religions of the oppressed; a study of modern messianic cults. Translated from the Italian by Lisa Sergio. New York, Knopf, 1963. 343p.

119. LINTON, R. "Nativistic movements." American Anthropologists. v.45, 1943: p230-240.

120. KATIYRETTE, Kenneth Scott. The Christian World Mission in our

day. New York, Harper, 1954. 192p.

121. LATOURETTE, Kenneth Scott. Christianity in a revolutionary age: a history of Christianity in the nineteenth and twentieth centuries. New York, Harper, 1958-1962. 5 vols.

122. LATOURETTE, Kenneth Scott. The twentieth century outside Europe, the Americas, the Pacific, Asia and Africa; the emerging world christian Community. London, Eyre & Spottiswoode, 1962. 568p.

123. LOVETT, R. The history of the London Missionary Society, 1795-1895. Oxford, Frowde, 1899. 2 vols.

124. LUCAS, William Vincent. "The Christian approach to non-christian customs." In W.G. de Lara Wilson, (ed) Christianity and native rites, London, 1950: p3-38.

125. MADDEN, A.F. "The attitudes of the evangelical to the Empire and imperial problems, 1820-1850." Thesis, Oxford University Press, (n.d.)

126. MAIR, L.P. "Independent religious movements in three continents". Comparative Studies in Society and History, v.1. No.2, 1959: p113-136. Also in God and ritual, Garden City, The Natural History Press, 1967: p307-335.
Comparative study of religious movements in America, Melanesia and Africa.

127. MASAMBA, Jean. "Une approche pastorale du probleme de la sorcellerie". Revue du Clerge Africain, v.26, No.1, January 1971: p3-26.

128. MAURIER, H. "Insertion de l'église dans le monde africain et
      problematique de la doctrine chrétienne." Revue du Clerge
      Africain. v.24, Nos 3/4, May-July 1969: p315-323.

129. MEHL, Roger. Decolonisation et missions protestantes.
      Paris, Societe des Missions Evangeliques. 1964.
      134p. (Collection: Presence de la Mission).

130. MEMBE, Rev. J.L.C. African Methodist Episcopal Church history.
      Luanshya, A.M.E. Church, 1969. (mimeographed).

131. MENDELSONN, J. God, Allah, and juju: religion in Africa today.
      Boston, Mass. Beacon. 1965. 245p.
      Seeks to show the spiritual conflict between Christianity,
      Islam and African traditional religion. The emphasis is
      on the new African tendency to revive traditional customs
      and beliefs suppressed by missionaries.

132. MERLE, Marcel (ed). Les églises chretiennes et la decolonisation.
      Paris, Armand Colin, 1967: 519p.

133. MILLER, Elmer S. "The Christian missionary: agent of secula-
      rization." Missiology, v.1., No.1, 1973: p99-107.

134. MITCHELL, Robert Cameron. "Christian healing." In V. Hayward
      (ed). African independent church movements. London,
      Edinburgh House Press, 1963. p47-51.

135. MITCHELL, Robert C. "Towards the sociology of religious
      independency." Journal of Religions in Africa. (Leiden)
      v.3, No.1, 1970: p2-21.
      A critical appraisal of the methodology used by D.B. Barrett

in his book Schism and renewal in Africa: an analysis of six thousand contemporary religious movements, 1968.

136. MOERMAN, J. "Catholic education and religious and apostolic training." In Catholic education in the service of Africa: report of the Pan-African Catholic Education Conference, Leopoldville, 16-23 August 1965. p292-304.

137. MOERMAN, J. and AUGER, G.A. "Catholic schools and Catholic environment." In Catholic education in the service of Africa: report of the Pan-African Catholic Education Conference. Leopoldville, 16-23 August 1965: p238-249.

138. MOERMAN, J. "Catholic schools and the state ."In Catholic education in the service of Africa: report of the Pan-African Catholic Education Conference, Leopoldville,16-23 August, 1965: p333-352.

139. MOURRET, Rev. Fernand. A history of the Catholic Church. St. Louis, Missouri, B. Herder Book Co., 1957. 8 vols.

140. MUHLMANN, W.E. Messianismes revolutionnaires du tiers monde. Paris, Gallimard, 1968.

141. NEELY, Thomas Benjamin. The Methodist Episcopal Church and its foreign missions. New York, The Methodist Book Concern, 1923. 341p.

142. NEIL, Stephen. Christian faith and other faiths: the Christian dialogue with other religions. London, Oxford University Press, 1961.

143. NEIL, Stephen Charles. A history of Christian Missions.
Harmondsworth, Penguin Books, 1964. 622p. (Pelican history
of the church, 6).

144. NIMO, John K. "Echec du laicat Chretien." Vivant Univers
(Brussels) No.269. July/August 1970: p27-30.

145. NISSEN, Karsten. "Mission and unity: a look at the integration
of the International Missionary Council and the World Council
of Churches." International Review of Missions, v.63,
No.252, October 1974: p539-550.

146. NYAMITI, Abbe Charles. "The transformation of the tribal
initiations into the rituals of initiation sacraments and
sacramentals." Cahiers des Religions Africaines, v.5,
January 1971: p5-57.
This thesis is concerned with the general problem of adapting
chrsitian liturgy to the realities of African cultural values.
This article is an extract from the author's thesis submitted
to University of Louvanium in 1969.

147. OLDHAM,J.H. "Christian missions and the education of the Negro."
International Review of Missions, v.8, 1918: p242-247.

148. OLDHAM, J.H. "The education work of missionary societies."
Africa, v.7, No.1, January 1934: p47-59.
Discusses the topic from three aspects, (1) the quality of
missionary education (2) missions and native society and
(3) missions and governments.

149. OLDHAM, J.H. ,ed. The modern missionary. A study of the human

factor in the missionary enterprise in the light of present day conditions. London, S.C.M. Press, 1935. 128p. Contains a chapter on Africa by M. Wrong.

150.   OLSON, Howard S. "The development of black theology in America." Africa Theological Journal, v.5, 1972: p8-18.

151.   OOSTERWAL,Gottfried. Modern messianic movements as a theological and missionary challenge. Elkhart, Institute of Mennonite Studies, 1973, 55p.

152.   OOSTHUIZEN, G.C. "The interaction between Christianity and traditional religion." In Fort Hare University. The Ciskei, 1971: p108-44.

153.   OOSTHUIZEN, G.C. Theological battleground in Africa and Asia: the issues facing the Churches and efforts to overcome Western Divisions. London, Hurst, 1970. 300p.

154.   PARRINDER, Edward Geoffrey. The Bible and polygamy: a study of Hebrew and Christian teaching. London, S.P.C.K. 1950. 78p.

155.   PARRINDER, Edward Geoffrey. Faiths of mankind: a guide to the world's living religions. New York, Crowell, 1964. 206p.

156.   PARRINDER, Edward Geoffrey. Worship in the world's religions. New York, Association Press, 1961. 239p.

157.   PASCOE, C.F. Two hundred years of the S.P.G. London, Society for the Propagation of the Gospel, 1901. v.1.

GENERAL WORKS

158. PARSONS, Robert T. "The missionary and the cultures of man."
International Review of Missions, v.45, 1956: p161-168.

159. PEETERS, E. "Confrontation entre Christianisme et communisme
(en Afrique), "Revue du Clerge Africain, v.22, 1967: p634-
644.

160. PERRYMAN, Leonard M. "The Churches, mass media and the developing nations." World Outlook, August 1967: p16-20.

161. PHILLIPS, Godfrey E. The transmission of the faith. London,
Lutterworth Press, 1946. 156p.
Chapter xii discusses the problems of the Christian way of
life in Africa with emphasis on the problems of Christian
marriage.

162. PRATT, Antoinette Marie. The attitude of the Catholic Church
towards witchcraft and the allied practices of sorcery and
magic. Ph.D. Thesis, The Catholic University of America,
1915. 138p.

163. PRICE, T. "The missionary struggle with complexity." In Baeta,
C.G. ed. Christianity in tropical Africa, studies presented
and discussed at the seventh international African Seminar,
University of Ghana, April 1965. London, Oxford University
Press, 1968. p100-122.

164. POBEE, J.S. "Christian responsibility in state and society."
In God's mission in Ghana, Accra, Asempa Publishers, 1974:
p67-78.
Outlines areas of life in a state to which the christians
can make a contribution for the benefit of all. These

31

include politics, the economy, morality, racism, tribalism
and sectionalism.

165. PORRO CARDENOSO, Julio. Cristo en el continente negro. Bilbao,
      Ediciones Paulinas, 1964. 245p.

166. POSNANSKY, M. "Archaeology, ritual and religion". In Ranger,
      T.O. and Kimambo, I.N. The historical study of African
      religion with reference to East and Central Africa. London,
      Heinemann, 1972.

167. ROE, J.M. A history of the British and Foreign Bible Society,
      1905 - 1954. London, British and Foreign Bible Society,
      1965. xii, 497p.

168. SARVIS, Guy W. "The missionary as a social changer". Christendom,
      v.6, 1936. p826-838.

169. SAWYER, Harry. "Quels sont les effets des religions traditionn-
      elles sur la foi chretienne? Quelle doit étre la reponse
      de l'église a cette situation?" Flambeau, v.25, February 1970:
      p35-46.

170. SAWYER, Harry. "Traditional sacrificial rituals and christian
      worship". Sierra Leone Bulletin of Religion, v.2, No.1,
      June 1960: p18-27.

171. SCHERER, James A. Missionary, go home! A reappraisal of the
      Christian world mission. Englewood Cliffs, N.J., Prentice
      Hall, 1964. 192p. Bibliography.

172. SCHMIDT, Nancy and GANN, Lewis H. "The neglected missionaries".

Africana Newsletter, v.2, No.2, 1964: p4-12.
A note on the contribution of protestant and Catholic
missionaries to the study of African ethnography.

173. "SEPARATIST church movements." In H.A. Gailey. *History of*
Africa from 1800 to present. New York, Holt, Rinehart &
Winston, 1972: p201-205.
Short notes on the history of syncretic movements in Africa.

174. SHEEN, Fulton J. Bp. *Missions and the world crisis*. Milwaukee,
Bruce Publishing Co. 1963. 273p.

175. SMALLEY, Stephen. "The Gospel of John in recent study". *Orita*;
v.4, No.1, June 1970.

176. SMITH, Charles Spencer. *A history of the African Methodist*
Episcopal Church. Philadelphia, Book concern of the A.M.E.
Church, 1922.

177. SMITH, Edwin Wilham. *The blessed missionaries*, with a foreword
by Sir Herbert Stanley. Cape Town, Oxford University Press,
1950. xx, 146p. (Phelps-Stokes lectures, 1949).

178. SMITH, J. "Theology in a hot climate". *New Blackfriars*,
v.47, No.545, November 1965: p96-100.

179. SOCIETY OF AFRICAN MISSIONS. *One hundred years of missionary*
achievement, 1856-1956. Cork, Ireland, African Missions,
1956. 93p.

180. TAYLOR, J.V. and LEHMAN, D. *The encyclopedia of the African*
Methodist Episcopal Church. Philadelphia, A.M.E. Book

Concern, 1947.

181. TCHIDIMBO, Raymond Marie. L' homme noir dans l'Eglise.
Paris, Présence Africaine, 1963. 124p. illus. (Culture et
religions).

182. TERRY-THOMPSON, Arthur Cornelius. The history of the African
Orthodox Church. New York, Beacon Press, 1956: 139p. illus.

183. THEYSSEN, Hansjosef. Lichter im schwarzen Kontinent. Zwischen
Marx, Mohammed und Christus. Limburg, Lahn-Verlag, 1965.
104p. (Taschenbucher fur wache christen, 12).

184. THOAMS, L.V. "Animisme et christianisme". Présence Africaine,
No.26, June-July, 1959.

185. THOMPSON, H.P. Into all lands: the history of the Society for
the Propagation of the Gospel in Foreign Parts, 1701-1950.
London, S.P.C.K., 1951.

186. THOMPSON, Thomas. An account of two missionary voyages.
Reprinted in facsimile with introduction and notes. Published
for the Society for the Propagation of the Gospel in Foreign
Parts. London, S.P.C.K. 1937. xiv, 87p. maps.

187. TOALDO, Ernesto. Chiesa e rivolusioni nel terzo mondo. Milano,
E.M.I., 1971. 88p. (Collana Anni '70 no.4).

188. TRUBY, David William. Not so much a story, more a work of God.
With a foreword by Gilbert W. Kirby. Worthing, Walter.
London, Unevangelized Fields Mission, 1968. 48p.

189. TUPPER, H.A. A decade of foreign missions 1880-1890. Richmond,
     1891.

190. TURNBULL, Thomas N. What God hath wrought: a short history of
     the Apostolic Church. Bradford, Puritan Press, 1959. 186p.

191. TURNER, Harold W. "Monogamy: a mark of the church?" Inter-
     national Review of Missions, v.55: No.219, July 1966:
     p313-321.

192. VAN DER WEIJDEN, A. "Libation: adapted rites and principles".
     African Eccle siastical Review, v.1, No.4, October 1959:
     p263-270.

193. VAN DER WEIJDEN, A. "Libation and the first commandment".
     African Eccles iastical Review, v.1, 1959: p160-168.

194. VANSINA, Jan Raymond M. and THOAMS, L.V. The historian in
     tropical Africa: studies presented and discussed at the
     fourth international African Seminar at the University of
     Dakar, Senegal 1961. London, Oxford University Press
     for International African Institute, 1964, 428p.

195. VAUGHAN, Benjamin Noel Y. The expectations of the poor: the
     church and the Third World. London, S.C.M. Press 1972.
     ix, 182p.

196. VON ALLMEN, Daniel. "The birth of theology: contextualization
     as the dynamic element in the formation of New Testament
     theology." International Review of Missions, v.64, No.253.
     This article tries to reaffirm that an African theology is

not only necessary, but also to show that it is possible on
the basis of a true fidelity to the New Testament.

197. WALKER, Williston. A history of the Christian Church. New York,
Scribner, 1959. 585p.

198. WARREN, Max. The missionary movement from Britain in modern
history. London, S.C.M. Press, 1965. 192p.

199. WELBOURN, F.B. "A note on types of religious society". In
Baeta, C.G. (ed) Christianity in tropical Africa, studies
presented and discussed at the seventh international African
seminar, University of Ghana, April 1965. London, Oxford
University Press, 1968: p131-137.

200. WELCH, Janet. "The missionary training of medical missionaries".
International Review of Missions, v.29, No.114 April 1940:
p262-269.

201. WESTGARTH, J.W. The Holy spirit and the Primitive Mind. London,
Victory Press, 1946.

202. WILBOIS, Joseph. L'action sociale en pays de missions. Paris,
Payot, 1938. 150p.

203. WILMORE, Gayraud S. "The black Messiah: revising the color
symbolism of Western Christology". The Journal of the Interdenominational Theological Center, v.2. No.1, Fall 1974.
p8-18.

204. WOODSTOCK CONFERENCE, March 1967. The word in the third world.
Edited by James P. Cotter. Washington, D.C., Corpus Books,

1968. 285p.

Collection of papers discussing missionary activities in
Africa, Asia, and Latin America.

205. YDEWALLE, Charles d'. L'Evangile sous les tropiques. Paris,
A. Fayard, 1958. 153p. (Bibliotheque Ecclesia, 47).

AFRICA (General)

206. "The AFRICAN continent: a Survey of ten years". International
Review of Missions. October, 1924: p481-499.

207. ADELAJA, B.A. "The Christian faith and African culture".
The East and West Review, v.22, 1956: p35-40.

208. AFRICAN theological intepretation". In Baeta, C.G. ed. Christianity in tropical Africa, studies presented and discussed
at the seventh international African seminar, University of
Ghana, April 1965. London, Oxford University Press, 1968:
p143-146.

209. AGOYA, W.H. "The Catholic attitude to nationalism in contemporary Africa". African Eccles iastical Review, v.2, No.4,
October 1960: p322-323.

210. AJAYI, Jacob F. Ade and AYANDELE, E.A. "Writing African church
history". In P. Beyerhaus and C.F. Hallencreutz, (eds).
The Church crossing frontiers: essays in honour of Bengt
Sundkler. Lund, Gleerup, 1969: p90-108. (Studia Missionalia
Uppsaliensia, xi).

211. ALL-AFRICA CHURCH CONFERENCE. Ibadan, Nigeria, 1958. The church
in changing Africa: report. New York, International Missionary Council, 1958. 106p.

212. ALL AFRICA CHURCH CONFERENCE. Salisbury, Southern Rhodesia,
1962-63.
Christian education in Africa: report. London, Published
for All Africa Churches Conference by the Oxford University
Press, 1963. VII, 120p.

213   ALL AFRICA CONFERENCE OF CHURCHES. Reports and statements
       at Second Assembly, Abidjan, 1969.   The Conference,
       1969. (mimeo).

214   ALLEN, Roland. Le Zoute: a critical review of "The Christian
       Mission in Africa." London, World Dominion Press, 1927.

215   ALTHAUSEN, Johannes. Christian Afrikas auf dem Wege sur
       Freiheit. Erlangen, Verlag d. Evangelisch Lutherischen
       Mission. 1971. 308p. (Erlanger Taschenbucher, bd. 17).

216   AMISSAH, S.H. "The present position and problems of the
       Church in Africa." In Consultation Digest. Geneva,
       World Council of Churches, 1965. p45-51.

217   AMU, Ephraim. "The position of Christianity in modern Africa."
       International Review of Missions, v.24, October 1940.
       p477-485.

218   ANDERSON, William T. "The Church in African Universities."
       Clergy Review, v.53, No.3, March 1968: p191-198.
       Discusses the role of the Catholic Church, its students,
       staff and chaplains in promoting University education
       in Africa.

219   ARNOT, Frederick Stanly. Arnot of Africa; a fearless pioneer,
       a zealous missionary, a true knight of the Cross, by
       Nigel B.M. Graheme, New York, George H. Doran, 1926. 59p.

220   ARNOT, Frederick Stanley. The life and explorations of
       Frederick Stanley Arnot: the authorised biography of a
       zealous missionary, intrepid explorer & self denying
       benefactor amongst the natives of Africa, by Ernest
       Baker. New York, Dulton, 334p.

221.   ASAMOA, E.A. "The Christian Church and African heritage".
       In Desai, Ram. Christianity in Africa as seen by Africans.
       Denver, Swallow, 1962: p124-135. Also in International
       Review of Missions, v.44, 1955: p292-301.
       Examines the question of the conflict between christian
       beliefs and the African heritage.

222.   ASHANIN, C.B. "Christianity and African nationalism"
       Universitas (Accra) v.4, No.3, June 1960.

223.   ASSIMENG, John Maxwell. "Jehovah's witnesses: a study in
       cognitive dissonance". Universitas, v.4, No.1. November
       1974: p130-150.
       This essay looks at the ways in which the Jehovah's witne-
       sses sect has sought to resolve the problem of unrealized
       expectations in the light of the theory of cognitive
       dissonance i.e. unfulfiled expectations.

224.   ASSIMENG, John Maxwell. "Religious and secular messianism in
       Africa". Research Review (Legon) v.6, No.1, 1969: p1-19.
       Attempts to demonstrate that there is considerable amount
       of underlying frustration and mental strain in messianism,
       and the consequent attempts by people to meaningfully
       restructure those social forces often give rise to such
       strains.

225.   ASSIMENG, John Maxwell. "A sociological analysis of the impact
       and consequences of some Christian sects in selected African
       countries". D. Phil. Thesis, St. John's College. Univer-
       sity of Oxford, 1968. 583p.

226. ASSIMENG, John Maxwell. "Sociological perspective on Christianity in Africa". Ghana Social Science Journal, v.1. No.2, 1971: p43-53.

227. ATAL, D. "New Testament eschatology in an African background". Cahiers des Religions Africaines, v.5, No.10, July 1971: p306-313.
A lengthy review article of John S. Mbili's book of the same title, reviewed in French by a Professor of Theology in Kinshasa.

228. ATTWATER, Donald. The white Fathers in Africa. London, Burns, Oates & Washbourne, 1937.

229. AUGER, G.A. "The factual position of Catholic education in Africa and Madagascar". In Catholic education in the service of Africa: report of the Pan-African Catholic Education Conference, Leopoldville, 16-23 August 1965: p43-104.

230. AUJOULAT, L.P. "L'évolution religieuse de l'Afrique du fetichisme au christianisme". Rythmes du Monde, v.1, 1948: p44-53.

231. AUJOULAT, L.P. "La place de l'ecole chrétienne dans l'evolution de l'Afrique noire". Etudes, v.291: No.9, October 1956: p32-46.

232. BAETA, Christian G. "The challenge of African culture to the church and the message of the church to African culture". In Christianity and African culture. Accra, Christian Council, 1955: p51-61.

41

233. BAETA, C.G. ,ed. Christianity in tropical Africa: studies
      presented and discussed at the 7th International African
      Seminar... University of Ghana, Legon, April 6-16. 1965.
      Foreword by Daryll Forde, London, International African
      Institute, 1968. 449p.
      A collection of eighteen studies on various aspects of
      the Christian religion in Africa.

234. BAETA, Christian G. "Some aspects of religious change in
      Africa". Proceedings of the Ghana Academy of Arts and
      Sciences, v10, 1972: p51-64.

235. BALANDIER, G. "Messianismes et nationalisme en Afrique Noire".
      Cahiers Internationaux de Sociologie, v.14, 1953: p41-65.

236. BALANDIER, Georges. "Movements messianiques et prophetiques
      en Afrique tropicale". Etudes Sociologiques, v.6, NO.1.
      p17.

237. BANTON, Michael. "African prophets". In Black Africa;
      its peoples and their cultures today, edited by John
      Middleton, London, Macmillan, 1970: Also in Race v.5,
      No.2, October 1963: p42-55.
      Attempts to explore some of the interrelations between
      political and religious factors in the growth of prophetic
      cults in Africa.

238. BARRETT, David Brian. "AD 2000: 250 million Christians in
      Africa". International Review of Missions. V.59,
      No.233, January 1970: p391-94.
      Uses the latest census figures concerning the present

number of Christians in Africa to predict the probable
numerical strengh of Christians in Africa in the year
AD 2000. Discusses the consequences of such growth in
terms of organizational problems and the probable shift
in the centre of gravity of theChristian World.

239.   BARRETT, David Brian. "The African independent churches".
        In H. Wakelin,Coxill and K. Grubb, (eds). World Christian
        handbook, 1968. London, Lutterworth, for Survey Application
        Trust, 1967. pp. 24-28, 98-99; 227-228.

240.   BARRETT, David Brian. "The African independent churches and
        the Bible". United Bible Societies. Bulletin, v.72, 1967:
        p184-192.

241.   BARRETT, David Brian. "The African independent churches:
        developments 1968-70". African Ecclesiastical Review,
        v.12, No.2, 1970: p123-126.

242.   BARRETT, David Brian, ed. African initiatives in religion.
        Nairobi, East African Publishing House, 1971. xxviii,
        288p. (Studies from Eastern and Central Africa, 21).
        Proceedings of the workshop on religious research in
        Africa.

243.   BARRETT, David B. "Analytical methods of studying religious
        expansion in Africa". Journal of Religion in Africa,
        v.3, No.1, 1970: p22-44.

244.   BARRETT, David Brian. "Church growth and independency
        as organic phenomena: an analysis of two hundred
        African tribes". In Baeta, C.G. (ed) Christianity in

tropical Africa, studies presented and discussed at the seventh International African seminar. University of Ghana, 1965. London, Oxford University Press, 1968: p269-288.

245. BARRETT, David Brian. "Inter disciplinary theories of religion and African independency". In Barrett, David Brian (ed) African initiatives in religion, Nairobi, East African Publishing House, 1971.

246. BARRETT, David Brian. "Reaction to mission: an analysis of independent church movements across 200 African tribes". In Baeta, C.G. (ed). Christianity in tropical Africa, studies presented and discussed at the Seventh International African Seminar, University of Ghana, 1965. London, Oxford University Press, 1968: p269-288.

247. BARRETT, David Brian. "Reaction to mission: an analysis of independent church movements across 200 African tribes". Ph.D. Thesis, Columbia University - Union Theological Seminary 1965. 238p.

248. BARRETT, David Brian. Schism and renewal in Africa; an analysis of six thousand contemporary religious movements. Nairobi, 1968 xx, 363p.
A survey of about 250 major African tribes in order to explain the factors which give rise to independent religious movements and to help predict future religious movements.

249. BARRET, David Brian. (ed). Theory and practice in church life and growth. 56 studies in Eastern, Central and Southern Africa over the last hundred years. Nairobi, Workshop in

Religious Research, 1968. 490p. (mimeo).

250. BARRETT, Leonard E. Soul-force: African heritage in Afro-
     American religion. Garden City, N.Y., Doubleday, Anchor,
     1974: viii, 251p. bibliog. (C. Eric Lincoln series on
     black religion.)

251. BASCOM, William R. "African culture and the missionary".
     Civilizations, v.3, No.4, 1953: p451-501.

252. BASSIR, Olumbe. "Le Quakerisme et la personalité africaine".
     In Colloque sur les religions, Abidjan, 5-12 Avril, 1961.
     Paris, Presence Africaine, 1962. p173-178.

253. BASTIDE, Roger. African civilizations in the new world.
     Translated from the French by Peter Green. With a foreword
     by Geoffrey Perrinder. London, Hurst, 1971. 239p. Bibliog.
     First published in 1967 as Les Ameriques noires. Contains
     a chapter on the mixtures of African religion with chris-
     tianity.

254. BATCHELOR, Peter G. and BOER, Harry R. Theology and rural
     development in Africa. (A reformed journal monograph).
     Grand Rapids, Michigan, Eerdmans, 1967. 24p.

255. BATES, Gerald E. "Mission/Church tensions in Africa as a
     function of goal discrepancy". Practical Anthropology.
     v.18, No.6 November-December, 1971. p269-278.

256. BAUNARD, Mgr. Le Cardinal Lavigerie. Paris, Poussielgue,1896.

257. BAUNIOL Joseph. The White Fathers and their missions. London,

Sands, 1929.

258. BEAVER, Robert Pierce. Christianity and African education: the papers of a conference at the University of Chicago. Edited by P. Pierre Beaver. Grand Rapids. Eerdmans Publishing Co., 1966. 233p.

259. BECKMANN, Johannes. Die katholische Kirchen in neuen Afrika. Koln, Benziger, 1947.

260. BEETHAM, T.A. Christianity in the New Africa. London, Pall Mall Press, 1967. 206p. Bibliog. (Pall Mall library of African Affairs).

261. BEETHAM, T.A. "The Churches and education in Africa today". Theology, v69. January 1966: p13-19.

262. BENNETT, George. "Christianity and African nationalism". Mawazo, v.1, No.3, June 1968: p63-68.
The interaction of Christianity with African nationalism is traced to the nationalist yearning expressed by some of the negro spirituals in the independent Churches of the African continent.

263. BENZ, E. "The contribution of Origen of Alexandria to an African theology". Abba Salama. (Athens). v.6, 1975: p17-36.

264. BENZ, Ernst (ed). Messianische Kirchen, Sekten und Bewegungen im heutigen Afrika. (Messianic churches, sects, and movements in present-day Afrika). Leiden, Brill, 1965. 128p. Bibliog.

265. BERKEL, C.V. "How to invigorate the African parish". <u>African Ecclesiastical Review</u>. V.2, No.3, July 1960: p225-229; v.2, No.4, October 1960: p285-294, v.3, No.3, July 1961: p203-211.

266. BERNARDI, Bernardo. <u>Le religioni in Africa</u>. Roma, Instituto Italiano per L'Africa, 1961. 95p.

267. BEYERHAUS, Peter. <u>The encounter with messianic movements in Africa</u>: Aberdeen, Dept. of Church History and Systematic theology, 1968. 12p. (Seminar on Christianity and the non-western world, paper 4).

268. BEYERHAUS, Peter. "Our approach to the African independent Church movement". <u>Ministry</u>, v.9, No.2, April 1969. p74-80.

269. BLAKE, Eugene Carson. <u>The ecumenical movement and Africa</u>: Address to All African Conference of Churches, Abidjan, 1969. (mimeo).

270. BLOMJOUS, J. "Africa and the Ecumenical Council". <u>African Ecclesiastical Review</u>, v.5, No.3, July 1963: p223-229.

271. BLOMOUS, J. "Christians and human development in Africa". <u>African Ecclesiastical Review</u>, v.14, No.3, 1972: p189-212.

272. BLOMOUS, J. "Ecumenism in Africa". <u>African Eccles iastical Review</u>, v.6, No.3, July 1964: p200-206.

273. BLOMOUS, J. "The function of the African layman in the Church". <u>African Ecclesiastical Review</u>, v.1. 1959: p146-152.

274. BLOMJOUS, J. "The position of the African layman in the Church". African Ecclesiastical Review, v.1, No.1, January 1959: p74-79.

275. BLOY, P.O. ,ed. Papers on urban industrial issues in Africa and the challenge for the Church. 66p. Bibliog. Privately printed by the Editor, former Urban Africa Secretary, All Africa Conference of Churches.

276. BLYDEN, Edward Wilmot. Christianity, Islam and the negro race. New ed., with an introduction by Christopher Fyfe. Edinburgh, University Press, 1967. xviii, 407p. (African heritage books, 1).
This study shows the spiritual struggles of the blackman at the time when white supremacy appeared as a natural landscape in the world.

277. BOIS, G. "L'Afrique, 1' Inde et le christianisme d'apres Raymond Panikkar". Monde Non-Chretien, no. 74, 1965: p102-106.

278. BOOTH, Newell Snow, Bp. This is Africa South of the Sahara. New York, Friendship Press, 1950. 40p. illus.

279. BOUCHARD, Joseph. L'eglise en Afrique noire. Paris, La Palatine, 1958. 189p.

280. BOWEN, Thomas J. Adventures and missionary labours in several countries in the interior of Africa 1849-1856. 2nd ed, with a new introduction by E.A. Ayandele. London, Frank Cass, 1968. 359p. illus.

281. BRANDETH, Henry R.T. Episcopi vagantes and the African church. London, Society for Promotion of Christian Knowledge, 1961. 140p. illus.

282. BRIAUD, M.   ,and others. Le clerge indigene de l'empire francais II, Afrique equatoriale francaise, Madagascar, les Antilles. Paris, Bloud & Gay, 1943. 32p.

283. BRENNECKE, Ursula. Christliche Frauen in Afrika unbernehmen Verantwortung. Bad Salzuflen, M.BK-Verlag, 1969. 36p. (Christus und die Welt, Heft 28).

284. BROU. "Le prophetisme dans les eglises protestantes indigenes d' Afrique". Revue d' Afrique". Revue d' Histoire des Missions, v.8, No.1, 1931: p71-84.

285. BROWN, Kenneth I. "An African experiment in Christian union". The Christian, v.103. No.4,1965: p4-5. No.5, p8-9, 24.

286. BROWN, Kenneth I. "Forms of baptism in the African Independent churches of tropical Africa". Practical Anthropology, v.19. No.4, p169-182.

287. BRYAN, George M. "Revolution and religion in Africa". Christian Century, v.78, January 1961: p12-14.

288. BUAKASA, Gerard. "Un centre d' études des religions africaines". Cahiers des Religions Africaines, v.1, No.1/2. January-July 1967: p5-8.

289. BUEHLMANN, O.F.M. "Africa today needs liturgical renewal". African Eccles iastical Review, v.2, No.2, April 1960:

p120-125.

290.   BUELL, Raymond Leslie. The native problem in Africa. New York,
        Macmillan, 1928. London, Cass, 1965. 2 vols.
        Contains discussions on various separatist and independent
        church movements across the African continent.

291.   BULHMANN, W. "La situation catechetique actuelle en Afrique:
        urgente necessité d' un approfondissement de la foi et
        d'un renouveau cetechetique en Afrique". Revue du Clergé
        Africain, v.19, 1964: p508.

292.   BURBRIDGE, W. Destiny of Africa: Cardinal Lavigerie and
        the making of the white Fathers. London, Chapman, 1966.
        195p.

293.   BURRIDGE, W. The missionary principles and work of Cardinal
        Lavigerie. Dublin, Chapman, 1965. 256p.
        A careful analysis of Cardinal Lavigerie's ideas and
        missionary principles.

294.   BUREAU, René. "Sorcellerie et prophetisme en Afrique noire".
        Etudes, April 1967: p467-481.

295.   BUREAU, René. "Syncretismes et messianismes en Afrique noire.
        Parole et Mission, v.24, 15 January 1964: p132-135.

296.   BURKLE, Horst. "Patterns of sermons from various parts of
        Africa". In Barrett, D.B. African initiatives in religion,
        Nairobi, East African Publishing House, 1971: p222-231.

297.   BURKLE, Horst ,ed. Theologie und Kirche in Afrika. Stuttgart,
       Evangelisches Verlagswerk, 1968, 311p.

298.   CAMPOR, Alexander Priestley. Missionary story sketches:
       folklore from Africa. With an introduction by M.C.B.
       Mason. Freeport, N.Y., Books for Libraries Press, 1971.
       346p. illus. (Black heritage library collection,).

299.   CARPENTER, George W. "Church and state in Africa today".
       Civilizations, v.3, 1953: p519-538.

300.   CARRINGTON, John F. "African music in Christian worship".
       International Review of Missions, v.37, No.146, April
       1948: p198-205.

301.   CARROLL, K. "Christian art in Africa". African Ecclesiastical
       Review, v.3, No.2, April 1961: p141-143.

302.   CATHOLIC CHURCH. (Pope Pius xii). The future of Africa:
       the encyclical, Fidei donum, of Pope Pius xii. London,
       Sword of the Spirit, 1957. 24p.

303.   CHANGING Africa and the Christian dynamic. Papers of a seminar
       of Mission Board Executives, February 15-18, 1960. Chicago,
       The Center for the study of the Christian World Mission,
       University of Chicago, 1960. 105p.

304.   CHILDS, S.H. The life of holiness: an introduction to Chris-
       ian morals for African students. London, Collins and
       Longmans, 1948. 243p.

305.   CHING, Donald Stanley. They do likewise: a survey of Methodist

medical missions in Africa. London, Cargate Press, 1951.
130p.

306. CHIRGWIN, A.M. An African pilgrimage. Glimpses of a church
in the making. London student Christian Movement Press,
1932. 158p.

307. CHRISTIAN action in Africa. Report of the Church Conference
on African Affairs. Ottenberg College, Waterville, Ohio,
African Committee of the Foreign Missions Conference of North
America, 1942. 194p.

308. CHRISTIAN education in Africa. Report of the Salisbury Conference. London, Oxford University Press, 1963.

309. CHRISTIAN occupation of Africa: the proceedings of a conference
of mission boards engaged in work in the continent of Africa,
held in New York City, November 1917. New York, Foreign
Missions Conference, 1917.

310. CHRISTIANITY and African culture: some psychological implications
of the encounter". In Baeta, C.G. ed. Christianity in
tropical Africa, studies presented and discussed at the
seventh international African seminar, University of Ghana,
April 1965: London, Oxford University Press, 1968: p126-
130.

311. "CHRISTIANITY in Africa". In African systems of thought, edited
by M. Fortes and G. Dieterlen. London, Oxford University
Press, 1965: p31-33.

312.   CHURCH CONFERENCE ON AFRICAN AFFAIRS. Christian action
        in Africa; report... Otterbein College, Westerville,
        Ohio, June 19-25, 1942. New York, African Committee
        of the Foreign Missions Conference of North America,
        1942.

313.   CHURCH MISSIONARY SOCIETY. Centenary volume of the Church
        missionary society for Africa and the East, 1799-1899.
        London, Church Missionary Society, 1902. 233p.

314.   "The CHURCH in the African States". Pro Mundi Vita.Special
        Note, 34, 1974.

315.   CICARWS. "Aid and the selfhood of the Church in Africa".
        Study Encounter, v9, No.3, 1973.

316.   CLARKE, Richard F. Cardinal Lavigerie and the African slave
        trade. London, Longmans, Green, 1889.

317.   COLUMBA, Fr. "Seminarians on Africanization of the liturgy".
        African Ecclesiastical Review, v.12, No.4, 1970: p309-317.

318.   COMHAIRE, Jean. "Religious trends in African and Afro-American
        urban societies". Anthropological Quarterly, New Series,
        v.1., No.4, October 1953: p95-108.

319.   CONFERENCE ON SOCIETY, DEVELOPMENT AND PEACE, Beirut, 1968.
        World development: challenge to the churches; the official
        report and papers. Edited by Denys Munby, Washington,
        Corpus Books, 1969. xvl, 208p.

320. CONSULTATION ON EVANGELIZATION OF WEST AFRICA TODAY. "The
     Evangelization of West Africa today". International Review
     of Missions: v.54, No.216, October 1965: p484-494.

321. COOKSEY, J.J. and McLEISH, A. Religion and civilization in
     West Africa: a missionary survey of French, British, Spanish
     and Portuguese West Africa, with Liberia. London, World
     Dominion. Press, 277p.
     A historical survey of missionary activities in West Africa,
     with a geographical anthropological account of the land and
     people.

322. COWAN, L. Gray J. and others. Education and nation building
     in Africa. London, Pall Mall Press, 1965. 403p.
     Many of the papers in this volume concern Christian
     education in Africa.

323. COUVE, Daniel. Sur la côte d' Afrique. Senegal, Togo,
     Cameroun et Gabon: journal de voyage, juin - novembre 1936.

324. CRANE, P. "The church in a changing Africa; reprint". Catholic
     Mind, v.59. February 1961: p59-63.

325. CUST, Robert Needham. Communication on the occupation of Africa
     by the Christian missionaries of Europe and North America.
     London, Stock, 1891. 67p.

326. DAMMANN, Ernst. Das Christentum in Afrika. Munich and
     Hamburg; Siebenstern Taschenbuch, 1968. 190p.

327. DAVIS, J. Merle. "The cinema and missions in Africa".
     International Review of Missions, July 1936: p378-383.

328.   DAVY, Yvonne. Campfire tales from Africa. Illustrated by
       Homer Norris. Takoma Park, Washington, Review and Herald
       Pub. Association, 1956. 156p.

329.   DEHONEY, Wayne. African diary. Nashville, Broadman Press,
       1968. 157p. illus.

330.   DERY, Peter P. "Message chretien et genie Africain". Vivant
       Univers, No.269, July/August, 1970: p22-26.

331.   DESAI, Ram. Christianity in Africa as seen by Africans.
       Edited with an introduction by Ram DeSai. Denver,
       Swallow, 1962. 135p.
       A collection of essays on christianity as seen and under-
       stood by various African scholars, with a running commen-
       tary by the author.

332.   DE SAINT-CHAMANT, Jean. "Sectes et christianisme en Afrique
       noire". La Revue des deux mondes, v.4, 1 August, 1962:
       p339-353.
       Discussion on the relationship between tribal tradition,
       politics and religion in Africa.

333.   DE SARAM, B.J.H. African independent churches. London, Church
       Missionary Society, 1964. 3p. (mimeographed).

334.   DESCHAMPS, Hubert. Les religions de l'Afrique noire.
       Paris, Presses Universitaires de France, 1954.
       A survey of religious cult groups, prophetism and inde-
       pendent churches in Africa.

335. DESROCHES, Henri ,ed. "Syncretisme et messianisme en
          Afrique noire". Archives de Sociologie des Religions,
          v.8, No.16, July-December 1963: p105-108.

336. DICKSON, Kwesi and ELLINGWORTH, Paul. Biblical revelation
          and African traditional beliefs. Maryknoll, N.Y. Orbis
          Books. 1970.
          Intended to explore ways African Christians can express
          their faith without denying their heritage and how the
          Church can best relate to Africans today.

337. DICKSON, Kwesi A. "Christian and African traditional cere-
          monies". Practical Anthropology, v.18, No.12, March-April
          1971: p64-71.

338. DOIG, Andrew B. "The Christian Church and demobilization in
          Africa." International Review of Missions, v.35, No.138,
          April 1946: p174-182.

339. DOUGALL, James W.C. "African separatist churches". Inter-
          national Review of Missions, v.45, No.179, July 1956:
          p257.266.

340. DOUGALL, James W.C. Christians in the African revolution.
          Edinburgh, Saint Andrew Press, 1963. (Duff missionary
          lectures - 1962).

341. DOUGALL, J.W.C. Christianity and the sex education of the
          African. London, Society for the Promotion of Christian
          Knowledge. 1937.

342. DOUGALL, J.W.C. "The relationship of church and school in

Africa". <u>International Review of Missions</u>, 1937: p204-214.

343.   DONOVAN, V.J. "The Protestant-Catholic scandal in Africa:
        a possible solution". <u>African Ecclesiastical Review</u>,
        v.1, 1959: p169-177.

344.   DONOVAN, V.J. "The Protestant-Catholic scandal in Africa-
        Answer to Father Slevin". <u>African Ecclesiastical Review,</u>
        v.2, No.3, July 1960: p242-245.

345.   DRAKE, St. Clair. <u>The redemption of Africa and black</u>
        <u>religion</u>. Chicago. Third World Press, Atlanta, Georgia:
        Institute of the Black World, 1970. 80p.

346.   D'SOUZA, Jerome. "Indian missionaries in Africa", <u>The Plyon,</u>
        v.26, No.2, 1964: p14-16: illus.

347.   DUBB, A.A. "Tribalism in the African Church". <u>In The</u>
        <u>multitribal society</u>... edited by A.A. Dubb. Lusaka,
        Rhodes-Livingstone Institute, 1962: p111-120.

348.   DUNCAN, Hall F. "African art and the Church". <u>Practical</u>
        <u>Anthropology</u>, v.13, No.3, 1966: p107-114.

        A study of the impact of Christianity on African art from
        the 15th and 16th centuries.

349.   EARTHY, E. Dora. "An African tribe in transition from
        paganism to Christianity". <u>International Review of</u>
        <u>Missions</u>, v.22, 1933: p367-376.
        Discusses the possibility of adapting certain heathen
        rituals in the life of Christian natives.

350   EDINBURGH. University. Centre for African Studies. Religion
       in Africa; proceedings of a Seminar held in the Centre
       of African studies, University of Edinburgh, 10th - 12th
       April, 1964. Edinburgh, 1964. 130p.

351.   EDMONDSON, L. "Africa and the Africa diaspora: intersections,
       linkages, and racial challenges in the future world order."
       In Mazrui, A.A. (and others, eds.) Africa in World
       Affairs, New York, 1973: p1-2.

352   EKOLLO, Pasteur. "Illustration du genie africain au sein de
       la communauté protestante en Afrique." In Colloque
       sur les religions, Abidjan, 5-12 Avril, 1961. Paris
       Presence Africaine, 1962: p147-154.

353   EMONTS, Joh. Ins steppen-und Bergland Innerkameruns: aus dem
       Leben und Wirken deutscher Afrikamissionare. Aachen:
       Missionsdruckerei, 1927.

354   "ENGAGEMENT of Christianity with African concepts and way of
       life." In Baeta, C.G., ed. Christianity in tropical
       Africa, studies presented and discussed at the seventh
       international African seminar, University of Ghana, April
       1965. London, Oxford University Press, 1968: p123.

355   ETHIQUE Chrétienne et valeurs africaines." Caheirs des
       Religions Africaines, v.3, No.5, 1969: p149-159.

356   FALCON, Paul. "Bilan historique de l'action des "Missions
       africaines' sur le continent noir." Revue Francais
       d' Etudes Politiques Africaines. (Paris) v.56. August
       1970: p12-36. Bibliog.

357. FASHOLE-LUKE, E.W. "An African indigenous theology: fact or
      fiction?" Sierra Leone Bulletin of Religion, v.11, 1969:
      p1-14.
      Suggests that instead of advocating   a specific
      indigenous African theology, African theologians should
      consider what contributions they themselves can make
      towards a universal theology, basing this contribution on
      the experience of man in Africa.

358. FASHOLE-LUKE, Edward W. "What is African Christian theology?"
      African Ecclesiastical Review, v.16, No.4, 1974: p383-388.

359. FEHDERAU, H.W. "Enthusiastic Christianity in an African church".
      Practical Anthropology, v.8, November 1961: p279-280.

360. FERNANDEZ, James William. "Contemporary African religion:
      confluents of enquiry". In G.M. Carter and A. Paden
      (eds). Expanding horizons in African studies: Proceedings,
      20th Anniversary Conference, Program of African Studies,
      1968. Evanston, Northwestern University Press, 1969.
      p27-45.

361. FERNANDEZ, James William. "Independent African Christianity:
      its study and its future". Journal of Asian and African
      Studies, v4, No.2, 1969: p132-147.

362. FERNANDEZ, James William. Microcosmogony and modernization
      in African religious movements. Montreal, McGill Univer-
      sity Centre for Developing Area studies, 1969. 21p.
      (Occasional Papers Series,3).

363. FERNANDEZ, James W. "Politics and prophecy: African religious

movements". Practical Anthropology, v12, No.2., March-
April 1965: p71-75.
Discussion on separatist, reformative, messianic and
nativist religious movements in Africa.

364. FISHER, Humphrey J. "Conversion reconsidered: some historical
aspects of religious conversion in black Africa". Africa,
v.43, No.1, 1970: p27-40. Bibliog.

365. FISHER, Lena Leonard. Under the crescent, and among the
kraals; a study of Methodism in Africa. Boston, Woman's
Foreign Missionary Society, M.E. Church, 1917. 159p.

366. FLASCHSMEIER, Horst R. Missionsarzt in afrikanischen Busch.
Giessen, Basel, Brunnen-verlag, 1966. 152p. (Brunnen
Taschenbuch, nr. 34).

367. FLATT, Donald C. "The cross-cultural interpretation of
religion in Africa: a study in methodology". Missiology
v.1, No.3, July 1973: p325-338.

368. FOSTER, Lizzie Rose. An historical sketch of the African
Mission of the Protestant Episcopal Church in the U.S.A.
New York, The Domestic and Foreign Missionary Society,
Protestant Episcopal Church, 1889. 80p.

369. FRASER, A.G. "Aims of African education". International
Review of Missions, v.4, 1925: p514-522.

370. FRASER, E. "Christianity in the tribal idiom: causes and
characteristics of African separation". African World,
November 1965: p4-5.

371. FROELICH, Jean-Claude. Le nouveau dieu d' Afrique. Paris,
     Orantes, 1969. 128p. (Collection Prismes). "The deve-
     lopment of traditional religions through Islam, chris-
     tianity, messianism and multiple syncretismes".

372. FUETER, P.D. "African genesis and western theology: comments
     on Robert Ardey's book". International Review of Missions,
     v.52, January 1963: p60-68.

373. GANTIN, B. "The Catholic Church in Africa". World Mission,
     v.12, No.3, Fall 1961. p33-42.

374. GANTIN, B. "Will Africa be Christian?" Mission Digest,
     v.19. May 1961: p27-32.

375. GAVAN DUFFY, T. Let's go: mission tours, Africa. London,
     Sheed & Ward, 1928.

376. GEOGHEGAN, G.M. "African sculpture and the Church". African
     Ecclesiastical Review, v.3, No.1, January 1961: p77-79.

377. GILLES DE PELICHY, Alexandre. "Vers une culture africaine
     chrétienne". Bulletin des Missions, v.24, No.1, 1950:
     p60-67. Grands Lacs, v.65, No.8/9, 1950: p60-67.

378. GILLILAND, Dean S. "The indigenous concept in Africa".
     Missiology, v.1, No.3, July 1973: p343-356.

379. GILSENAN, M. "Myth and the history of African religion".
     In Ranger, T.O. and Kimambo, I.N. The historical study of
     African religion with reference to East and Central Africa.
     London, Heinemann, 1972.

380.   GODIANISM proposed as a new African religion".. Muslim World,
       v.55, No.2, 1965: p172-174.

381.   GOODALL, Norman and NIELSEN, Eric. Survey of the training of
       the Ministry in Africa. London, 1954.

382.   GOODLOE, R.W. "Missionaries as transmitter of western civi-
       lization in nineteenth century Africa". Ph.D. thesis.
       St. Andrew's University, 1955-56.

383.   GOODY, Jack. "Tribal, racial, religious and language problems
       in Africa". In Man and Africa; Ciba Foundation Symposium.
       London, Churchill, 1965: p98-120.

384.   GRANGETTE, G. "Syncretises et messianismes en Afrique noire".
       Parole et Mission, v.4, No.4, 15 July 1961: p343-370.

385.   GRAY, Ernest. "Some present day problems for African Chris-
       tian marriage". International Review of Missions, v.45,
       1956: p267-277.

386.   GRAY, Richard. "Problems of historical perspective: the
       planting of Christianity in Africa in the nineteenth and
       twentieth centuries". In Baeta, C.G. ed. Christianity in
       tropical Africa, studies presented and discussed at the
       seventh International African Seminar, University of Ghana,
       April 1965. London, Oxford University Press, 1968: p18-33.

387.   GRESCHAT, Hans-Jurgen. "Understanding African religion".
       Orita, v.2, No.2. December 1968: p59-69.

388.   GRIMES, M.S. "Life out of death; or, the story of the African

inland mission". London, African Inland Mission, 1917.
91p.

389. GRIMWOOD, E.M. Faith and works in an African village.
(Yoruba tribe). Oxford, Oxford University Press, 1949.
46p.

390. GROVES, C.P. The planting of Christianity in Africa. London,
Redhill, Lutherworth Press, 1948-1958. 4 vols. illus.
(Lutherworth library vols. 26, 43, 44, 50).
A detailed historical study of the origin and growth of
Christianity in Africa.

391. GUILCHER, Rene F. La société des Missions Africaines: ses
origines, sa vie, ses oeuvres. Lyon, Missions Africaines,
1956.

392. HALE, Charles. Early history of the Church missionary society
for Africa and the East to the end of A.D. 1814. London,
Church Missionary Society, 1896. 677p.

393. HARLIN, Tord. Spirit and truth: religious attitudes and
life involvements of 2,200 African students. Scandinavian
Institute of African Studies, 1972.

394. HARR, Wilber C. "The Christian mission since 1938: Africa
south of the Sahara". In Frontiers of the Christian World
Mission since 1938 edited by W.C. Harr. New York, Harper,
1962: p83-114.

395. HARR, Wilber C. "The Negro as an American protestant missionary in Africa". Ph.D. Thesis, 1945: University of

63

Chicago, 1945. 214p.

396. HARLOW, Robert E   and   SMART, John. Who is my neighbour?
Assembly missionaries in Africa. New York, The Fields,
Inc., 1962. 94p. illus.

397. HARRIES, Lyndon. "Mission research and the African marriage
survey". International Review of Missions, v.39, No.153,
January 1950: p94-99.

398. HARRISON, W.P. The gospel among the slaves. A short account
of missionary operations among the African slaves of the
southern states. Reprinted from the 1893 ed. Nashville,
Tenn, New York, 1973.

399. HASTINGS, Adrian. Christian marriage in Africa. (Cape Town?)
S.K.C.K., 1973. 180p.
A report commissioned to be written by the Anglican
Archishops of Cape Town, Central Africa, Kenya, Tanzania
and Uganda. The author is a Catholic priest of sound
theological and sociological education.

400. HASTINGS, Adrian. "Christianity and African cultures". New
Blackfriars, v.48, December 1966, p127-136.

401. HASTINGS, A. "Christianity in independent Africa". African
Affairs, v.73, No.291, April 1974: p229-232.

402. HASTINGS, Adrian. Church and mission in modern Africa.
London, Burns & Oates, 1967. 263p.
A personal assessment of the work of the Roman Catholic
Church in Africa today by a missionary. Its aim is to

provoke discussion, further investigation and critical
assessment, so that effective decisions in relation to
the mission of the Church can be made.

403.   HASTINGS, Adrian. The Church in Africa (Roman Catholic Church).
        Dublin Review, No.507, spring 1966: p34-47.

404.   HASTINGS, Adrian. "The Church in Afro-Asia today and
        tomorrow". African Ecclesiastical Review, v.6. No.4,
        October 1964: p287-298.

405.   HASTINGS, Adrian. "The Church's response to African marriage".
        African Ecclesiastical Review v.13, No.3, 1971: p193-203.

406.   HASTINGS, Adrian. "Ecumenical development in Africa". African
        Ecclesiastical Review, v.7, No.2, April 1965: p113-120.

407.   HASTINGS, Adrian. "Patterns of African mission work. African
        Ecclesiastical Review, v.8, No.4, October 1966: p291-298.
        Outlines 4 different phases of missionary work in Africa,
        the first is the Christian village mission approach, then
        to a network of catechism schools before the war, after
        the war Governments cooperated with the missions in the
        establishment of schools, but after independence the
        backbone of African Church life is no longer the schools,
        but the Church.

408.   HATTON, Desmond J. ed. Missiology in Africa today: thought-
        provoking essays by modern missionaries. Dublin, Gill,
        1961. 151p.

409.   HAYWARD, V.E.W. "African independent church movements".

International Review of Missions, v.52, April 1963:
p163-172. Ecumenical Review, v.15, No.2, Jan. 1963:
p192-202.

410   HAYWARD, Victor E.W. ed.   African independent church movements.
       London, Published for the World Council of Churches.
       Commission on World Mission and Evangelism, by Edinburgh
       House Press, 1963. 94p. (C.W.M.E. research pamphlets,
       no.11).

411   HEARNE, Brian. "Roman Catholicism or African Catholicism?"
       African Ecclesiastical Review, v.14, No.2, 1972: p97-107.

412   HEILGERS, J. Die Grundung der Afrikanischen Mission durch
           den Ehrwurgdigen P. Libermann. Paderborn, Schoningh.

413   HEMMER, C. and HEMMER, P. Crane. "Catholic programs for
           African leaders." Social Order. v.11. December 1961:
           p444-450.

414   HENNERMANN, Franziskus. Werden und wirken eines Afrika-
           missionars. Limburgh, Pallottiner, 1922.

415   HEARSKOVITS, M. "African Gods and Catholic Saints in New World
           Negro beliefs." American Anthropologist, v.39, No.4,
           1937: p635-643.

416   HETHERWICK, Alexander. The gospel and the African. Edinburgh,
           T & T. Clark, 1932.

417   HEY, P.D. "The influence of Christianity on a rural African
           area." Teacher Education in New Countries, v.1, No.2,

November, 1960: p23-32.

418.   HODGE, Alison. "The training of missionaries for Africa:
       the Church Missionary Society's training college at
       Islington, 1900-1915". Journal of Religion in Africa.
       v.4, 1971/72: p81-96.

419.   HOFFMAN, Paul E   ,ed. Theological education in today's
       Africa. Geneva, Lutheran World Federation, 1969.
       183p.

420.   HOLLENWERGER, Walter J. "Ministry of Ministers: an outreach
       to African independent Churches". The United Church Review,
       June 1967: p129-132. Also in The Christian Minister, v.3,
       No.5, 1967. p154.
       A plea for the theological education of ministers in
       African independent churches.

421.   HOPKINS, Raymond F. "Christianity and socio-political change
       in sub-saharan Africa". Social Forces, v.44, No.4, 1966
       p555-562.

422.   HOWITT, William. Colonisation and Christianity; a popular
       history of the treatment of the natives by the Europeans
       in all their colonies. London, Longmans, Green, 1838. xi,
       508p.

423.   HUGHES, W. Dark Africa and the way out; or, A scheme for
       civilizing and evangelizing the Dark Continent. New York,
       Negro Universities Press, 1969, xiv, 155p. illus.

424.   HYND, J. "African music in church". All African Conference of

Churches Bulletin, v.3, No.2, February, 1966: p303-307.

425. INTERNATIONAL MISSIONARY COUNCIL. A survey of the training of
the ministry in Africa. Reports. Part I: East and West
Africa, by Stephen Neill. Part II: Angola, Belgian Congo,
French West Africa, French Equatorial Africa, Liberia,
Mozambique and Ruanda-Urundi, by a commission under the
chairmanship of M. Searle Bates. London, New York, 1951.

426. JOHNSON, Hildegard Binder. "The location of Christian missions
in Africa". Geographical Review, v.57, No.2, April 1967:
p168-202p maps.
The complex factors behind the selection of sites, and the
general distribution of pioneer missions during the 19th
century, are summarized under four themes, illustrated by
four case studies of missions in Ghana, S.W. Africa and
Tanzania. Contains a map showing the distribution of
missions in 1925.

427. JOHNSON, Hildegard Binder. "The role of missionaries as
explorers in Africa". Terrae Incognitae, v.1, 1969: p68-76.

428. JOHNSON, William Percival. My African reminiscences, 1875-1895.
Westport, Negro Universities Press, 1970. 236p. illus.

429. JONES, F.M. "The future of the Church in Africa". East and
West, v.22, April 1924: p125-136.

430. JONES, Thomas Jesse. Education in Africa: a study of West,
South and Equatorial Africa by the African Education
Commission, under the auspices of the Phelps-Stokes Fund
and Foreign Mission Societies of North America and Europe.

Report prepared by Thos. Jesse Jones. New York, Phelps-Stokes Fund, 1922.

431   JORDAN, Artishia Wilkinson. The African Methodist Episcopal Church in Africa. New York, African Methodist Episcopal Church, 1960.

432   JOUBERT, L. "La prise de contact entre l' Afrique et la mission chrétienne." Monde Non-Chrétien, v.14, April-June, 1950: p201-208.

433.   JOWITT, H. "Education in a changing Africa: today's challenge to the church" African Ecclesiastical Review, v.1, Nu.1, January 1959: p92-104.

434   JUBILEE volume of the Church Missionary Society for Africa and the East, 1848-1849. London, Seey, Service & Co., 1849. 400p.

435   KABAZZI-KISIRINYA, S. "Towards dialogoe within the African Church." African Ecclesiastical Review, v.13, No.3 1971: p204-212.

436   KALANDA, P. "Christ in African art". African Ecclesiastical Review, v.2, No.4, October 1960: p324-326.

438   KAMBEMBO, Daniel. "Schisme et renouveau en Afrique (analyse de 6000 mouvements religieux contemporains." Cahiers des Religions Africaines, v.2, No.4, July 1968: p337-341. A review of David Barrett's "schism and renewal in Africa."

439   KAREFA-SMART, Joh. The halting kingdom: Christianity and the African revolution. New York, Friendship Press, 1959. 86p.

440. KAUFMAN, L. "The first African martyr Bishop". African Ecclesiastical Review, v.1, No.1, January 1959: p43-46.

441. KAUFFMAN, Robert A. "Impressions of African Church music".
African Music, v.3, No.3, 1964: p109-110.

442. KELDANY, H. H.E. Cardinal Hinsley's travels in Africa, 1928-9.
London, Catholic Truth Society, 1939.

443. KENDALL, R. Elliott. "On the sending of missionaries: a call for
restraint". International Review of Missions, v64, No.253,
January 1975: p62-66.
The Rev. R.E. Kendall is Secretary for Africa and the
Caribbean of the Conference of Missionary Societies in Great
Britain and Ireland. The author cautions that there must be
some restraint on the influx of Foreign missionaries into
Africa.

444. KING, Noel Q. Christian and Muslim in Africa. New York, Harper
& Row, 1971, 153p. Bibliog.
A survey of the history and present position of the two
religions on the African continent. Intended as an introductory guide, it summarises the successive advances and
retreats of the two religions in Africa from the earliest
times.

445. KINGSWORTH, J.S. "The changing role of missionary societies in
Africa". Royal Society of Arts Journal, v.111, February 1963:
p224-238.

446. KINGSNORTH, John S. Come back, Africa: the review of the work of
1962. London, Universities' Mission to Central Africa, 1963

72p. illus.

447. KINOTI, Cyprian A. "An African approach to ecumenism." African Ecclesiastical Review, v.13, No.2, 1971: p145-154.

448. KOLARZ, W. Religion and communism in Africa. Published for the African Centre by the Sword of the Spirit. 1963.

449. KRUGER, Etienne and others. "Les eglises protestantes en Afrique." Revue Francaise d' Etudes Politiques Africaines, v.32, August 1968: p22-78.

450 KUBAY, Laurel Betty. "Christian women in Africa want their place in the Church." Ministry. v.3., No.4, July 1963: p180-184.

451 KUNENEKE, R. "To see ourselves: nationalism and Christianity in Africa." Practical Anthropology, v.8, March 1961: p85-86.

452 LAMBERT, John C. Missionary heroes in Africa. London, 1923.

453 LANTERNART, Vittorio. "Syncretismes, messianismes, neotraditionalismes: postface à une étude des mouvements religieux de 1' Afrique noire." Archives de Sociologie des Reli ions. v.19, January - June 1965: p99-116: v21 January - June 1966: p101-111.

454 LAROCHE, R., "Some traditional African religions and Christianity" in Christianity in tropical Africa, studies presented and discussed at the seventh International African Seminar, University of Ghana, 1965. London, Oxford University Press, 1968: p289-307.

455.   LATOURETTE, Kenneth Scott. "The spread of Christianity:
       British and German missions in Africa." In Britain
       and Germany in Africa: imperial rivalry and colonial rule,
       edited by P. Gifford and W.R. Louis. New York, Yale
       University Press, 1967: p393-416.

456.   LAUDRIE, Marie Le Roy. Paques africaines: de la communaute
       clanique a la communaute chretienne. Paris, Mouton,
       1965. 231p. illus. (Monde d' Outre-Mer Passe et Present).

457.   LAWRENCE, V. and WARR, W. Coming and going in Africa: true
       life stories of African and European Christians showing
       how God has called and commissioned them for his service
       with teaching notes and practical work. Edinburgh House
       Press. 1963. (Discoveries series - no. 21).

458.   LEDOUX, Marc-Andre. "Force et faiblesses des eglises protes-
       tantes africaines". Revue Francaise d' Etudes Politiques
       Africaines, v.32, August 1968: p69-73.

       Lists, among other things, the weaknesses of African
       Protestant Churches as follows: unreadiness for autonomy,
       financial dependence on foreign missions, heavy burden of
       educational expenditure, inappropriate methods of recruiting
       priests, and failure to find answer to the problem of
       polygamy.

459.   LEE, Anabelle. "African nuns: an anthropologist's impressions".
       New Blackfriars, May 1968: p401-409.

460.   LEENHARDT, Maurice and MERCOIRET, (Mmme). "Prophetisme
       Africain". Le Monde non-chretien, nos 79/80: 1966:p53-62.

461. LEHMANN, Dorothea. "Women in the independent African churches". In Victoria E.W. Haywood, (ed) African independent church movements, London, Edinburgh, Edinburgh House Press, 1963: 65-69.

462. LESOURD, Paul. Les Peres Blancs du Cardinal Lavigerie. Paris, Grasset, 1935.

463. LEWIS, John. "The literary theological equipment of the Church in Africa". Books for Africa, v.18, No.2, April 1948: p20-22.

464. LEWIS, L.J. and WRONG, Margaret. Towards a literate Africa: report of a conference held under the auspices of the International Committee on Christian Literature for Africa and the Colonial Department of the University of London Institute of Education, December 1974. London, Longmans, 1948.

465. LIENHARDT, R.G. "Some African Christians". Blakfriars. v.33, No.382. January 1952: p14-21.

466. LOPETEGUI, Leon. El despertar cristiano de Africa. Bilbao, El Siglo de las Missiones, 1945.

467. LOUW, Johan K. "African music in Christian worship". African Music, v.2, No.1, 1958: p51-53.

468. LUFULUABO, Francois-Marie. "Mentalité religieuse Africaine et Christianisme". Revue du Clergé Africain, v.22, 1967: p318-341.

469. LUFULUABO, F. Valeur des religions africaines selon la bible
      et selon vatican. Kinshasa, Edition St. Paul Afrique,
      1968. 96p.

470. LUGIRA, Aloysius M. "African Christianity". African Eccle-
      siastical Review, v.12, No.2, 1970: p138-142.

471. LUGIRA, A. "Christ in African art". African Ecclesiastical
      Review, v.4, No.2, April 1962: p127-134.

472. LUNTADILA, Jean- C. Lucien. "Has christianity a future in
      present-day Africa? Ministry, v.9, No.4, 1969: p155-157.

473. LUPI, D. Giovanni Beltrame, missionario ed esploratore
      italiano in terra d' Africa. Verona, 1938.

474. LUYKX, Boniface. "Christian worship and the African Soul".
      African Ecclesiastical Review, v.7, No.2, April 1965:
      p133-143. v.7, No.3, July 1965: p220-225.

475. McCALLUM, F.V.I. "African ideas and the Old Testament".
      Nada, v.10, No.2, p5-11.

476. MACDONALD, A.J. Trade, politics, and Christianity in Africa
      and the east. With an introduction by Sir Harry Johnston.
      London, Longman, 1916. New York, Negro Universities Press,
      1969. 296p.

477. MAC GREGOR, J.K. "Christian missions and marriage usage in
      Africa". International Review of Missions, v.24, 1935:
      p184-191.

478. MACINNES, G. "Preaching and teaching in the African Parish".
African Ecclesiastical Review, v.13, No.1, 1971: p53-61.

479. McKENNA, J.C. and SANUSI, A. "The sociological aspects
of Catholic education in Africa". In Catholic education
in the service of Africa: report of the Pan-African
Catholic Education Conference, Leopoldville, 16-23
August 1965: p179-190.

480. MAcKENZIE, Jean K. African adventures. London, Religious
Tract Society, n.d. 112p. illus.

481. MAHIEU, Wauthier de. "Anthropologie et théologie africaines".
Revue du Clergé Africain , v.25, 1970: p378-387.

482. MAIER, Jean-Louis. L' episcopat de l' Afrique romaine,
vandale et byzantine. Rome, 1973. 453p. (Bibliotheca
Helvetica Romana, 11).

483. MAKUNIKE, E.C. ed. Christian press in Africa: voice of
human concern. Lusaka: Multimedia Publications, 1973.
61p.

484. MAKUNIKE, Ezekiel C. "Evangelism in the cultural context
of Africa". International Review of Missions, v.63,
No.249, 1974: p57-63.

485. MALULA, Joseph. "The Church and the hour of Africanisation".
African Ecclesiastical Review, V.16, No.4, 1974: p565-371.

486. MANGEMATIN, B. "Biblical catechesis in Africa today".
African Ecclesiastical Review, v.6, No.4, October 1964:

p366-373.

487. MANGEMATIN, B. "Catechese biblique en Afrique". Revue du
Clergé Africain, v.19, 1964: p549-560.

488. MANGEMATIN, B. "Making an African catechism". African
Ecclesiastical Review, v.6, No.3, July 1964: p233-238.

489. MARANTA, E. "The Catholic African and the present social
evolution in Africa: Christian social teaching as regards
class, nation, state and international community". African
Ecclesiastical Review, v.1. No.4, October, 1959: p225-238.

490. MARKUS, R.A. "Imperial administration and the Church in
Byzantine Africa". Church History, March 1967: p18-23.

491. MARSHALL, Thomas W.M. Christian missions: their agents and
their results. 2nd ed. London, Longman, Green, 1863.
2 vols.
A general survey of missionary enterprise. Pages 546-644
are devoted to Africa.

492. MATEENE, Kanombo. "Concepts of God in Africa". Cahiers des
Religions Africaines, v.5, No.10, July 1971: p302-305.
A review of John S. Mbiti's book of the same title,
written in French.

493. MATHESON, Elizabeth M. African apostles. Staten, New York,
Alba House, 1963. 224p. Includes bibliography.

494. MAUNY, Raymond. "Le judaisme, les juifs et l' Afrique
occidentale". Bulletin de l' IFAN, v.11, Nos. 3/4,

495.   MAURIER, Henri. "Approche theologique des religions
       traditionnelles africaines". Revue du Clerge
       Africain, v.24, No.1, January 1969: p5-15.

496.   MAURIER, Henri. Religion et developpement. Tradi-
       tions africaines et catecheses . Tours, Maison
       Mame, 1965. 190p. (Esprit de Mission).

497.   MAZE, J. La collaboration scolaire des gouvernements
       coloniaux et des missions. Afrique britannique,
       Afrique belge, Afrique francaise. Alger, Maison
       - Carree. 1933.

498.   MAZE, R. P. "Le prophetisme dans les Eglises prote-
       stantes d' Afrique". Revue des Grands Lacs,
       April, 1936.

499.   MBITI, John S. "Afrikanische Beitrage zur Christo-
       logie". In P. Beyerhaus (et al) (eds) Theolo-
       gische Stimmen aus Asien, Afrika und Lateinamer-
       ika. III. Munich, Kouser Verlag, 1968: p72-85.

500.   MBITI, John S. Afrikanische religion und weltansch-
       auung. Berlin, Gruyter, 1974. xv, 375p. bib-
       liog. (Studienbuch).

501.   MBITI, John S. "Christianity and traditional reli-
       gions in Africa". International Review of
       Missions. v. 59. No. 236p. October 1970:p430-
       440.
       The author concludes that if christianity in
       Africa is to expand, then it must adapt itself

77

to the local context. This would make it appear
more as a universal religion rather than as a
Western religion, and make it more tolerant
toward African traditional religions.

502. MBITI, John. "Church and state: a neglected element
of Christianity in contemporary Africa". African
Theological Journal v.5, 1973: p31-45.

503. MBITI, John S. "La contribution protestante à l'
expression culturelle de la personalité africaine". Colloque sur les religions, Abidjan,
5-12 Avril, 1961. Paris, Presence Africaine.
1962: p137-146.

504. MBITI, John S. The crisis of mission in Africa.
Kampala, Uganda Church Press, 1971, 10p.

505. MBITI, John S. New Testament eschatology in an African
background: a study of the encounter between New
Testament theology and African traditional concepts.
London, Oxford University Press, 1971. 244p.
In this book, Professor Mbiti is skeptical about
the capacity of African languages to sustain New
Testament teaching, even though he thinks that
Africans can make a contribution in the form of
music, dance and ritual.

506. MBITI, John S. "The ways and means of communicating
the Gospel". In Baeta, C.G. ed Christianity in
tropical Africa, studies presented and discussed

at the seventh International African Seminar, University of Ghana, 1965: London, Oxford University Press, 1968. p329-352.

507. MBONYINKEBE, Deogratias. "Un visage africain du christian-isme: l' union vitale bantu face a l' unite vitale eccle-siale". Cahiers des Religions Africaines, v.3, No.5, 1969: p143-147.
A review of Vincent Mulago's book published by Presence Africaine in 1965.

508. MBUNGA, Stephen. "Le role de la musique dans l' apostolat catechetique en Afrique". Revue du Clergé Africain, v.20 No.1, January 1965: p69-85.

509. MEINHOF, C. "Changes in African conceptions of law due to the influence of Christian missions". International Review of Missions, v.3, 1929: p430-435.

510. MELADY, P. "The impact of Africa on recent developments in the Roman Catholic Church". Race, v.7, No.2, 1965: p147-156.

511. MENSAC E, Pierre de. "La doctrine sociale catholique et les missions d' Afrique". Acta Tropica, v.2, No.3, 1945: p193-210.

512. MERLO, M. "Perspectives chretiennes en Afrique et a Madagascar". Civilisations, v.6, No.1, 1956: p91-95.

513. MITCHELL, Sir Philip and ALLCOCK, Ruth. Governments and missions in Africa. Part I. The case for cooperation by

Sir Philip Mitchell. Part 2. The contribution of missions, by Ruth Allcock. London, Church Missionary Society, 1943.

514. MITCHELL, Robert Cameron. "Africa's prophet movements". The Christian Century, v.81, No.47, 18 November 1964: p1427-1429.

515. MITCHELL, Robert C and MITCHELL, Charles B. "Chronicle of recent literature on religion in Africa, religion, Christianity in Africa". Journal of Religion in Africa, v.1, 1968: p150-152.

516. MITCHISON, N. "The future of Christian missions in Africa". Listener, v.70. 18 July 1963. p80-81.

517. MOERMAN, Canon J. "First Pan-African Catholic Education Conference (PACEC)." In Catholic Education in the service of Africa: report of the pan-African Catholic Education Conference, Leopoldville 1623 August 1965: p13-14.

518. MORRISON, James H. The missionary heroes of Africa. New York, Negro Universities Press, 1969. 276p.

519. MPONGO, Laurent. "La liturgie du marria dans la perspective africaine". Revue du clerge Africain, v.26, 1971: p177-197.

520. MSHANA, Eliewaha. "The challenge of black theology and African theology. Africa Theological Journal, v.5, 1973: p19-30.

521. MSHANA, Eliewaha E. "Church and state in the independent states in Africa". African Theological Journal, v.5,

1973: p46-58.

522. MSHANA, Eliewaha E. "Nationalism in Africa as a challenge
and problem to the Christian Church". African Theological
Journal, No.1, February 1968: p21-29.

523. MUCHABAIWA, Alexio. Church and African values, by Alexio
Muchabaiwa, Chaca Kosta, and Raphael Nweke. Edited by
Denys Lucas. Kampala, Gaba Publications, 1974. 26p.
(Pastoral papers no. 31)
Extracts from papers by a Rhodesian, a Sudanese, and a
Nigerian writer.

524. MUKENGE, Godefroid. "Une approche d' une spiritualite du
mariage chretien en Afrique". Revue du Clerge Africain,
v.26, 1971: p162-176.

525. MULAGO, Vincent. "Christianisme et culture africaine: apport
a la theologie. "In Baeta, C.G. (ed) Christianity in
tropical Africa; studies presented and discussed at the
seventh International African Seminar, University of Ghana,
1965. London, Oxford University Press, 1968: p308-328.

526. MULIRA, E.M.K. Thoughts of a young African. London, United
Society for Christian Literature. (Africa's own Library,
no. 14).

527. MUSHANGA, Musa T. "Church leadership in a developing society".
African Eccle siastical Review, v.13, No.1, 1971: p33-40.

528. MVENG, Englebert. "Les survivaneces traditionnelles dans les

81

sectes chrétinnes africaines". v.7, No.13, 1973: p63-74.

529. MVENG, Englebert. "Traditional remnants in modern African
sects". Bulletin Secretairatus pro Non-Christianis. v.20,
1972: p45-55.

530. MWASARU, Dominic. "The challenge of Africanising the Church".
African Eccle siastical Review, v.16, No.3, 1974: p285-294.

531. NASSAU, Robert H. Historical sketch of the Missions in Africa
under the care of the Board of Foreign Missions of the
Presbyterian Church. Philadelphia, Woman's Foreign
Missionary Society of the Presbyterian Church, 1881. 24p.

532. NCUBE, Pins A. "A Christian feast of tabernacles in Africa?"
African Eccle siastical Review, v.16, No.3, 1974: p269-276.

533. NDINGI, Bishop Raghael S. "To take deep roots: thoughts on
making the church truly African". World Mission, v.22,
No.4, Winter 1971-72.

534. NEWINGTON, David and PHILLIPS, H.C. The shape of African
Christian leadership: (a series of personality portraits
showing christian leadership in modern Africa). Nelspruit,
Emmanuel, 1962. iv, 59p. illus.

535. NGINDU, A. "L' efferverscence des eglises africaines". p437-445.

536. NIELEN, J. "For an African Christianity". Abbia, v.7, October
1964: p101-108.

537. NIELSEN, J. "Baptising the African mentality." African

Ecclesiastical Review, v.5, No.3, July 1963: p249-255.
Contends that in spite of the fact that christianity
has been introduced in Africa for over one hundred years
it has not succeeded in being accepted as an African
religion.

538. NILES, D.T. "The All African conference of Churches". International Review of Missions, v.52.
October 63: p409-413.

539. NKETIA, J.H. Kwabena. "The contribution of African culture to
Christian worship". International Review of Missions.
v.47, 1958: p265-278.
There are conflicting opinions about African culture and
Christian worship which emphasise the value of tradition
and change. This paper examines the problem of christian
worship in Africa against this background.

540. NORTHCOTT, William C. Christianity in Africa. Philadelphia,
Westminister Press, 1963. 125p. illus.

541. NORTHCUTT, C. "Modern missions and Africa". West African
Review, v.13, No.181: October 1942: p25-28.

542. NWOSU, S.N. "Mission schools in Africa". World Year book of
Education, 1966. p186-199.

543. NYAMITI, Charles. The scope of African theology. Kampala.
Gaba Publications, 1973. 51p.

544. NYERERE, J.K. "The Church in Africa in the 1970s". Mbioni
(Dar es Salam) v.6, No.4, 1970. p20-44.

545. O'CONNELL, J. "The Church and modernisation in Africa".
African Ecclesiastical Review, v.5, No.4, October 1963.:
p326-337.

546. OELSCHNER, Walter. Da fanden wir Brudder. Mission im Lichte
der Afrikareise. Duisburgh-Ruhrort, Brendow, 1967. 214p.

547. OJIKE, Mbonu. "Christianity in Africa". In Desai, Ram.
Christianity in Africa as seen by Africans. Denver,
Swallow, 1962: p60-66.

548. OJIKE, Mbonu. "Religious life in Africa". In Desai, Ram.
Christianity in Africa as seen by Africans. Denver,
Swallow, 1962. p49-59.

549. OLDHAM, John H. "The Christian opportunity in Africa".
International Review of Missions, v.2, 1925: p173-187.

550. OLDHAM, John H. "The Christian mission in Africa as seen at
the International Conference at Le Zoute". International
Review of Missions, v.16, January 1927: p24-35.

551. OLDHAM, J.H. "Christian missions, and African labour". International Review of Missions, April, 1921: p183-195.

552. OLIVER, R. How Christian is Africa? London, The Highway Press,
1956: 23p.

553. OLSON, H.S. "African music in Christian worship". In Barrett,
David Brian, (ed). African initiatives in religion.
Nairobi, East African Publishing House, 1971: p61-72.

84

554.   OLUMIDE, Y. "Christian broadcasting in Africa". International
       Review of Missions. v.60, No.420, October 1971: p505-511.

555.   ONAN, H. "African culture and ideology (vis a vis implanting
       socialism". African Communist, v55, 1973: p71-82.

556.   OOSTHUIZEN, G.C. "Causes of religious independentism in Africa".
       Fort Hare Papers, v.4, No.2, June 1968: p13-28.
       Examines the political, economic, historical, denominational,
       religious, ethnic, ecclesiastical, non-religious, and
       biblical factors that lead to the rise of independent
       churches in Africa.

557.   OOSTHUIZEN, G.C. "The Church among African forces" Practical
       Anthropology, v.11, No.4, July-August 1964: p162, 164-165.

558.   OOSTHUIZEN, G.C. "Independent African Churches; sects or
       spontaneous development?" Ministry. v.5, No.3, April 1965:
       p99-107.

559.   OOSTHUIZEN, G.C. "The misunderstanding of the Holy spirit in
       the independent movements in Africa". In Christuspredi-
       king in de wereld. Kampen, (Holland), Kok, 1965. p172-197.

560.   OOSTHUIZEN, G.C. Post-christianity in Africa: a theological and
       anthropological study. London, Hurst, 1968. xiv, 273p. ll
       illus.

561.   OOSTHUIZEN, Gerhardus C. "Sondebegrip by die separatistiese
       bewegins in Africa". Nederduitsch Gereformeerde Teolog-
       iese Tydskrif (S. Africa). v.5, No.4, 1964: p219-225.

562.   OTTO, S. "Francis Libermann, Apostle of Africa". African
        Ecclesiastical Review, v.4, No.3, July 1962: p226-231.

563.   OUMA, Joseph P.B.M. "The Christian and the integral deve-
        lopment of Africa". African Ecclesiastical Review, v.13,
        No.1, 1971: p12-17.

564.   OVERS, Walter Henry. The Church's investment in Africa.
        New York, National Council of the P.E.C., U.S.A. Dept.
        of Missions, 1924. 12p.

565.   PARRINDER, E.G. "Africa's churches advance". West African
        Review. v.33, No. 40p: January 1962: p5-9.

566.   PARRINDER, E.G. "Monotheism and pantheism in Africa".
        Journal of Religion in Africa, v.3, No.2, 1970: p82-88.
        bibliog.
        The author's overall impression is that much of African
        religious thought is both theistic and unitary, in that
        a single 'vital force' is conceived to animate a hierarchy
        of beings running from God through lesser spirits,
        ancestors, men, etc., to inanimate objects.

567.   PARRINDER, E.G. "The scriptures of African art". Orita,
        v.2, No.1, June 1968: p3-10.

568.   PARSONS, Ellen C. Christian liberator, an outline study of
        Africa, New York, London, Macmillan, 1905. viii, 309p.

569.   PARSONS, Robert T. "Missions-African relations". Civiliza-
        tions, v.3, 1953; p505-518.

570. PAYNE, Denis ,ed.' African independence and Christian freedom; addresses delivered at Makerere University College, Uganda, in 1962. London, Oxford University Press, 1965. 89p. (A Three Crowns book). Bibliog. Considers the problems of independence, church and state relationships, education and the family in Africa.

571. PAYNE, Roland J. "The influence of the concept of the traditional African leadership on the concept of Church leadership (some personal impressions)". African Theological Journal No.1, February 1968: p69-74.

572. PEILLON, P. "The pastoral aspects of Catholic education in Africa". In Catholic education in the service of Africa: report of the Pan-African Catholic Education Conference, Leopoldville, 16-23 August 1965: p191-202.

573. PENDER-CUDLIP, Patrick. "Religion and change in African history". International Journal of African Historical Studies, v.7, No.2, 1974: p305-311. A discussion and critique of Jan Vansina's review of the book The historical study of African religions, London, 1972; which appeared in vol. 6, No.1, 1973: p178-180 ∩f the abcve journal.

574. PENICK, Charles Clifton. Our mission work in Africa. (n.p) Protestant Episcopal Church, (n.d). 16p.

575. PERRAUDIN, Jean. Les principes missionnaires du Cardinal Lavigerie. Rapperswil, Berti, 1941.

576. PERRIN-JASSY, M.F. and others. Basic community in African

Churches. Maryknoll, N.Y., Orbis Books, 1973. xvl, 257p.
illus, bibliog.

577.   PERRIN-JASSY, Marie-France. La communaute de base dans les
églises africaines. Bandundu: Centre d' Etudes Ethnolo-
giques. 1970: 231p. Bibliog.
Review article by Gaston Mwene Baton in Cahiers des Religions Africaines, v.6, January 1972: p109-112.

578.   PHELPS STOKES FUND. Committee on Africa. The War and Peace
Aims. The Atlantic charter and Africa from an American
standpoint, a study. New York, 1942.

579.   "The PHENOMENON of independent churches in Africa". Ecumenical
Press Service (Geneva) v.1, 1970: p11-14.
Also in African Ecclesiastical Review, v.12, No.12, 1970;
p120-122.

580.   PHIPPS, W.E. "Christianity and nationalism in tropical Africa.
Civilizations, v.22, No.1, 1972: p92-100.

581.   POWER, E. "Black nuns in Africa". New Blackfriars, v.48,
December 1966: p143-146.

582.   PRAEM, Boniface Luykx O. "Christian worship and the African
soul. II. Worship adapted to African needs". African
Ecclesiastical Review. 1965, p220-225.

583.   PRICE, Thomas. "The task of mission schools in Africa". The
International Review of Missions, v.27, 1938: p223-228.

584.   PURY, R. de. Les eglises d' Afrique entre l' Evangile et la

coutume. Paris, Societe des missions evangeliques
de Paris, 1958. 96p. (Presence de la mission).

585   RAWSON, David P. "Africa's social and political demands
      on the church." Practical Anthropology. March-April
      1966: p75-83.

586   REDDINGTON, Anthony. "African Worship." Clergy Review,
      v.53, No.3, March 1968: p199-207.

587   "RELATIONS between the African communities, missions, traders,
      and the colonial administrations." In Baeta, C.G. ed.
      Christianity in tropical Africa, studies presented and
      discussed at the seventh International African Seminar,
      University of Ghana, April 1965. London, Oxford Univ.
      Press, 1968: p7-13.

588   RELIGION in Africa; proceedings of a similar held at the
      Centre of African studies, University of Edinburgh, 9th-
      12th April, 1974: 130p. (Mimeographed).

589   RENAULT, Francois. Lavigerie, l' esclavage africain, et l'
      Europe, 1868-1892. Paris, E. de Boccard, 1971. 2 vols.

590   RETIF, A. "Au service de l' Afrique chretienne. Le personnel
      missionnaire catholique en Afrique noire." Etudes,
      v.299, vol.1, October 1958: p32-42.

591   RICHTER, Julius. Geschichte der evangelischen Mission in
      Africa. Gutersloh, Bertelsmann, 1922.

592   RICHTER, J. "Missionary work and race education in Africa."

International Review of Missions, 1929: p74-82.

593. RIGBY, Mary John, Sister. Aflame for Africa: the white
     Sisters in Africa. Foreword by Douglas Hyde Billinge,
     Lancashire, Birchley Hall Press 1953. 83p. illus.

594. ROBINSON, James H. Africa at the crossroads. Philadelphia,
     Westminster Press, 1962: 83p.
     Analysis of Christian perspectives on social problems.

595. ROBINSON, John M. The family apostolate and Africa. Dublin,
     Helicon, 1964, xvi, 278p.
     This study attempts to present a synthesis of the aspects
     and implications of the family apostolate - the effort to
     build up christian married and family life in Africa, as
     well as a survey of its principal methods and organisations,
     with suggestions as to how to extend and improve family
     apostolate activity in Africa.

596. ROBINSON, John M. "Political cooperation between Catholics,
     non-Catholics and others: an urgent necessity in the new
     African states". African Ecclesiastical Review, v.2,
     No.4, October 1960: p319-322.

597. "Le ROLE de l' eglise chretienne. "Afrique noire: les Missions
     protestantes". Monde Non-Chretien, No.5, January-March
     1948: p582-613, No.6, April-June 1948: p694-721.

598. ROMMELAERE, Andre. "La preparation au bapteme dans les missions
     de l' Afrique noire". Neue Zeitschrift fur Missionswissen-
     schaft, v.4, 1950: p161-174.

599. ROSEVEARE, Richard. "The role of the church in the new Africa". New Times, no. 1, August 1967. p25-26.

600. ROSS, Emory. "Christianity in Africa". Annals of the American Academy of Political and Social Sciences. 1955: p161-169.

601. ROSS, Emory. "Impact of Christianity in Africa". Annals of the American Academy of Political and Social Sciences, v.298: March 1955: p161-169.

602. ROTBERG, Robert I and MAZURI, Ali A. ,eds. Protest and power in black Africa. New York, Oxford University Press, 1970. 127p. maps. Comparative study of resistance movements to European domination in Africa and their impact upon post-colonial developments. The study includes some African religious movements; especially the Christian separatist churches.

603. ROUTH, Jonathan. The nuns go to Africa. London, Methuen, 1971. 32p.

604. RUDOLPH, Ebermut. Schwarze Volker suchen Gott. Afrikas Christen auf eigenen wegen. Munchen, Claudius - Verl. 1969. 256p.

605. RWEYEMAMU, Robert. People of God in the missionary nature of the church. A study of concilian ecclesiology applied to the missionary pastoral in Africa. Rome, 1968. xiv, 132p.

606. RYTZ, Otto. "Das wiedererwachende religiose selbstbewusstsein der nicht-Christlichen volker und die mission in Afrika".

Evangelisches Missions Magazin. January 1947: p12-13.

607   SANON, A. "Communication sur les responsabilities de la
       theologie africaine." Revue du Clergé Africain, v.24,
       v.24, Nos 3/4, May-July 1969: p337-350.

608   SASTRE, Abbe. "Contribution de l' Eglise catholique à l'
       expression culturelle de la personalité africaine."
       In Colloque sur les religions, Abidjan, 5+12.Avril,
       1961. Paris, Presence Africaine: 1962: p183-194.

609   SASTRE, Robert. "Christianisme et cultures africaines."
       Tam - Tam, v.6, No.7, 1957: p12-23. Presence
       Africaine, Nos. 24/25 February-May 1959: p142-152.

610   SARPONG, Peter. "African theology and worship." Ghana
       Bulletin of Theology, v.4, No.7, December 1974: p1-9.

611   SARPONG, Peter. "The search for meaning: the religious
       impact of technology in Africa." Ecumenical Review,
       July 1972: p300-309.

612   SAWYERR, Harry. "The basis of theology for Africa. Inter-
       national Review of Missions, v.52, July 1963: p266-278.

613   SAWYERR, Harry. Creative evangelism: towards a new chris-
       tian encounter with Africa. London, Lutterworth Press,
       1968, 183p.

614   SAWYERR, Harry. "Theological Faculty Conference for Africa:
       an appreciation." African Theological Journal, No.3,

March 1970: p7-10.

615.   SCANLON, David G. ed. Church, state, and education in
        Africa. New York, Teachers College Press, Teachers
        College, Columbia University, 1966. 313p. Contri-
        butions stress the transfer of church and school lead-
        ership to African administrators by former colonial
        powers.

616.   SCHLOSSER, Katesa. "Les sectes d' Afrique du sud en tant
        que manifestation de la tension raciale". In Syncre-
        tisme et messianisme en Afrique noire. Paris,
        Editions du Seuil, 1963.

617.   SCHUTTE, I. "The Catholic church and agriculture in Africa".
        Neue Zeitschrift fur Missionswissenschaft, v.14,No.1,
        1958: p1-11.
        States that the Catholic Church in Africa can contri-
        bute much to agricultural development because of her
        widespread missions. It could build an Agricultural
        Institute which would train Africans to collect and
        interpret agricultural information for the missions.

618.   SCOTT, Clifford H. Protestant missionary images of Negro
        Africans, 1900-1940. Fort Wayne, Indiana University.
        Dept. of History, 1968. 19p.
        Paper presented at Annual Meeting of Organization of
        American Historians, Texas, April 1968.

619.   SCOTT, H.S. "Cooperation between Government and missions
        in African education". East and West Review, v.8,

No.4, October 1942: p207-211.

620.   SEATS, V. Lavell. Africa: arrows to atoms. Tennessee,
        Convention Press, 1967. 127p. illus. A popular
        account of the work and problems of Christian missions
        in Africa.

621.   SEMI-BI ZAN, "Messianismes et retour aux sources religieuses
        africaines, (evolution historique)". Afrique Litteraire
        et Artistique, April 28, p36-41.

622.   SETILOANE, Gabriel M. "Graduate school of ecumenical stu-
        dies and the younger churches in Africa". Ecumenical
        Review, v.14, October 1961; p65-68.

623.   SEUMOIS, Xavier. "Adaptation de la catechese moderne a 1'
        Afrique du' aujourd'hui". Revue du Clergé African,
        v.19, 1964: p532-546.

624.   SHEJAVALI, Abisai. "The influence of the concept of the
        traditional African leadership on the concept of Church
        leadership". African Theological Journal (Makumira)
        v.1, No.1, February 1968: p75-82.

625.   SHENK, Wilbert R. "Mission agency and African independent
        churches". International Review of Missions, v.63,
        No.252, October 1974: p475-491.

626.   SHEPPERSON, George. Joseph Booth and the Africanist diaspora.
        Evanston, Illinois, Northwestern University, 1972. 19p.
        The tenth Melville J. Herkovits Memorial lecture

delivered under the auspices of the program of African Studies.

627. SHEPPERSON, George. "Religion and the city in Africa: a historians observations". In Urbanization in African Social change. Centre of African Studies, Edinburgh, 1963: p141-150.

628. SHORTER, A. The African contribution to world church, and other essays in pastoral anthropology. Kampala, Gala Publishers, 1972. 73p. (Pastoral papers, 22).

629. SHORTER, Alward. African culture and the Christian Church: an introduction to social and pastoral anthropology. London, Chapman, 1973. xi, 229p. Invaluable study of the importance of African anthropology to the work of the christian Church in Africa. Includes facts, examples, ease-studies and practical applications.

630. SHORTER, A. "An African eucharistic prayer". African Ecclesiastical Review, v.12, No.2, 1970: p143-148.

631. SHORTER, A. and KATAZA, Eugene. "The churches' research on marriage in Africa". African Ecclesiastical Review v.14, No.2, 1972: p145-149.

632. SHORTER, A. "Dialogue with African traditional religions: an account of the GABA consultation". African Ecclesiastical Review, v.16, No.4, 1974: p425-428.

633. SHORTER, Aylward and "KATAZA, Eugene. Missionaries to

yourselves: African Catechists today. Maryknoll,
New York, Orbis Books, 1972: p212.

634.   SHORTER, A. "Prayer in African tradition". African Eccle-
         siastical Review. v.14, No.1, 1972: p11-17.

635.   SITHOLE, Ndabaningi. "An African Christian view". In
         Christianity in the non-western world, edited by
         Charles W. Forman, Englewood Cliffs, N.J. Prentice-Hall,
         1967. p111-114.

636.   SITHOLE, Ndabaningi. "African nationalism and christianity".
         Transition, v.10, September 1963: p37-39.
         Looks at Christianity from two angles, namely; culture-
         centred and christ-centered Christianity. States that
         both Christianity and African nationalism have two
         different roles to play, because neither dependence nor
         independence can put the religious function of christi-
         anity out of action.

637.   SLEVIN, Thomas B. "The Protestant-Catholic scandal in Africa
         a reply". African Ecclesiastical Review, v.2, No.2,
         April 1960: p126-1313.

638.   SMITH, Edwin Wikam. African beliefs and Christian faith.
         London, Lutterworth Press, 1944.

639.   SMITH, Edwin William. The christian message in Africa. A
         study based on the work of the International Conference
         at Le Zoute, Belgium, September 14-21, 1926. London,
         The International Mission Council, 1926. Collection of
         various views and opinions about the spread of christ-

ianity in Africa.

640.   SMITH, Edwin. The Christian mission in Africa. New York,
        The International Missionary Council, 1926. 188p.

641.   SMITH, Judson. History of the American board of missions
        in Africa. Boston, American Board Commissioners for
        missions, 1905. 85p.

642.   SMYKE, Raymond. "Christianity in Africa". Africa Report.
        May 1968: p8-12. illus.
        Review essay on twelve recent books on the theme of
        religion in Africa.

643.   "SOVIET Views on the Christian churches in Africa". The
        Mizan Newsletter, (Oxford) v.3, No.7, 1961: p16-23.

644.   SPITZ, Dom Maternus. "The growth of Roman Catholic missions
        in Africa". International Review of Missions, v.13,
        July 1924: p360-372.

645.   STEPHENS, A. John (ed). African attitudes to health and
        healing. Ibadan, The Editor, 1964. 71p. (mimeo).

646.   STEWART, James. Dawn in the dark continent, or, Africa
        and its missions. Edinburgh, Oliphant, 1903. 400p.
        (Duff missionary lectures for 1902).

647.   STORME, M.B. Evangelisatiepogingen in de binnenlanden van
        Afrika gedurende de de xix^e eeuw. Bruxelles, Institut
        Royal Colonial Belge, 1951.

648.   STUDER, Basile. "Encore 'la theologie africaine"
             Revue du clerge Africain, v.16, No.2, March 1961:
             p105-129.

649.   SUNDKLER, Bengt Gustaf Malcolm. The Christian Ministry in
             Africa. Uppsala. Swedish Institute of Missionary
             Research, 1960. 346p. illus. bibliog.
             (Studia missionalia upsaliensia, 2).

650.   SUNDKLER, Bengt Gustaf Malcolm. The concept of Christianity
             in the African independent Churches. Seminar Programme,
             1958. Durban, University of Natal, Institute for Social
             Research, 1958. 22p. Also in African Studies, v.20,
             No.1, 1961.

651.   "SURVEY of missionary work in Africa". International Review
             of Missions, v.24, No.93. January 1935: p65-82.

652.   SWORD OF THE SPIRIT. The Church to Africa: pastoral letters
             to the African hierachies. London, Sword of the spirit
             for the Africa Office, 1959. 136p.

653.   TAYLOR, John Vernon. "An African Christianity". C.M.S.
             Newsletter, (London) No. 331, October 1969: p1-4.

654.   TAYLOR, John Vernon. Christianity and politics in Africa.
             London, Penguin Books, 1957. 127p. (Penguin African
             Series, W.A. 9)

655.   TAYLOR, John V. "The development of African drama for
             education and evangelism". International Review of

Missions, v.39. No.155, July 1950. p292-301.

656. TAYLOR, John V. The primeval vision: christian presence
amid African religion. London, S.C.M. Press, 1963.
(Christian presence series).

657. TAYLOR, John V. Were you there? an African presentation of
the passion story. London, Highway Press, 1950.

658. TEMPLE, David G. and JONES, A.M. Africa praise: hymns
and prayers for schools. London, Lutterworth Press,
1968. 156p.

659. THOMAS, Louis-Vincent. "L' Africain et le sacré (reflexions
sur le devenir des religions". Bulletin de l' Institut
Fondamental d' Afrique Noire v.29, (B), Nos 3/4, July-
October 1967: p619-677.
A study based on questionnaires in 1955-66 to estimate
and evaluate the resistance of animistic, Islamic
Christian religions to new ideologies (Socialism and
Communism) in Africa.

660. THORNTON, D.M. Africa waiting; or, The problem of Africa's
evangelization. New York, Student Volunteer movement
for Foreign Missions. 1903. 148p.

661. THORNTON, M. "The work of the Catholic Church in British
tropical Africa: a study in cooperation".
Ph.D. Thesis. University of London, 1932-33.

662. TIELEMANS, A.M. "L' art chretien dans l' Afrique Septentri-
onale". L' Artisan liturgique. v.40, 1938: p844-845.

663.   TOBERT, R.G. "Maintaining the light in Africa" In Venture
         of faith, by Robert Tobert. Philadelphia, The Judson
         Press, 1955: chapter xvii.

664.   TOPPENBERG, Valdemar E. Africa has my heart. Mountain
         View, California, Pacific Press Pub. Association, 1958.
         168p. illus.

665.   "The TRAINING of village teachers in Africa: a memorandum".
         International Review of Missions, v.2, 1929: p231-249.

666.   TROBISCH, W.A. "Church discipline in Africa". Practical
         Anthropology, v.8, September 1961: p200-208.

667.   TROWEL, H.C. The passing of polygamy: a discussion of
         marriage and sex for African Christians. London, Oxford
         University Press, 1940. viii, 90p. (African Welfare
         Series).

668.   TURNER, Harold Walter. "African prophet movements".
         Hibbert Journal, v.61, No.242, April 1963: p112-116.

669.   TURNER, Harold Walter. "African religious movements and
         Roman Catholicism". in H.J. Greschat and H. Jungraith-
         mayr (eds) Wort und religion: Kalima na Dini, Stuttgart,
         Evangelisches Missionsverlag, 1969: p255-264.

670.   TURNER, Harold Walter. "A methodology for modern African
         religious movements". Comparative studies in Society
         and History, v.7, No.3, 1966: p281-294.

671.   TURNER, Harold W. Modern African religious movements: an

introduction for the Christian Churches. Nsukka,
University of Nigeria, 1965. 10p. (Mimeograph).

672. TURNER, Harold W. "The place of independent religious
movements in the modernizations of Africa". Journal
of Religion in Africa v.2, No.1: p43-63.
Argues that independent religious movements in Africa
have contributed immensely to the development of political nationalism and assisted political unification
by disregarding territorial frontiers in Africa.
By undermining the mystical beliefs of chieftaincy and
tribalism, independency has helped the transition to
secular society.

673. TURNER, Harold Walter. "Problems in the study of African
independent churches". Numen, v. 13, No.1, 1966:
p27-42.

674. TURNER, Harold W. "Religion today: African prophet
movements". Hibbert Journal, v.61, April 1963: p112-
116.

675. TURNER, Philip. "The wisdom of the fathers and the Gospel
of Christ: some notes on Christian adaptation in Africa".
Journal of Religion in Africa', v.4, 1971/72: p45-68.

676. VANNESTE, Alfred. "Debat sur la theologie africaine:"
Revue du Clergé Africain, v.15, No.4, July 1960:
p333-352.

677. VANNESTE, Alfred. "Ou en est le probleme de la theologie
africaine? Cultures et Developpement, v.6, No.1, 1974:

p149-167.

678. VANNESTE, Alfred. "Theologie universelle et théologie
      africaine". Revue du Clergé Africain, v.24, Nos. 3/4,
      May-July 1969: p324-336.

679. VANNESTE, Alfred. "Valeurs des religions africaines selon
      la Bible et selon vatican". Cahiers des Religions
      Africaines, v.2, No.4, July 1968: p343-346. Review
      article of a book by F. Lufuluabo.

680. VANNESTE, Chanoine Alfred. "People of God in the missionary
      nature of the church: a study of concilian ecclesiology
      applied to the missionary pastoral in Africa.".
      Cahiers des Religions Africaines, v.3, No.6, July 1969:
      p321-323.
      A review of a book of the same title by Robert Rweye-
      mamu.

681. VAN THIEL, Paul. "Divine worship and African Church music".
      African Ecclesiastical Review, v.3, No.1, January 1961:
      p73-76; v3, No.2, April 1961: p144-147.

682. VAN THIEL, Paul. "Text, tone and tune of African sacred
      music". African Ecclesiastical Review, v.6, No.3,
      July 1964: p250-257.

683. VILAKAZI, Absalom. African religious concepts and the
      separatist movements. Paper read to the Second
      Annual Conference, American Society of African Culture,
      New York City, 1959. 10p. (mimeograph).

684.   VONCK, Pol. J. "Theological Faculty Conference for Africa:
         personal comment". African Theological Journal, No.3,
         March 1970: p11-16.

685.   VOORN, J. "Africanisation of theology". African Eccle-
         siastical Review, v.8, No.4, October 1966: p309-316.

686.   WALIGORSKI, A. The Jews in Africa. Caorp, American
         University Press, 1966.

687.   WALKER, F.D. Call of the dark continent; a study in
         missionary progress, opportunity and urgency. London,
         Foreign Missions Conference, 1923. 34p.

688.   WALLS, Andrew Finlay. "The theological faculty and local
         studies in Africa". In Christian theology in indepen-
         dent Africa, edited by Harry Sawyerr. Freetown,
         Fourah Bay College, 1961: p24-29.

689.   WARREN, Max A.C. Christianity in the new Africa. London,
         Prism Pamphlets, (1964). 18p.

690.   WATT, W.M. Religion in Africa. Edinburgh, University Centre
         of African Studies, 1964. 130p. (mimeograph).

691.   WEBSTER, J.B. "Independent Christians in Africa". Tarikh,
         v.3, No.1, 1969: p56-81.

692.   WELBOURN, F.B. "Missionary stimulus and African responses".
         In Colonialism in Africa, 1870-1960, edited by V.
         Turner. New York, Cambridge University Press, 1971.
         p310-345.

Attempts to assess changes in colonial Africa as a product of Western Culture of which Christian missionaries were important representatives.

693.   WELBOURN, F.B. "Some problems of African Christianity: guilt and shame". In Baeta, C.G. ed. Christianity in tropical Africa, studies presented and discussed at the seventh International African Seminar, University of Ghana, 1965. London, Oxford University Press, 1968: p182-200.

694.   WELCH, J.W. "Can Christian marriage in Africa be African?" International Review of Missions, v.22, No.85, January 1933: p17-32.

695.   WEMAN, H. African music and the Church in Africa. Stockholm, Swedish Institute of Missionary Research, 1960.

696.   WENZEL, Kristen. "Clergymen's attitudes toward black Africa: role of religious beliefs in shaping them. Washington, D.C., Center for Applied Research in the Apostolate, 1971. 183p. illus.

697.   WENZEL, Kristen. "The relationship between beliefs and missionary attitudes held towards black Africa: a study of protestant and Catholic clergymen serving churches within the five boroughs of New York City". Ph.D. thesis, Catholic University of America, 1970: 263p.

698.   WESENICK, Jurgen. "On the crisis concerning the office of evangelist in Africa". African Theological Journal,

No.3, March 1970: p37-52.

699.   WESTERMANN, D. Africa and Christianity. London, Oxford
          University Press, 1937. x, 221p. A general survey
          of missionary tasks in relation to changes in African
          culture and needs.

700.   WIEGRABE, Paul. Christus auf der Sklavenkuste: Bilder aus
          hundert Jahren deutscher Missionsarbeit in Afrika.
          Hamburg, Reich und Heindrich, 1947.

701.   WIELAND, Robert J. For a better Africa. 6th ed. Kendu
          Bay, Kenya, Africa Herald Publishing House, 1967.
          93p. illus.

702.   WIELAND, Robert J. Pour une meilleure Afrique. Dammarie-
          les-Lys, Seine-et-Marne, Editions Signes des Temps,
          1965. 95p. illus.

703.   WILHELM, R.A. Modern Africa. New York, Society for the
          Propagation of the Faith, 1945.

704.   WILLIAMS, Walter B. "Fighting the devil in Africa".
          Missionary Review of the world, v.29, August 1916:
          p597-601.

705.   WILLIS, J.J. An African church in building. London,
          Church Missionary Society. 1952.

706.   WILSON, Frank T. "The future of missionary enterprise in
          Africa south of the Sahara". Journal of Negro
          Education, v.30. Summer 1961: p324-333.

707.   WILSON, Monica (Hunter). "An African Christian morality".
        Africa, v.10, 1937: p265-291.

708   WILSON, Monica (Hunter). Religion and the transformation
        of Society in Africa - a study in social change in
        Africa. Cambridge, Cambridge University Press, 1971.
        165p. (The Scott Holland memorial lectures, 1969).

709.   WILSON, William J. ed.   The Church in Africa: Christian
        mission in a context of change. Maryknoll, N.Y.
        Maryknoll Publications, 1967. xii, 177p.

710.   WORLD STUDENT CHRISTIAN FEDERATION. A new look at Christ-
        ianity in Africa. Geneva, World Student Christian
        Federation, 1972. 82p.

711.   WRIGHT, Marcia. "African history in the 1960's: religion".
        African Studies Review, December 1971: p403-424.
        Explores the problems of religious studies as a sub-
        field of African history.

712.   WRONG, Margaret. "The Church's task in Africa south of the
        Sahara". International Review of Missions, April 1947:
        p201-231.

713.   ZEITZ, Leonard. Some African messianic movements and their
        political implications. Paper read to the second
        Annual Conference, American Society of African Culture.
        New York City, 1959. 42p. (mimeograph).

714.   YOUNG, T. Cullen. "How far can African ceremonies be
        incorporated in the Christian system?" Africa, v.8,

No.1. January 1935: p210-217.
Discusses the possibility of adapting certain African
ceremonies to Christian worship.

715.   ALDERSON, C. "The church in Central Africa". East and
        West Review, v.29, January 1963.

716.   ANDERSON- MORSHEAD, A.E.M. The history of the universities
        Mission to Central Africa, 1859-1909.
        London, Office of the Universities Mission to Central
        Africa. 1909. 448p. illus.

717.   BAINES, Thomas. The Northern goldfields: diaries of Thomas
        Barnes, 1862-1872. Edited by J.P.R. Wallis. London,
        Chatto & Windus. 1947. 3 vols. (Central African
        Archives, Oppenheimer series, no. 3).

718.   BALDWIN, Arthur. A missionary outpost in Central Africa.
        London, 1914.

719.   BLOOD, A.G.B. The history of the Universities mission
        to Central Africa. London, Universities Mission to
        Central Africa, 1957.

720.   BLOOD, Arthur Gordon. Spearhead of Africa's progress,
        a review of the word of the Universities mission to
        Central Africa in 1943. London, Universities Mission
        to Central Africa. 1943. iv. 43p.

721.   BOLINK, Peter. Towards church union in Zambia: a study of
        missionary cooperation and church-union efforts in
        Central Africa. Franeker, Netherlands., Wever, 1967,

427p. Bibliog.
A thorough study of the movement towards church unity
in Zambia by a Missionary of the Dutch Reformed Church
(Orange Free State) in South Africa.

722.   BOWEN, T.J. Central Africa: adventures and missionary
        labors in several countries in the interior of Africa,
        from 1849 to 1856. Charleston, Southern Baptist
        Publication Society, 1857. xii, 359p.

723.   BRIAULT, "L' art chrétien en Afrique equatoriale". L'
        Artisan liturgique, v.40. 1938: p841-843.

724.   BROOMFIELD, Gerald Webb. Towards freedom. With a foreword
        by the Archbishop of York, London, Universities' Mission
        to Central Africa, 1957.

725.   CARPENTER, George W. "Church, state and society in Central
        Africa". Ph.D. Thesis, Yale University, 1937.

726.   CATRICE, Paul. Un audacieux pioneer de l' Eglise en Afrique:
        Mgr. Comboni et l' evangelisation de l' Afrique Centrale:
        vie et caractère d' un precurseur, idées et methodes
        missionnaires, le drame de l' Eglise du Soudan, les
        Comboniens. Lyons, Editions Vitte, 1964. viii, 139p.

727.   COILLARD, Francoise and Christine. Coillard of the Zambesi:
        the lives of Francois and Christine Coillard of the
        Paris Missionary Society, in South and Central Africa,
        1858-1904, by Catherine W. Mackintosh. London, T.
        Fisher Unwin, 1907. 848p.

728.   COLLIARD, Francois. On the threshold of Central Africa:
        a record of twenty years pioneering among the Batsi
        of the Upper Zambesi. Translated from the French and
        edited by Catherine Winkworth Mackintosh. 3rd ed.
        with a new introduction by Max Gluckman. London, Frank
        Cass, 1971. illus. (Cass library of African studies,
        missionary researches and travels, no. 19).

729.   CUNNINSON, Ian. "Jehova's witnesses at work: expansion in
        Central Africa". The Times British Colonies Review,
        v.29, No.1, 1958: p.13.

730.   CUNNISON, Ian. "A Watchtower Assembly in Central Africa".
        International Review of Missions, v.40, No. 160:
        October 1951: p456-469.

731.   DALLACIACOMA, Florentiono. I missionari camilliani con
        Mons. Comboni nell'Africa centrale 1867-77 (con
        riposta al Prof Michelangeo Crancelli, biografia di
        Comboni. Verona, La Tripografica Veronese, 1924.

732.   DAVY, Yvonnee. Going with God: on missions of mercy in
        Central Africa. Illustrated by Robert W. Nicholson.
        Washington, Review & Herald Publishing Association,
        1959. 192p. illus.

733.   DU PLESSIS, Johannes. The evangelization of Pagan Africa:
        a history of Christian missions to the pagan tribes
        of Central Africa. (Yao, Ngoni, Tonga). London,
        Walker. xll, 408p.

734.   ELSTON, P. "A note on the Universities' Mission to Central

Africa, 1857-1914". In B. Pachai, (ed). The early
history of Malawi. London, Longman, 1972: p344-364.
bibliog.
Early history of the Anglican mission in Malawi during
the period 1859-1914.

735. FERNANDEZ, James W. "African religious movements; types
and dynamics". Journal of Modern African Studies,
v.2, No.4, 1964: p531-549.
Describes the elementary forms of religious movements
in Africa, the Syncretic type of religious movement in
equatorial Africa, and the present and future role of
religious movements in the progress toward nationalism
and pan-Africanism.

736. FRAY, Marion. "New church members' orientation in Central
Africa in the light of biblical and historical back-
grounds". Ph.D. Thesis, Southwestern Baptist Theological Seminary, 1968. 254p.

737. GOOD, Adolphus Clemens. Life for Africa; Rev. Adolphus
Clemens Good, American missionary in equatorial Africa,
by Ellen C. Parson, 2nd ed. New York, Fleming H.
Revell, 1898. 316p.

738. HANNA, A.J. The beginnings of Nyasaland and North-Eastern
Rhodesia, 1859-1895. Oxford, Clarendon Press, 1956.
viii, 281p. illus.
Pages 1 - 106 of this book treat "Christianity,
commerce, and civilization, versus the slave trade"
in the context of Nyasaland and Rhodesia.

739.   HANNA, A.J. "The role of the London Missionary Society in
the opening up of East Central Africa".
Transactions of the Royal Historical Society, v.5,
1955. p41-59.

740.   HANNA, A.J. _The story of the Rhodesias and Nyasaland_.
London, Faber & Faber, 1960. 288p. illus.
This is the first attempt to survey the history of the
Rhodesias and Nyasaland in a single book. Chapter 3
is an account of the development and growth of Chris-
tianity and commerce in the country.

741.   HOOKER, J.R. "Witnesses and watchtower in the Rhodesias
and Nyasaland". _Journal of African History_, v.6, No.1,
1965: p91-106.
Jehovah's witnesses in general have been suppressed in
Southern Rhodesia and kept under close surveillance in
Nyasaland and Northern Rhodesia. They are regarded as
subversives, conservatives and non-political in a
predominantly political world.

742.   INTERNATIONAL MISSIONARY COUNCIL. _Modern industry and the
African: an inquiry into the effect of the copper
mines of Central Africa upon native society and the
work of Christian missions_, by J. Merle Davis. New York,
Negro Universities Press, 1969. xxxviii, 425p.

743.   JACK, James. _Daybreak in Livingstonia: the story of the
Livingstonia mission, British Central Africa_. New York,
Fleming H. Revell, 1900, 371p.

744.   JENKINS, D. and STEBBING, D. _They led the way: Christian_

pioneers of Central Africa. London, Oxford Univ. Press, 1966: 80p.

745.   KAGAME, Alexis. "Poesie chretienne en Afrique Centrale". Revue de l' Aucam, 1946/47, p209-213.

746.   LIVINGSTONE, David. Livingstone's missionary correspondence, 1841-1856, edited with an introduction by I. Schapera. London, Chatto & Windus 1961. xxvi, 342p. illus.

747.   LIVINGSTONE, David. Some letters from Livingstone, 1840-1872. Edited by David Chamberlain. London, Oxford University Press, 1940.

748.   MACKINTOSH, Catharine W. Some pioneer missions of Northern Rhodesia and Nyasaland. Livingstone, Northern Rhodesia, Rhodes-Livingstone Museum, 1950. 42p. illus. (The occasional papers of the Rhodes-Livingstone Museum, new series, no.8).

749.   MAcMIN, R.D. "The first wave of Ethiopianism in Central Africa". The Livingstone News, v.4, 1909: p56-59.

750.   McNAIR, James I. Livingstone the liberator. London, Collins, 1940.

751.   MARTIN, Marie-Louise. "Face aux mouvements prophetiques et messianiques en Afrique meridionale". Monde Non Chrétien, v.64. October-December 1962: p226-255.

752.   MILFORD, T.R. "In Central and Southern Africa for theological education fund". The International Review of

Missions.   v.50, July 1961: p286-292.

753.   MILLS, D.Y. The quest of the mighty: a short history of the
          Universities mission to Central Africa for young
          people. London, Universities Mission, 1920. 128p.

754.   MWAMBA, Simon. "Mission in a Watch Tower area". Central
          Africa (London) v.73, No.866, 1955: p42-44.

755.   OLIVER, E.W. and WALLS, Andrew F. "The Livingstone inland
          mission and the McCall papers". Bulletin of the Society
          for African Church history, v.1,   No.1, 1963: p21-23.

756.   "The PIONEER missions". In A.J. Willis, An introduction
          to the history of Central Africa. 3rd ed. London,
          Oxford University Press, 1973: p97-114.
          Historical account of the first two missionary expedi-
          tions to the Zambezi following Livingstone's appeal in
          Britain.

757.   "La PREMIERE conference intermissionnaire d' apres-guerre d'
          Afrique Equatoriale, Leopoldville, 1946" Monde Non-
          Chrétien, v.7, July-September 1948; p813-850.

758.   RAGOEN, J. "De Watch-Towers of Getuigen Van Jehova in
          Midden-Afrika" Nieuw-Afrika v.72, No.3, 1956: P111-
          115, No.4, 1956: p157-161.

759.   RANGER, Terrence O. Aspects of Central African history.
          London, Heinemann, (1968). 291p.

760.   RANGER, T.O. and Weller, John ,eds. Themes in the
         Christian history of Central Africa. Berkeley,
         University of California Press, 1974: 304p.
         Case histories on a number of religious cults and
         political Institutions such as the Nyan Society and
         the Mbona Cult in Central Africa.

761.   ROOME, William J.M. Through Central Africa for the Bible.
         London, Marshall, Morgan & Scott, 1928. 209p.

762.   ROTBERG, Robert. "The rise of nationalism in Central Africa:
         the making of Malawi and Zambia, 1873-1974".
         Cambridge, Mass., Harvard University Press, 362p.
         Chapter vi deals with "The Religious Expression of
         dissatisfaction" in which account is given of the
         watch Tower Movement and other Millenial sects.

763.   ROWLEY, Henry. The story of the Universities Mission to
         Central Africa: from its commencement under Bishop
         Mackenzie, to its withdrawal from the Zambezi. 2nd
         ed. New York, Negro Universities Press, 1969. 424p.
         illus.

764.   SAMARIN, W.J. "Religion and modernization in Africa"
         Anthropological Quarterly, v.39, No.4, 1966: p288-297,
         bibliog.
         Based on data drawn from the Gbeya of the Central
         African Republic, this paper examines and challenges
         the thesis that life in Africa is becoming increasingly
         secularised.

765.   SCHMID, Erich. "L' erezione del vicariato apostolico dell'

Africa centrale (1846)". (The establishment of the
Vicariate Apostolic of Central Africa) Euntes Docete,
v.22, 1969: p99-127.

766.   SEAVER, George. David Livingstone, his life and letters.
London, Lutterworth Press, 1957. 650p.

767.   SHEPPERSON, George. "Church and sect in Central Africa".
Journal of the Rhodes-Livingstone Institute, v.33,
1963: p82-94.

768.   SHEPPERSON, George. "David Livingstone 1813-1873: a
centenary assessment". Geographical Journal, v.139,
No.2, 1973: p207-219.

769.   SHEPPERSON, G. "The politics of African Church Separatist
Movements in British Central Africa, 1892-1916". Africa,
v.24, 1954: p233-246.

770.   SHEPPERSON, George. "Religion in British Central Africa".
In W.M. Watt, Religion in Africa. Edinburgh, Univer-
Centre of African Studies, 1964. p47-51.

771.   SODERBERG, Gustav. Missionsresa i Centralafrika. Orebro,
Evangeliipress, 1970. 157p. illus.

772.   SPRINGER, John McKendree. The heart of Central Africa;
mineral wealth and missionary opportunity. Cincinati,
Jennings & Graham, 1909. 223p.

773.   STEWART, James. Livingstonia, its origin; an account
of the establishment of that mission in British

Central Africa. Edinburgh, Elliot, 1894. 138p.

774.   TILSEY, G.E. Dan Crawford, Missionary and pioneer in
        Central Africa. London, Oliphant, 1929: xix, 609p.

775.   TINDAL, P.E.N. A history of Central Africa. London,
        Longman, 1968. 348p. illus.
        An outline history of Central Africa, covering Malawi,
        Zambia and Rhodesia. Chapter 7 outlines the work of
        the early missionaries from 1850 -1890 which preceeded
        the effective establishment of government by European
        powers. It also considers the achievements of the
        missionaries and the reasons for the degree of
        success they obtained.

776.   TONIOLO, E. "The first centenary of the Roman Catholic
        Mission to Central Africa, 1846-1948". Sudan Notes
        and Records, v.27, 1946: p99-126.

777.   TUTTLE, Sarah. The African traveller; or, Prospective
        missions in Central Africa. Boston, Massachusetts
        Sabbath School Society, 1832. 150p.

778.   VAN DER BURGT, J.M.M. Het kruis geplant in een onbekend
        Negerland van Midden-Afrika: verhaal van de stichting
        der Sint- Antonius-Missie in het koningrijk oeroendi.
        Boxtel, Witte Paters, 1921.

779.   VANSINA, Jan. "Religions et sociétes en Afrique centrale".
        Cahiers des Religions Africaines. January 1968: p95-
        107.

780.   WADDELL, Hope Masterton. Twenty nine years in the West
       Indies and Central Africa: a review of missionary work
       and adventure, 1829-1858. With a new introduction by
       G.I. Jones. 2nd ed. London, Cass, 1970. xxvi, 681p.
       illus. (Cass Library of African Affairs. Missionary
       Researches and Travels, no. 11).

781.   WILKINSON, F.O. Green. "Christianity in Central Africa".
       African Affairs, v.62. October 1963: p300-308.

782.   WILLS, A.J. An introduction to the history of Central
       Africa. 2nd ed. London, Oxford University Press,
       1967: 412p. bibliog.
       Pages 97-114 contains an account of the pioneer
       missions to Central Africa.

783.   WILSON, George Herbert. The history of the Universities'
       Mission to Central Africa. London, Universities
       Mission to Central Africa, 1936. 228p.

784.   WORSLEY, Peter M. "Religion and politics in Central Africa".
       Past and Present, v.15, April 1959: p73-81.

                            ANGOLA

785.   ALVES CORREIA, Joaquim. Civilizando Angola e Congo; os
       missionarios do Esprito Santo no padroado espiritual
       portugues. Sousa Cruz, 1922.

786.   BEATON, Kenneth I. Angola now: a brief record of the program
       and prospects of the West Africa Mission of the United
       Church of Canada. Toronto, Committee on Missionary

Education, United Church of Canada. 1945. 64p. illus.

787.   BRIAULT, Maurice. Une soeur missionnaire, la soeur St.
        Charles de l' Immaculée-conception de Castres, missio-
        nnaire au Gabon pendant 50 ans, de 1859 a' 1911. Tequi,
        1914.

788.   BRINDA, Matthieu. La Bible secrète des noirs selon le
        Bouity, Paris, Omnium Litterarum, 1952. 148p. illus.

789.   CARDOSO, Carlos Lopes. "Ethnographic and linguistic aspects
        of baptism in Angola". Occidente (Lisbon) v.50, 1971.
        p67-76.

790.   CHILDS, Gladwyn M. "The Church in Angola: a few impressions"
        International Review of Missions, v.186, April 1958:
        p186-192.
        The Protestant church has been established for over
        80 years. Out of a population of 4 million in 1950,
        1,912,747 were estimated as Protestants. This paper
        analyses the role of the Church in Angola in bringing
        about social change.

791.   COLE, C. Donald. "The trial of Sachilama (umbundu church
        leader, Angola)" Practical Anthropology, v.14, No.5,
        September-October, 1967: p228-231.

792.   CUVELIER, J. "Missionnaires capucins des missions de
        Congo et d' Angola du xvii^e et xviii^e siecle". Congo.
        v.1, No.4, November 1932: p504-522: v.2, No. 5, Decem-
        ber 1932: p684-703.

793.   "L'EGLISE et la crise Angolaise" Revue du Clerge Africain,
        v.16, No.3, 1961: p439-449.

794.   LECOMTE, Pere. "Para a historia das missoes catolicas en
        Angola". Portugal em Africa v.157, January-February
        1970: p17-26.

795.   MARGARIDO, Alfredo. L' eglise toko et le mouvement de
        liberation de l'Angola". (The Toko church and the
        liberation movement in Angola) Moisen Afrique, v.5,
        Mai, 1966: p80-97.
        Tokoism started in 1949 in the Congo after Simon Toko,
        the Angolan founder of the movement, broke away from
        the Baptists. Tokoism absorbed a large number of the
        practices of the Kimbanguist church.

796.   MONNIER, Henri. Mission Philafricaine en Angola, 1897-1947.
        Lausanne: Mission Philafricaine en Angola, 1947.

797.   ROONEY, C.J. "Catholic Portuguese missions of Angola".
        Journal of Race Development. (Worcester) v.2,
        January 1912: p282-308.

798.   "SECTES nouvelles en Angola". In Devant les sectes non-
        chré. tiennes xxxie semaine de Missiologie, Louvain
        1961. Louvain, Desclée de Brouwer, 1961: p140-143.

799.   SOREMEKUN, . "Religion and politics in Angola: the American
        Board Missions and the Portuguese government 1880-1922".
        Cahiers d' Etudes Africaines, vii, No.3, 1971: p341-
        347.

800   TASTEVIN, R.P. "Nouvelles manifestations du prophetisme
         en Afrique equatoriale en Angola." Comptes Rendus
         Mensuels des seances de l' Academie des Sciences
         Coloniale, v.16, No.3, 1956: p149-154.

801   VAN OVERSCHELDE, A. Monseigneur Leon-Paul Classe, premier
         Vicaire Apostolique du Ruanda. Imprimerie de Kabgayi.
         1945.

802   WILSON, Thomas Ernest. Angola beloved. Sketches by J. Boyd
         Nicholson, Neptune, N.J. Loizeaux Bros., 1967. 254p.
         illus.

CONGO BRAZZAVILLE AND ZAIRE

803   AFONSO, Dom. "An African response to Christianity" In
         William H. McNeill and Mitsuko Iriye. Modern Asia
         and Africa, London, Oxford University Press, 1971: p43-
         71.
         Translated version of King Afonso I of the Congo's
         letter to King Dom Manuel of Portugal, dated 15th
         October 1514, on African response to christianity in
         the Congo.

804   ALDEN, K. "The prophet movement in Congo." International
         Review of Missions, v.25, No.99, July 1936: p347-353.

805   ALEXIS, Frere M. Gochet. La barbarie africaine et l'action
         civilisatrice des missions catholiques au Congo et dans
         l' Afrique equatoriale. Liege, H. Dessain, 1889. 208p.

806.   ANCKAER, Leopold. De evangelizatiemetode van de mission-
        arissen van Scheut in Kongo, 1888-1907. Brussel, Kon.
        Aca, voor overzeese wetensehappen, 1970. 307p.

807.   ANDERSON, Efraim. Churches at the grass-roots: a study in
        Congo-Brazaville. London, Lutterworth Press, 1968.
        296p.

808.   ANDERSON, Efraim. Messianic popular movements in the Lower
        Congo. Uppsala & Stockholm, Almquist & Wicksell, 1958.
        x111, 287p. illus. (Studia ethnographica Uppsaliensia,
        14). Bibliography.
        A study of the major prophetic movements in the former
        French & Belgian Congo from 1921 to the 1950.
        Inlcudes Kimbanguism, Ngunzism, Matswanism, Salvation
        Army and the Munkykusu Movement.

809.   ANET, H. and ANET, Mrs. H. Message of the Congo Jubilee
        and West African Conference, Leopoldville, September
        15-23, 1928. Leopoldville, Conseil Protestant du
        Congo, 1929.

810.   ANET, Henri. "A propos du Kibangisme". Congo, v.5, No.2,
        1924: p771-773.
        A refutation of charges that Protestant missionaries
        prompted the formation of Kimbanguism.

811.   ANET, Henri. "Protestant missions in Belgian Congo".
        International Review of Missions. July 1939: p415-425.

812.   ANNA, Andrea d'. De cristo a Kimbangu. Traductor. Manuel

de la Cera. Madrid Ediciones. Combonianas, 1966.
1966. 146p.

813. ANSTEY, Roger T. "Christianity and Bantu philosophy:
observations on the thought and work of Placide Tempels".
International Review of Missions, v.52. July 1963:
p316-322.

814. ANSTEY, Roger. King Leopold's legacy: the Congo under
Belgian rule, 1908-1960. London, Oxford University
Press for International Institute of Race relations,
1966. 293p.

815. ANTOINE, N. "Vicariat Apostolique de Baudouinville - pères
Blancs". Lovania, v.8, 1945/46: p9-33.

816. ANYENYOLA, Jacques-Oscar. "Leadership dans les movements
prophetiques de la ville de Lumumbashi". Problemes
Sociaux Congolais.
The three prophetic movements discussed in this paper
are the Kitawala (a Congolese branch of the Watchtower
Association), Kimbanguism, and the Lumumbashi Apostolic
Church of Africa.

817. ARNOT, Frederick Stanley. Garenganze; or Seven years'
pioneer mission work in Central Africa. New ed. with
a new introduction by Robert I. Rotberg. London, Cass,
1969. xxiv, 276p. (Cass Library of African Studies,
Missionary Researches and travels, no. 10).

818. AUFFRAY, A. En pleine brousse equatoriale: histoire de la
Mission Salesienne du Katanga (Prefecture Apostolique

du Luapula Superieur) Congo Belge. Turin, Societe Internationale d' Editions, 1926.

819. AUGOUARD, Prosper Philippe. Un explorateur et un apôtre du Congo francais. Mgr. Augouard, archeveque titulaire de Cassiopée, vicaire apostolique du Congo francais, sa vie, par le baron Jehan de Wilte, ses notes de voyage et sa correspondance. Paris, Emile-Paul Freres, 1914. 375p.

820. AXELSON, Sighert. Culture confrontation in the lower Congo. From the Old Congo kingdom to the Congo independent state with special reference to the Swedish missionaries in the 1880's and 1890's. Stockholm, Gummesson, 1970. 339p. (Studia missionalia Uppsaliensia, 14).

821. AZOMBO, Soter. "Quelques reflexions a propos de la jamaa' au Congo". Tam-Tam (Paris) v. 5/6, 1965: p79-87.

822. BAESTEN, Victor S.J. Les anciens Jesuites au Congo 1548-1648. Bruxelles, Vromant, 1898.

823. BALLANDIER, G. "Breves remarques sur les Messianismes del Afrique congolaise". Archives de Sociologie des Religions: v.3, No.5, 1958: p91-95.

824. BALLANDIER, Georges. "Messianisme des Ba-Kongo". Encyclopedie Coloniale et Maritime Mensuelle, v.1. No.12, August, 1951. p216-220.

825. BALLANDIER, Georges. "Naissance d' un mouvement politico-

religieux chez les Ba-Kongo du Moyen-Congo". Proceedings of the third International West African Conference,
held at Ibadan, Nigeria, December 1949. Lagos, Nigeria,
Museum, 1956: p334-336.

826.   BAYLY, Joseph T. Congo crisis: Charles and Muriel Davis
relive an era of missions during weeks of imprisonment
in Stanleyville, Africa. London, Eastbourne, Victory
Press, 1966: 224p.

827.   BAZOLA, Etienne. La conversion au Kimbanguisme et ses
motifs. Leopoldville. Université Lovanium. (Memoire
de Licence en Sciences Pedagogiques. 199p.

828.   BAZOLA, Etienne. "Le Kimbanguisme". Cahiers des Religions
Africaines". v.2, No.3, January 1968: p121-152: v.2,
No.4, July 1968: p315-336.
Kimbanguism is a doctrine which is still in the process
of elaboration. It involves a belief in God, the
Trinity, Jesus, Salvation, Heaven and the divine mission
of Simon Kimbangu.

829.   BERTSCHE, James E. "Kimbanguism: a challenge to missionary
statesmanship". Practical Anthropology v.13, No.1,
1966: p13-33. Also in Congo Mission News, v.209.
July-September 1965: p24-29.
Reviews the development of Kimbanguism, a form of
prophetic, separatist christian religion in the Congo,
whose leader Simon Kimbangu of Bakongo, was born around
1890.

830.   BERTSCHE, James. "Kimvabgyyism: a separatist movement".
        M.A. Thesis, Northwestern University. 1963.

831.   BEGUIN, Willy. "Decouverte... et actualite du Kimbanguisme
        et son histoire". Le Monde non-chretien. n.s. 89/90.
        January - June 1969. p4-7. p14-26. maps.

832.   BENTLEY, William Holman. Pioneering on the Congo. With a
        map and 206 illustrations from sketches, photos, and
        materials supplied by the Baptist Missionary Society,
        several of their missionaries and the Govt. of the
        Congo Free State. London, Religious Tract Society,
        1900. New York, Johnson Reprint Corp. 1970. 2v. illus.

833.   BERNARD, Guy. "Diversité des nouvelles églises congolaises".
        Cahiers d' Etud es Africaines, v.10, No.2, 1970: p203-
        227.
        Account of the proliferation and diversity of politico-
        religious movements in the Congo since the attainment
        of independence.

834.   BERNARD, Guy. "Les eglises congolaises et la construction
        nationalé. Revue de l' Institut de Sociologie. v.40,
        No.2/3 1967: p241-247.
        Apart from the Kimbanguist church in the Congo which
        participates in all national events, the imported
        sects like the Jehovah's Witnesses and the Seventh
        Day Adventists generally refuse any participation in
        all efforts towards national growth.

835.   BERNARD, G. and CAPRASSE, P. "Religious movements in the
        Congo: a research hypothesis". Cahiers Economiques et

Sociaux, v.3, No.1, March 1965. p49-60.
Comparative study of Jehova's Witnesses, the Mpadist
Church, and the Kimganguist Church of Jesus Christ.

836. BIEBUYCK, M.O. "La societe Kumu face au Kitawala". Zaire,
v.11, No.1, January 1957: p7-40.
A study of the relationship between Jehovah's Witnesses
and the political, social and religious aspects of Kumu
society.

837. BOKEIEALE, Itofo Bokambanza. "From missions to mission: the
church in Zaire and new relationships". International
Review of Mission, v.62, No.248, 1973: p433-436.

838. BONTINCK, F. "Le conditionnement historique de 1' implanta-
tion de 1' eglise Catholique au Congo". Revue du clerge
Africain, v.24, No.2, March 1969: p132-145.

839. BROAMANN, Martin. Zwischen Kreuz und fetisch; die Geschichte
einer Kongomission. Bayreuth, Hestia, 1965. 386p.
illus.

840. BOSSCHE, Jean Venden. Sectes et associations secretes au
Congo belge. Leopoldville, Editions du Bulletin
Militaire, 1954. 101p.

841. BOUCHARD, J. "Messianisme de Ba- Kongo". Encyclopedie
Coloniale et Maritime Mensuelle. v.1, No.12, August,
1951.

842. BOUCHER, A. Mgr. Au Congo francais, les missions catholiques.

Paris, Tequi, 1928.

843.   BRAEKMAN, E.M. Histoire du protestantisme au Congo.
        Bruxelles, Librairies des Eclaireurs. Unionistes,
        1961. 391p. illus. (Collection Histoire du
        Protestantisme en Belge et au Congo Belge.

844.   BROUSSARI, N. "Watch Tower Oder Kitawala im Kongo.
        (Watch Tower or Kitawala in the Congo)". Hemecht a
        Mission, No.1, 1947:p19-20;No.2, 1947: p50-51; No.3,
        1947: p85-87.

845.   BROWN, A.R. "An examination of the educational system of
        the American Baptist Mission in the Belgian Congo,
        with special attention to government policy". B.D.
        Thesis, Berkeley Baptist Divinity School, 1951.

846.   BROWN, W.H. "A critical and historical study of the evange-
        listic work of the American Baptist Mission in the
        Belgian Congo". B.D. Thesis, Berkeley Baptist Divinity
        School, 1957.

847.   BROWN, Wesley H. "Eglise evangeliques et societes
        missions au Congo". Revue du Clerge African, v.23,
        No.1, January 1968: p42-55.

848.   BROWNE, Stanley G. "The indigenous medical evangelists in
        Congo". International Review of Missions. v.35,
        No. 137, January 1946: p59-67.

849.   BUKASA, Gerard. "Notes sur le Kindoku chez les Congo".

Cahiers des Religions Africaines. No.3, January 1968: p153-169. Tables.

850 CAMBIER, J. "Nouveauté du Christ et renouveau chrétien dans l' église du Christ." Revue du Clergé Africain, v.24, No.2, March 1969: p146-161.

851 CAMPS, Arnulf. "New ways of realizing a Christian togetherness in non-western countries." Internationales Jarbuch fur Religions-soziologie. (Koln) v.5, 1969: p182-94.

852 CARPENTER, George Wayland. Les chemins du seigneur au Congo; commemorant soixante-quinze ans de missions protestantes 1878-1935. Leopoldville, Librairie evangelique au Congo, 1953. 91p. illus.

853 CARLSON, Lois. Monganga Paul; the Congo ministry and martyrdom of Paul Carlson, M.D. New York, Harper & Row, 1966. viii, 197p.

854 CHESTERMAN, C.C. "Medical missions in Belgian Congo." International Review of Missions, v.26, No.26, No.103 1937; p378-389.

855 CHRIST and the Congo: findings of conferences held under the leadership of Dr. John F. Mott at Leopoldville, Mutoto and Elizabethville, Congo Belge, 1934. Leopoldville-Ouest, Conseil Protestant du Congo, London & New York, International Missionary Council, 1934.

856.   CHURCH OF JESUS CHRIST (Kimbanguist Church) Office du
        Prophète Simon Kimbangu. (Nkanda Bisambu bis tata
        Simon Kimbangu). Leopoldville, La Reunion des
        Pasteurs Kimbanguistes, n.d.). 115p. illus.
        Contains a biographical account of Kimbangu, the
        liturgy of the Kimbanguist Church and ten hymns in the
        Kikongo language.

857.   CLINE, Catherine Ann. "The Church and the movement for
        Congo reform". Church History, v.32, No.1, 1963: p46-
        56.

858.   COMHAIRE, Jean. "Societes secrètes et mouvements prophe-
        tiques au Congo Belge". Africa, v.25, No.1 1955: p54-
        59.

859.   CONGO Missionary Conference, 1st. Report of the United
        Missionary Conference on the Congo. Leopoldville,
        January 19-21, 1902. Matadi, Swedish Mission Press,
        1902.

860.   CONGO Missionary Conference, 2nd. Report of the Conference
        of Missionaries of the Protestant societies working in
        Congoland. Leopoldville, January 29-31, 1904. Bolobo,
        Hannah Wade Press, 1904.

861.   CONGO Missionary Conference. 3rd. Report of general
        conference of missionaries of the Protestant Societies
        working in Congoland, Kinshasa, January 9-14, 1906.
        Bongandanga, Congo Balolo Mission Press, 1906.

862.   CONGO Missionary Conference. 4th. Report of general confe-

rence of missionaries of the Protestant Missionary Societies working in Congoland. Leopoldville, September 17-22, 1907. Bolobo, Baptist Mission Press, 1911.

863   CONGO Missionary Conference. 5th. Report of general conference of missionaries of the Protestant Societies working in Congoland, Kinshasa, September 14-19, 1909.

864   CONGO Missionary Conference, 6th. Report of general conference of missionaries of the Protestant Societies working in Congoland, Bolenge, Haut Congo, October 11-17, 1911. Bolobo, Baptist Mission Press, 1911.

865   CORNELIS, Jos. "Lettera pastorale dell' Arcivescovo di Elizabethville sul moviemento africano della Jamaa." Le Missioni Francescane. (Rome) v.41, 1965: p28-31.

866   COXHILL, H. Wakelin. "Enseignement a dispenser aux indigenes du Congo Belge, tel que le concoivent les Missions Protestantes." Congo Mission News, No.151, July 1950: p8-9, 19.

867   CRABBE, R. "La situation religieuse au Congo." Congo An.V. Eurafrica et Tribune du Tiers-Monde, v.8, No.7/8, July-August, 1964: p48-50.

868   CRAWFORD, John R. "Aspects of culture clash in the Congo, 1878-1920." Missiology, v.1, No.3, July 1973: p367-375.

869   CRAWFORD, John R. "Protestant missions in Congo, 1960-1965".

International Review of Missions v.55, No.217: p86-95.

A review of the activities of the Protestant missions in the Congo from the point of view of evangelical work, education and training, medical and relief work, and prospects for the future.

870.   CRAWFORD, John R. Protestant missions in Congo, 1878-1969. Black Mountain, North Carolina, The Author, (n.d.) 26p.

871.   CROSS, A.J. "Katanga copper and indigenous evangelism". World Dominion, v.3, No.4, October 1929:

872.   CUYPERS, L. "La politique fonciere de l' etat Independent du Congo a l'égard des missions catholiques". Revue d' Histoire Ecclesiastique, v.57, No.1, 1962: p45-65. No.2, 1962: p446-469.

873.   DAVIS, Jackson and others. Africa advancing; a study of rural education and agriculture in West Africa and the Belgian Congo. New York, The Friendhsip Press, London, International Committee on Christian Literature for Africa. 1945. ix, 230.
Report of a survey on the missionary efforts in West Africa and the Congo in the rural development schemes of the people.

874.   DECAPMAEKER, R.L. "Le Kimbanguisme". In Devant les sectes non-chrétiennes, xxxle semaine de Missiologie, Louvain, 1961. p52-66.
An account by a Roman Catholic missionary in the Congo, describing contemporary Kimbanguism with quotations from Kimbanguist documents.

875. DE COCKER, M. "Essai de parallelisme biblico-congolais".
Zaire, v.4, No.3, 1950: p277-298.

876. DE CRAEMER, Willy et al. Analyse sociologique de la jamaa.
Kinshasa, Centre de Recherches Sociologiques (Episcopat
Catholique du Congo) 1965. 79p. (mimeo).

877. DE CRAEMER, Willy. "The Jamaa movement in the Katanga and
Kasai regions of the Congo". Review of Religious
Research, v.10, No.1, 1968: p11-23.

878. DECRAENE, Philippe. "Les incidences politiques des
religions syncretiques et des mouvements messianiques
en Afrique noire." Afrique Contemporaine, v.17,
January-February 1965: p19-22.
A historical study of syncretic and messianic movements in the Congo from the 17th century, especially
Matswanism and the growth of pan-African religious
consciousness.

879. DEGRYSE, O. "The lay apostolate in the Congo; the formula
best suited to Africa". Christ to the World, v.6,
1961: p350-358.

880. DE HEMPTINNE, J.F. La politique des missions protestantes
au Congo. Elizabethville, Editions de L' Essor du
Congo, 1929.

881. DE JONGHE, Edward. "Formations recentes des sociétes
secrètes au Congo belge," Africa, v.9, No.1, January
1936: p56-63. Also in Congo, v.1, 1936: p233-242.

CONGO BRZZAVILLE AND ZAIRE

882.   DEKEN, Constant de. Twee jaar in Congo   Heruitg. op
        initiatief van het Conite de Pater de Deken-Feesten
        te Wilrijk op 15 Juni 1952. Antwerpen, De Vlijt, 1952.
        203p.

883.   DEL VASTO, Lanza. "Simon Kimbangu et la non-violence
        africaine". Jeune Afrique, (Paris) v.385, 20-26 May
        1968: p

884.   DE MOEUS, Fr. and STEENBERGHEN, R. Les missions religie-
        uses du Congo Belge. Bruxelles, Editions Zaire, 1947.

885.   DENIS, Leopold. "les Jesuites au Congo belge". Lovanica,
        v.7, 1945: p7-58.

886.   DENIS, Leopold. Les Jesuites belges au Kwango 1893-1943.
        Bruxelles, L' Edition Universelle, 1943. 127p.

887.   DE WAELE, Frank. "La catechèse dans les jamaas a Leopold-
        ville". Kinshasa, 1965. (unpublished manuscript).

888.   DE WITTE, Jehan. Un explorateur et un apôtre du Congo
        francais: Monseigneur Augouard, Archevèque Titulaire
        de Cassiopée, Vicaire Apostolique du Congo francais.
        Paris, Emile-Paul Freres, 1924.

889.   DIANGENGA, J. "Le Kimbanguisme". Courrier Hebdomodaire,
        No. 60, 29 January 1960: p16-17.

890.   DIEU, Leon. Dans la brousse congolaise: les origines des
        Missions de Scheut au Congo. Liege, Marcechal, 1946.

891.   DODSON, James R. "Some proposals for the development of
        the educational program of a theological school in the
        Belgian Congo". Ph.D. Thesis, Columbia University.
        Teachers College, 1958.

892.   DOUTRELOUX, Albert. "Prophetism and development". Africa
        Quarterly: v.6, No.4, 1967: p334-342.
        History of Kimbanguism in the Congo and the Prophetic
        Church of Mayumbe.

893.   DOUTRELOUX, Albert. "Prophetisme et culture Kongo". Africa
        Kring, v.2, 1961: p169-174.

894.   DOUTRELOUX, Albert. "Prophetisme et leadership dans la
        societe Kongo". In Devant les sectes non-Chrétiennes,
        xxxie semaine de Missiologie, Louvain, 1961.
        Louvain, Desclee et Brouwer, 1961: p52-66.

895.   "Foi chretienne et langage humain: Compte rendu de la
        septieme semaine theologique de Kinshasa, organisée
        par la Faculte de Theologie de 1' universite Natio-
        nale du Zaire, du 24 29 Juillet 1972". Cahiers des
        Religions Africaines v.6, July 1972: p239-254.

896.   FABIAN, Johannes. "Charisma and cultural change: a study
        of the Jamaa movement in Katanga". Ph.D. Thesis,
        University of Chicago, 1969.

897.   FABIAN, Johannes. "Charisma and cultural change: the case
        of the Jamaa Movement in Katanga (Congo Republic)".
        Comparative studies in Society and History, v.11,
        No.2, April 1969: p155-173.

The author concludes after a lenthy analysis, that
certain aspects of the Jamaa movement indicate that
current theories about the relationship of charismatic movements and cultural change need to be
revised and modified.

898.   FABIAN, Johannes. "Dream and Charisma: 'theories of
         dreams' in the Jamaa - movement (Congo)". Anthropos,
         v.61, Nos 3/6, 1966.: p544-560.
         The Jamaa is a charismatic family movement in the
         Catholic communities of Katanga and South-eastern
         Congo. A specific theory of dreams appears to be
         an important element in the ideology of the movement.

899.   FABIAN, Johannes. Jamaa: a charismatic movement in Kata-
         nga. Evanston, Ill., Northwestern University Press,
         1971. xi, 284p.
         Based on intensive field work, this detailed study of
         the movement begins with a biography of Father
         Tempels, centering on those aspects of his life that
         led to his special role. The author then character-
         ises the members of the movement and the social and
         personal factors contributing to their participation.
         Includes a detailed examination of the jamaa system
         of thought.

900.   FILESI, Teobaldo. Le relazioni tra il regno del Congo
         e la Sede apostolica nel xvi secolo. Como, P. Cairoli,
         1968. 249p. illus. (Publicazioni de 11' Instituto
         italiano per 1' Africa, Quaderni Africa, no.10).

901. FILESI, Teobaldo. Roma e Ceongo all'inizio del 1600.
Nuouve testimonianze. Como, P. Cairoli, 1970. 103p.
illus. (Quaderni d' Africa, 11).

902. FORD, W.H. "Conversion and its recognition in Congo converts".
International Review of Missions v.22,
No.87, 1933: p377-387.

903. GERARD, O. "Christian life in the Jamaa". Christ to the
World, v.9, 1964: p22-32.

904. GERARD, O. "A remarkable case of fruitful adaptation in
Africa: the Jamaa in the Congo; with reports by Fathers
Mulago Piette and Tempels". Christ to the World (Rome)
v.9, 1964: p16-32: p119-131.

905. GIOVANNI FRANCESCO DA ROMA. Breve relation de la fondation
de la mission des freres mineurs capucins du seraphique
pere saint Francois au Royaume du Congo, et des parti-
cularites, coutumes et facons de vivre des habitants
de ce royaume. Louvain, Editions Nauwelaerts, 1964.
xxviii, 149p.

906. GRENFELL, George. George Grenfell: pioneer in Congo. London,
Student Christian Movement, 1927. 248p. (Modern
series of missionary biographies).

907. GROSJEAN, J. "Que pensent les Chretiens Congolais de leur
eglise et de leur clerge". Revue du Clergé Africain,
v.23, No.3, May 1968: p358-372.

908.   HAES, René de. "Pour une anthropologie chrétienne du
         mariage au Congo". Cahiers des Religions Africaines,
         v.3, No.5, 1969: p131-132.
         A review article of a book with the same title by
         Laurent Mpongo, published in Kinshasa in 1968.

909.   HARRISON, Mary. Mama Harri - and no nonsense: missionary
         memories of a Congo casualty. Foreword by Norman P.
         Grubb, London, Oliphants, 1969: 128p. (Lakeland pub-
         lications).

910.   HEIMER, Haldor Eugene. "The Kimbanguists and Bapostolo:
         a study of two African independent churches and in
         the context of Lulua traditional culture and religion".
         Ph.D. Thesis, Hartford Seminary Foundation, 1971. 496p.

911.   HERTSENS, L. "Christianisme et conversion au Lac Albert".
         Revue de l'Aucana, v.23, January 1948: p89-93.

912.   HOLAS, B. "Compte rendu du livre de Efraim Anderson,
         Messianic Popular Movements in the Lower Congo",
         Uppsala, 1958. Also In Bulletin de 1' Institut
         Francais d' Afrique Noire. v.21, No. 3/4 Juillet-
         Octobre, 1959.

913.   IDOTI. With God in the Congo: Priests during the perse-
         cution under rebel occupation, as told by an African
         Pastor to David M. Cavies. Gerrards Cross, Bucks,
         England, Worldwide Evangelisation Crusade, 1971.

914.   IGLESIAS ORTEGA, Luis Maria. Los simbas llaman a meurte;

dominicas espanolas en el Congo. Villava Espanca,
Editorial OPE, 1965. 238p. illus.

915.   "INFLUENCE politico-religieuse au Congo belge - expansion
du Kumbanguisme". Notes et Documents, v.1, January
1960: p39-40.

916.   IRVINE, Cecilia. "The birth of the Kimanguist movement in
the Bas-Zaire 1921". Journal of Religion in Africa,
v.6, No.1, 1974: p23-76.
Traces the history of the movement in the light of
current research findings which have added significantly to the scant body of knowledge about the
movement.

917.   JACOBSSON, Per-Olof. Hemma hos oss i Kongo. Stockholm,
Filadelfia, Solna, Seeling, 1968. 47p. illus.

918.   JADIN, Louis. "Apercu de la situation du Congo et rite
d' election des rois en 1775, d' apres le P.
Cherubino da savona, missionaire au Congo de 1759 a
1774". Bulletin de I'Institut Historique Belge de
Rome, v.35, 1963: p347-419.

919.   JADIN, Louis. "Le clerge seculier et les capucins du Congo
et d' Angola aux xvi[e] et xvii[e] siecles". Bulletin de
1' Institut Historique Belge de Rome, v.36, 1964:
p185-419.

920.   JADIN, Louis. "Le Congo et la secte des Antoniens: restauration du royaume sous Pedro IV et la 'Sainte Antoine'
congolaise (1694-1718)". Bulletin de 1' Institut

Historique Belge de Rome, v.33, 1961. p411-615.

921.   JADIN, Louis. "Les sectes religieuses secretes des Antoniens
        au Congo (1703-1709)". Cahiers des Religions Africaines,
        v.2, No.3, 1968: p109-120.

922.   JANSSEN, T.M. "Religious encounter and the Jamaa" Heythrop
        Journal, v.8, 1967: p129-151.

923.   JEANROY, Vincent. Vingt-cinq ans de mission au Congo:
        histoire de la mission des Falls fondee et dirigee
        par les pretres du Sacre-Coeur de Jesus. Bruxelles,
        Action Catholique, 1923. 208p.

924.   JOSET, Paul-Ernest. "Quelques mouvements religieux au Bas-
        Congo et dans l' ex-Afrique-Equatoriale francaise".
        Journal of Religions in Africa, v.1, No.2, 1967.
        p101-128.
        Discusses Kimbanguism, Ngouzism, les Missions des Noirs,
        and the Tansi, Bola-Manonga and Mayangi sects, as well
        as the influence of the Salvation Army.

925.   JUMP, Chester and JUMP, Margaret. Coming-ready or not;
        Congo Baptists advance. Illustrated by John Savidge,
        Philadelphia, Judson Press, 1959. 100p.

926.   KIA-MAHANIAH, Kimpianga. "The building of the first Baptist
        Church in the Congo". Cahiers des Religions Africaines,
        v.5, No.10, July 1971: p197-230.

927.   KIBONGI, R. Buana. "L' evolution du Kimbanguisme".
        Flambeau (Yaounde) 10, May 1966: p75-81.

928 KIBONGI, R.B. "Le reveil spirituel au Congo-Brazaville."
   Flambeau, v.11, August 1966: p143-157.

929 KARLSSON, Elsa. Med Gud i Kongo; personliga minnen och
   upplevlser. Orebro, O.Ms forlag, 1956. 170p.

930 KELLER, Jean. "Le protestantisme au Congo-Kinshasa."
   Revue Francaised' Etudes Politiques Africaines, v.32,
   August 1968: p52-62.
   Traces the origins and spread of Protestantism in the
   Congo from the first efforts of private individuals
   in the 1880s to independence, showing the work of the
   missions in the fields of education and health.

931 KENYON, Albert. Congo crusade: the story of Henri and
   Paula Becquet. London, Salvationist Pub. & Supplies,
   1955. 94p. illus.

932 "KIMBANGUISME." Afrique Ardente, v.31, No.110, 1959: p1-7.

933 KOPYTOFF, Igor. "Suku religion: a study in internally
   induced reinterpretation." Ph.D. Thesis, Northwestern University, 1960.

934 KRATZ, Michael. La mission des redemptoristes belges au
   Bas-Congo; la periode des semailes (1899-1920)
   Bruxelles, Academie royale des sciences d' outremer,
   1970. 402p.

935 KREMER, Eva Maria. Mutter am Kongo; Lebensbild der Gresch-
   wister Falter. Bayreuth, Hestia. 1963. 248p.

936.   LABRIQUE, J. "Etudes du movement Kitawala". Belcopresse,
          v.3, 1956: p88-99.

937.   LAGERGREN, David. Mission and state in the Congo: a study
          of the relations between Protestant missions and the
          Congo Independent state authorities with special
          reference to the Equator district, 1885-1903. Lund:
          Gleerup, 1970. 366p. Bibliog. map. (Studia Mission-
          alia Uppsaliensia, 13).

938.   LANZAS, A. and BERNARD, G. "Les fideles d' une nouvelle
          église au Congo". Genève-Afrique, v.5, No.2, 1966:
          p189-216.
          Description of 'L' Eglise Apostolique Africaine,
          founded in Lusaka in 1927, drawn mainly from Protes-
          tantism, with vague and unwritten doctrines based on
          the Bible, which is interpreted with the aid of the
          Holy Spirit by so called 'apostoles'.

939.   LASSERRE, J. "L' église Kimbanguiste africaine et non-
          violente". Cahiers de la Reconciliation". Nos 5/6,
          May-June 1966: p1-52.

940.   LASSERRE, Jean. "L' église Kimbanguiste du Congo". Monde
          Non-Chrétien, Nos 79/80, July/December, 1966: p45-52.
          A study of the history, organisation, doctrines and
          social activities of the Church of Jesus Christ,
          founded by Simon Kimbangu.

941.   "L' EGLISE au Congo et au Ruanda Urundi". Bulletin des
          Missions, v.24, No.1, 1950: xvi, 106p. illus.

942.   "L'EGLISE du Congo dans la tourmente"   Vivante Afrique,
         May-June 1965. 48p.

943.   "L' EGLISE du prophète Kimbangu". Reforme (Paris). v.20,
         No.1192, 1968: p10-11.

944.   "L' EGLISE et le Congo independant". Revue du Clergé
         Africain, v.15, No.5, September 1960: p437-446.

945.   LEGRAND, Pierre and THOREAU, Benoit. Les Benedictions au
         Katanga: vingt-cinq ans d' apostolat 1910-35.
         Lophem-Les-Bruges, Abbaye de Saint-Andre.

946.   LELONG, Maurice Hyacinthe. Mes frères du Congo. Préface
         de George Hardy. Illustré de Paul Henri Durand.
         Alger, Beconnier, 1946. 2 vols. illus.

947.   LEPAGE, Andre. "L' organisation du prophetisme Kongo".
         Cultures et Developpement. (Louvain) v.2, No.2, 1969-
         70: p407-425.

948.   LERRIGO, P.H.J. "Protestant missions in relation to the
         future of Congo". International Review of Missions,
         April 1936: p227-234.

949.   LERRIGO, P.H.J. "The prophet movement in Congo". The
         International Review of Missions, v.11, No. 42, April
         1922: p270-277.
         Account of the origins of the Kimbanguist movement.

950.   LIBERT, Evelyne. "Les missionnaires chrétiens face au
         mouvement Kimbanguiste: documents contemporains (1921)"

Etudes d' Histoire Africaine, (Louvain) v.2, 1971: p121-154.

951. LUFULUABO, Francois-Marie. Mariage coutoumier et mariage chretien indissoluble. Kinshasa, Les Editions St. Paul Afrique, 1969. 46p.

952. LUNTANDILA, Lucien. "L' eglise Kimbanguiste est-elle une veritable église". L' Essor-Reconciliation (La Chaux de Fonds, Switzerland). v.61, No.18, 1966. p2.

953. LUYKX, Boniface. "Le directoire pour la messe à l'usage des dioceses du Congo". Revue du Clerge Africain, v.18, No.3, May 1963: p237-248.

954. LWAKALE, Celestin M. "Initiation africaine et initiation chrétienne. Kinshasa, Editions du C.E.P. 1966: 101p.

955. MABIE, C.L. Our work in the Congo; a book for mission study classes and for general information. Boston, American Baptist Publication Society.

956. MACBEATH, Andrew. "The revival in Bolobo, Belgian Congo". International Review of Missions; v.27, July 1938: p415-423.

957. MACGAFFEY, Wyatt. "The 'Beloved City': comments on a Kimbanguist text". Journal of Religion in Africa, v.2, No.2, 1969: p129-147.

958. MACGAFFEY, Wyatt. "Autobiography of a prophet". Cahiers Economiques et Sociaux (Kinshasa) v.4, No.2, June

1966: p231-235.
A biography of Mabwaaka Mpaka Gabriel, a Congolese
prophet.

959.   McINTOSH, Ducan. "The church and Kimabnguism" Congo
        Mission News (Kinshasa). No.222,
        January - March 1969: p24-25; No.223, April- June 1969:
        p22-25.

960.   MAHANIAH KIMPIANGA, J.W. "Kingunzu of Simon Kimbangu: a
        case study of the protonationalism movement in the
        Democratic Republic of the Congo". Ph.D. Thesis,
        Temple University, 1970.

961.   MAKENGERE. "Vigilance! Kitawala ou Watch-Tower" Revue
        Coloniale belge, v.1, No.8, February 1964: p4-7.

962.   MANICOM, Peter J. "Will Kimbanguism lead to a deeper
        understanding of the Christian faith?" Missionary
        Herald. (London). Janaury 1970: p10-11.

963.   MARKOWITZ, Martin D. Cross and sword: the political role
        of Christian missions in the Belgian Congo, 1880-1892.
        London New York, Oxford University Press, 1973. 586p.
        illus.

964.   MARKOWVITZ, Marvin D. Cross and sword: the political role
        of Christian missions in the Belgian Congo, 1908-1960.
        Stanford, California, Hoover Institution Press, 1973.
        223p.

965.   MARKOWITZ, Marvin D. "The missions and political develop-
        ment in the Congo". Africa, July 1970: p234-247.

966.   MARTIN, Marie-Louise. "Christus im Kongo; aus Geschichte
        und Leben der Kimbanguisten-Kirchen". Das Wort in der
        Welt (Hamburg), v.6, December 1968: p161-164. illus.

967.   MARTIN, Marie-Louise. "Confessing Christ in the Kimbanguist
        Church". International Review of Missions, v.64,
        No.253, January 1975: p25-29. The author is the Prin-
        cipal of the Kimbanguist Theological Seminary, Kinshasa,
        Zaire. This article which reviews the history and
        activities of the Kimbanguist Church, is based on a
        report given at the Congress of International Asso-
        ciation for Mission Studies, 29th July to 2 August,
        Frankfurt, Germany.

968.   MARTIN, Marie-Lovise. "L' eglise independantes et 1' Eglise
        de Jesus-Christ sur la terre par le prophete Simon
        Kimbangu en particulier". Flambeau, v.29 February
        1971; p41-49.

969.   MARTIN, Marie-Louise. "L'eglise Kimbanguiste". Congo-
        Afrique, (Kinshasa) v.9, No.39, November 1969: p441-
        450.

970.   MARTIN, Marie-Louise. "Notes sur l'origine et 1' histoire
        de l'eglise Kimbanguiste" Congo-Afrique (Kinshasa)
        v.9, No.39, 1969: p442-450.

971.   MARTIN, Marie-Louise. Prophetic Christianity in the Congo.
        The Church of Jesus Christ on Earth through the

Prophet Simon Kimbangu. Johannesburg, Christian
Institute for Southern Africa, n.d. (1968?) 40p.
illus.

972   MARTIN, Marie-Louise. "Prophetism in the Congo: origin
        and development of an independent African church."
        Ministry v.8, 1968: p154-163.

973   MARTIN, Marie-Louise. "Sa situation actuelle, une inter-
        pretation theologique." Le Monde Non-Chretien, n.s.
        v. 89/90, January-June 1969: p7-13: p26-37.
        Report on Kimbanguism made to the Swisss Moravian
        Mission Committee on a visit in 1968.

974   MARTHINSON, A.W. "Les sociétés bibliques au Congo: leur
        but; leur action." Revue du Clergé Africain, v.23,
        No.1, January 1968: p35-41.

975   MASSAMBA-DEBAT, A. Congo. De la revolution messianique
        à la revolution politique. Brazzaville, Librairie
        Populaire, B.P. 577. 1968. 107p.

976   MASSON, J. Le roi Albert et les missions. Louvain,
        Editions de l'Aucam.

977   MASSON, J. "Simples reflexions sur des chants Kibanguistes,"
        In Devant les sectes non-chrétiennes, xxxie semaine de
        Missiologie, Louvain, 1961. Louvain, Desclee et
        Brouwer, 1961: p82-90.

978   MATISON, Elon. "Rapport sur l'oeuvre medicale des Missions
        Protestantes Au Congo Belge pendant 1941." Congo

Mission News, No.120, October 1942: p12-14.

979.   MAVUMILUSA, Makanzu. L'histoire de l'église du Christ au
        Zaire. Nous n'avons pas trahi l'Evangile de Jesus
        Christ. Kinshasa, Centre Protestant d' Editions et
        de Diffusion, (n.d.) 101p.

980.   MEERT, J. "Quelques considerations sur la 'Jamaa".
        Orientations Pastorales, v.13, 1961: p17-28.

981.   MELS, B. "An example of fruitful adaptation in Africa -the
        'Jamaa' at Luluabourg". Christ to the World, v.9,
        1964: p500-504.

982.   MEEUS, Franciscus de: Les missions religieuses au Congo
        belge, par Fr de Meeus et R Steenberghen. Anvers,
        Editions Zaire, 1947. 209p. illus.

983.   MINJAUW, Leon. Les redemptoristes belges: cinquante ans
        au Bas-Congo. 1899-1949. Louvain, St. Alphonse, 1949.

984.   "MISSIONS Catholiques au Congo belge". Congo, v.2, No.3,
        October 1932: p378-390.

985.   MITHERRUTZNER, J.C. Dr. Ignnaz Knoblecher, Apostolischer
        Previkar der Katholischen Mission in Central Afrika:
        eine Lebensskize. Wien, Weger, 1869.

986.   MOSMANS, G. "Les imperatifs de l'action missionnaire en
        Afrique belge". Revue Nouvelle, v.12, July-August
        1956: p3-21.

987.   MOULES, Leonard C. ed. This is no accident; testimonies
        of a trial of Faith in Congo, 1964. Told by the missi-
        onaries. London, Worldwide Evangelization Crusade.
        1965. 111p. illus.

988.   MOUVEMENT INTERNATIONAL DE RECONCILIATION. "L'église
        Kimbanguiste africaine et non-violente". Cahiers
        de la Reconciliation v.5/6, 1966: p1-52. Bibliog.

989.   MOYSAN, N. "Apropos the Jamaa - a wonderful and feasible
        experience". Christ to the World, v.9, 1964: p239.

990.   MOYSAN, N. "A wonderful and feasible experience: the Jamaa".
        Christ to the World, (Rome). v.9, 1964. p239-240.

991.   MPONGO, Laurent. Pour une anthropologie chrétienne du
        mariage au Congo. Vers un rituel du mariage conforme
        au genie des Ntombee Njale. Kinshasa, Editions du
        C.E.P. 1968. 201p. illus.

992.   MUKENDI, Placide. "La Jamaa et son avenir". Revue du Clergé
        Africain, v.26, No.2, March 1971: p142-168.

993.   MUKENGE, Godefroid. "Le prêtre face à la jamaa et à l'
        apostolat des laics". Orientations Pastorales (Limete-
        Kinshasa). No.98, January-February 1965: p24-33.

994.   MULAGO, Vincent. "Autour du mouvement de la jamaa".
        Orientations Pastorales, Cahier No.1, 1960: p3-28.

995.   MULAGO, Vincent. "A visit to the Jamaa". Christ to the
        World, v.9, 1964: p17-19.

996.   MWENE-BATENDE, Gaston. "La dynamique socio-culturelle des
        mouvements prophetiques dans le Bas-Zaire" Cahiers
        des Religions Africaines, v.7, No.13, 1973: p43-62.

997.   MWENE-BATENDE, Gaston. "Quelques aspects du prophetisme au
        Zaire". Cahiers des Religions Africaines, v.6,
        January 1972: p69-9.

998.   MWENE-BATENDE, Gaston. Le phenomène de dissidence des
        secrets religeuses d'inspiration Kimbanquiste.
        Bruxelles, Centre des Etudes et Documentation africaines,
        1971. 37p. (Cahiers du CEDAF.6)

999.   NEILS, M. Le prophetisme au Congo belge". Ph.D. Thesis,
        Protestant Theological Faculty, Aix 1956.

1000   NELSON, Robert G. Congo crisis and Christian mission. St.
        Louis, Bethany Press, 1961. 112p. illus.

1001   NEUFELD, Elmer. Kimbanguism: An African prophet movement.
        Nsukka, E. Nigeria, Department of Religion, Univer-
        sity of Nigeria, 1963. 15p. (mimeograph).
        Theological evaluation of the evolution and growth of
        Kimbanguism in the Congo.

1002.   NGINDU, Alphonse. "La quatrième semaine theologique de
        Kinshasa et la problematique d'une theologie africaine".
        Cahiers des Religions Africaines, v.2, No.4, July 1968:
        p353-372.

1003   NGINDU, Alphonse. "Simon Kimangu et le Kimbanguisme. une
        lecture historique a propos d'un colloque recent".

Cahiers des Religions Africaines, v.6, January 1972: p91-102.

1004.   NGOYI, Louis. "Le mariage chrétien vu par un Congolais critique". Revue du Clergé Africain, v.26, 1971: p153-161.

1005.   NOIRHOMME, Guy. "Vocations to the priesthood in the Congo". In Barrett, D.B. (ed) African initiatives in religion, Nairobi, East African Publishing House, 1971.

1006.   NOIRHOMME, G. and CRAEMER W. de. L'église au Congo en 1963: rapport d'une enquête socio religieuse. Leopoldville, Centre de Recherches-Sociologiques. 1964. 186p.

1007.   NOTHOMB, Dominique M. "Une nouvelle forme de catechèse". Nouvelle Revue Theologie (Louvain). No.86, 1964: p725-744.
        On the catechism of the Jamaa movement.

1008.   PAULUS, Jean-Pierre. "La kitawala au Congo belge (mouvement indidene à caractère politico-religieux)". Revue de 1' Institut de Sociologie Solvay, v.2, No.3, 1956: p257-270.

1009.   PETERSEN, William J. Another hand on mine: the story of Dr. Carl K. Becker of the Africa Inland Mission. New York, McGraw-Hill, 1967. viii, 228p. illus.

1010.   PIETTE, A. "Fruits yielded by the 'jamaa' in Luluabourgh" Christ to the World, v.9, 1964: p19-21.

1011.   PIROTTE, Jean. "Une experience chrétienne au Congo: la
         jamaa". Neue Zeitschrift fur Missionswissenschaft,
         v.24n 1968: p282-283.

1012.   POSTIOMA, Adalbert de. "Methodologie missionnaire des
         Capucins au Congo-Matamba-Angola, 1645-1834". Revue du
         Clergé Africain, v.19, 1964: p359-384.

1013.   "POSTCRIPT on the Lumpa movement. Newsletter, London,
         Institute of Race Relations), September 1964: p25-28.

1014   QUELQUES notes sur le Kimbanguisme". La Revue de l'Aucan,
         v.6, March 1931: p66-74.

1015   RAYMAEKERS, P. "L'église de Jesus-Christ sur la terre par
         le prophete Simon Kimbangu". Zaire, v.13, No.7, 1959:
         p679-756.

1016   RAYMAEKERS, Paul and BOKA, Simon. 250 chants de l'Eglise
         de Jesus-Christ sur la terre par le prophète Simon
         Kimbangu. Leopoldville, Institut de Recherche
         Economique et Sociales, Université Lovanium, 1960. 43p.
         (mimeograph).

1017.   REA, W.F. "Christian missions in Central Africa, 1560-1890
         and modern missiology". Rhodesian History, v.3, 1972:
         p1-10.

1018.   REARDON, Ruth Slade. "Catholics and Protestants in the Congo"
         In Baeta, C.G. ed. Christianity in tropical Africa,
         studies presented and discussed at the seventh inter-
         national African Seminar, University of Ghana, April

1965. London, Oxford University Press, 1968. p83-100.

1019.   REID, Alexander James. Congo drumbeat: history of the first
        half century in the establishment of the Methodist
        Church among the Atetela of Central Congo. New York,
        World Outlook Press, 1964. 158p.

1020.   RENAULT, L. "Abbe Fulbert Youlou et Matsou". Bulletin
        d'Information de la France d'Outre-Mer. v.324.
        November 1956.

1021.   "Le RETOUR du prophète". Zaire, v.36, 14 April 1969: p10-16.
        illus.
        A survey of the past and present history of Kimbanguism,
        with reference to its admission to the World Council of
        Churches.

1022.   REYNOLDS, W.E. The past fifty years in Congo of the Baptist
        Missionary Society. London, Carey Press, 1947. 56p.

1023   RIZVI, Seyyid Saeed Akhtar. "Some East African ithna-asheri
        jamaats (1840-1967). Journal of Religion in Africa.
        v.5, No.1, 1973: p12-22.

1024   ROELANDT, R. "The situation of the Church in the Congo".
        African Ecclesiastical Review, v.3, No.3, July 1961:
        p212-220.

1025.   ROELENS, Victor. Notre vieux Congo 1891-1917: souvenirs du
        premier evêque du Congo Belge. Namur: Collection
        Lavigerie, 1948. 2 vols.

1026   ROELENS, Victor. <u>Instructions aux missionnaires Peres</u>
<u>Blancs du Haut Congo</u>. Baudouinville; 1920.

1027   ROEYKENS, Auguste. "Les capuchins et les missions congolaises au xix siecle." Aequatoria, v.11, No.4, 1948:
p128-136.
History of the Capuchin mission in the Congo from the
17th to the 20th century.

1028   ROEYKENS, Auguste. <u>La politique religieuse de l'etat</u>
<u>independent du Congo; documents</u>. Bruxelles, 1965-
vols. (Academie royale des sciences d'outre-mer.
class des sciences morales et politiques. memoires.
ouv. ser. t. 32. fase. 1).

1029   ROSEVEARE, Helen. <u>Give me this mountain; an autobiography</u>.
Grand Rapids, Eerdmans, 1966. 166p.

1030   ROSEVEARE, Helen. <u>Doctor among Congo rebels</u>; with a foreword
by Norman Grubb. London, Lutterworth Press, 1965. 104p.

1031   ROTBERG, Robert I. "Plymouth Brethren and the occupation
of Katanga, 1886-1907." Journal of African History, v.4.
1964: p285-297.

1032   RYCKMANS,Andre. "Les mouvements prophetiques Kongo en 1958."
<u>Ngonge Kongo</u>, v.7, 1964.

1033   SADIN, Fernand. <u>La mission des Jesuites au Kwango: notice</u>
<u>historique</u>. Kisantu, Imprimerie de Bergeyck S. Ignace,
1918.

1034   SCHOMER, Mark. "Report from the Congo - the Kimbanguist
        Church; where now?" Ministry, v.9, No.4, 1969: p178-
        179.

1035   SHEPPARD, W.H. Presbyterian pioneers in the Congo. Richmond,
        Va. Presbyterian Committee of Publications. 1917.
        157p.

1036   SINDA, Martial. Le messianisme congolais et ses incidences
        politique: Kimbanguisme, matsouanisme, autres mouve-
        ments. Paris, Payot, 1972. 390p. Bibliog.

1037   SINDA, Martial. "Le messianisme congolais et ses incidences
        politiques depuis son apparition jusqu' a' l' époque de
        l'independance, 1921-1961". Ph.D. Thesis, Université
        de Paris, 1961.

1038   SLADE, R. "L' attitude des missions protestantes vis-à-vis
        des puissances européennes au Congo avant 1885".
        Bulletin de l'Academie Royale des Sciences Coloniales,
        v.35, 1959: p684-721.

1039   SLADE, R. "English missionaries and the beginning of the
        anti-Congolese campaign in England". Revue Belge de
        Philogie et d' Histoire, v.33, No.1, 1955: p37-73.

1040   SLADE, Ruth M. English-speaking missions in the Congo
        independent state (1878-1908). Bruxelles, 1959.
        432p. (Academie royale des sciences coloniales.
        Classes des sciences morales et politiques. memoires,
        8.)

1041   SLADE, R. "King Leopold II and the attitude of English and
        American Catholics towards the anti-Congolese campaign".
        Zaire, v.11, 1957: p593-612.

1042   SPINDLER, Marc. "Le mouvement Kitawala en Afrique centrale".
        Monde Non-Chrétien. v.87, July-September, 1968: p30-41.

1043   SASA, Lusangu. "Le messianisme Congolais et ses incidences
        politiques". Cahiers des Religions Africaines, v.6,
        July 1972: p235-238.
        Review article of Mr. Sinda's book with the same title.

1044   STONELAKE, A. "Missionary situation in Congo". International
        Review of Missions, v.8, March 1919: p314-330.

1045   STRIJBOSCH, Alfons. Missionar im Tross der Kongo-Rebellen;
        Tatsachenbericht nach 33 Monaten Gefangenschaft bei den
        Simbas. Trier, J.J. Zimmer, 1970. 211p.

1046   STORMS, Arnold. "Famille chrétienne et société matriarcale
        au Katanga". Zaire, v.2, No.3, March 1948: p239-248.

1047   STUART, C.H. "The lower Congo and the American Baptist
        Mission". Ph.D. Thesis, Boston University, 1969.

1048   SWIDERSKI, Stanislaw. "Notes sur le Ndeya Kanga; secte
        syncretique du Bouiti au Gabon". Anthropos (Freibrugh).
        v.66, Nos. 1/2, p81-119. illus.
        Brief notes on the history of the Ndeya Kanga sect of
        the Fang, derived from the bwiti cult of Mitsogo and
        Apindji.

1049   TANNER, Ralph E.S.   "The Jamaa movement in the Congo: a
            sociolog ical comment on some religious interpretations".
            Heythrop Journal   (Oxford) v.9. No.2, April, 1968:
            p164-178.

1050   THEUWS, T.   The jamaa movement in Katanga.   London, Mission
            Press, 1961.

1051   THEUWS, T.   "Le mouvement jamaa au Katanga".   Rythemes du
            Monde, v.34, Nos 3/4, 1960: p201-212.
            'Jamaa' is a movement of parochial origin in the Katanga
            province of the Congo.   It is a vital union for those
            who fully accept the Catholic message.

1052   TRITTON, Joseph.   Baptist missionary society: Rise and
            progress of the work on the Congo river by the treasurer.
            London, Baptist Missionary society, 1884.   63p.

1053   UBRUN, A.   "Le mouvement Kimbanguiste ou ngounziste au Bas-
            Congo".   Annales des Peres du Saint-Esprit, No.51,
            November 1935: p272-278.

1054   ULWOR, Paul.   "Une acculturation religieuse en echec dans
            l' ancienne colonie belge du Congo".   Revue de Psycho-
            logie des Peuples, v.23, No.4, 1968: p390-421.
            A questionnaire circulated among 100 students who had
            studied under missionaries revealed that the majority
            believed that the missionaries and the colonial powers
            were in collusion.   They suspect the priests who have
            destroyed African culture and denied them access to
            higher white culture.

1055   VAN ACKER, Gustaaf. By de Baloebas in Congo. Reisverhaal
        Bladzijden uit de geschiedenis der eerst jaren van het
        bokeeringswerk in opper-Congoland. Antwerpen, Witte
        Paters, 1924.

1056   VANNESTE, Alfred. "Catholic-Protestant relationships at
        Lovanium University, Leopoldville". One in Christ,
        No.2, 1965: p166-168.

1057   VANNESTE, Alfred. "La Faculté de Theologie de 1' Université
        Lovanium de Leopoldville". Revue du Clergé Africain,
        v.18, 1963: p260-268.

1058   VANSINA, Jan. "Les mouvements religieux kuba (kasai)
        a l'époque coloniale". Etudes de l'Histoire Africaine
        (Louvain) v.2, 1971: p155-187.

1059   VAN WING, J. "Notes sur quelques problemes congolais"
        Institut Royal Colonial Belge, Bulletin des Seances,
        v.21, No.21, No.1, 1950: p176-195.

1060   VERBEKEN, A. "A propos du Kimbanguisme et de son auteur".
        Revue Congolaise, v.31, No.3, March 1959: p25-27.

1061   VERMEERSCH, Arthur. Les missionnaires au Congo Belge:
        surnegres ou chrétiens. Bruxelles, Goemare, 1911.

1062   VERMEERSCH, Arthur. Les missions catholiques au Congo
        Belge: étude critique de leur action. Bruxelles,
        Hayez, 1909.

1063   VERSTRAELEN, F..T.J. Le patriomoine religieux des Baluba
        et de quelques autres peuplades dans le sud-est du
        Congo. Fribourg, Pontifica Universitas Gregoriana,
        1964. 49p.

1064   VIDAL, Claudine. "Passe et present des innovations religieu-
        ses au Congo-Leopoldville".(New religious movements in
        Congo-Leopoldville, in the past and present time).
        Mois en Afrique, v.5, May 1966: p61-79.

1065   VINCENT, Jean-Francoise. "Le mouvement Crois-Koma: une
        nouvelle forme de la lutte contre la sorcellerie en
        pays Kongo". Cahiers d'Etudes Africaines, v.6, No.4,
        1966: p527-564.

1066.   VITTOZ, Pierre. "Une esperance au Congo? L'église Kumban-
        guiste". L'Actualité Missionnaire, (Lausanne) v.13,
        No.1, 1968: p10-13. ilius.

1067   WAINWRIGHT, Geoffrey. "Theological reflections on the
        catechism concerning the prophet Simon Kimbangu of
        1970". Orita, v.5, No.1, June 1971: p18-35.

1068   WAUTHION, R. "Le mouvement Kitawala au Congo belge".
        Bulletin de l'Association des Anciens Etudiants de
        l'Institut Universitaire des territoires d'outremer.
        v.3, No.8, 1950: p3-10.

1069   WITTE, Baron Jehan de. Les deux Congo, trente-cinq ans
        d'apostolat au Congo francais: Mgr. Augouard. Les
        origines du Congo belge. Preface de M. le Compte A
        de Mun. Paris, Plon, 1913. 408p.

1070   WING, J. Van and GOEME, V. Annuaire des missions
            catholiques au Congo belge et au Ruanda - Urundi
            Bruxelles, Edition Universelle, 1949: 671p.

1071   ZOLA, E. "A la recherche de principale cause du Kimbangisme".
            Pour Servir, v.4, No.2, January-February, 1960: p6-11,
            v.4, No.7, 1960: p8-13.

GABON

1072   BRIAULT, Rev. P. La soeur Saint-Charles, missionnaire au
            Gabon pendant cinquante ans: 1859-1911. Paris, Peres
            du Saint Esprit, 1922. 228p.

1073   ESPARRE, Paul Louis. "Quelques aspects metaphysiques du
            'bouiti' Mitshogo". Geneve-Afrique, v.7, No.1, 1968:
            p53-57.

1074   FERNANDEZ, James W. "Christian acculturation and Fang
            witchcraft". Cahiers d'Etudes Africaines, v.2, No.2,
            1961: p244-270.

1075   FERNANDEZ, James W. "The idea and symbol of the saviour in
            a Gabon syncretic cult". International Review of
            Missions, v.53, No.211, 1964: p281-289.
            Describes the various ideas and symbols of Christ in
            the 'bwiti' syncretic cult in Gabon and the underlying
            basis of the mythology of messianism.

1076   FERNANDEZ, James W. "Symbolic consensus in a Fan reformative
            cult". American Anthropologist, v.67, No.4, August
            1965: 902-929.

Discusses the relationship between the concepts 'consensus' and 'symbol' with reference to the 'Bwiti' reformative cult, which is practiced among about 10% of the Fang of Northern Gabon and Rio Muni.

1077   MBENG, Jean-Marie. "Ella-Akou, prophète ou charlatan? Liaison (Brazaville) v.44, 1954: p25-26.

1078   SCHWEITZER, Albert. More from the primeval forest. Translated by C.T. Campion. London, A & C. Black, 1956. 128p.

1079   SCHEWITZER, Albert. On the edge of the primeval forest: experiences and observations of a doctor in Equatorial Africa. 2nd ed. London, Hodder & Stoughton, 1938.

1080   SEAVER, George. Albert Schweitzer: Christian revolutionary. London, J. Clarke, 1944. 111p.

1081   SEAVER, George. Albert Schweitzer: the man and his mind. London, Black, New York, Harper, 1947.

1082   SINGER, Kurt D. and SHERROD, Jane. Dr. Albert Schweitzer, medical missionary, a biographical sketch of a man who has dedicated his life to others. Minneapolis, Denison, 1962. 163p. (Dennison's men of achievement series.)

1083   VERNAUD, G. Etablissement d'une mission du plein evangile au Gabon. Pesaux Editions Evangeliques, 1957.

GABON

1084   WALDOW, Rene. "Planning for change and social action: the
        role of an African church". International Review of
        Missions, v.56, No.224, October 1967: p489-498.
        On the role of "L'Eglise Evangelique du Gabon" which
        created a Bureau of Plans to find out what could be
        done in a national five-year plan.

MALAWI

1085   BISHOP Mackenzie's grave". Nyasaland Journal v.15, No.2,
        1962: p12-13.

1086   CARDEW, C.A. "The Universities Mission". Nyasaland Journal
        v.2, No.1, January 1949: p35-37.

1087   CHRINSIDE, A. The Blantyre missionaries: discreditable
        disclosures. London, W. Ridgway. 1880.

1088   DEBENHAM, Frank. Nyasaland: the land of the lake. London,
        Her Majesty's Stationery Office, 1955. 239p. (The
        Corona Library).
        Pages 130-144 give an account of the missionary effort
        in the conquest and development of Nyasaland.

1089   DOUGLAS, Arthur Jeffreys. Arthur Douglas, missionary on
        Lake Nyassa; the story of his life, compiled by
        B.W. Randolph. Westmister, 1912. 311p.

1090   DUFF, H.L. Nyasaland under the foreign office. London,
        Bell, 1903. New York, Negro Universities Press, 1969.
        422p.
        Chapter xx is an account of "Religious Missionary

160

activities in Nyasaland".

1091   ELMSLIE, Water Angus. Among the wild Ngoni, being some
         chapters in the history of the Livingstonia Mission
         in British Central Africa. 3rd ed. with a new intro-
         ductory note by Ian Nance. London, Cass, 1970. xii,
         319p. illus. (Cass library of African studies.
         Missionary researches and travels, no. 12).

1092   ELMSLIE, Walter Angus. "Ethiopianism in Nyasaland". The
         Livingstonia News, v.2, No.5, 1909; p72-74.

1093   EMTAGE, J.E.R. "The first mission settlement in Nyasaland".
         Nyasaland Journal, v.8, No.1, January 1955: p16-24.

1094   FRANKLIN, H. "Zambia's Holy War". Spectator, (London)
         Short account of the Lumpa uprising of 1964.

1095   FRASER, Donald. African idylls: portraits and impressions
         of life on a central African mission station. With an
         introduction by Jean Mackenzie. New York, Negro
         Universities Press, 1969. 229p. illus.

1096   FRASER, Donald. Winning a primitive people; sixteen years'
         work among the warlike tribe of the Ngoni and the Senga
         and Tumbuka peoples of Central Africa. With an intro-
         duction by John R. Mott. Westport, Conn., Negro Uni-
         versities Press, 1970. 320p. illus.

1097   GAUNDU-LANSQUET, Madeleine. Matilda, fille du Nyasaland.
         Paris, Edition Alsatia, 1964. 204.
         The history of a Christian marriage in Malawi.

161

1098   GELFAND, Michael. Lakeside pioneers: a socio-medical study
        in Nyasaland (1875-1920). Oxford, Blackwell, 1974. 330p.

1099   HAMILTON, J.T. Twenty years of pioneer missions in Nyasaland,
        a history of Moravian missions in German East Africa.
        Bethlehem, Pa. Society for Propagating the Gospel. 1912.
        192p.

1100   HENDERSON, James. Forerunners of modern Malawi; the early
        missionary adventures of Dr. James Henderson 1895-1898.
        Edited by M.M.S. Ballantyne and R.H.W. Shepherd. Alice,
        Lovedale Press, 1968. 297p. illus.

1101   JACK, James W. Daybreak in Livingstonia, the story of the
        Livingstonia Mission, British Central Africa. Edinburgh,
        1901.

1102   KATOKE, I.K. "Karagwe (Kafuro) and the founding of the
        Nyanza Mission". Tanzania Notes and Records,v.66,
        December 1966: p155-162.

1103   LEBLOND, M.A. Le Pere Auguste Achte, des missionnaires
        d'Afrique, missionaire au Nyanza septentrional.
        Paris, Procureur des Missionnaires d'Afrique, 1912.

1104   LEHMANN, Dorothea. "Sectarianism in Nyasaland". Interna-
        ional Review of Missions, v.55, No.220, October 1966:
        p503-505.
        A review article of R.L. Wishdale's Sectarianism in
        Southern Nyasaland: 1965.

1105   LINDEN, Ian and LINDEN, Jane. Catholics, peasants and
        Chewa resistance in Nyasaland 1889-1939. London,
        Heinemann, 1974. 223p.

1106   LINDEN, Ian. "Mponda mission diary, 1889-1891: daily life
        in a Machinga village". International Journal of
        African Historical Studies. v.7, No.2, 1974: p272-303.
        "The historical value of the Mponda dairy lies both
        in the dearth of information about the Yao of Malawi
        in the 19th century and in the absence of a similar
        day-by-day description of life in a Machinga town
        before the suppression of the slave trade".

1107   LIVINSTONE, W.P. Laws of Livingstonia: a narrative of
        a missionary adventure and achievement. London,
        Hodder and Stoughton, 1922. 385p.

1108   LIVINGSTONE, W.P. A prince of missionaries: the Rev.
        Alexander Hetherwick of Blantyre, Central Africa.
        London, Clark, 1931. 205p.

1109   McCRACKEN, K.J. "Livingstonia as an industrial mission,
        1875-1900: a study of commerce and christianity in
        Nyasaland". Religion in Africa; proceedings of a
        seminar held in the Centre of African Studies, Univer-
        sity of Edinburgh, 10th - 12th April, 1964. 130p.
        (mimeographed).

1110   MAcCRACKEN, K.J. "Livingstonia mission and the evolution
        of Malawi, 1875-1939". Ph.D. Thesis, Cambridge Univer-
        sity, 1967.

1111   McCRACKEN, K.J. "Religion and politics in northern
        Ngoniland, 1881-1904." In B. Pachai, (ed). The early
        history of Malawi. London, Longman, 1972: p215-236.
        bibliog.
        The impact of Christianity on the modern history of
        Malawi.

1112   MAcDONALD, L.J. "Bishop MacKenzie's grave." Nyasaland
        Journal, v.14, No.2, 1962: p12-13.

1113   MAcDONALD, Roderick J. "Religious independency as a means
        of social advance in Northern Nyasaland in the 1930's.
        Journal of Religion in Africa, v.3, 1970: p106-129.

1114   MAcDONALD, Roderick J. "Reverend Hanock Msokera Phiri and
        the establishment in Nyasaland of the African Methodist
        Episcopal Church." African Historical Studies, v.3,
        No.1, 1970: p75-87: v.4, No.1, 1970.
        Biographical account of Rev. Phiri, including the
        history and progress of the A.M.E. Church at Kasungu
        in the Central Province of Nyasaland.

1115   MILLER, W.R.S. A great emancipation: a missionary survey
        of Nyasaland. London, 1927.

1116   MORRISON, James Horne. Streams in the desert; a picture of
        life in Livingstonia. New York, Negro Universities
        Press, 1969. vii, 174p. illus.

1117   PACHAI, Bridglal. "Christianity and commerce in Malawi:
        some pre-colonial aspects." In Smith, G. (and others
        eds.) Malawi, past and present: selected papers from the

University of Malawi History Conference, 1967,
Blantyre, Christian Literature Association of Malawi,
1971: p114-136. illus.

1118   PINEAU, Henry. Eveque roi des brigands, monseigneur Dupont,
premier Vicaire Apostolique du Nyassa (1850-1930)
Paris, Peres Hlancs, 1930.

1119   PRETORIUS, J.L. "An introduction to the history of the
Dutch Reformed Church Mission in Malawi 1889-1914".
In B. Pachai, (ed) The early history of Malawi.
London, Longman, 1972: p365-383.

1120   PRETORIUS, J.L. "The story of the Dutch Reformed Church
Mission in Nyasaland". Nyasaland Journal, v.10, No.1,
January 1957: p11-22.

1121   PRETONIUS, Pauline. "An attempt at Christian initiation in
Nyasaland". International Review of Missions, v.39,
No.155, July 1950: p284-291.

1122   ROBERTSON, W. The martyrs of Blantyre. London, Nisbet,
1892.

1123   RIDDEL, A. A reply to "the Blantyre Missionaries: discreditable disclosures by Andrew Chirinside, F.R.G.S.
Edinburgh, Blackwood, 1880.

1124   ROSS, A.C. "The African - a child or a man: the quarrel
between the Blantyre Mission of the Church of Scotland
and the British Central African Administration, 1890-
1905". In Stokes, E. and Brown, R. (eds) The

Zambezian past: studies in Central African history.
Manchester, Manchester University Press, 1966: p352-
375.

1125   SCHOFFELERS, M. and LINDEN, Ian. "The resistance of the
        Nyau Societies to the Roman Catholic missions in
        colonial Malawi". In Ranger, T.O. and KIMAMBO, I.N.
        The historical study of African religion with reference
        to East and Central Africa. London, Heinemann, 1972.
        p252-273.

1126   SHEPPERSON, George. "Education sponsors freedom - the story
        of African native John Chilembwe". The Negro History
        Bulletin, v.15, No.4, January 1952: p69-73.

1127   SHEPPERSON, George and PRICE, Thomas. Independent African:
        John Chilembwe and the origins, setting and signifi-
        cance of the Nyasaland native rising of 1915. Edinburgh,
        University Press, 1958. x, 564p. illus. (Edinburgh
        University Publications; history, philosophy and
        economics, no.8).
        A massive book with detailed biography of Chilembwe,
        rich in information about the background to the revolt.

1128   SHEPPERSON, George. "Nyasaland and the millennium".
        Comparative Studies in Society and History.
        Supplement II. 1962: p144-159.

1129   STONE, W. Vernon. "The Livingstonia mission and the Bemba".
        Bulletin of the Society of African Church History,
        v.2, No.4, 1968: p311-322.

1130   STUART, Richard G. "Christianity and the Chewa in Malawi - the Anglican case, 1885-1950". Ph.D. Thesis, University of London, 1974.

1131   VAN VELSEN, J. "The missionary factor among the Lakeside Tonga of Nyasaland". Human Problems in Central Africa, No.26, 1959: p1-22.
A discussion on the role of missionaries as an important factor in Tonga-Nyoni politics and diplomacy in the 1870s. They brought material benefits to the area, increased the political status of the chiefs and became agents in the rivalries between Tonga and Ngoni leaders.

1132   VELSEN, Jaap Van. "The missionary factor among the Lakeside Tonga of Nyasaland". Rhodes-Livingstone Journal, v.26. 1960: p1-22

1133   WALDMAN, Marilyn R. "The Church of Scotland mission at Blantyre, Nyasaland: its political implications". Bulletin of the Society of African Church History, v.2, No.4, 1968: p299-310.

1134   WELLENS, Stephen C. "The influence of village environment on the stability of Roman Catholic marriages in a rural parish of Malawi". African Theological Journal, No.2, February 1969: p84-93.

1135   WINSPEAR, Canon Frank. "A short history of the Universities Mission to Central Africa". Nyasaland Journal, v.9, No.1, January 1956: p11-50.

MALAWI

1136   WISHDALE, Robert Leonard. Sectarianism in Southern
            Nyasaland. London, Oxford University Press for
            International African Institute, 1965. 162p. illus.
            bibliog.
            A study, by a social anthropologist, of the connexion
            between the process of sectarianism, the splitting of
            Christian groups into smaller and smaller sects, and
            the mechanism of social organization in the southern
            part of Malawi.

1137   TANGRI, Roger. African reaction and resistance to the early
            colonial situation in Malawi, 1891-1915. Salisbury,
            Rhodesia, 1969. (Central Africa Historical Association.
            Local series, 25).

RHODESIA

1138   AQUINA, Sister Mary. Christianity in a Rhodesian tribal trust
            land. Kampala, Institute for Social Research, 1966.
            Also in African Social Research, v.1, June 1966: p1-40.

1139   AQUINA, Mary. "A note on missionary influence on Shona
            marriage." The Rhodes-Livingstone Journal, v33, 1963:
            p68-79.

1140   AQUINA, Mary. "The people of the spirit: an independent
            church in Rhodesia." Africa, v.37, No.2, April 1967:
            p203-219.
            Deals with the system of beliefs of an independent
            African Church, the Apostoles, founded in 1932 in the
            eastern province of Rhodesia by John Maranke.

168

1141   AQUINA, Mary. "Zionists in Rhodesia". Africa, v.39,
         No.2, 1969: p113-136. illus. bibliog.
         Account of the organisation and liturgy of the Zionist
         Church movement in Rhodesia, and its relation to Euro-
         peans.

1142   BRODERICK, Rev. Canon G.E.P. "History of the Diocese of
         Southern Rhodesia (formerly the Diocese of Mashonaland)".
         (Unpublished typescript).

1143   BERLYN, Phillippa. "The Mashona people of Central Africa:
         traditional religion's affinity with Christianity".
         African World, November, 1968: p6.

1144   "Portuguese priests and soldiers in Zimbabwe, 1560-1572: the
         interplay between Evangelism and trade". International
         Journal of Africa Historical Studies, v.6, No.1, 1973:
         p36-48.

1145   CLINTON, Iris. Hope Fountain story; a tale of one hundred
         years. Gwelo, Rhodesia, Mambo Press, 1967. 101p.

1146   CORBISHLY, T. "The Church in Southern Rhodesia". Wiseman
         Review, no. 495: Spring 1963: p87-93.

1147   DACHS, Anthony J. ed. Christianity south of the Zambezi.
         Gwelo, Rhodesia, Mambo Press, 1973. 213'.
         A collection of essays on Christian history and the
         contact of Christian and traditional religion, mainly
         in Rhodesia.

1148   DANEEL, M.L. The background and rise of the Southern Shona
independent churches. The Hague, Mouton, 1971, 2v.
A notable contribution to the literature on the history
and culture of the Shona peoples of Rhodesia, research
for which was centered on the Chikaranga-speaking
region of Rhodesia.

1149   DANEEL, M.L. Old and new in Southern Shona independent
churches. I. Background and rise of the major movements. The Hague, Mouton for Afrika-Studiecentrum,
Leiden, 1971. xviii, 557p. illus. Bibliog.
(Change and continuity in Africa). A work in two parts.
Part I deals with the history and socioeconomic background of the area, shona traditional religion, and
Roman Catholic and Dutch Reformed Church. Part II
deals with the rise of independent churches and their
early history.

1150   DANEEL, Marthinus L. "Shona independent churches and
ancestor worship". In Barrett, D.B. (ed) African
initiatives in religion. Nairobi, East African
Publishing House 1971: p160-170.

1151   DANEEL, M.L. Zionism and faith healing in Rhodesia, aspects
of African independent churches. Translated from the
Dutch by V.A. February. Afrika Studiecentrum, Leiden,
Mouton, 1970. 64p.

1152   DOMINION SISTER. In God's white robed army: the chronicle
of the Dominican Sisters in Rhodesia, 1895-1934.
Cape Town.

1153   EVANS, H. St. John T. The Church in Southern Rhodesia. London, S.P.G. and S.P.C.K. 1945. 80p. illus.

1154   FARRANT, J.C. Mashonaland matry: Benard Mizeka and the pioneer church. London, Oxford University Press, 1966: 258p. Bibliog.

1155   FAVRE, Edourd. Francois Coillard: Missionnaire au Zambeze, 1882-1904. Paris, Société des Missions Evangeliques, 1913.

1156   FRIPP, Constance. "Bishop Knight-Bruce's journey to the Zambesi, 1888". NADA, 1939: p71-91.

1157   FRIPP, C. and HILLER, V.W. Gold and the Gospel in Mashonaland, 1888. London, Chatto & Windus, 1959.

1158   GANN, Lewis Henry. A history of Southern Rhodesia: early days to 1914. London, Chatto & Windus, 1965. 354p.

1159   GALVIN, Patrick. The formation of christian communities in the rural area. Gwebo, Rhodesia, Mambo occasional papers - Missio-pastoral series, 1).

1160   GELFAND, Michael ed. Gubulawayo and beyond: letters and journals of the early Jesuit missionaries to Zambesia. (1879-1887) London, Chapman,1968, 496p.

1161   GELFAND, Michael. "Mother Patrick and her nursing sisters: based on extracts of letters and journals in Rhodesia of the Dominican sisterhood 1890-1901. Cape Town, Juta, 1964, 281p.

1162   GELFAND, Michael A. "A Nganga who has adopted two faiths".
Nada, v.10, No.3, 1971: p73-76.
Description of the training and practices of a Shona
Christian who is also an accredited diviner relying
on traditional methods for healing patients.

1163   HASSING, P.S. "Christian missions and the British expansion
in Southern Rhodesia, 1888-1923". Ph.D. Thesis,
American University, 1960.

1164   KAPENZI, Geoffrey Z. "A study of the strategies and methods
used by the American Methodist Missionary Society in its
religious education program in Mashonaland from 1896-
1967". Ph.D. Thesis, Boston University, 1969/70.

1165.   KNIGHT-BRUCE, Bishop G.W.H. Journals of the Mashonaland
mission of Bishop Knight-Bruce, London. S.P.G., 1892.

1166   LENHERR, J. "Advancing indigenous church music". African
Music, journal of the African Music Society, v.4, No.3,
1968: p33-39.
The author compares experiences in Taiwan and Rhodesia
in guiding the creation of new indigenous church music
by local composers.

1167   McPHERSON, Alexander. James Fraser: the man who loved the
people: a record of missionary endeavour in Rhodesia
in the twentieth century. London, Banner of Truth
Trust, 1967. ix, 224p.

1168   MARTIN, Marie-Louise. "The Mai Chaza church in Rhodesia".

In Barrett. David Brian, (ed). African initiatives
in religion. Nairobi, East African Publishing House,
1971: p109-121.

1169   NUBAKO, Simbi V. "The southern Shona independent churches".
        African Affairs, v.73, No.290. January 1974: p108-111.
        A review article of M.L. Daneel's the background and
        rise of the Southern Shona independent churches, 1971.

1170   MURPHREE, Marshall W. Christianity and the Shona. London,
        Athone Press, 1969. viii, 200p.
        Bibliog. maps. (London School of Economics.
        Monographs on social anthropology, 36).
        This book is concerned with an analysis of the relation-
        ship sustained between the different forms of religious
        life found in contemporary Shona Society.

1171   PEADEN, W.R. Missionary attitudes to Shona culture, 1890-
        1923. Salisbury, Rhodesia, Central African Historical
        Association, 1970. 41p. (Central African Historical
        Association. Local series, 27).

1172   PELLY, D.R. "Bernard Mizeki: the first Mashonaland martyr".
        Mashonaland Quarterly, February 1897.

1173   RANGER, Terrence O. "African attempts to control education
        in East and Central Africa, 1900-1939". Past and
        Present. v.32, December 1965: p57-85.

1174   RANGER, Terrence O. "The early history of independency
        in Southern Rhodesia". Religion in Africa, 1964: p52-
        74.

1175   RANGER, Terrence Osborn. "The Ethiopian episode in Barotse-
        land, 1900-1950 ". Rhodes-Livingstone Journal, v.37.
        1965: p26-41.

1176   REA, W.F. "Agony on the Zambezi; the first Christian
        mission to southern Africa and its failure. 1580-
        1759". Zambezia, v.1, No.2, 1970: p46-53. Bibliography.

1177   REA, W.F. Loyola Mission, Chishawasha 1892-1962. Chishawasha,
        Rhodesia, 1962. 23p.

1178   SMITH, E.W. The way of the white fields in Rhodesia; a
        survey of Christian enterprise in Northern and
        Southern Rhodesia, London, World Dominion Press, 1928.
        166p. Short notes on the establishment and development
        of mission stations by various societies, supported
        with statistics.

1179   SODERSTROM. Hugo. "En forenad protestantisk Kyrka i
        Rhodesia? (A untied non-Roman Catholic Church in
        Rhodesia). Svensk Missionstidskrift, v.62. No.2,
        1974: p88-91.

1180   SPILLMAN, Joseph. Vom Cap zum Zambesi, die Anfange der
        Zambesi. Aus den Tagebuchern des P. Terorde S.J.
        und aus den Berichten der andern Missionare
        dargestellet. Freiburg, Herder, 1882.

1181   STEWART, James. The Zambesi journal of James Stewart,
        1862-1863, with a selection of his correspondence.
        Edited by J.P.R. Wallis. London, Chatto & Windus,
        1953. (Central African Archives, oppenheimer series,
        no.6.

1182   THOMAS, Norman Ernest. "Christianity, politics and the
        Manyika: a study of the influence of religious
        attitudes and loyalties on political values and activi-
        ties of Africans in Rhodesia". Ph.D. thesis, Boston
        University, 1967/68.

1183   THOMPSON, H.P. The Martry of Mashonaland: the story of
        Bernard Mizeki. London, S.P.G. 1937.

1184   VAMBE, Lawrence. An ill-fated people: Zimbabwe before and
        after Rhodes: with a foreword by Doris Lessing. London,
        Heinemann, 1972. xxxiv, 254p.

1185   VERMEULEN, J. "Scripture translations in Northern Rhodesia".
        African Eccle siastical Review v6, No.1, January 1964:
        p67-73.

1186   WALLIS, J.P.R. ed. Gold and the gospel in Mashonaland,
        1888. London, Chatto & Windus.
        Central African Archives, Oppenheimer series, no.4).

1187   WALLIS, J.P.R (ed) The Matabele Mission: a selection from
        the correspondence of John and Emily Moffat, David
        Livingstone and others, 1858-1878. London, Chatto &
        Windus, 1945. (Govt. Archives of S. Rhodesia, Oppen-
        heimer series, no.2).

1188   WELD, A. Missions of the Zambezi. London, Burns & Oates,
        1878.

1189   ARNOUX, A. Les Pères Blancs aux sources du Nil. Paris, Edition Saint Paul, 1948. 189p. illus.

1190   "BURUNDI Chrétien", Vivante Afrique, No.233, 1964: 61p. (Special number).

1191   BUSHAYIJA, Stanislas. "Indifference religieuse et neopaganisme au Ruanda". Rythmes du Monde, v.9, No.1, 1961: p58-67.
        Account of the revival of neopagan beliefs following the superficial nature of Catholic influence in Ruanda.

1192   CHURCH, Joseph E. William Nagenda: a great lover of Jesus. London, Ruanda Mission CMS, 1973. 12p.

1193   CHURCH, Joseph E. William Nagenda: an appreciation. London, Ruanda Mission CMS, 1973: 12p.

1194   GRAVEL, Pierre Bettez. Remera: a community in Eastern Ruanda. The Hague, Paris, Mouton, 1968. 226p.

1195   GRAVEL, Pierre Bettez. Remera: a community in Eastern Ruanda. The Hague, Paris, Mouton, 1968. 226p.

1195   GUILLEBAUD, Lindesay. A grain of mustard seed: the growth of the Ruanda Mission of C.M.S. London, Ruanda Mission C.M.S., n.d. (1959?). 136p. illus.

1196   KUHN, Pia and ENGEL, Ignatia. Auf Gottes Saatfeld: Erlebnisse und Beobachtungen aus der Ruanda-Mission. Trier, Paulinus-Druckerei, 1928.

1197   LORY, Marie Joseph. Face à l' avenir: L'Eglise au Congo
        belge et au Ruanda Urundi. Tournai, Casterman, 1958.
        210p. illus.

1198   PERRAUDIN, Jean. Naissance d' une église: histoire du
        Burundi chrétien.   Usumbura, Presses Lavigerie 1963.
        228p.

1199   ST. JOHN, Patricia Mary. Breath of life: the story of the
        Ruanda Mission. With a foreword by the Archishop of
        York. London, Norfolk Press, 1971. 238p.

1200   SCHUMACHER, Pierre. "Un cours de theologie dans la brousse
        africaine (les attributs de dieu au Ruanda". Grands
        Lacs, March 1935: p163-175.

1201   SCHUMACHAER, Pierre. "Les debuts de l' apostôlat au Ruanda:
        souvenirs d' un missionnaire". Bulletin des Missions,
        v.21, Nos 3/4 1947: p86-99. illus.

1202.   SMITH, A.C.S. Road to revival: the story of the Ruanda
        Missions. London, Church Missionary Society, 1946.

1203   SMITH, A.C.S. Supplement to read to revival. The story
        of the Ruanda Mission continued from 1946 to 1951.
        London, Ruanda Mission C.M.S. n.d. 30p. illus.

1204   WINGERT, Norman A. No place to stop killing. Chicago,
        Moody Press, 1974. 125p.
        The effect of massacres on Burundi and its church.

1205   BUTT, George E. My travels in Northwest Rhodesia. London,
        1921.
        An account of a visit to primitive Methodist missions
        by a fellow missionary from the Cape Colony.

1206   HANS-JURGEN, Greschat. "Legend?" Fraud?, Reality?, Alice
        Lenshina's prophetic experience: notes from some
        sources." Africana Marburgensia, v.1, No.1, 1968:
        p8-13.

1207   CAVE, Sigrid. "Von der Lumpa-Sekte in Zambia." Mittellungen
        der Norddeutchen Mission. (Breman), February, 1965:
        p1-2.

1208   CHERY, H.C. "Les sectes en Rhodesie du Nord." Parole et
        Mission (Paris),v.2, No.7, October 1959: p578-594.
        Survey of syncretic churches in Northern Rhodesia
        (Zambia) including the Lumpa Church and the Church of
        the Sacred Heart.

1209   COURTOIS, Padre Victor Jose. Notes chronologiques sur
        les anciennes Missions Catholiques au Zambezi. Lisbon
        1889.

1210   DU PLESSIS, Johannes. A thousand miles in the heart of
        Africa; a record of a visit to the Boer Missions of
        Central Africa. Edinburgh, 1905.
        A contemporary and sympathetic view of the first Dutch
        Reformed Church mission establishments in Northern
        Rhodesia.

1211   FERNANDEZ, James W. "The Lumpa uprising: why?" Africa
        Report, v9, No.10, November, 1964: p30-32.

1212   GRENVILLE; Grey W. "Mindolo: a catalyst for Christian
        participation in nation building in Africa."
        International Review of Missions, v.58, No. 229,
        January 1969: p110-117.
        Describes the activities of the first ten years of
        the Mindolo ecumenical foundation at Kitwe, Zambia,
        which was founded in 1958.

1213   GRESCHAT, Hans-Jurgen. "Legend? Fraud? Reality? Alice
        Lenshina's prophetic experience: notes from some
        sources." Africana Maburgensia, v.1, No.1, 1968:
        p8-13.   An analysis of seven sources based on
        information collected between 1953 and 1960 leads to
        the conclusion that Lenshina's experience in September
        1953 is to be classed as a "dream" or 'inspiration'
        not as a 'possession'.

1214   HAY, Hope. Literacy technique in Northern Rhodesia."
        The Rhodes-Livingstone Journal, v.9, 1950: p1-13.

1215   HAY, Hope. "Mass literacy in Northern Rhodesia." Quarterly
        Bulletin of Fundamental Education, v.1, 1949: p11-17.

1216   HEWARD, Christine. "The rise of Alice Lenshina." New
        Society (London) v.4, No.98, 13 August, 1964: p6-8.

1217   KERSWELL, Mrs. Kate L. Romance and reality of missionary
        life in Northern Rhodesia. London, 1913.
        Life in the Zambezi valley and the Mumbwa District
        of Zambia from the point of view of a missionary's
        wife.

1218   KING, E.R.G. "On educating African girls in Northern
          Rhodesia". Rhodes-Livingstone Journal. v10, 1950:
          p65-74.

1219   LALONDE, Leopold. "The Mwakalenga: African National
          Church". Notes et Documents (Rome) No.40, September/
          October 1963: p385-386.

1220   LEHMANN, Dorothea A. "Alice Lenshina. Die Lumpa Bwegung
          in Zambia". Das Wort in der Welt (Hamburg) v.3,
          June 1966: p41-47. illus.

1221   "LENSHINA" Nigrizia, v.83, No.9, September 1964: p20-23.
          Short account of Alice Lenshina of Zambia and her
          Lumpa sect.

1222   LONG, Norman. "Religion and socio-economic action among
          the Serenje-Lala of Zambia". In Baeta, C.G. ed.
          Christianity in tropical Africa, studies presented
          and discussed at the seventh International African
          Seminar, University of Ghana. 1965. p396-416.

1223.   "The LUMPA Cult". In Murder for magic: witchcraft in
          Africa. London, Cassell 1965: p155-172.
          A account of the confrontation between Zambia troops
          and the followers of Alice Lenshina's Lumpa sect in
          Zambia.

1224   "LUMPA prophetess seeks to join United Church". Ministry,
          v.5, No.4, July 1965: p200.

1225   "LUMPA sect uprising". Africa Diary (New Delhi), v.4,

No.37, September 1965: p5-11.

1226   MAKULU, H.F. "Origins of a nation". International Review
        of Missions, v.55, No.220, October 1966: p506-507.
        A review article of R.I. Rotberg's book Christian
        missionaries and the creation of Northern Rhodesia,
        1966.

1227   MARTIN, Marie-Louise. "The conflict between the Lumpa
        Church and the government in Zambia". Ministry, v.5,
        No.1, October 1964: p46-48.

1228   MORRIS, Colin. The end of the missionary? a short account
        of the political consequences of Missions in Northern
        Rhodesia. London, Cargate Press, 1962. 61p.

1229   MUWAMBA, E.A. "An indigenous native church". In Evange-
        lization: a report of the General Missionary Confe-
        rence of Northern Rhodesia held in Broken Hill, July
        15-21. 1931.

1230   NORTH-WEST Rhodesia General Missionary Conference. 1st.,
        Report of the proceedings. Livingstone, June 29-
        July 2, 1914. Kasenga, via Kalsmo, Northern Rhodesia,
        Book Room of the Baila-Batonga Mission, 1914.

1231   NORTH-WEST Rhodesia General Missionary Conference. 2nd.,
        Report of the proceedings, Livingstone, July 1919.

1232   "OFFICIAL description of development of Lumpa church,
        Lenshina opposition to witchcraft and political
        parties". East Africa and Rhodesia. v.40, No.2080,

ZAMBIA

20 August 1964, p941-942, 950.

1233   OGER, Louis. "Le mouvement Lenshina en Rhodesie du Nord".
        Eglise Vivante, v.14, No.2, March-April 1962: p128-
        138.

1234   PHEKO, S.E.M. Christianity through African eyes. Lusaka,
        Daystar Publications, 1969. 133p. illus.

1235   QUICK, G. "Some aspects of the African Watch Tower movement
        in Northern Rhodesia". International Review of Missions,
        v.29, No.114, April 1940: p216-225.

1236   RANDALL, Max Ward. Profile for victory: new proposals for
        missions in Zambia. South Pasadena, Calif., William
        Carey Library, 1971. x, 395p. illus.

1237   ROBERTS, Andrew D. "The Lumpa church of Alice Lenshina".
        In Protest and power in Black Africa, edited by R.
        Rotberg and A. Mazuri, New York, Oxford University
        Press, 1970. p513-568 map.

1238   ROBERTS, Andrew. "The Lumpa tragedy". Peace News, (London)
        No.1471, September 4, 1964: p6-7.

1239   ROTBERG, R.I. Christian Missionaries and the creation of
        Northern Rhodesia, 1880-1924. Princeton, Princeton
        University Press, 1965. xi, 240p. illus. bibliog.
        A survey of the history of the planting of Christianity
        in the Republic of Zambia and the role of missionaries
        in the introduction of western civilization in that
        country.

1240   ROTBERG, R.I. "Christian missions in Northern Rhodesia, 1882-1924, with special reference to the history of the London Missionary Society, the South African General Mission, the Plymouth Brethren and the Universities Mission to Central Africa". D.Phil. Thesis, Oxford University, 1960.

1241   ROTBERG, Robert I. "The emergence of Northern Rhodesia: the missionary contribution, 1885-1924". St.Anthony Papars, v.15, 1963: p101-129.

1242   ROTBERG, Robert I. "The Lenshina Movement of Northern Rhodesia". Rhodes-Livingstone Journal, v.29, 1961: 63-78.
           Brief history of the movement, its nature, especially its hatred of foreigners.

1243   ROTBERG, Robert I. "Missionaries as chiefs and entrepreneurs: Northern Rhodesia, 1882-1924". Boston University Papers in African History, edited by Jeffrey Butler, Boston, Boston University Press, 1964: p197-215.

1244   ROTBERG, Robert I. "The missionary factor in the occupation of trans-Zambezia". Northern Rhodesian Journal, v.4, 1964: p330-338.
           Historical role and influence of missions in the occupation of the trans-Zambezian region.

1245   JAMIESON, Gladys. Zambia contrasts: a page in the story of Christian education in Zambia. Illustrations and

London, Missionary Society, 1965. 87p. illus.

1246   JOHNSON, Walton R. "The history of the A.M.E. Church in
        Zambia". The Journal of the Interdenominational
        Theological Center. v.2, No.1, Fall 1974: p55-68.

1247   "La SECTA Lumpa". Actualidad Africana, (Madrid) No. 151,
        January 1965: p10+.

1248   SHAW, John R. "Nkala: an abondened mission on the Kafue
        flats". Northern Rhodesia Journal, v.4, No.5, 1961:
        p484-486.

1249   SHEWMAKER, Stan. Tongo christianity. South Pasadena,
        Calif. William Carey Library, 1970. xvl, 199p. illus.
        bibliog.

1250   STEFAISZYN, B. "Intertribal relations in the Catholic
        church in Northern Rhodesia". In The multitribal
        society... edited by A.A. Dubb. Lusaka, Rhodes-
        Livingstone Institute, 1962: p105-110.

1251   TAYLOR, J.V. LEHMAN, Dorotea. Christians of the Copper
        belt. London, Student Christian Movement Press, 1961.
        308p. illus. (World mission studies).

EASTERN AFRICA (General)

1252   BARRETT, David Brian. "The meaning of money in an Anglican
        diocese of East Africa: Masasi". Social Compass, v.1.
        1969: p77-90.

1253   BARRETT, David Brian. "Two hundred independent church
         movements in East Africa". Social Compass. (The
         Hague) 1968: p101-106.

1254   BARRETT, David Brian. "Two hundred independent church
         movements in east Africa: a survey, analysis and
         prediction". Makerere Institute of Social Research.
         Conference Paper, 1967: January, p29-39. illus. map.
         Bibliog.

1255   BAUMANN, Oswin. "Songo, der schwarze Prophet, ein
         Beitrag zum Prophetentum in Ostafrika". (Songo the
         black prophet; a contribution to the study of prophets
         in East Africa.) Missionsbote, v.30, No.2, 1950:
         p20-29.

1256   BEDFORD, Francis John. The Bible in East Africa. London,
         British and Foreign Bible Society, 1954. 61p. illus.

1257   BENNET, N. "The Holy Ghost Mission in East Africa, 1858-
         1890". In Studies in East African history, edited
         by N. Bennett. Boston University Press, 1963: p54-
         75.

1258   BERNANDER, Gustav. Addik. The rising tide; Christianity
         challenged in East Africa. Translated by H. Daniel
         Friberg. Rock Island, III., Augustana Press, 1957.
         70p.

1259   BESSEM, J. "Scripture translations in East Africa".
         African Ecclesiastical Review, v.4, No.3, July 1962:
         p201-211.

1260   BROWN, Gerald Grover. Christian response to change in
            East African traditional societies. London, Friends
            Home Service Committee for Woodbroke College, 1973.
            52p. (Woodbroke occasional papers, 4).

1261   CATHOLIC directory of Eastern Africa. 1965. Tabora,
            Tanzania, T.M.P. Book Department, 1965.

1262   CRAWFORD, Mrs. E.M. By the equator's snowy peak.   A
            record of medical missionary work and travel in
            British East Africa. London, Church Missionary
            Society, 1913. 176p.

1263   DOENS, Irene. "L' église orthodoxe en Afrique orientale
            dans et hors le cadre du patriarcat grec orthodox
            d' Alexandre". Revue du Clergé Africain, v.24, 1969:
            p543-576.

1264   EHRET, C. "Language evidence and religious history". In
            Ranger, T.O. and Kimambo, I.N. The historical study
            of African religion with reference to East and Central
            Africa. London, Heinemann, 1972.

1265   ELWES, Columba Carey. "Some reflections on the church in
            East Africa". African Ecclesiastical Review. v.13,
            No.1, 1971; p69-75.

1266   FRERE, Sir H.B. Eastern Africa as a field for missionary
            labour; four letters to his Grace, the Archbishop of
            Canterbury, by the Rt. Hon. Sir Bartle Frere. London,
            Murray.

1267   GRAY, J.R. "The missionary factor in East Africa". In
        Africa in the Nineteenth and twentieth centuries,
        edited by J.C. Anene and G. Brown. London, Nelson,
        1966: p458-471.

1268   GREAVES, L.B. "The educational advisership in East
        Africa". International Review of Missions, July
        1947: p329-337.

1269   GUTTMAN, B. "Sektenbildung und Rassener lebnis in
        Ostafrica". (The development of sects in East
        Africa) Evangelisches Missions Magazin, New series,
        v.78, No.9, September 1934: p277-292.

1270   HAKE, Andrew. "The decolonization of the Church in East
        Africa". East African Journal v.3, No.11 February
        1967: p7-12.
        The Churches of East Africa face a massive task of
        decolonisation which involves not only the appointment
        of African church leaders, but the discovery and
        expression of a new integrity, identity and appre-
        ciation of past tradition, and the development of a
        new pattern of life to meet the challenges of the
        future.

1271   HARRIES, Lyndon. "The missionary on the East African
        Coast". International Review of Missions, v.35,
        No. 138, April 1946: p183-186.

1272   HARTWIG, Gerald W. "Bukerebe, the Church Missionary
        Society and East African politics, 1877-1878"
        African History Studies, v.1, No.2, 1968: p211-232.

In 1877 two members of the British Church Missionary
Society were killed on Bukerebe Island in Lake
Victoria. This study examines the ramifications of
the disaster and its effects upon African leaders.

1273   HASTINGS, Adrian. "Vocations for priesthood in Eastern
        Africa". In Barrett, David Brian, (ed). African
        initiatives in religion, Nairobi, East African
        Publishing House, 1971: p188-197.

1274   HOLLAND, Frederick E. Kulikuwa Hatari: a way, walk and a
        warfare of forty-three years in Africa as Nimrod,
        named and missionary. New York, Exposition Press,
        1963. 85p. Autobiography of 43 years in East Africa
        as a missionary of the African Inland Mission.

1275   HORNSBY, George. "German educational achievements in East
        Africa". Tanganyika Notes and Records, v.62, 1964:
        p83-90.

1276   JASPER, Gerhard. "The East African Church Union discuss-
        ions". African Theological Journal No.1, February
        1968: p49-58.

1277   JOHANSSEN, Ernst. Ruanda; kleine anfange-grosse aufgaben
        der evangelischen mission im Zwischen seengebiet
        Deutsch-Ostafrikas. Bethel bei Bielefeld, Verlags-
        handlung der anstalt, 1912. 210p.

1278   JONES, Thomas Jesse. Education in East Africa: a study of
        East, Central and South Africa by the second African
        Education Commission under auspices of the Phelps-

Stokes Fund, in cooperation with the International
Education Board. New York, Phelps-Stokes Fund, 1925.

1279   KENYON, E.R. "Missions in Eastern Equatorial Africa".
        The East and the West: Quarterly Review for the
        study of Missionary problems. v.7, 1909: p323-343.

1280   KIERAN, John A.P. "The Christian church in East Africa in
        modern times". Neue Zeitscrift fur Missionwissenschaft.
        (Schoneck-Beckenried). v.25, No.4, 1969: p273-287.

1281   KIERAN, J.A.P. "Christian villages in northeastern
        Tanzaina". paper for U.S.S.C. conference 1968-69.
        Kampala, M.I.S.R. 1970. History papers: p84-95.
        Also in Trans Africa Journal of History, v.1, No.1,
        January 1971: p24-38.

1282   KIERAN, J.A.P. "The Holy Ghost fathers in East Africa,
        1863-1914". Ph.D. Thesis, University of London. 1966.

1283   KIERAN, J.A.P. "Some Roman Catholic missionary attitudes
        to Africans in nineteenth century East Africa". Race,
        v.10, No.3, January 1969: p341-359.
        A study based on the allegation that East African
        missionaries were guilty of racial and cultural
        arrogance, condemning African religious beliefs
        without understanding them.

1284   KING, K.J. "The American Negro as missionary to East Africa:
        a critical aspect of evangelism". University of East
        Africa; Social Science Council Conference, History
        Paper, 1968/9: p96-110. Bibliog. Also in African

History Studies, v.3, No.1, 1970: p5-22.

1285   KING, Noel. "The East African revival movement and
evangelism". Ecumerical Review,v.20, No.2, 1968:
p159-182.

1286   KIWOVELE, Judah B.M. "Polygamy as a problem to the
church in Africa". African Theological Journal,
No.2, February 1969: p7-26.

1287   KNAPPERT, Jan. "The first Christian Ultenzi, a new
development in Swahili literature". Afrika und
Ubersee, v.47, No.3/4, June 1964: p221-232.

1288   KRAPF, J. Lewis. Travels, researches, and missionary
labours during an eighteen years' residence in Eastern
Africa, together with journeys to Jagga, Usambara,
Ukambani, Shoa, Abessinia and Khartum... With an
appendix by E.G. Ravenstein. 2nd ed. London, Frank
Cass, 1968. 566p.

1289   AMGFPRD-SMITH, N. "Revival in East Africa". International
Review of Missions, January 1954: p77-81.

1290   LEYS, Norman. Religion and common life: a problem in East
African missions". International Review of Missions,
v.8, February 1919-172.

1291   MAZRUI, A.A. "The sacred and the secular in East African
politics". Cahiers d' Etudes Africaines, v.13, No.4,
1973: p644-681.

1292   MILLER, Paul M. Equiping for ministry in East Africa.
        Dodoma, Tanzania, Central Tanganyika Press, Scottdale,
        Heralrd Press, 1969. 231p.
        Study and teaching of christianity in East Africa.

1293   MIHAYO, Mark. "African clergy". Clergy Review, v.53, No.3,
        March 1968: p170-177.
        Discusses the method of training African clergymen in
        Kenya, Uganda, Tanzania, Malawi and Zambia, emphasising
        on the need to train more Africans to play the role of
        missionaries.

1294   MITCHELL, Sir Philip. "Governments and missions in East
        Africa". East and West Review, July 1941: p134-140.

1295   MORGER, Othmar. Die blume der wildnis: Lebensbild der Sr.
        M. Magdalena Mwinuka, O.S.B. aud der   kongregation
        der eingeborenen Schwestern von der hl. Agnes in
        Peramiho, Ost Afrika. Uznach, Benediktinor-Missionare,
        1945.

1296   MOSHI, Stefano R. "Lutheranism today". African Theological
        Journal, No.1, February 1968: p59-61.

1297   MURRAY, F. "The Diaconate in East Africa". African Eccle-
        siastics Review, v.7, No.4, October 1965-350.

1298   MANJI. Azim. "Modernization and change in the Nizari Ismaili
        community in East Africa - a perspective". Journal of
        Religion in Africa, v.6, No.2, 1974: p123-139.
        Analyses how the concept of modernization of techno-
        logically backward and traditional societies has been

reflected within the Nizari Ismaili community of East
Africa, relating this to the processes by which a spe-
cific Muslim group has been able to effect change.

1299   NANKYAMAS, Theodorus. "On the Orthodox Church in Uganda
        and Kenya". Porefthendes   (Athens) v.3 1961, p43-44.

1300   NEW, Charles. Life, wanderings and labours in Eastern
        Africa, with an account of the first successful ascent
        of the equatorial snow mountain, Kilma Njaro, and
        remarks upon East African slavery. 3rd ed; with a
        new introduction by Alison Smith. London, Cass, 1971.
        (Cass Library of African Studies. Missionary Researches
        and Travels, no. 16).

1301   OKANLANON, T. "The diaconate in East Africa". African
        Ecclesiastical Review, v.4, 1965: p346-350.

1302   OLIVER, Roland Anthony. The missionary factor in East
        Africa. London, Longmans, 1952. xviii, 302p.
        bibliog.
        An authoritative survey of the work of Christian
        missions, of all denominations, throughout East Africa.
        This book shows how far the missionaries were respon-
        sible for the growth of European interests in East
        Africa and how in later years the churches they
        founded have affected the subsequent histories of
        East African states.

1303   PARKER, F. "Early church-state relations in African
        education in Rhodesia and Zambia". World Yearbook
        of Education, 1966: p200-216.

1304   PASSOTH, Richard. "Religion and a science of man: the
        study of religion in a university". East African
        Journal, September 1971: p15-24.
        Examines the question of religious studies in
        relation to university and to the wider society in
        the contemporary secular age.

1305   PASTORAL INSTITUTE OF EASTERN AFRICA. Development projects:
        examples of Church involvement in Eastern Africa.
        Kampala, The Institute, 1972. xii, 65p.

1306   P'BITEK, Okot. "De-hellenising the church". East Africa
        Journal. August 1969: p8-10. Relevance of world
        wide theological debate to the study of traditional
        African belief and customs.

1307   PIROUET, M. Louise. "Recovering the sources for Church
        history in East Africa". Bulletin of the Society of
        African Church History, v.2, No.2, 1966: p193-196.

1308   "PLANNING for the Church in Eastern Africa in the 1980's.
        African Ecclesiastical Review, v.16, Nos 1/2, 1974:
        (whole issue is devoted to above topic.)

1309   RANGER, Terrence O and KIMAMBO, I.N. eds. The historical
        study of African religion with reference to East and
        and Central Africa. London, Heinemann, 1972: 307p.
        This volume grew out of the Dar Es Salaam conference
        on the historical study of African religious systems,
        held in June 1970.

1310   SCHAPPI, Franz Solan. Die katholische Missionsschule im
        ehemaligen Deutsch-Ostafrika. Paderborn, Schoningh,
        1937.

1311   SMITH, N. Langford. "Revival in East Africa". Inter-
        national Review of Missions, v.43, No.169, 1954:
        p77-81.

1312   SMOKER, E.W. "Decision making in East African revival
        movement groups". In Barrett, David Brian (ed)
        African initiatives in religion. Nairobi, East
        African Publishing House, 1971.

1313   SODEPAX CONFERENCE ON THE CHURCHES IN DEVELOPMENT,
        PLANNING AND ACTION, Limuru, Kenya, 1971.
        Picking up the pieces. A report of a Sodepax
        Conference on the Churches in Development Planning
        and Action, Limuru, Kenya, January 1971. Photograph
        and graphics by Victor and Rowena Lamont. Geneva,
        Ecumenical Centre, World Council of Churches, 1971.
        77p.

1314   STRAYER, Robert and others. Protest movements in colonial
        East Africa: aspects of early African response to
        European rule, by Robert Strager, Edward I. Steinhart
        and Robert Maxon. Syracuse, Program of Eastern
        African Studies, Syracuse University, 1973. 100p.

1315   THOMAS, H.B. "Church missionary society boats in East
        Africa". Uganda Journal, v.25, No.1, March 1961:
        p43-53. illus.

Short descriptive accounts of the sailing vessels
in which the pioneering activities of the early
missionaries were carried out.

1316   VERSTEYNEN, F. "Pioneer days in East Africa - 1860-1869".
        African Ecclesiastical Review, v.10, No.4, October
        1968: p362-366.

1317   WARREN, Max. Revival: an enquiry. London, S.C.M. Press,
        1954. 123p.
        Analyses the causes of the revival movement in East
        Africa from 1935 onward and why the church members
        did not form an independent church in spite of their
        dissatisfaction.

1318   WELBOURN, F.B. East African Christian. London, Oxford
        University Press, 1965. 232p. (Student's Library).

1319   WELBORUN, F.B. and OGOT, B.A. East African rebels; a study
        of some independent churches. London, S.C.M. Press,
        1961, xii, 258p.

1320   WELBOURN, F.B. "Independency in East Africa". Ecumenical
        Review, v.11, No.4, July 1959: p430-436.

1321   WENTINCK, D.E. "The Orthodox Church of East Africa".
        Ecumenical Review, v.20, No.1, 1968:
        History of the African Greek Orthodox Church and its
        relationship with the Pariarch of Alexandria.

1322   AGATANGELO DA CUNEO, C.M. Nelle terre d' Ethiopia: quasi
        cent' anni di storia missionaria. Roma, Scuolo
        Tipografica Piox, 1939.

1323   ASANTE, S.K.B. "The Catholic missions, British West African
        nationalists, and the Italian invasion of Ethiopia,
        1935-36". African Affairs, v.73, No. 291: April 1974:
        p234-243.

1324   AIMONETTO, Lydia. Nell' Africa inesplorata con Guglielmo
        Massaia. Padova, Edizioni Messaggero, 1964. 232p.
        illus.

1325   ALOYS, O.M. Capucins missionnaires en Afrique orientale,
        pays Galla en Ethiopie, Cote Francaise des Somalis.
        Toulouse, Les Voix Franciscaines, 1931.

1326   BAETMAN, J. Au pays du roi Menelik: croquis noirs. Lyon,
        Vitte, 1930.

1327   BAETMAN, J. Le bienheureux Justin de Jacobis, Lazariste,
        apôtre de l' Abyssinie. Bellevue, Librairie Vincen-
        tienne & Missionnaire, 1939.

1328   BARSOTTI, Giulio. Ethiopia cristiana. Milano, Editrice
        Ancora, 1929.

1329   BENT, J. Theodore. The sacred city of the Ethiopians.
        London, Longmans, 1893. xv, 309p.

1330   BERNOVILLE, Gaetan. L' épopée missionnaire d' Ethiopie,
        monseigneur Jarosseau et la mission des Gallas. Paris,

Librairie St. Francois, 1950.

1331 BERNOVILLE, Gaetan. Monseigneur Jaroseau et la Mission des
      Galls: L' epopee missionaire d' Ethiopie". Paris,
      Michel, 1950. 381p. illus.

1332 BESHAM, Grima and AREGAY, Merid W. The question of the Union
      of the churches in Luso - Ethiopian relations. (1500-1632)
      Lisbon, Junta de Investigacoes do Ultramar/Centre de
      Estudos Historicos Ultramarinos, 1964. 115p.

1333 BIDDER, I. Laliabala: the monolithic churches of Ethiopia.
      New York, Praeger, 1960. 137p.

1334 BROWN, Clifton F. The conversion experience in Axum during
      the fourth and fifth centuries. Washington, Howard
      University, Dept. of History, 1973. 30p.
      Attempts to examine an important period in the history
      of the Ethiopian Orthodox Church, the conversion
      experience of Ethiopia or Axum during the fourth and
      fifth centuries.

1335 BURNET, Amos. "Ethiopianism". Church Missionary Review.
      v.73, No. 837, March 1922: p29-34.

1336 BUXTON, D.R. "Ethiopian rock-hewn churches". Antiquity, v.20,
      June 1946: p60-69.
      Description of two ancient Ethiopian churches, the Debra
      Damo, which is the oldest surviving Christian church in
      Ethiopia, and Debra Libanos, accross the Eritrean border.

ETHIOPIA

1337   CAQUOT, Andre. "Preliminary views on the Mashafa Tefut of
       Gechen Amba". (Apercu preliminaire sur les Mashafa
       Tefut de Gechen Amba). Annales d' Ethiopie, v.1, 1955:
       p89-108.
       Christian legends in Ethiopia account for the arrival
       of a fragment of the cross and pictures of the Virgin
       during the reign of Emperor Dawit (1380-1409). These
       items are described in this paper.

1338   CAQUT, Andre. "The reign of Saba and the wood of the Cross,
       according to Ethiopian tradition". (La reine de Saba
       et le bois de la croix selon une tradition Ethiopienne"
       Annales d' Ethiopie, v.1, 1955: p137-147.
       Christian Ethiopians firmly believe in the narratives
       that trace the origin of their kingship to the reign of
       Saba (the Queen of Sheba).

1339   CAULK, R.A. "Religion and the state in nineteenth century
       Ethiopia". Journal of Ethiopian Studies, v.10, No.1,
       1972: p23-41.

1340   CERULLI, Enrico. "Two Ethiopian tales on the Christians of
       Cyprus". Journal of Ethiopian Studies, v.5, No.1,
       January 1967: p1-8.
       Written in Amharic with parallel English translation.

1341   CHOJNACKI, S. "The iconography of Saint George in Ethiopia".
       Journal of Ethiopian Studies, v.11, No.1, January 1973;
       No.2, July: p51-92. v.12, No.1, January 1974: p71-132.
       illus.

1342   COTTERELL, F. Peter. Born at midnight. Chicago. Moody Press,

198

1973. 189p.
History of the evangelical church in Southern Ethiopia.

1343   COTTERELL, F. Peter. "Dr. T.A. Lambie: some biographical
notes". Journal of Ethiopian Studies, v.10, No.1,
1972: p43-53.
Biography of Sudan Interior mission pioneer in Ethiopia.

1344   COWLEY, R.W. "Old Testament in the Andemta Commentary
tradition". Journal of Ethiopian Studies, v.12, No.1,
1974: p133-175.

1345   CRUMMEY, Donald E. "Foreign missions in Ethiopia, 1829-
1868". Bulletin of the Society for the African Church
History, v.2, No.1, 1965: p15-36.

1346   CRUMMEY, Donald. Priests and politicians: Protestant and
Catholic Missions in Orthodox Ethiopia 1830-1886.
New York, Oxford University Press, 1973: 176p. illus.
Traces the development of relations between European
missionaries and Orthodox Ethiopia during that period
of Ethiopian history known as the era of the Princess
and the subsequent reign of Emperor Tewodoros.

1347   CULBEAUX, T.B. Histoire politique et religieuse de l'
Abyssinie depuis les temps les plus recules jusqu' a l'
avenement de Menelick II. Geunther, 1929. 3 vols.
A detailed history of Ethiopia from the origins to the
time of Theodore.

1348   DAVIS, Asa J. "The church-state ideal in Ethiopia: a synopsis
        (Pt.1) Ibadan, v.21, October 1965: p47-52.

1349   DAVIS, Raymond J. Fire on the mountains: the story of a
        miracle - the church in Ethiopia. Grand Rapids, Zonder-
        van Publishing House, 1966. 253p.
        A study of the establishment, expansion and conversions
        of the Wollams Evangelical Church of Ethiopia, including
        accounts of prominent personalities and converts.

1350   DEMIMUID, Mgr. Vie du Venerable Justin de Jacobis, de la
        Congretation de la Mission (dite des Lazaristes)
        premier Vicaire Apostolique de 1' Abyssinie. Paris,
        Tequi, 1904.

1351   DE CAROUGE, Alfred. Une mission en Ethiopie d' apres les
        memoires du Cardinal Massaia et d' autres documents.
        Paris, Poussielgue, 1902.

1352   FARGHER, Brian L. "Tribal power structure and church
        government". (Darassa tribe) Practical Anthropology.
        v.17, No.6, November-December. 1970: p280-284.
        In this article, the author points out that it would
        be surprising if a church organization based on a
        pattern other than that which already exists in the
        society could succeed.The Darassa tribe is found in
        Ethiopia.

1353   FINDLAY, Louis. "The monolithic churches of Lalibila in
        Ethiopia". Bulletin de la Société d' Art Copte, v.9,
        1943: p1-58. illus.

1354   GIACOMO, d' Albano. "Historia" della Missione francescana
        in Alto Egitto-Fungi-Ethiopia, 1686-1720. Edita
        dal p. Gabriele Giamberardini.
        Cairo, Edizioni del Centro francescano di studi
        orientali cristiari, 1961. xii, 212. (Studia
        orientalia cristiana Aegyptica).

1355   GIDADA, Negaso and CRUMMEY, Donald. "The introduction
        and expansion of Orthodox Christianity in Qelem
        Awraja, Western Wallaga, from about 1886 to 1941".
        Journal of Ethiopian Studies, v.10, No.1, 1972:
        p103-112.

1356   GIEL, R. and others. "Faith-healing and spirit-possession
        in Ghion, Ethiopia". Social Science and Medicine,
        v.2, No.1, March 1968: p63-79.

1357   HABERLAND, E. "The influence of the Christian Ethiopian
        empire on Southern Ethiopia" Journal of Semitic
        Studies, v.9, No.1, Spring 1964: p235-238.

1358   HANSON, Herbert M. and HANSON, Della. For God and emperor.
        Mountain View, Calif. Pacific Press Pub. Association,
        1958. 188p. illus.

1359   HERBERT, Lady. Abyssinia and its apostle: (Giustino
        de Jacobis, J.M.) London, Burns & Oates, 1868.

1360   HUNNESTAD, Steiner. "Sidamo, morgenlys. I misjonaerenes
        spor etter 20 ar i Ethiopia." Oslo, Lunde, 1969.
        275p.

ETHIOPIA

1361   HUNTINGFORD, G.W.B. "The lives of Saint Takla Haymanot".
       Journal of Ethiopian Studies, v.4, No.2, July 1966:
       p35-40.

1362   HYATT, Harry Middleton. The Church of Abysssinia. London,
       Luzac, 1928. 302p.
       A descriptive work on the introduction of christianity
       into Ethiopia in 340 A.D. and the evolution of the
       coptic church.

1363   ISENBERG, Karl Wilhelm. The journals of C.W. Isenberg
       and J.L. Krapf detailing their proceedings in the
       kingdom of Shoa and journeys in other parts of
       Abyssinia in the years 1839, 1840, 1841 and 1842,
       to which is prefixed a geographical memoir of
       Abyssinia and North Eastern Africa by James M'Queen,
       grounded on the missionaries journals and the
       expedition of the Pacha of Egypt up the Nile...
       London, Cass, 1968. 529p.

1364   KORABIEWICZ, W. The Ethiopian cross. Addis Ababa, Holy
       Trinity Cathederal, 1973. 152p. illus.

1365   KRAPF, Ludwig. Travels, researches and missionary labours,
       during an eighteen years' residence in Eastern Africa,
       together with journeys to Usambara, Ukambani, Shoa,
       Abessinia and Khartoum; and a coasting voyage from
       Mombaza to Cape Delgado. London, Trubner, 1860.
       566p.

1366   LASS-WESTPHAL, Ingeborg. "Protestant Missions during

202

and after the Italo-Ethiopian War, 1935-1937".
Journal of Ethiopian Studies, v.10, No.1, 1972:
p89-101.

1367   LEROY, Jules. "Les étapes de la peinture ethiopienne
        revelées par les manuscripts illustrés et les
        églises peintes". Journal of Semitic Studies,
        v.9, No.1, Spring 1964: p245-246.

1368   LEROY, J. "Objectives of the researches on religious
        Ethiopian painting" (objectifs des recherches sur
        la peinture religieuse ethiopienne". Annales d'
        Ethiopie, v.1, 1955: p127-136. illus.
        By the second half of the 16th century, Ethiopian
        painting had lost its traditional character because
        of the introduction of iconoclastic elements by
        Spanish and Portuguese missionaries.

1369   LESLAU, Wolf. "The black Jews of Ethiopia". Commentary
        v.7, No.3, March 1949: p216-224.
        Until very recently, the Falasha of Ethiopia
        believed themselves to be the sole surviving Jews
        of the world. Since their rediscovery in the 18th
        century they have constituted an unending mystery to
        the scientific investigator.

1370   LINTINGRE, Pierre. "Le concept judéo-chrétien de la
        monarchie ethiopienne" (The Judeo-Christian concept
        of the Ethiopian monarchy). Afrique Documents, v.78,
        1965: p31-44.
        This myth enumerates 35 names, from Adam to Solomon,
        of Kings who reigned de facto over Israel and de jure

over Ethiopia.

1371   LORIT, Sergio C. Abuna Messias. Costi quel che costi.
        Roma, Citta nouva, 1968. 199p. (Minima di Citta
        nuovo, 33).

1372   MCLURE, Bryan. "Religion and nationalism in Southern
        Ethiopia". Current Bibliography on African Affairs,
        September-November 1972: p497-508.
        Case study of three of southern Ethiopia's ethnic
        groups in relation to their modes of nationalist
        expression.

1373   MASSAIA, Gugliemo. I miei trentacinque anni di missione
        nell' alta Ethiopia: memoire storiche. Roma,
        Propaganda Fide, 1885-95. 12 vols.

1374   MATTHEW, A.F. "The Church of Ethiopia". Ghana Bulletin
        of Theology, v.1, No.7, Decembe 1959: p11-17.
        Short historical account of the Ethiopian church
        starting from 1968.

1375   MATTHEW, Rev. A.F. The teaching of the Abyssinian Church.
        London, The Faith Press, 1936.

1376   MATTHEWS, D.H. "The restoration of the monastery church of
        Debra Damo, Ethiopia". Antiquity, v.23, No.92, Dec.,
        1949: p188-200.
        Description of the most ancient Church in Ethiopia
        by the author who was in charge of restoration works,
        and was privileged to enter other parts normally
        closed to Europeans.

1377   MAURO DA LEONESSA, O.F.M. Santo Stefano maggiore
delg' Abissini e le relazioni romanoetiopiche.
Citta del Vaticano, 1929.

1378   METODIO de Nembro, Father. La missione dei Minori
cappuccini in Eritrea (1894-1952). Romae,
Institutum Historicum Ord. Fr. Min. Cap., 1953.
xxiv, 503p. (Bibliotheca seraphico-capuccina.
sectio historica, 13).

1379   MOLGAARD, Lausten A. Gammel kirke og ny mission i
Ethiopien. Kobenhavn, Dansk Ethioper Mission,
1969. 81p. illus.

1380   MONTANO, Giovanni Maria. Ethiopia Francescana nei
documenti dei secoli xvii e xviii. La missione
di Akhmin, Fungi ed Ethiopia, prefectura del P.
Francesco Passalacqua Da Salemi. Quaracchi,
Collegio di S. Bonaventura, 1948.

1381   O'LEARY, De Lacy. The Ethiopian Church. London,
society for Promoting Christian Knowledge, 1936.

1382   PANKHURST, Richard. "A cave church at Kistana, south
of the River Awash", Ethiopia Observer, v.16.
No.3, 1973: p216-219.

1383   PANKHURST, Rita. "Mikael Argawi, Ethiopia's first
Protestant Missionary". Ethiopia Observer v.10,
No.3, 1966: p215-217.
Biography of Mikael Argawi (1848-1931), a Falasha

who spent 50 years in missionary work in Ethiopia
and helped to prepare an Amharic edition of the
New Testament.

1384   PANKHURST, Richard. "The rock church of Tulu Lemen near
        Adadi south of the Awash".
        Ethiopian Observer, v.17, No.1, 1974: p226-227.
        Description of an antiquarian Church of Shoa
        situated at Tulu Lemen.

1385   PANKHURST, Richard. "The rock-hewn Church of Gufti
        Gabriel, South of Tulu Bolo". Ethiopia Observer,
        v.17, No.1, 1974: p222-235, illus.
        Description of an ancient rock-hewn church of
        Gufti Gabriel, in the town of Tulo Bolo, near
        Addis Ababa. It was used for housing the "holy
        of holies" during the annual Timkat or Epiphany.

1386   PERETRA DE QUEROZ, Maria Isaura. "Mauria Leenhardt
        et les églises ethiopiénnes". Monde Non-Chrétien,
        new series, v.74. April-June 1965: p84-101.

1387   RICCI, Lanfranco. "The legend of the Holy Virgin in
        Lebanon and of St. Gigar". Rass studi Ethiopici
        v.8, 1949: p83-118.
        This legend, originating in Lebanon, was brought
        to Ethiopia by the Ethiopian monks who were
        stationed in Lebanon for a short period during
        the second half of the 15th century.

1388   RUBENSON, G. "The lion of the tribe of Judah: christian
        symbol and/or Imperial title?". Journal of

Ethiopian Studies, v.3, No.2, July 1965: p75-85.
This article seeks to explain the myth and the rationale
behind the use of this title by various imperial rulers
of Ethiopia.

1389   SAGE, Clive B. M.E.G.M. education: an introduction to six
        schools in Eritrea where the scriptures are used by or
        through their education programme. London, Middle East
        General Mission, 1973. 20p.

1390   SAUTER, R. "L' église monolithe de Yekka-Mikael" Annales
        d' Ethiopie, v.2, 1957: p15-36. illus.

1391   SCHULTZ, Harold J. "Reform and reaction in Ethiopia's
        orthodox church". Christian Century, January 1968:
        p142-143.

1392   SOMIGLI DE S. DETOLE, Teodosia. Ethiopia Francescana nei
        documenti dei secoli xvii e xviii prededuti da conni
        sorici sulle relazioni con l' Ethiopia durante i sec
        xix e xv Tomo 1, 1633-81. Quaracchi, Collegio di S.
        Bonaventura, 1928.

1393   SUMNER, Claude. "The Ethiopic luturgy: an analysis".
        Journal of Ethiopic studies, v.1, January 1963:
        p40-46.

1394   TAMRAT, Taddesse. Church and state in Ethiopia, 1270-1527.
        Oxford, Clarendon Press, 1972. xv, 327. bibliog.
        illus.
        A detailed study of the rise of the medieval chrstian
        kingdom in Ethiopia from the middle of the thirteenth

century to the period just before the invasion of
Ahmad Gragn.

1395   TAMRAT, Taddesse. "A short note on the traditions of
          pagan resistance to the Ethiopian Church (14th and
          15th centuries)". Journal of Ethiopian Studies,
          v.10, No.1, 1972: p137-150.

1396   TRIMINGHAM, John S. The Christian Church and missions
          in Ethiopia (including Eritrea and the Somalilands.
          London, World Dominion, 1950. 73p.
          Concise and informative study of the relationship
          of the Coptic Church to other Christian missions.
          Examines the proselytizing efforts of the christian
          missionaries among pagans and muslims.

1397   ULLENDORF, Edward. "Hebraic - Jewish elements in
          Abyssinian (monophysite) Christianity". Semitic
          Studies, v.1, No.3, July 1956: p216-256.

1398   WRIGHT, S. "Notes on some cave churches in the province
          of Wallo". Annales d' Ethiope, v.2, 1957: p7-13.
          Description of a visit to sites of archeological
          interest. The eight sites described are (1) Dabra
          Abuna Aron, (2) Estifanos, (3) Dabra Abuna Muse,
          (4) Yagarata Giyorgis, (5) Sagwara Qirqos, (6)
          Dabra Karbe, (7) Dabra S'ege. (8) Gassetcha Abba
          Giyorgis.

1399   ANDERSON, John. The struggle for the school; the inter-
        action of missionary, colonial and nationalist
        enterprise in the development of formal education
        in Kenya. London, Longman, 1970. 192p. (Develop-
        ment texts) Examines the impact of the expatriate
        missionaries, government officials, traders and
        technical experts on African education in the Central
        province of Kenya.

1400   BARRA, Giovanni. "Le frontiere dell' amore. Testimonianze
        sulle Missioni del Kenya". Torino, Missioni Consolata.
        1969. 199p.

1401   BARNETT, Anne. "Christian home and family life in Kenya
        today". International Review of Missions, v.49,
        No.196, October 1960: p420-426.
        Analysis of the causes of family breakdown by
        the Christian Council of Kenya in 1959 in an effort
        to find solution to the problem.

1402   BEECHER, Leonard J. "African separatist churches in
        Kenya". World Dominion, v.31, No.1, January - February
        1953. p5-12.

1403   BEECHER, Leonard. "The revival movement in Kenya".
        World Dominion. January-February, 1951, p29-34.

1404   BENNETT, Norman Robert. "The church Missionary Society
        at Mombasa 1873-1894". In Boston University Papers
        in African History, edited by Jeffrey Butler. Boston
        University Press, 1964: p159-194.

1405   BENSON, Stanley. "Christian communication among the
Masai". African Theological Journal, No.4, August
1971: p68-75.

1406   BERNARDI, B. The Mugwe, a failing prophet; a study of a
religious and public dignitary of the Meru of Kenya.
With a foreword by Daryll Forde. London, New York,
Published for the International African Institute by
the Oxford University Press, 1959. xiv, 211p.

1407   BEWES, T.F.C. "The Christian revival in Kenya". World
Dominion, v.34, No.2, April 1956. p110-114.

1408   BEWES, T.F.C. Kikuyu conflict: mau mau and the Christian
Witness, London, The Highway Press, 1953: 76p.

1409   BEWIS, T.F.C. "Kikuyu religion: old and new" The African
world, April 1953: p14, 16. Account of Kikuyu
Christians' religion and Mau Mau persecution, by an
Anglican missionary.

1410   BEWES, T.F.C. "The work of the Christian Church among
the Kikuyu" International Affairs, v.29, No.3,
1953: p316-325.

1411   BEWES, T.F.C. "The work of the Christian Church among
the Kikuyu". International Affairs, v.29, 1953:
p316-325.

1412   CAPON, M.G. Towards unity in Kenya: the story of cooperation between missions and churches in Kenya
1913-1947. Nairobi, Christian Council of Kenya,

1962. 101p.

1413   CONFERENCE ON THE ROLE OF THE CHURCHES IN INDEPENDENT
        KENYA. Limuru, Kenya, 1964.
        Report of the conference held at Limuru Conference
        Centre, Kenya, 28th - 31st January, 1964 on the role
        of the church in independent Kenya. Nairobi,
        Christian Council of Kenya, 1964. 76p.

1414   DAIN, F.R. "Church and state in education: Kenya".
        World Yearbook of Education, 1966: p375-377.

1415   DPMPVAM. V.J. "Preaching the gospel to the Masai".
        African Ecclesiastical Review, v.9, No.3, July 1967:
        p204-215.

1416   DOUGAL, J.W.C. Missionary education in Kenya and Uganda:
        a study of co-operation. London, International
        Missionary Council, 1936.

1417   GOGARTY, H.A. Kilmanjaro: an East African Vicariate.
        New York, Society for the Propagation of the Faith,
        1927.

1418   HARJULA, Raimo. "On the role of the laity and their
        equipping". African Theological Journal, No.1,
        February 1968: p30-48.

1419   HARRIES, Lyndon. "Bishop Lucas and the Massai experiment".
        International Review of Missions, v 34, No.136,
        October 1945: p389-396.

1420   HOLWAY, James D. "The religious composition of the
        population of the coast province of Kenya".
        Journal of Religion in Africa, v.3, 1970:
        p228-239.

1421   IRVINE, Cecilia. "Toward a profile of the African
        independent churches (separatist) in Nairobi city,
        July 1967". M.A. Thesis, Columbia University, 1968.
        210p.

1422   KENYATTA, Jomo. "Christianity and clitoridectomy".
        In Desai, Ram. Christianity in Africa as seen by
        Africans. Denver, Swallow, 1962: p84-88.

1423   KENYATTA, Jomo. "The new religion in East Africa"
        In Desai, Ram. Chrisitianity in Africa as seen
        by Africans. Denver, Swallow, 1962: p99-102.

1424   KIBICHO, Samuel G. "The interaction of the traditional
        Kikuyu concept of God with the Biblical concept".
        Cahiers des Religions Africaines. v.2, No.4,
        July 1968: p223-238.
        Analysis of references to God in Kikuyu proverbs,
        and of their traditional names of God, shows that
        the Kikuyu concept of God is monotheist, and is
        comparable in many ways with the Hebrew concept
        of God.

1425   KIBUE, David N. "The African Greek Orthodox Church in
        Kenya". Porefthendes (Athens). v.3, 1961:
        p54-55. v.4, 1962: p40-41.

1426   KITAGAWA, Daisuke. African independent church movements
        in Nyanza Province: kenya, Nairobi Christian Council
        of Kenya, 1962. (mimeograph).

1427   LEMA, Anza Amen. "The Lutheran churh's contribution to
        education in Kilimanjaro, 1893-1933". Tanzania Notes,
        v.68, February 1968: p87-94.
        An account of the development and growth of Lutheran
        church schools and their present day contribution to
        the overall development of education in the region.

1428   LONSDALE, J.M. "European attitudes and government in Kenya
        between the wars". Hadith. (Annual Conference of the
        Historical Association. Kenya, Nairobi), v.2, 1970:
        p229-242.

1429   McINTOSH, Brian G. "Kenya 1923: the political crisis and
        the missionary dilemma". University of East Africa;
        Social Science Council Conference, History Paper,
        1968/9· p138-56.

1430   MBITI, J.S. "New Testament eschatology and the Akamba of
        Kenya". In Barrett, David Brian (ed.) African ini-
        tiatives in religion. Nairobi, East African Publishing
        House, 1971: p17-28.

1431   MURRAY, Jocelyn. "The Kikuyu spirit Churches". Journal
        of Religion in Africa, v.5, No.4, 1973: p198-234.
        Gives an introductory and historical outline of the
        development of the Kikuyu spirit churches, followed
        by a preliminary sociological and theological analysis.

213

1432   NASS, Eef A.H. "Christian communication among the Masai".
African Theological Journal, No.4, August 1971: p56-67.

1433   NEWING, Edward G. "The baptism of polygamous families:
theory and practice in an East African church (in Kenya)"
Journal of Religions in Africa (Leiden),v.3, No.2,
1970: p130-141. A survey of the attitude of polyamous
families to baptism among christians of the Anglican
Province of East Africa to find out the place of
monogamy in Christian belief and discipline.

1434   NEWING, Edward G. "A study of Old Testament curricula in
Eastern and Central Africa". African Theological
Journal, No.3, March 1970: p80-98.

1435   PICH, V. Merlo. "Les apsects religieux du mouvement
Mau-Mau". In Devant les sectes non-Chrétiennes xxl^e
semaine de Missiologie, Louvain, 1961. Louvain,
Desclée de Brouwer 1961: p125-139.

1436   PIROUET, M. Louise. "A comparison of the response of
three societies to Christianity (Toro, Teso, Kikuyu)".
Paper in Religious Studies Papers for University of
East African Social Science Conference,1969. Kampala,
Makerere Institute of Social Research, 1970: p36-50.

1437   PRESBYTERIAN CHURCH OF EAST AFRICA. Nendeni; adventure in
social service. Nairobi, Presbyterian Church of East
Africa, n.d. 16p.

1438   RANGER, Terrence O. "Missionary adaptation of African
religious institutions; the Massai case. In Ranger,

T.O. and Kimambo, I.N. The historical study of African religion with reference to East and Central Africa. London, Heinemann, 1972.

1439   SCHOFFELERS, M. "The history and role of the Mbona cult among the Mang'anya". In Ranger, T.O. and Kimambo, I.N. The historical study of African religion with reference to East and Central Africa, London, Heinemann, 1972.

1440   SPENCER, Leon P. "Defence and protection of converts: Kenya missions and the inheritance of Christian widows, 1912-1931". Journal of Religion in Africa, v.5, No.2, 1973: p107-127.

1441   SPENCER, Leon P. "Kenya missions and African interests, 1905-1924". Ph.D. Thesis, Syracuse University, 1974.

1442   STRAYER, R.W. "Missions and African protest: a case study from Kenya, 1875-1935". In Strayer, R.W. Protest movements in colonial east Africa, Syracuse, 1973: p1-37. Also in International Journal of African Historical Studies, v.6, No.2, 1973: p229-248.

1443   TEMU, A.J. British protestant missions. London, Longman, 1972. 184.
A study of Kenya missions from 1874 to 1929. Based on the authors doctoral thesis at the University of Albesia. It claims to reinterprete the role of the missions from an African perspective.

1444   WANYOIKE, E.N. An African Pastor: the life and work of
        the Rev. Wanyoike Kamawe. 1888-1970. Nairobi, East
        African Publishing House. 1974. 256p.

1445   WEATHERBY, J.M. "The Sabei prophets". Man, v.63. No.223.
        November, 1963: p178-179.
        Account of 19th century prophets among the Sabei-
        speaking peoples of Mt. Elgon, Kenya.

1446   WELBOURN, F.B. and OGOT, B.A. A place to feel at home;
        a study of two independent churches in Western Kenya.
        London & Nairobi, Oxford University Press, 1966. xv,
        157. illus., bibliog.

1447   WELBOURN, F.B. "Separatism in East Africa". In Religion
        and social change in modern East Africa. Kampala,
        Makerere College, 1956?, p68-82. (mimeograph).
        An account of the Bamaliki, African Greek Orthodox
        Church and the Kikuyu movements.

1448   WILLIS, J.J. The Kikuyu conference: a study in Christian
        unity, together with the proposed scheme of federation
        embodied in the resolutions of conference. London,
        Longmans, 1914.

1449   WILSON, Bryan R. "Jehovah's witnesses in Kenya". Journal
        of Religion in Africa, v.5, No.2, 1973: p128-149.

1450   YANNOULATOS, Anastasios. "Brief diary of a tour among the
        Orthodox of West Kenya". Porefthendes (Athens)
        v.7, No.2, 1965: p24-28. v.7, Nos 3/4, 1965: p48-52.
        illus.

SUDAN

1451   ADAMS, W.Y. "Introductory classification of Christian Nubian pottery". Kush, v.10, 1962.

1452   ALLISON, O.C. Bishop in the Sudan: a pilgrim Church's progress. London, Highway Press, 1966: 94p.

1453   ALLISON, O.C. Different religious influences in the Sudan. World Dominion, 1948: p235-238.

1454   ANDERSON, W.B. "The role of religion in the Sudan's search for unity". In Barrett, David Brian, (ed). African initiatives in religion. Nairobi, East African Publishing House.

1455   ARKELL, Anthony John. "The influence of Christian Nubia in the Chad area between AD 800-1200". Kush, v.11, 1963: p315-319.
        New archaeological evidence from Koro Toro in Chad seems to support the theory of the influence of Christian Nubia in the Chad area.

1456   ARKELL, A.J. "Persian geographer throws light on the extent of the influence of Christian Nubia in the 10th century AD". Kush, v.11, 1963: p320-21.

1457   BATTLE, Vincent M. "The American mission and educational development in the Southern Sudan". In Vincent M. Battle and Charles H. Lyon, (eds). Essays in the history of African education. New York, Teachers College Press, 1970. p63-83.

SUDAN

1458   BLACK book on the Sudan on the expulsion of the missionaries
        from southern Sudan: an answer. Milan, Verona Fathers,
        1964. 217p.

1459   CAPOVILLA, Agostino. Il serve di Dio Daniele Comboni,
        Vicario Apostolico dell' Africa Centrale, foundatore
        delle Missioni Africane di Verona e delle Pie Madri
        della Nigrizia. Verona, Missioni Africane, 1944.

1460   CHITTICK, H.N. "The last Christian stronghold in the Sudan".
        Kush, v.11, 1963: p264-272.

1461   COOK, C.L. "The Church in Southern Sudan". East and
        West Review, 1953: p119-125.

1462   DANIEL, N.A. "Bishop Gwynne and General Gordon". Sudan
        Notes and Records, v.48, 1967: p62-70.
        A study contrasting General Gordon's published
        opinions about Islam with the attitude of Bishop
        Gwynne, first leader of the Church of England in the
        Sudan, relating the letter's views to his contemporary
        situation.

1463   FORSERG, Malcolm. Last days on the Nile. Philadelphia,
        Lippincott, 1966. 216p.

1464   GADALLAH, F.F. "The Egyptian contribution to Nubian
        Christianity". Sudan Notes, v.40, 1959: p38-43.

1465   GELSTHORPE, A.S. "The Church in the Southern Sudan".
        East and West Review, 1944: p16-21.

218

1466   GRANCELLI, Michelangelo. Daniele Comboni e la missione
        dell' Africa centrale: memoire biografico-storiche.
        Verona, Instituto Missioni Africane, 1923.

1467   CRAWFORD, O.G.S. Castles and Churches in the Middle Nile
        region. With a note on the inscriptions by M.F.
        Laming MacAdam. Khartoum, 1953. (Sudan Antiquities
        service - occasional papers, no.2).

1468   GRAY, R. "Christian traces and a Franciscan Mission in
        Central Sudan, 1700-1711". Journal of African History.
        v.8, No.3, 1967: p383-393.

1469   HELSER, Albert D. The land of God in the Sudan: more
        demonstrations of divine power in the Sudan. New York,
        London, Fleming H. Revell, 1946. 146p. illus.

1470   HILL, R. "Government and the missions in the Anglo-
        Egyptian Sudan". Middle Eastern Studies, v.1, No.2,
        1965: p113-134.

1471   HUNTER, James D. A flame of fire: the life and work of
        R.V. Bingham. Toronto and London, Sudan Interior
        Mission, 1961. 320p.

1472   KAMIL, el BAGIR. Freedom of religions in the Sudan.
        Khartoum, Religious Affairs Department. 1964. 59p.

1473   JOHNSTON, J.W. Mission work among the Azande. London,
        African Inland Mission, n.d. 53p.

1474   MAAN, W.J. "Church and state in the Sudan". Frontier;

v.7, No.1, 1964: p36-40.

1475   MAZRUI, Ali. "Religion and democracy in the first
        Republic of the Sudan". Makerere Journal, v.11,
        1965: p39-50.

1476   MICHALOWSKI, Kazimierz. "La Nubie chrétienne". Africana
        Bulletin, (Warsaw) v.3, 1965: p9-26.

1477   MONTEIL, Vincent. "Problems du Soudan occidental: juifs
        et judaises". Hesperis, v.38, Nos. 3/4. 1951-298.

1478   OATES, J.F. "A Christian inscription in Greek from Nubia".
        Journal of Egyptian Archeology, v.49. 1963: p161-171.

1479   SANDERSON, Lilian M. "The modern Sudan 1820-1950: the
        present position of historical studies". Journal
        of African History. v.4, No.3, 1963: p435-461.

1480   SHINNIE, P.L. "A note on some fragments of stamped
        pottery from Christian Nubia". Sudan Notes, v.31,
        No.2, December 1950: p279-299.

1481   TRIMGHAM, John Spencer. The Christian Church in post-war
        Sudan. London, New York, World Dominion Press,
        1949. 44p. (Post-war survey series, no.44).

1482   VANDEVORT, Eleanor. A leopard tamed: the story of an
        African pastor, his people, and his problems.
        Drawings by James Howard. New York, Harper & Row,
        1968. xii, 218p. illus.

SUDAN

1483   VANTINI, Giovanni. The excavations at Faras: A contribution to the history of Christian Nubia. Belogna, Nigrizia, 1970. 311p. (Museum Combonianum, No.24).

1484   VEENSTRA, Johanne. Pioneering for Christ in the Sudan. Grand Rapids, Mich., Smitter Book Co., 1926. 233p.

UGANDA

1485   ALL AFRICA CONFERENCE OF CHURCHES. Drum beats from Kampala. London, Lutterworth Press for Christian Literature, 1963. 77p.

1486   ANDRE, Marie. Lumiere sur l' Ouganda: Recits missionnaires. Lyon, Librairie Saint-Paul, Editions La Bonté, 1964. 96p.

1487   ASHE, Robert Pickering. Chronicles of Uganda. 2nd ed. with a new introduction by John A. Rowe. London, Cass, 1971. xvi, 480p. illus. (Cass Library of African Affairs. Missionary researches and travels, no.20).

1488   ASSIMENG, John Max. "Sectarian allegiance and political authority: the Watch Tower Society in Zambia, 1907-35". Journal of Modern African Studies. v.8, No.1, April, 1970: p97-112.
A study of the hostilities and tensions between the state and the Watch Tower Society in Zambia in the pre-independence and the post-independence era.

1489   BEOBIDE, Ricardo de. La conjuraction de Katikiro; narracion historica africana, por un sacerdote salesiano. 6th ed. Barcelona, Libreria Salesiana, 1958. 93p. illus. (Bibliotheca "Horas serenas", v.10).

1490   BISSCHOP, E. "The Catholic priest in the pluralistic society". African Ecclesiastical Review, v.4, No.4, October 1962: p300-310.
Lecture organised for the Uganda clergy, based on a questionnaire circulated among participants

1491   BIERMANS, J. A short history of the vicariate of the Upper Nile, Uganda. Nsambya, Kampala, Mill Hill Fathers' Mission, 1920.

1492   BOUCHARD, Richard and LEJEUNE, M. Eucharist and community: parish: of Mushanga. Kampala, Pastoral Institute of Eastern Africa. 1973. 26p.

1493   BRAZIER, F.S. "The Nyabingi cult: religion and political scale in Kigezi 1900-1930". Makerere Institute of Social Research: Conference Paper (D), January 1968. 17p.

1494   BUERKLE, Horst. "The message of the 'false prophets' of the independent churches of Africa". Makerere Journal, v.11, December 1965. p51-55.

1495   BYARUHANGA-AKIIKI, A.B.T. "Religion in Bunyoro" Ph.D. Thesis, Makerere, 1971. 564p.

1496   CALLIS, John Samuel. In Uganda for Christ; the life story
        of the Rev. John Samuel Callis of the Church Missionary
        society by R.D. Pierpont. London, Church Missionary
        Society, 1898. 196p.

1497   CARTER, Fay. "Cooperation in education in Uganda: mission
        and government relations in the inter-war period".
        Bulletin of the Society for African Church History.
        v.2, No.3, 1967: p259-275.
        An account of the principles of cooperation between
        the British Colonial government and missionary socie-
        ties in the establishment of schools in Uganda between
        1917 and 1940.

1498   CHARSLEY, Simon. Churches in Kigumba. Kampala, Makerere
        Institute of Social Research, 1966. 10p. (Sociology
        working papers, 10) (mimeo).
        Discusses the size of church congregations and the
        relation of the churches to tribe and mobility.

1499   COOK, Sir Albert. The Church in Uganda. Kampala, Uganda
        Society, 1945.

1500   CHURCH, J.E. (and others). Forgive them: the story of
        an African martyr, by J.E. Church and colleagues
        of the Ruanda Mission (C.M.S.). London, Hodder and
        Stoughton, 1966. 126p.

1501   DOORNBOS, Martin R. "Protest movements in Western Uganda;
        some parallels". Kroniek Van Afrika, v.3, 1970:
        p213-229.
        Account of the Kumanyana movement of Ankole and the

Rwenzururu movement in Toro, Uganda.

1502   DAHINDEN, Justus. "Quartre monuments aux martyrs de l'
        Ouganda". Art d' Eglise, v.3, No.133, 1965: p258-
        261.

1503   DOERR, L. "The relationship between the Benedictine Mission
        and the German colonial authorities". Dini na Mila,
        (Kampala), v.4, No.1, October 1969: p1-11.
        (cyclostyled).

1504   FAUPEL, J.F. African holocaust: the story of the Uganda
        Martyrs. London, Chapman, 1962. 242p.

1505   GRUPPO UGANDA TERZO MONDO. Dove va la missione? La Lesione
        dell' Uganda. Milano, Jaca book, 1969. 171p. illus.

1506   GALE, H.P. "The work of the Mill Hill Fathers in relation
        to the spread of Roman Catholicism from Nsambya
        throughtout the Vicariate of the Upper Nile (Uganda)
        from 1895 to 1914". Ph.D. Thesis., University of
        London, 1954-55.

1507   GALE, H.P. Uganda and the Mill Fathers. London, Macmillan,
        1959. xi, 334p.

1508   HALLFELL, M. Die Neger-martyrer: nach den ersten geschich-
        tlichen quellen dargestellt. Trier, Paulinus
        Druckerei, 1931.

1509   HANSEN, Holger B. "British administration and religious
        liberty in Uganda". Proceedings of East African

Institute of Social Research Conference, Kampala,
January 1966. 15p.

1510 HARRISON, Mrs. J.W. A.M. Mackay: pioneer missionary of the
Church Missionary Society to Uganda, by his sister.
1st ed. reprinted with a new introductory note by
D.A. Low, London, Frank Cass, 1970: viii, 488p. illus.
(Cass library of African Studies, missionary researches
and travels, no. 14).
A biographical work of one of the early pioneer
missionaries to Uganda. Originally written in 1890.

1511 HATTERSLEY, Charles W. The Baganda at home. London,Franks
Cass, 1968. 227p. illus.
Chapter VIII is about religion in Uganda. Gives short
historical sketch of the various religious denominations,
including Mohammedanism.

1512 HUNNERMANN, G. La flamme qui chante: les martyrs de l'
Ouganda. Mulhouse, Salvator, 1963. 170p.

1513 KALANDA, Paul. "Adaptation of Church law to the Ganda
marriage prohibitions". African Ecclesiastical Review,
v.5, No.1, January 1963: p39-49.

1514 KAVULU, David. The Uganda martyrs. Kampala, Longmans of
Uganda, 1969. 38p.

1515 KIBIRA, J. "The church in Buhaya: crossing frontiers".
In The Church crossing frontiers edited by P.
Beyerhaus and C.F. Hallencreutz. Lund, Gleerups,
1969: p189-205.

1516   KING, Anne. "The Yakan cult and Lugbara response to
        colonial rule". Azania, No.5, 1970: p1-24. bibliog.

1517   KIWANUKA, M.S.M. "Religion in Uganda: a discussion arising
        from F.B. Welbourn's Religion and politics in Uganda".
        East African Journal, v.3, No.11, February 1967. p3-6.

1518   LANGLANDS, B.W. and NAMIREMBE, G. "Studies on the geography
        of religion in Uganda". Kampala, Makerere, University
        College, Dept. of Geography. 1967. 65p. maps.
        (cyclostyled).
        Three essays on the historical background to the
        distribution of religion in Buganda, the religious
        divisions of Buganda into dioceses and deaneries,
        and the expansion of missionary activity in Uganda.

1519   LANGLANDS, B.W. and NAMIREMBE, G. "The historical backg-
        ground to the distribution of religion in Buganda".
        In Studies in the geography of religions in Uganda;
        Kampala, Makerere University, 1967.
        (Department of Geography- occasional paper no. 4.)

1520   LARIDAN, P. "The wonderful life of the Uganda martyrs.
        London, Chapman, 1965. 26p.

1521   LAURAND, Luce. Une semence de chrétiens en terre africaine;
        les martyrs de l' Ouganda. Genval, Belgique, Editions
        Marie Mediatrice, 1966. 173p. illus.

1522   LEDOGAR, R.J. ed. Katigondo; presenting   the Christian
        message to Africa. London, Deacon Bcoks, 1965.
        Proceedings of the first Pan-African Cathechetical study

week, held at Katigondo Seminary in Uganda from
27 August to 1 September 1964.

1523   LEYSBETH, A. Les martyrs de l' Uganda. Leopoldville,
        Bibliotheque d' Etoile, 1964. 55p.

1524   LOCKARD, Kathleen G. "Religion and political development
        in Uganda, 1962-1972". Ph.D. Thesis, University of
        Wisconsin, 1974.

1525   L'OUGANDA et les agissements de la Compagnie Anglaise
        "East Africa". Paris, A la Procure des Missions d'
        Afrique, 1892.

1526   LOW, D.A. Religion and society in Buganda, 1875-1900.
        Kampala. East African Institute of Social Research,
        1957.
        A historical study of the arrival and involvement
        of European missionaries in the politics of Buganda.

1527   LOW, D.A. "Converts and matyrs in Buganda". In Baeta,
        C.G. (ed). Christianity in tropical Africa, studies
        presented and discussed at the seventh International
        African Seminar, University of Ghana, April 1965.
        London, Oxford University Press, 1968: p150-164.

1528   LOW, D.A. "Church and political reforms in Buganda".
        In Forman, C.F. (ed.) Christianity in the non-
        Western world. Englewood Cliffs, N.J. Prentice-Hall,
        1967: p75-78.

1529   LUCK, A. African Saint: the story of Apolo Kivebulaya.

London, S.C.M. Press, 1963. 188p. illus.
The first authoritative account of a pioneer
Ugandan Missionary into the Congo.

1530   MARIE ANDRE DU SACRE-COEUR, Uganda, terres des Martyrs.
Paris, Castermann, 1963. 296p.

1531   MATHESON, Elizabeth Mary. An enterprise so perilous.
Dublin, Mellifont, 1962. 128p. illus.
A history of the white fathers Mission to Uganda.

1532   MBITI, John S. Death and the hereafter in the light of
Christianity and African religion: an inaugural
lecture. Kampala, Makerere University, Dept.
of Religious Studies and Philosophy. 1973. 22p.

1533   MBITI, John S. The voice of nine Bible trees. Mukono,
Uganda: Uganda Church Press, 1972. vii,
31p.

1534   MERCUI, Joseph. L' Ouganda, la mission catholique et
les agents de la compagnie Anglaise. Paris, A la
Procure des Missions d' Afrique, 1893.

1535   MPUGA, W. "A challenge: looking towards the canonization
of the martyr's of Uganda." African Ecclesiastical
Review, v.6, No.3, July 1964: p225-228.

1537   NANKYAMA, T. "Orthodoxy in Uganda". African Ecclesiastical
        Review, v.9, No.2, 1967: p124-127.

1538   O'BRIEN, Brian. That good physician: the life and work of
        Albert and Katherine Cook of Uganda. London, Hodder
        & Stoughton, 1962. 264p.

1539   OKULU, H. "Towards unity in Uganda". African Ecclesiastical
        Review, v.9, No.2, April 1967: p108-110.

1540   PHILIPPE, Anthony. Au cours de l' Afrique; Ouganda: un
        demisiècle d' apostolat au Centre africain, 1878-1928.
        Paris, Gaume, 1880.

1541   PIROUET, L. "The spread of Christianity in and around
        Uganda". Uganda Journal, v.32, No.1, 1968: p220-22.
        A brief note with a table showing the year in which
        effective evangelization was undertaken in various
        areas, giving the names of the missionaries and the
        various missions.

1542   POTTS, M. Ancestors in Christ (the living dead in African
        traditional and Christian religion). Kampala. Gaba
        Publishers, 1971: xii, 19p. Pastoral papers, 17).

1543   POULTON, J. "Like father, like son: some reflections on
        the Church of Uganda". International Review of Missions,
        v.50, July 1961: p297-307.

1544   ROWE, J.A. "The purge of Christians at Mwanga's court: a
        reassessment of this eipisode in Buganda history".
        Journal of African History, v.5, No.1, 1964: pp55-72.

A study of events which culminated in the massacre
of Christians in Buganda in 1886 during the reign of
Kabaka Mwanga.

1545   RUSSELL, J.K. Men without God? A study of the impact of
        the Christian message in the north of Uganda. London,
        Highway Press, 1965. 95p.

1546   SANGREE, Walter H. Contemporary religion in Tiriki. Kampala,
        Makerere Institute of Social Research, 1956. 7p.
        (Conference papers, 64) (mimeo).
        Discusses the relation between traditional society
        and Christian missions with reference to the Pente-
        costal church, Dini Israel, Dini Yawoaha and their
        leadership.

1547   SEMAKULA, P. A brief history of Uganda Martyrs. Gulu,
        Catholic Press, 1964. 32p. illus.

1548   SLOAN, W.W. What is the Old Testament?; a review from
        Africa. Lusaka, Multimedia Publications, 1973. 132p.

1549   STEANNING, D.J. "Salvation in Ankole". In African systems
        of thought, edited by M. Fortes and G. Dieterlen.
        London, Oxford University Press, 1965: p258-275.

1550   STOCK, Sarah Geraldina. The story of Uganda and the Victoria
        Nyanza mission. New York, Fleming H. Revell, 1829.
        223p.

1551   TAYLOR, John Vernon. Processes of growth in an African church.
        (Uganda) London, S.C.M. Press, 1958. 30p. (I.C.M.

research pamphlets, no.6).

1552   TAYLOR, John Vernon. The growth of the Church in Buganda;
        an attempt at understanding. London, S.C.M. Press,
        1958. 288p. illus. (World missionary studies).

1553   "The KITGUM Pastoral Community". Bodija Bulletin, v.16, 1973:
        p21-26.
        Describes an experimental training school for the
        priesthood in Northern Uganda.

1554   THOONEN, J.P. Black martyrs (Uganda). London, Sheed and
        Ward, 1941.

1555   VAN DE CASTEELE, J.J. "Le voyage du Pope Paul vi en Uganda".
        Revue du Clergé Africain, v.24, No.6, November 1969:
        p623-645.

1556   VAN DEN EYNDE, (Pere). "L' action protestante dans les
        districts du Lac Albert et de l' Uganda". Bulletin
        de l' Union du Clergé (Brussels) v.5, April 1925:
        p53-61.

1557   VITTORINO, Dellagiacoma. An African martyrology. Verona,
        Nigrizia Printing Press, 1965. 244p.

1558   WALSER, F. "Theological precision in African languages:
        Is our Luganda baptismal formula theologically correct?"
        African Ecclesiastical Review, v.1, No.1, January
        1959: p47-49.

1559   WANDIRA, Asavia. Early missionary education in Uganda: a
        study of purpose in missionary education. Kampala,
        Makerere University, Dept. of Education, 1972.
        356p.

1560   WELBOURN, F.B. "Spirit initiation in Ankole and a Christian
        Spirit movement in Western Kenya". In J. Beattie
        and J. Middleton (eds) Spirit mediumship and society
        in Africa. London, Routledge and Kegan Paul, 1969:
        p290-306.

1561   WELBOURN, F.B. Religion and politics in Uganda. 1952-1962.
        Nairobi, East African Publishing House. London,
        Deutsch. 1965.

1562   WHISSON, M.G. The will of God and the wiles of men. Kampala,
        East African Institute of Social Research, 1962?
        34p.

1563   WILLIAMS, Trevor. "The coming of Christianity to Ankole"
        Bulletin of the Society of African Church History,
        v.2, No.2, 1966: p155-173.

1564   WRIGLEY, C.C. "The Christian revolution in Buganda".
        Comparative studies in Society and History, v.2, no.1
        October 1959: p33-48.
        Account of a Christian and Muslim revolt against
        King Mwanga of Buganda in 1889 which led to his
        overthrow and led to the establishment of Christianity
        in the Kingdom by 1900.

1565   ALTENMULIER, D. "Observations after a year's study at the
       Lutheran Theological College Makumira". Lutheran
       World, v.12, No.2, April 1965: p169-172.

1566   AUF DER MAUR, I. "Beitrag der Benediktiner Missionare von
       St. Ottilen in Tanzania zur liturgischen Erneuerung
       1887-1970". Neue Zeitschrift fur Missionwissen-
       schaft. v.27, No.2, 1971: p126-135. No.3, 1971.

1567   BEIDELMAN, T.O. "Social theory and the study of Christian
       missions". Africa, v.44, No.3, July 1974: p235-249.
       A study based on the Church Missionary Society in
       Ukaguru, Tanzania.

1568   BENNETT, N.R. "The London Missionary society at Urambo,
       1878-1898". Tanzania Notes, v.65, March 1966: p43-52.
       This historical account of a European mission in
       Western Tanzania, includes some notes on local headmen.

1569   BERNANDER, G. Lutheran wartime assistance to Tanzanian
       Churches, 1940-1945. Gleerup, Lund, 1968. 170p.
       bibliog. (Studia missionalia Upsaliensia, 9.).

1570   BUHAYA - et hjorne of Tanzania. Religion og kultur skildrest
       of afrikanere. Red of Finn Allan Petersen, Knud Lange
       og Jorgen B. Svendsen. Kobenhavn, D.M.S. Forlag, 1971.
       68p. illus.

1571   DI MARTINO, A. "Tizania: vento di urbanesimo nella steppa".
       Missioni Consolata, v.71,No.11, June 1969: p18-26.

1572   FLETCHER, Jesse C. Wimpy Harper of Africa. Nashville,

TANZANIA

Broadman Press, 1967. 142p.

1573 FOUQUER, Roger, Le docteur Adrien Atiman; medecin-catechiste au Tanganyika; sur les traces de Vincent de Paul, Spes, 1964. 166p.

1574 GRAY, R.F. "Some parallels in Sonjo and Christian mythology". African Systems of thought, edited by M. Fortes and G. Dieterlen. London, O.U.P. for International African Institute, 1965. p49-63.

1575 HASSING, ". "German missionaries and the Maji Maji rising". African Historical Studies, v.3, No.2, 1970: p373-389. An account of a rising in September 1905 in which the rebels murdered seven Benedictine missionaries in Tanganyika, and destroyed several Catholic and Lutheran Berlin Missionary Society stations.

1576 HASTINGS, A. "The Catholic church in Tanzania". African Ecclesiastical Review, v.11, No.2, April 1969: p125-130. v.11, No.3, 1969: p310-311.

1577 HELLBERG, Carl Johan. Missions on a colonial frontier West of Lake Victoria: Evangelical Missions in North-West Tanganyika to 1932.
Lund, Gleerup, 1965. 256p.
Primarily, a historical account of the Protestant missions in Bukoba district, Tanzania.

1578 HELLBERG, Carl Johan. "The German Evangelical Mission and the north western boundaries of Tanganyika".Tanganyika Notes and Records, v.58/59, 1962: p207-210.

234

1579   HELLBERG, John Hakan. John Hakan. "The Makumira consultation on the healing ministry of the church." African
Theological Journal, No.1, February 1968: p62-68.

1580   HEREMANS, R. Les etablissements de l' Association Internationale Africaine au lac Tanyanika et les peres
blancs Mpale et Karema, 1877-1885. Tervuren, Musee
Royal de l' Afrique Centrale, 1966. 139p.

1581   HERTLEIN, S. Die kirche in Tanzania ein Kurzer Uberblick
uer Geschichte uber Gegenwart. Munster, Vier-Turner-
Verlag, 1971. 160p. illus. (Munsterschwarzacher
Studien, bd. 17).

1582   HOFGREN, Allan ed. Tanganyika; ett bildverk om svenska
insatser i Afrika Forord av Tage Erlander. Stockholm,
E.Fs-forlaget, 1963. 45p. illus.

1583   HOKORORO, A.M. "The influence of the Church on tribal
customs at Kukuledi." Tanganyika Notes and Records.
1960: p1-13.

1584   HUDDLESTON, Trevor. "The Christian churches in independent
Africa." African Affairs, v.68. No.270, January 1969;
p42-48.
Based mainly on the author's experience as Bishop of
Masasi, Tanzania.

1585   HUNTER, Monica. "An African Christian morality." Africa
v.10, No.3, July 1937: p265-292. This study, based
on observations of the Nyakusa of South Tanganyika,
analyses the problem as to how far belief in traditional

religious sanctions remains in the Christian
community, how far it is replaced or modified,
and how far changes affect christian moral behaviour.

1586   JOINET, B.A. The image of Christ among Catholic adolescents
in Tanzania. Paper for U.S.S. c. Conference, 1968-69,
Kampala, Makerere Institute of Social Research, 1969.
23p. (M.I.S.R. conference paper).

1587   ILIFFE, J. "The organization of the Maji-Maji rebellion".
Journal of African History. v.8, No.3. 1967: p495-
512.

1588   The IMPACT of social change on the life and structure of
the church. Dodoma, Central Tanganyika Press, 1968.
32p.

1589   INGVARSSON, B. "Dar es Salaam: en ny stad". Den Evangeliska
Missionen, v.1, 1970: p28-37.

1590   KITTLER, G. "Black prince (Cardinal Laurian Rugambwa)".
Negro Digest. v.10, July 1961: p27-32.

1591   LAMBOURN, R. "Zanzibar to Masasi in 1876: the founding of
Masasi mission". Tanganyika Notes, v.31, July 1951:
p42-46.

1592   LARSON, L. Der funfarmige Leuchter. vol. 1 - Grundung und
Grundlegung der Kongregation von St. Ottilien. vol.2 -
Kloster und Missionen der Kongregation. Eos Verlag,
Benedictine Missions in Tanzania, 1971.

1593   LUNDMARK, E. "Religions forskring: Tanzania". Svernsk
        Missiontidskrift. v.3, 1970: p128-132.

1594   "MAKUMIRA, Lutheran Theological College". Africa Theologigical
        Journal, No.2, 1969 and No.3, 1970.

1595   MATSON, A.T. "The Holy Ghost mission at Kosi on the Tana
        river." Bulletin of the Society of African Church History,
        v.2, No.2, 1966: p174-179.
        A history of the Zanzibar mission founded in 1860 from
        Reunion which was transferred to the Holy Ghost Fathers
        in 1863.

1596   MIHALYI, Louis J. "German missionary acivity in the Usambara
        Highlands, 1885-1914". East African Journal v.8, No.2,
        February 1971: p26-32. Bibliog.

1597   MURRAY, F. Short report and reflections on the personnel
        and financial survey of the Catholic Church in Tanzania.
        Mwanza, Pastoral Orientation Service, 1970. 24p.
        (Report no.5).

1598   MURRAY, F. "1969 - A study year for the Church in Tanzania."
        African Ecclesiastical Review. v.12, No.1, 1970: p71-73.

1599   NEILL, S. Colonialism and Christian missions (Tanzania).
        London, Lutterworth, 1966. 445p.
        A study on cooperation between colonial administration
        and the missionaries.

1600   NYBLADE, Orville W. "An idea of theological education in
        Tanzania". African Theological Journal, No.3, March

1970: p69-79.

1601   OCHSNER, Knud. Church, school and the clash of cultures:
        examples from North-west Tanzania". Journal of
        Religion in Africa. (Leiden) v.4, No.2, 1971: p97-
        118.

1602   OCHSNER, K. "The consecration of Bishop Josiah Kibira".
        Lutheran World, v.12, August 1965: p283-286.

1603   OGOT, Bethwell A. "British administration in the Central
        Nyanza district of Kenya, 1900-6o." Journal of
        African History. v.4, No.2, 1963: p249-273.
        Includes discussion on missionaries and the Mumbo
        cult.

1604   PAVECE, F. "Tanzania un delicato problema pastorale"
        Missioni Consolata (Rome). v.69, No.6, April 1967:
        p19-22.

1605   PELTOLA, M. "Ostafrikansk Kyr kohistora". Svensk Mission
        stidskrift, v.3, 1970: p121-128.

1606   PERRIN-JASSY, M.F. Forming Christian communities: an
        evolution of experiments in North Mara, Tanzania.
        Kampala, Pastoral Institute of Eastern Africa, 1969.
        76p. (Gaba Institute Pastoral Papers, no.12).

1607   PETERSEN, F.A. and others. Buhaya - et Hjorne of Tanzania
        religion og kultur skildret af afrika nere. Kellrup,
        D.N.S. Forlag, 1971. 68p.

1608   RANGER, T.O. The African Churches of Tanzania.
        Nairobi, East African Publishing House, 1968. 28p.
        (Historical Association of Tanzania, paper no.5).

1609   RANGER, Terrence O. "Christian independency in Tanzania".
        In Barrett, D.B. ed. African initiatives in religion,
        Nairobi, East African Publishing House, 1971: p122-
        145.

1610   RICKLIN, L.A. La mission catholique du Zanguebar: travaux
        et voyages du R.P. Horner, missionnaire de la Congre-
        gation du St. Esprit et du St. Coeur de Marie Vice-
        Prefet Apostolique du Zanguebar, membre honoraire
        correspondant de la societe Royale de Geographie de
        Londres. Paris, Gaume, 1880.

1611   ROBINSON, D.W. "The Church in Tanzania: African socialism".
        African Ecclesiastical Review. v.5, No.3, July 1963:
        p256-264.

1612   RUGAMBWA, Laurian, Cardinal. "African Cardinal". Negro
        History Bulletin, v.24. January 1961: p94-95.

1613   RUGAMBWA, Laurian, Cardinal and others. "Catholics in
        a plural society; excerpts from pastoral letter on
        Tanganyika" Commonweal, v.74, July 1961: p374-375.

1614   RWEYEMANU, S. and MSAMBARE, T. The glories of the
        Catholic Church in Tanganyika. Rome, Pontificea
        Universita Urbaniana de Propaganda Fide, 1963. 96p.

1615   SCHNEIDER, Gebhard. Die katholische Mission von Zanguebar:

thatigkeit und reisen des P. Horner. Regensburg, Joseph Manz, 1877.

1616   SEROTE, S.E. "Sect and church in the city". In The Missionary outreach in an urban society. Mapumulo, Missiological Institute, Lutheran Theological College, 1967: p94-103.

1617   SHORTER, A. "Form and content in African sermon: an experiment". African Ecclesiastical Review, v.11, No.3, 1969: p265-279.

1618   SHORTER, Alyward. "The migawo: peripheral spirit possession and Christian prejudice", Anthropos, v.65, No. 1/2, 1970: p110-126.
        Description of a spirit possession guild known as "Migawo" among the Kimbu and Nyamwezi of Tanzania and the attitude of Christian missionaries towards the sect.

1619   SHORTER, A. "Religious value in Kimbu history charters". Africa, v.39, No.3, July 1969: p227-237.

1620   SICARD, Siegvard von. "The Lutheran Church on the coast of Tanzania 1887 - 1914 with special reference to the Evangelical Lutheran Church in Tanzania, Synod of Uzaramo - Uluguru. Lund, Gleerup, 1970: 260p. (Studia missionalia Upsaliensia, 12).

1621   SMEDJEBACKA, Henrik. Lutheran Church autnomy in Northern Tanzania 1940-1963. Akad. Avh. Abo adadeni. (Acta Academiae Aboensis. Serie A. Humaniora, 44).

TANZANIA

1622   SMITH, A. "The contributions of the Missions to the educational structure and administrative policy in Tanganyika, 1818-1916". M.A. Thesis, University of Sheffield, 1962-63.

1623   SMITH, Anthony. "The missionary contribution to education (Tanganyika) to 1914." Tanganyika Notes and Records, v.60, 1963: p91-110.

1624   SOUTHON, Ebenezer John. "The history, country and people of Unyamwesi." In N.R. Bennet, Studies in East African history, Boston, Boston University Press, 1963: p81-88.

1625   SUNDKLER, B.G.M. "Marriage problems in the Church in Tanganyika." International Review of Missions, July 1945: p253-266.

1626   SWANTZ, Lloyd W. Church, mission and state relations in pre and post independent Tanzania, 1955-1964. New York, Syracuse university, 1965. 50p. illus. bibliog. (Program of East African Studies. Occasional paper 19).

1627   SWEETING, Rachel. "The growth of the church in Buwalasi". Bulletin of the Society of African Church History, v.2, No.4, 1968: p311-322.

1628   TANNER, Ralph E.S. "Christianity in Usukuma". African Ecclesiastical Review, v.10, No.4, October 1968: p383-390. Part II; v.11, No.2, April 1969: p149-158. Part III; v.11, No.3, 1969: p284-293. Research carried out in 1967 in the dioceses of Mwanza and Shinyanga into the comparative failure of Christianity to attract the Sikuma in large numbers.

1629   TANNER, Ralph E.S. Transition in African beliefs; traditional religion and Christian change; a study in
Sikumaland, Tanzania, East Africa: 1967. xii, 256p.

1630   WHITE, P. Jungle doctor's progress: a sequel to "Doctor of
Tanganyika," highlighting more than a quarter of a
century of progress in missions, medicine and nation-
hood; with photographs by Emery, and drawings by G. Wade.
London, Pater-Noster.

1631   WILLIS, R.G. Kaswa: oral tradition of a Fipa prophet.
Africa. v.40. No.3, July 1970: p248-256. Bibliography.

1632   WRIGHT, Maria. "German Evangelical Missions in Tanganyika,
1891-1939, with special reference to the Southern Highlands." Ph.D. Thesis, University of London, 1966.

1633   WRIGHT, Marcia. German missions in Tanganyika. 1891-1941.
Lutherans and Moravians in the Southern highlands.
London, Oxford University Press, 1971: xiv, 249p.
Bibliog. (Oxford studies in African Affairs).
A historical study of the interaction of Africans and
German missionaries in the southern highlands of
Tanzania.

1634   VON SICARD, S. "The first ecumenical conference in Tanzania,
1911." Bulletin of the Society of African Church History,
v.2, No.4, 1968: p323-333.

1635   VON SICARD, S. The Lutheran on the coast of Tanzania, 1887-

TANZANIA

1914. Uppsala, Gleerup, 1970. 360p.

WESTERN AFRICA (General)

1636   AGBEBI, Mojola. An account of Dr. Mojola Agbebi's work in
        West Africa, comprising Yorubaland, Fantiland, the
        Ekiti country, Central Nigeria, Southern Nigeria and
        the Cameroons. New Calabar, n.p. n.d. (1940?) 40p.
        illus.
        Reprints of the author's letters and press articles.

1637   AGBEBI, Mojola. Inaugural sermon delivered at the celebration
        of the first anniversary of the "African Church", Lagos,
        West Africa, December 21, 1902. Yonkers, N.Y. Horworth,
        1903. (Schomburg Collection, N.Y.C.) 31p.

1638   ANDERSON, Vernon A. "Indigenous churches in West Africa".
        Congo Mission News, No. 143/145, July 1948 - January
        1949.

1639   BANE, Martin J. Catholic pioneers in West Africa. Preface
        by James R. Knox, with a foreword by Patrick J. Cornish.
        Dublin, Clonmore and Reynolds. 1956. 220p. illus.,
        bibliography.
        This is the best available book in English on Catholic
        missionaries as a whole.

1640   BANE, Martin J. The Popes and western Africa: an outline
        of mission history, 1460s - 1960s. Preface by O.
        Carlos Stoetzer. Foreword by Sergio Pignedoli. Staten
        Island, N.Y.Alba House, 1968. xv, 187p.

242

1641 BARRET, Leonard E. "Religious rejuvenation in Africa: some
impressions from West Africa". <u>Journal of Ecumenical</u>
<u>Studies</u>, v.3, No.1, Winter 1970.

1642 BARROW, Alfred Henry. <u>Fifty years in Western Africa: being</u>
<u>a record of the work of the West Indian Church on the</u>
<u>banks of the Rio Pongo</u>. New York, Negro Universities
Press, 1969. iv, 157p. illus.

1643 BERTHO, J. "Le probleme du mariage chrétien en Afrique
occidentale francaise". <u>Africa</u>, v.17, No.4, 1947:
p252-

1644 BIRTHWHISTLE, Allen. "Missionary administrator: the story
of Thomas Birch Freeman". <u>West African Review</u>,
December, 1951: p1392-1395. illus.
Account of Freeman's missionary activities in Ghana,
Nigeria and Dahomey in the 19th century.

1645 BIRTWHISTLE, Allen. <u>Thomas Birch Freeman, West African</u>
<u>pioneer</u>. London, the Cargate Press, 1950: xvi, 112p.
Tells the story of Freeman's missionary activities
in West Africa. It contains an account of the history
of the Methodist Church in Cape Coast and Ashanti.

1646 BLYDEN, Edward Wilmot. <u>The return óf the exiles and the</u>
<u>West African Church</u> (A lecture at Breadfruit School
House, Lagos, 2/1/91). London, W.B. Whittigham 1891.
39p. Also in <u>African Repository</u>, v.68, 1892: p1-18.

1647 BRASIO, Antonio C.C. <u>Monumenta missionaria Africana</u>.
<u>Africa occidental</u> (1471-1531) vol.1. (1532-69) vol.II

(1570-99) vol. III, (1469-1599). Lisbon, Agencia Geral do Ultramar, Segunda Serie. 1963-64.

1648   CLARKSON, Thomas. Review of the Rev. Thomas B. Freemans journals of visits to Ashanti, etc., with remarks on the present situation of Africa and its spiritual prospects. London, Nisbet, 1845. 15p.
Reviews the practice of human sacrifice and the prevalence of superstition among the natives of West Africa in the light of Freeman's experiences in Ashanti, Dahomey and Nigeria.

1649   COLE, J. Augustus. A revelation of the Secret Orders of Western Africa. Dayton, United Brethren Publishing House, 1886. 99p.

1650   DEBRUNNER, Hans W. "Sieckentroosters, Predikants and chaplains: A documentation of the history of Dutch and English chaplains to the Guinea coast before 1750". Bulletin of the Society for African Church History. (Nsukka) vi. 1964: p73-89.

1651   DICKSON, K.A. "Hebrewism of West Africa - the Old Testament and African life and thought". Legon Journal of Humanities. v.1, 1974: p23-34.

1652   "The EVANGELIZATION of West Africa today." International Review of Missions, v.54, No.216, October 1965: p484-494.

1653   FISHER, Humphrey J. "Separatism in West Africa". in J. Kritzeck and W.H. Lewis (eds). Islam in Africa,

New York, Van Nostrand - Reinhold Co., 1969: p127-
140. bibliog.

1654   FLASCHE, Rainer. "Ein fruher versuch einer Gesamstrsd-
        tellung der westafrikanischen reliogionen". (An early
        attempt at describing West African religions in general)
        Africana Marburgensia, v.3, No.1, 1970: p24-32.

1655   FLICKINGER, D.K. Ethiopia; or, Twenty years of missionary
        life in Western Africa. Dayton O. United Brethren
        Publishing House, 1885. 329p.

1656   FREEMAN, Thomas Birch. Extracts from a journal of various
        visits to the kingdoms of Ashanti, Yariba and Dahomi
        in Western Africa to promote the objects of the
        Wesleyan Missionary Society. (London, Printed by J.
        Nicholas, 1843). 24p.

1657   FREEMAN, Thomas Birch. Journal of various visits to the
        kingdoms of Ashanti, Aku, and Dahomi in Western
        Africa, together with an historical introduction by
        Rev. John Beecham. 2nd ed. London, Mason, 1844. x,
        298p. illus.
        .n authentic record of Freeman's missionary work in
        Ashanti and other parts of West Africa.

1658   FORTES, Meyer. Oedipus and Job in West Africa. Cambridge,
        Cambridge University Press, 1959. 81p.

1659   FOX, William. A brief history of the Wesleyan Missions on
        the Western Coast of Africa; including biographical
        sketches with some account of the European settlements,

and of the slave trade. London, Aylott & Jones,
1851. xx, 624p. illus.
Historical account of the activities of the Wesleyan
missionaries including biographical sketches of the
missionaries who died in the course of their work.

1660   GOLLMER, Charles Andrew. Charles Andrew Gollmer, his
life and missionary labours in West Africa. Compiled
from his journals and Church missionary Society's
publications by his eldest son. London, Church
Missionary Society, 1899. 220p.

1661   GRESCHAT, Hans-Jurgen. Westafrikanische Propheten.
Morphologie einer religionen Spezialisierung.
Marburg/Lahn, im Selbsteverlag, 1974. 113p.
(Marburger studien zur Africa - und Asien Kunde,
A.4).

1662   GOOD health! the Church's ministry of healing. London,
World Student Christian Federation, 1961. 16p.
(West African Project, no.6).

1663   GROCKER, William G. Memoir of William G. Grocker, late
missionary in West Africa among the Bassas, including
a history of the Bassa mission by R.B. Medbery. 1848.
300p.

1664   HAIR, Paul Edward Hedley. "C.M.S. 'native clergy' in
West Africa to 1900". Sierra Leone Bulletin of
Religion, v.4, No.1, June 1962: p71-72.

1665   HAIR, Paul Edward Hedley. "Native clergy in West Africa
        to 1900". Sierra Leone Bulletin of Religion. v.4, No.2,
        1962: p71-72.

1666   HAYFORD, Mark C. West Africa and Christianity. London,
        Baptist Tract and Book Society. 1900.

1667   HOLAS, Bohumil T. "Sur la position des religions
        traditionnelles dans l' ouest africain". Monde Non-
        Chrétien, N.S. June - July, 1953: p183-192.

1668   ITALIA, N.B. The most Rev. James George Campbell,
        D.B.P., Senior Patriach of the West African Episcopal
        Church and the presiding Patriach of the Christ Army
        Church G.B.C. Nigeria; a brief account of his missionary
        labours. Lagos, Oluwole Press, 1945. 16p.

1669   JACOBSON, Stiv. Am I not a man and a brother? British
        missions and the abolition of the slave trade and
        slavery in West Africa and the West Indies 1786-1883.
        Uppsala, Lund, 1972. (Studia missionalia Upsaliensia,
        17).

1670   KRAS , A.C. "A strategy for primary evangelism in West
        Africa." Ministry, v.8, no.2, April 1968: p74-76.

1671   LYNCH, W. Blyden: pioneer West African nationalist".
        Journal of African History, v.6, No.3, 1965: p373-388.

1672   MACARTHY, J.A. The prospects of Christianity in West Africa.
        London, 1887.

1673   MALDANT, B and HAUBERT, M. Croissance et conjoncture dans
        l' Ouest africain. Paris, Presses Universitaires de
        France, 1973. 350p.

1674   NAGAR, O. The pilgrimage tradition in West Africa.
        Khartoum- Khartoum University Press, 1973. 192p.

1675   NASSAU, Robert Hamil. Corisco days; the first thirty
        years of the West African mission. Philadelphia,
        Allen, Lane & Scott, 1910. 192p.

1676   PARIS. UNIVERSITE. Centre de Hautes Etudes. Administration
        sur l' Afrique et Asie Modernes.
        Cartes des religions de l' Afrique de l' ouest: notice
        et statistiques. Paris, La Documentation Francaise,
        1966. 135p.

1677   PARRINDER, E.G.S. "Christian marriage in French West Africa".
        Africa, v.17, No.4, 1947: p260-

1678   PARRINDER, E.G. "The religious situation in West Africa".
        African Affairs, v.59. No.234, January 1960: p38-42.

1679   PLATT, William J. From fetish to faith. London, Livingstone
        Press, 1935. 159p. map. bibliog.
        A study on the origin and growth of the Church in
        West Africa.

1680   REECK, Darrell Lauren. "A socio-historical analysis of
        modernisation and related mission influences in two
        chiefdoms in West Africa. 1875-1940". Ph.D. Thesis,
        Boston University, 1970. 343p.

1681   SHAW, Trevor and SHAW, Trevor. Through ebony eyes: evangelism through journalism in West Africa. With an introduction by Norman Grubb and an epilogue by Claude de Mestral. London, United Society for Christian Literature, Lutterworth Press, 1956. 96p.

1682   SLATER, Eleanor C. Afiong: a story of West Africa. Illustrated by Mary Paschal. Milwaukee, Bruce Publishing Co., 1959. 96p.

1683   THOMPSON, E.W. "Christian education in British West Africa." Church Missionary Review, v.66, 1924: p61-7.

1684   THOMPSON, George. The palm land; or West Africa illustrated: being a history of missionary labours and travels, with descriptions of men and things in Western Africa- also a synopsis of all the missionary work on that continent. 2nd ed. reprinted. London, Dawsons, 1969. 456p. illus. (The colonial history series).

1685   THOMPSON, George. Thompson in Africa: or, an account of the missionary labors, sufferings, travels, and observations of George Thompson in western Africa at the Mendi mission. 2nd ed. New York, Printed for the author, 1852. 356p.

1686   TILDSLEY, Alfred. The remarkable work achieved by Rev. Dr. Mark C. Hayford in promotion of the spiritual

and material welfare of the natives of West Africa,
and proposed developments. London, Morgan and Scott,
1926. 36p.

1687   TODD, John M. African mission- a historical study of the
Society of African Missions whose priests have
worked on the Coast of West Africa and Inland, in
Liberia, the Ivory Coast, Ghana, Togoland, Dahomey
and Nigeria, and in Egypt since 1856. With a preface
by David Mathew. London, Burns & Oates, 1962. 230p.
illus. Includes bibliography.

1688   TURNER, H.W. "The catechism of an independent West African
Church". Sierra Leone Bulletin of Religion, v.2,
No.2, 1960: p45-57.
Comparative analysis of the catechisms of the
Aladura and Kimbanguist Churches with two Ghanaian
independent churches.

1689   TURNER, Harold W. "Pagan features in West African independent churches". Practical Anthropology. v.12,
No.4, July - August 1965: p145-51.
Discusses the relationship between pagan and
christian elements in independent African churches.
The pagan features include the practice of divination
through revelation, ecstatic worship and spirit
possession, purification procedures, etc.

1690   WILLIAMS, Joseph John. Hebrewish of West Africa: from
Nile to Niger with the Jews. London, Allen & Urwin
1930: viii, 443p. illus. bibliog.

1691   YATES, Walter Ladell. "The history of the African
            Methodist Episcopal Zion Church in West Africa:
            Liberia, Gold Coast (Ghana) and Nigeria. 1900-1939".
            Ph.D. Thesis, Hartford Seminary Foundation, 1967.
            398p.

1692   YOUELL, George. Africa marches. London, S.P.C.K.
            1949. 144p.
            West African Christian soldiers during the war.

                        CAMEROONS

1693   ALLEGRET, Elie. La mission de Cameroon. Recits
            missionnaires. Paris, Société des missions
            evangeliques. 1924. 60p.

1694   BAHOKEN, V.C. "La contribution des religions a' l' expre-
            ssion culturelle de la personalité africaine". In
            Colloque sur les religions Abidjan, 5-12 Avril 1961.
            Paris, Presence Africaine, 1962: p155-168.
            A discussion on the role of the protestant church in
            the social, literary and health needs of the
            Cameroons.

1695   BAYART, J.F. "La fonction politique des eglises au
            Cameroun". Revue Francaise de Science Politique,
            June 1973: p514-536.

1096   BOETZKES, William. "West Cameroon: a success story."
            World Mission, v.15, No.3, 1964: p83-87.

1697   BOUBA, Bernard. "Is God Veneb or Yaama?". Missiology, v.1,
No.1, 1973: p109-111.
Samba religion, North Cameroon.

1698   BRUTCH, Jean R. "A glance at missions in Camerron". International Review of Missions, v.39, No.155, July 1950:
p302-310.

1699   BUREAU, Rene. "Influence de la Christianisation sur les
institutions traditionnelles des ethies cotieres du
Cameroun". In Baeta, C.G. ed. Christianity in tropical
Africa, studies presented and discussed at the seventh
International African Seminar, University of Ghana,
1965. London, Oxford University Press, 1968: p166-181.

1700   BUREAU, Rene. "Flux et reflux de la christianisation
Camerounaise". Archives de Sociologie des Religions,
v.9, No.17, 1964: p97-112.

1701   CAMEROUN francais: la mission de   Foumban des pretres du
sacrecoeur de Saint-Quentin. Paris, Dillen, 1931.

1702   CERETI, Giovanni. Rapporto sull' Africa nera. Impressioni
di un viaggio in Camerun. Milano, Pontifico Instituto
missioniestere, 1969. 117p.

1703   CHRISTOL, Jacques. Quatre ans au Cameroun. Paris,
Societe des Missions Evangeliques, 1922.

1704   GRAINES d' Evangile; apercu des eglises independantes
africaines. Yaounde, Cameroun: Editions Cle,
1973. 63p.

1705   GROOT, N. "God's people of Cameroon: a forward look."
         African Ecclesiastical Review, v.12, No.1, 1970:
         p63-70.

1706   HABERLE, Wilhelm. Trommeln Machte und ein Ruf.
         Erzahlungen aus Kamerun. Stuttgart, Evangelischer
         Missionsverlag, 1966. 93p.

1707   HALLDEN, Erik. The culture policy of the Basel Mission in
         the Cameroons 1886-1905. Uppsala, Uppsala University,
         1968. (Studia Ethnographica Uppsaliensia, 31).

1708   HARRIS, B. "The Methodist Church Women's Training Centre -
         Kwadaso". Community Development Bulletin, v.4, No.2,
         March 1953: p35-36.
         A description of the Centre and an analysis of the
         course content.

1709   HEGBA, M. ,and others. Croyance et guerison (chrétiennes).
         Yaounde, Cle, 1973. 148p.

1710   MBOCK, Pierre. La vie d' une église au Cameroun. Paris,
         Société des Missions Evangeliques, 1934.

1711   REYBURN, William D. "The Church, male and female". Practical
         Anthropology, v.4, No.4, 1957: p140-145.
         Among certain tribes in the Cameroons (Bulu, Yaounde,
         Bafia, Meka Gbaya, Kaka), membership of the Christian
         church is predominantly female.. Church membership is
         sought by women only after they have gained sufficient
         status or have shown that they are of little productive
         value.

1712   REYBURN, William D. "Polygamy, economy and Christianity in the Eastern Cameroun." Practical Anthropology, v.6, No.1, January - February 1959: p1-19.
Among the Kaka, Yengele, Mponpong, Bizom, Ngounabam, Bangando and Mpoman tribes in the Cameroons, the relevance for the practice of polygamy is mainly economic. A woman who has more work than she can handle is often anxious to see her husband take on another wife.

1713   REYBURN, William D. "Quelques reflexions sur les mouvements ecclesiastiques independants en Afrique". Flambeau (Yaounde) v.22, May, 1969: p95-100.

1714   SKOLASTOR, Herman. Bishof Heinrich Vieter, erster Apostilischer Vikar von Kamerun. Limburg, Pallottiner, 1925.

1715   SKOLASTER, Hermann. Die Pallotiner in Kamerun: 25 Jahre Missionsarbeit. Limburg, Pallottiner, 1924.

1716   SLAGEREN, J. Van. Les origines de 1' église evangelique du Cameroun. Missions européennes et christianisme autochtone. Leiden, 1972. 297p.

1717   TRIMUA, D.J. "Le nom africain dans le baptême chrétien." Flambeau, v.39, August 1973: p149-158.

1718   TROBISCH, W.A. "Pre-marital relations and Christian marriage in Africa". Practical Anthropology v.8, November 1961: p257-261.
Based on data collected from male students of a missionary school in the Cameroons, this paper

attempts to reconsturct the traditional attitudes and
motives of the Bassa, Bulu and Bamileke tribes
regarding pre-marital sexual practices.

1719   TRUB, A. "A study of the traditional outlook of the native
community in the Cameroons Province of Nigeria and its
impact upon the thought and practice of the Christian
Church in that province." PH.D. Thesis, Edinburgh
University, 1960.

1720   VAN SLAGEREN, J. Les origines de 1' église evangelique du
Cameroun: missions Européennes et christianisme
autochtone. Leiden, Brill, 1972. ix, 301p. Bibliog.

DAHOMEY

1721   DESCRIBES, E. Abbe, L' evangile au Dahomey et à la Côte
des Esclaves, ou, histoire des Missions Africaines de
Lyon. Paris, Emile-Paul Freres. 1924.

1722   ELLINGWORTH, Paul. 'As others see us': non - Methodist
sources for Methodist history in Ouidah, Dahomey".
Bulletin of the Society for African Church History.
v.1, No.1, 1963: p13-17.

1723   ELLINGWORTH, Paul. "As they sat themselves : more about
the beginnings of Methodism in Ouideh" Bulletin of the
Society for African Church History, v.1, No.2, 1963:
p35-41.

1724   ELLINGWORTH, Paul. "Christianity and politics in Dahomey

1843-1867". Journal of African History, v.5, No.2,
1964: p209-220.

1725   ELLINGWORTH, Paul. "Methodism on the slave Coast, 1842-
        1870". Bulletin of the Society For African Church
        History, v.2, No.3, 1967: p239-248.
        Discusses the developments of the Methodist missionary
        activities in Dahomey to the west at Anecho and
        Agoue and to the east at Porto Novo by Thomas Birch
        Freeman.

1726   LABOURET, Henri et RIVET, Paul. Le royaume d' Ardra et
        son evangelisation au xvll^e siecle. (Gunet Aizo).
        Paris, Institut d' Ethnologie, 1929. 63p. illus.
        (Travaux et memoires, 8).

1727   MERLO, Carlo. "Les sectes au Dahomey". In Devant les
        sectes non- chretiennes, xxi^e semaine de missiologie,
        Louvain 1961. Louvain, Desclee de Brouwer, 1961:
        p102-119.

1728   ABRAHAM, Philip. "Spiritual Churches in Ghana." The
        Ghanaian, v.5. No.8, August 1962, p27.
        The author asserts that the multiplicity of spirit-
        ual churches in Ghana today shows the African's
        inherent belief in God.

1729   ADIKU, E.T. "Settling disputes among the Ewe". Missiology,
        v.1., No.2, 1973: p67-70.

1730   ADJEI, Ako. "Imperialism and spiritual freedom." In
        Desai, Ram. Christianity in Africa as seen by Africans.
        Denver, Swallow, 1962: p67-83.

1731   AFRIFA, A.A. The Church in our society: an address by
        Brigadier A.A. Afrifa at the 7th Annual Conference
        of the Methodist Church of Ghana at Kumasi in August
        1968. Accra, Ministry of Information, 1968. 8p.

1732   AGBETI, J.K. "The history of the training of African
        Christian Ministers in Ghana, 1842-1965". Ph.D.
        Thesis. London University, 1969.

1733   AGBETI, J.K. "New perspectives in theological education
        with special reference to Ghana". Ghana Bulletin of
        Theology, v.4, No.6, June 1974: p19-36.

1734   AGBETI, J.K. 'Religious education in Ghana'. Insight
        and Opinion, v. No.3, 1970: p13-21.

1735   AGBETI, J.K. "Theological education in Ghana". Ghana
        Bulletin of Theology, v.3, No.10, June 1971:

1736   AGYEMFRA, L.S.G. Ghana Church union: an opinion. Accra,
        Waterville Publishing House, 1969. 50p.

1737   ALLEYNE, Cameron. Gold Coast at a glance, especially
        adapted to missions study classes. New York, Hunt
        Printing Co., 1931. 143p.

1738   AMICE, Laurie. "The first time a Bishop visited Teppa."
        Ghana Radio and T.V. Times, v.4, No.29, September 1963:

p7+15.

Account of the welcome ceremony on the occasion of
the first visit of a Bishop to a village in Brong-Ahafo.

1739   AMISSAH, S.H. "A missionary strategy for this decade".
        In God's mission in Ghana. Accra, Asempa Publishers,
        1974: p88-94.

1740   AMPOFO, Oku. "The traditional concept of disease, health
        and healing with which the Christian Church is
        confronted" Ghana Bulletin of Theology, v.3, June 1967:
        p6-7.

1741   ANNOBRAH-SARPEI, J. Operation help Nima: five years of
        christian involvement in urban renewal, Accra.
        Operation Help Nima, 1974. 30p.

1742   ANQUANDAH, James R. "The Christian torn between the world
        and his faith". In God's mission in Ghana... Accra,
        Asempa Publishers, 1974. p48-59.
        The author firmly believes that many Ghanaian Christians
        have one foot in the church and another foot in some
        pagan rite, cult, festivity, or in Kramo spiritualism
        or in some wayside private church that practices
        idolatory in the name of Christ. This work is supported
        with authentic account of personal observations and
        interviews.

1743   ANSAH, J.K. The centenary history of the Larteh Presbyterian
        Church, 1853-1953. Larteh, Presbyterian Church, 1955:
        111p.

1744   ANSRE, Gilbert. "The Church in mission." In God's mission
         in Ghana.   Accra, Asempa Publishers, 1974: p31-39.
         Puts forward suggestions that for the Church to perform
         its mission effectively there must be better knowledge
         of the scriptures and of Ghanaian society. The church
         must also be sensitive politically and must be ready
         to participate in state affairs. It must also evolve
         moral and ethical norms and must take part in the
         educational process.

1745   ARHIN, Kwame. "The missionary role on the Gold Coast and
         in Ashanti: Reverend F.A. Ramseyer and the British
         take-over of Ashanti, 1869-1894". Research Review
         (Legon), v.4, No.2, 1968: p1-15.

1746   ARMSTRONG, Charles W. The winning of West Africa. London,
         Wesleyan Methodist Missionary Society, 1920. 64p.
         Contains a summary of the work of Prophet Harris in
         Ghana.

1747   ARTHUR, J.B. "The christian faith and African culture,
         especially its liturgical expression." Ghana Bulletin
         of Theology, v.2, No.1, 1962. p1-12.

1748   ARYEE, A.F. "Christianity and polygamy in Ghana: the role
         of the Church as an instrument of social change".
         Ghana Journal of Sociology. v.3, no.2, 1967. p98-105.
         Based on data collected from the 1960 census report,
         this paper reveals that the rate of polygamy is lower
         for Anglicans, Catholics and members of Apostolic
         Churches than for those professing traditional beliefs
         and those belonging to African independent christian
         sects.

1749   ASAMOA, E.A. "The influence of fetichism." In Christianity
          and African Culture. Accra, Christian Council, 1955:
          p39-45.

1750   ASHANIN, C.B. "The social significance of religious
          studies in West Africa." Universitas. (Legon) v.4,
          No.1, December 1959: p9-11.

1751   BAETA, Christian G. In W. Birmingham (and others) (ed.)
          A study of contemporary Ghana. v.2, Evanston,
          Northwestern University Press, 1967: p240-250
          Analysis of traditional, Islamic and Christian
          religions in Ghana.

1752   BAETA, Christian G. "Challenge of the Ghana Church Union
          proposals." Reformed and Presbyterian World, v.28,
          June 1964: p69-74.

1753   BAETA, C.G. "Christianity and healing." Orita: December
          1967: p51-61.
          The concept of the 'healing church' in Ghana is to
          be viewed with reference to the healing practices of
          indigenous religious and healing sects, which employ
          physical, magical and religious approaches to healing.

1754   BAETA, C.G. "Conflict in mission: historical and separa-
          tist churches." In The theology of the christian
          mission, edited by G.H. Anderson. New York, McGraw-
          Hill, 1961. p290-299.
          Analysis of the relationship between Mission churches
          and the independent churches in Ghana.

1755   BAETA, C.G. "Cultes sycretiques au Ghana." In
        Syncretisme et messianisme en Afrique noire; papers
        presented to the seminar at Bouake, Ivory Coast
        1963. Paris. Edition du Seuil, 1963.

1756   BAETA, Christian G. "Is there still a role for European
        and American missionaries in Africa." Central
        Africa, v.81, January, 1963, p12-15.

1757   BAETA, Christian G. "The mission of the church is
        christ's mission." In God's mission in Ghana...
        Accra, Asempa Publishers, 1974: p12-19.

1758   BAETA, G.G.K. Prophetism in Ghana; a study of some
        spiritual churches. London, S.C.M. Press, 1962,
        xiii, 169p.
        A study based on the multiplicity of spiritual
        churches in Ghana. This is a slightly revised
        version of the original thesis submitted and
        approved for the Ph.D.

1759   BAETA, C.G.K. "Prophetism in Ghana". Ph.D. Thesis,
        University of London, 1958/59.

1760   BAETA, C.G. The relationship of Christians with men of
        other living faiths: a valedictory lecture delivered
        before the University at the Auditorium, Legon, on
        Thursday, 13th May, 1971. Accra. Ghana Universities
        Press, 1971: 27p. Bibliography.

1761   BAETA, Christian G. Report of Rev. C.G. Baeta on his
        tour of the Gold Coast, July-September, 1938, at

the meeting of the Council held on 21st October 1938.
Accra, Christian Council of the Gold Coast, 1939.

1762   BAMFO, Godfried A. "Winning the nation for Christ. In
        God's mission in Ghana. Accra, Asempa Publishers,
        1974. p79-87.
        A discussion on the strategy of the church in mobilising
        available potential resources, material and human, to
        achive its evangelical mission in Ghana.

1763   BAPTIST CHURCH. Gold Coast. The year-book and report of
        the Baptist Church and Mission and the Christian Army
        of the Gold Coast. Cape Coast.

1764   BARTELS, F.L. The beginning of Africanisation... the dawn
        of the missionary motive in Gold Coast education: Rev.
        Thomas Thompson, 1751-1951. Gold Coast, Methodist
        Book Depot, 1951. 12p.

1765   BARTELS, Francis L. "Jacobus Eliza Johannes Capitein, 1719-
        1747". Transactions of the Historical Society of
        Ghana, v.4, Part 1, 1959, p3-13.

1766   BARTELS, F.L. "Philip Quacue." Transactions of the Gold
        Coast and Togoland Historical Society. v.1. No.5.
        1955: p153-177.
        Biography of the first Ghanaian chaplain in the Gold
        Coast, at Cape Coast.

1767   BARTELS,F.L. The roots of Ghana Methodism. Cambridge
        and Accra. Cambridge University Press, 1965. xiii,
        368p. Bibliog.

Historical account of the Methodist Church in Ghana, based on documentary sources and oral tradition. Gives useful account on the role of the Church in the educational development of the country.

1768   The BASEL Evangelical Mission on the Gold Coast, Western Africa from 1828-1893.   Basel, Basel Mission, 1894.

1769   BASE1 Mission centenary, 1828-1928.   Accra, Scottish Mission, 1928. 27p.

1770   BEECHAM, John.   Ashantee and the Gold Coast: being a sketch of the history, social state, superstitions of the inhabitants of these countries with a notice of the state and prospects of Christianity among them. London, Dawsons, 1968. 378p. (Colonial history series).

1771   BEETHAM, T.A.   "Religious education in the Gold Coast". International Review of Missions, July 1945: p267-272.

1772   BENTLEY, M.   "Philip Quaque".   Church Quarterly Review, No.167. April/June 1966: p151-165.
        Biographical sketch of the first Cape Coast citizen to be ordained a priest.

1773   BELSHAW, Harry.   "Church and state in Ashanti."   International Review of Missions, v.35, No.140, October 1946: p408-415.
        Highlights the conflict between the Christian church and the Ashanti confederacy council on the decision

of the latter that Thursdays are to be observed
as sacred days during which farming will be prohibited.

1774   BIELBY, N.R. Alone in the city of blood. London,
Edinburgh House Press, 1941. 32p. (Eagle books,
no.34).
An account of the first two missionary journeys of
Thomas Birch Freeman to Kumasi in 1839 and 1941.

1775   BOAHEN, A. Adu. "James Richardson: the forgotten
philanthropist and explorer." Journal of the
Historical Society of Nigeria, v.3, No.1, 1964:
p61-71.

1776   BREWER, John H. "The ordination of Philip Quaque
1765." Bulletin of the Society for African
Church History, v.1, Nos. 3-4, 1964: p89-91.

1777   BRIEF history of the Methodist Church, Winneba, 1899-
1959. Cape Coast, Mfantsiman Press, 1959: 15p.

1778   BROKENSHA, David. Christianity and change. Pittsburgh
Duguesne University Press, 1961.
An account of religion and social change in Larteh,
situated in the Akwapim Ridge, 35 miles North of
Accra.

1779   BUCHNER, H. "Die allgemeine und kirchliche lage auf
der Goldkuste". Evangelische Missions-Magazine,
January 1944: p8-19.

1780   BULCK, G. Van. "Le prophete Harris vu par lui-même

(Cote d' Ivoire, 1914)". In Devant les sectes non-
chrétiennes xxie semaine de Missiologie. Louvain
Desclée de Brouwer, 1961: p120-124.

1781   BURKE, F.L. and McCREANOR, F.J. Training missionaries for
community development; a report on experiences in
Ghana. Princeton, New Jersey, Jill de Grazia, 1960.
86p.

1782   BUSIA, K.A. "Christianity and Ashanti." In Desai, Ram.
Christianity in Africa as seen by Africans. Denver,
Swallow, 1962: p94-98.

1783   BUSIA, K.A. "Freedom and unity in Christ - in society."
International Review of Missions. v.52, October 1963:
p447-452.

1784   BUSIA, K.A. "Has the christian faith been adequately
presented?". International Review of Missions, v.50.
January 1961: p86-89.

1785   BUSIA, Kofi Abrefa. Urban churches in Britain: a question
of relevance. London, Lutterworth Press, 1966. 175p.

1786   CHAMPAGNE, Gabriel. Catholic hymnal. Accra, Diocese of
Tamale, 1965. 73p.

1787   CHRISTIAN COUNCIL OF GHANA. The Brause Committee.
Religious broadcasting survey, by Peter Edwards.
Accra. The Author, 1967. Variously paged. (Report
no.2)

1778   CHRISTIAN COUNCIL OF THE GOLD COAST.
Christianity and African culture: the proceedings of
a Conference held at Accra, Gold Coast, May 2nd - 6th,
1955, under the auspices of the Christian Council.
Accra, the Council, 1955: 80p.

1779   CHRISTIAN COUNCIL OF THE GOLD COAST.
The Church in town: addresses given at a conference in
Accra, Gold Coast, May 15th - 18th, 1951. Accra,
Christian Council, 1951. 63p.

1780   CHRISTENSEN, James Boyd. "The adaptive functions of Fanti
priesthood." In W. Bascom and M.J. Herskovits,
(eds). Continuity and change in African cultures:
Chicago, University of Chicago Press, 1959: p257-278.
An analytical study of the impact of christianity upon
traditional Fanti religion.

1781   CREEDY, L.A. "News of the Churches; Presbyterian Church of
Ghana". Reformed and Presbyterian World, v.20,
December 1968: p173.

1782   DEBRUNNER, Hans W. A history of Christianity in Ghana.
Accra, Waterville Publishing House, 1967.

1783   DEBRUNNER, Hans Werner. A history of Sampson Opong, the
prophet. Accra. Waterville Publishing House, 1965.
37p. illus.

1784   DEBRUNNER, Hans. "The Moses of the Ghana Presbyterian
Church: an historical meditation on Reverend Andreas
Riis , 1804-1854." Ghana Bulletin of Theology.

v.1, No.3, December 1957: p10-16, No.4, June 1958:
p12-19.

1785   DEBRUNNER, H. "Notable Danish chaplains on the Gold Coast".
       Transactions of the Gold Coast and Togoland Historical
       Society, v.2, 1956: p13-29.
       The chaplains discussed here include Wilhelm Johann
       Mueller, Johann Rask and H.C. Monrad.

1786   DE WILSON, George. The biography of Prophet John Mensah.
       Cape Coast, The author. (c.1960). 42p.
       Biography of the founder of independent Church of
       Christ, at Cape Coast, Central Region of Ghana.

1787   DICKSON, Kwesi A. "The Methodist Society; a sect."
       Ghana Bulletin of Theology. v.2, No.6, June 1964:
       p1-7.

1788   DOVLO, Christian K. Africa awakes: some of the problems
       facing Africa today as seen from the Christian point
       of view. Accra. Scottish Mission Book Depot, 1952.
       77p.

1789   DOVLO, C.K. Christianity and family life in Ghana.
       Accra, Waterville Publishing House, 1962. (Books for
       further reading).

1790   DOVLO, Christian K. "The Gold Coast Church". Africana.
       v.1. No.2, April 1949: p12-13.

1791   DOVLO, E.K. Yevuga. "Our culture and Christianity."

GHANA

The Ghanaian, No.12, June 1959: p21-22.
A study into the problem of the conflict of African culture and the Christian religion, with an attempt to reconcile the differences.

1792   DZOBO, N.K. "Christian citizenship and politics in Post-coup Ghana". Ghana Bulletin of Theology, v.3, No.7, 1969: p1-7.

1793   ELLIOT, C.H. "Miscellanea Anglicana: some events in the history of the Diocese of Accra". Ghana Bulletin of Theology, v.1, No.4, June 1958: p5-12.

1794   FERGUSON, Duncan. "The cosmic Christ and African culture". Ghana Bulletin of Theology, v.1. No.8, 1960: p1-2.
A discussion on whether the Ghanaian can become a Christian without losing his African identity.

1795   FERNANDEZ, James W. "Rededication and prophetism in Ghana." Cahiers d' Etudes Africaines (Paris) v.10. No.2, 1970: p228-305. illus.
A detailed account of the history and teaching of Prophet Wovenu, leader of the Apostles Revelation Society in the Volta Region of Ghana. Traces his emergence as a spiritual leader, the development, practices and the organization of the sect, and the relevance of the Prophet and his sect to Ghanaian politics.

1796   FIAWOO, D.K. "From cult to church: a study of some aspects of religious change in Ghana." Ghana Journal of Sociology, v.4, October 1968: p72-87.

Description of 'Atike' or medicine cults among the coastal Ewe as an example of social adjustment through syncretic adaptation.

1797   FIAWOO, D.K. "The influence of contemporary social changes on the magico-religious concepts and organization of Southern Ewe-speaking people of Ghana". Ph.D. Thesis, Edinburgh University, 1959.

1798   FIAWOO, D.K. "Urbanization and religion in Eastern Ghana". Sociological Review. N.S. v.7, No.1, July 1959: p83-97.

1799   FIELD, Margaret Joyce. "Ashanti and Hebrew Shamanism". Man, v.58, No.7, 1958: p14.
        Discusses the similarity between Ashanti and Hebrew shamanism.

1800   FREMPONG, Isaac. "Schism and division - help or hindrance to mission?". In God's mission in Ghana... Accra, Asempa Publishers, 1974: p60-66.
        Defines Schism and gives the causes for it as doctrinal differences, spiritual decadence, inclination to different forms of worship, personal grounds or language differences

1801   GABA, Christian R. Scriptures of an African people. New York, Nok publishers, 1973. 100p.

1802   GABA, Christian R. "Sociological factors with regard to ordination of women: an African view". Ghana Bulletin of Theology (Legon) v.3, No.10, June 1971. p35-41.

1803   GARTLAN, J. "Christening of pagan customs in Ghana."
         Catholic World, November 1959: p101-106.

1804   GBEWONYO, James K. "Architecture of the catholic Missions
         in Ghana". M.Sc. Thesis, Kumasi, University of Science
         and Technology. Faculty of Architecture. 1965. 27p.

1805   GHANA CHURCH UNION COMMITTEE. An order for divine worship
         with Holy Communion. Accra, Church Union Committee,
         1970. 18p.
         This order has been prepared by the Committe for use
         by its member churches. It has two purposes in mind -
         the need to help members from various churches to worship
         together, and also as a contribution to the worship of the
         United Church.

1806   GHANA CHURCH UNION COMMITTEE. Proposed basis of Union.
         Accra, Ghana Church Union Committee, 1965. 28p.

1807   GHANA CHURCH UNION COMMITTEE. Proposed constitution of the
         United Church. Accra, Ghana Church Union Committee,
         1967. 70p.

1808   GHANA CHURCH UNION COMMITTEE. Proposals for Church Union
         in Ghana. Prepared by the Ghana Church Union Committee
         and submitted to the negotiating churches. Accra,
         Ghana Church Union Committee, 1973. 194p.

1809   GHANAIAN studies for priesthood." Sepia, v.2, August 1962:
         p59-61.

1810   GILDEA, R.Y. "Religion in the Ashanti province of Ghana."

<u>Social Sciences</u>, v.38, October, 1963: p209-212.

1811 <u>GOD's mission in Ghana; talks given at a conference on the</u>
   <u>mission of the Church in Ghana, held in Kumasi in</u>
   <u>January 1973</u>. Accra, Asempa Publishers, 1974: 96p.
   illus.
   A collection of eleven speeches by prominent Ghanaian
   Church leaders and laymen of the "mission of the Church
   in Ghana Today.".

1812 GRAU, E.E. "The Evangelical Presbyterian Church (Ghana
   and Togo) 1914-1946: A study in European mission
   relations affecting the beginning of an indiginous
   church". Ph.D. Thesis. Hartford Seminary Foundation,
   1964. xi, 251p.

1813 GRAU, Eugene. "The German Protestant heritage of the
   Church in Ghana." <u>Ghana Journal of Theology</u>, v.3,
   No.1, December 1966: p10-18. v.3, No.4, June 1968: p14-

1814 GRAU, Eugene. "Missionary policies as seen in the work of
   missions with Evangelical Presbyterian Church, Ghana."
   <u>In</u> Baeta, C.G. ed. <u>Christianity in tropical Africa,</u>
   <u>studies presented and discussed at the seventh Inter-</u>
   <u>national African Seminar, University of Ghana, April</u>
   <u>1965</u>. London, Oxford University Press, 1968. p61-82.

1815 HALL, <u>Rev. Peter</u>. <u>Autobiography of Rev. Peter Hall</u>. Accra,
   Waterville Publishing House, 1965. 74p. (Pioneer
   series).
   Biographical account of the first moderator of the
   Presbyterian Church in Ghana.

1816   HALIBURTON, G.M. "The Anglican Church of Ghana and the
        Harris movement of 1914." Bulletin of the Society for
        African Church History. v.1. December 1964: p101-106.
        The Anglican Church in Ghana gained many adherents
        after the visit of Harris, due to the influence of one
        of his disciples, John Swatson.

1817   HALLIBURTON, Gordon M. "The calling of a prophet: Sampson
        Oppong". Bulletin of the Society of African Church
        History, v.2, No.1, December 1965: p84-96.
        Biography of a prophet who started work as a labourer
        and fetish priest, and was imprisoned in the Ivory
        Coast where he saw a vision which led to his conversion
        into the Christian faith before turning to be a prophet.

1818   HALIBURTON, G.M. "The late Sampson Oppong: Ashanti prophet."
        West African Religion, v.5, February 1966: p1-3.
        From 1916 until 1923, Sampson Oppong was a leading
        Christian evangelist, whose charismatic powers led to
        the conversion of many people in Ashanti. He worked
        mainly in association with the Methodist Mission,
        although he disclaimed membership of any christian sect.
        He died in 1964.

1819   HAYFORD, Mark C. ,ed. The year-book and report, the Baptist
        Church and Mission and the Christian Army of the Gold
        Coast. London, the Church, 1913. 127p.

1820   HORN, K. "The first hundred years of the Methodist Mission."
        Teachers' Journal (Accra) v.7, No.2, 1935: p58-61.
        A brief account of the development of the Methodist
        missions in Ashanti.

1821   HORNER, G.S. "Thomas Birch Freeman - pioneer missionary".
West African Review, v.13, No.181. October 1942: p29-31.

1822   HUBER, Hugo. "Das totentritual einer Ewe-Gruppe des sudost-
lichen Ghana". Ethnos, v.30, 1965: p79-104.

1823   HULSEN, C. Unbaptized infants. Cape Coast, Catholic Press,
1965. 236p.

1824   INTERNATIONAL MISSIONARY COUNCIL. The Ghana Assembly of the
International Missionary Council, 28th December, 1957
to 8th January, 1958. Selected papers, with an essay
on the role of the I.M.C. Edited by Ronald K. Orchard.
London. Published for the International Missionary
Council by Edinburgh House Press, 240p.

1825   JACKSON, Rex. Guide to Christian growth. Accra. Assemblies
of God Mission. 1968. 50p.

1826   JACKSON, Rex. Our sure foundation. Accra, Assemblies of
God Mission. 1968. 54p.

1827   JEHU-APPIA, Metapoly Moses. The constitution of the Musama
Disco Christo Church. Mazano, Po. Box 3, Gomoa Eshiem,
via Swedru, Ghana: The Church, 1959. 58p.

1828   JENKINS, Paul. "A comment on M.P. Frempong's history of
the Presbyterian Church at Bompata". Ghana Notes and
Queries, No.12, June 1972: p23-27.

1829   KELLEHALS, E. "Staat und Kirche auf der Goldkuste".
Evangelische Missions-Magazin. January 1944: p19-29.

1830   KEMP, Rev. Dennis. Nine years at the Gold Coast. London,
        Macmillan, 1898. xv, 279p. illus.
        Descriptive account of the author's missionary work in
        the Gold Coast with observations on topics of anthro-
        pological interest.

1831   KETEKU, H.J. Biography of Rev. Nathaniel Victor Asare.
        Accra, Waterville Publishing House, 1965. 24p. (Pioneer
        series).
        Rev. Asare was a Presbyterian Minister who was stationed
        in Ashanti from 1902 to 1911.

1832   KIMBLE, David. A political history of Ghana: the rise of
        Gold Coast nationalism 1850-1928. Oxford, Clarendon
        Press, 1963. xviii, 587p.

1833   KITTLER, Glenn D. The White Fathers. Introduction by
        Lourian Rugambwa. New York. Harper, 1957. 229p. illus.

1834   KIVENGERE, Festo. When God moves you move too. Accra.
        Asempa Publishers, 1973. 46p.

1835   KRASS, A. "Toward a more indigenous liturgy". Ghana Bulletin
        of Theology, v.3, No.7, December 1969: p20-28.
        Discusses aspects of life among the Chokosi and Konkomba
        of Northern Ghana, with a suggestion that some elements
        of life in the area should be integrated into the
        Christian liturgy.

1836   KUDAJIE, J.N. "Does religion determine morality in African
        societies? - a view point". Ghana Bulletin of Theology,
        v.4, No.5, December 1973: p30-49.

1837   KUMEKPOR, Tom K. "Evaluation of the family planning services
        of the Christian Council of Ghana 1967-1969". Legon,
        Department of Sociology, 1970. (Current Research
        Report Series, no.4).

1838   KYEREMATEN, E.A. "History of the Presbyterian Church at
        Bompata in Asante Akyem". (Translated from the original
        twi of M.P. Frempong by E.A. Kyerematen). Ghana Notes
        and Queries, No.12, June 1972: p20-23.

1839   McKENZIE, R.P. "Thomas Freeman's attitude to other faiths".
        Ghana Bulletin of Theology. (Legon) v.3, no.8, June
        1970: p21-31.

1840   McNULTY, J. "Credit unions in Northern Ghana: the Church
        goes to the people". Month, v.24, October 1960: p255-
        258.

1841   McTORKLE, W.F. The Assemblies of God of Ghana: constitution
        and laws. Accra. Assemblies of God Mission. 1968.
        66p.

1842   "MAKING man whole: the report of the the Legon consultation
        on the Healing Ministry of the Church". Ghana Bulletin
        of Theology. v.3. nos. 1 & 2. 1967. 80p.

1843   MARSHALL, M.J. "Christianity and nationalism in Ghana: an
        analysis of the role of Christian Missions in the
        political development of the Gold Coast, with special
        reference to the early movement". M.A. Thesis, Univer-
        sity of Ghana, 1965. vi, 118p.
        A study conducted to find out to what extent nationalism

in the Gold Coast was generated by the work of
Christian missionaries.

1844   MARTINSON, A.P.A. Biography of Rev. Benjamin A. Martinson.
         Accra, Waterville Publishing House, 1965. 31p.
         (Pioneer series).

1845   MARWICK, R.P. "Thomas Freeman's attitude to other faiths".
         Ghana Bulletin of Theology (Legon) v.3, No. 8, June
         1970. p21-31.

1846   MAXWELL, Arthur S. Your Bible and you: priceless treasures
         in the Holy Scriptures. Accra, the Advent Press, 1966.
         302p.

1847   MAXWELL-LAWFORD, F. Catholics at Achimota: an account of
         the first six years. Achimota, Achimota College Press,
         1933. 25p.

1848   MILUM, John. Thomas Birch Freeman, missionary pioneer to
         Ashanti, Dahomey and Egba. London, S.W. Patridge,
         (1893) 160p. illus. (Popular missionary biographies).
         Account of Freeman's pioneering missionary work in
         Ashanti and other parts of West Africa.

1849   MOBLEY, Harris Witsel. "The Ghanaian's image of the
         missionary: an analysis of the published critiques of
         Christian missionaries by Ghanaians, 1897-1965". Ph.D.
         Thesis, Hartford Seminary Foundation, 1966. 350p.

1850   MOBLEY, Harris W. The Ghanaian's image of the missionary:
         an analysis of the published critiques of Christian

missionaries by Ghanaians, 1897-1965. Leiden, Brill,
1970. 180p. (Studies on Religion in Africa, vol.1).

1851   MOISTER, William. Henry Wharton: the story of his life and
missionary labours in the West Indies, on the Gold
Coast, and in Ashanti; with a brief account of Wesleyan
missions in Western Africa. London, Wesleyan Conference
Office, 1875. vi, 216p. illus.
Detailed biographical account of the man and his
missionary work.

1852   MENSAH, Annan Attah. "The Akan church lyric". International
Review of Missions, v.49, April 1960: p183-188.

1853   METHODIST CHURCH OF THE GOLD COAST. "I will build my church":
the report of the Commission appointed by the Synod of
the Methodist Church, Gold Coast, to consider the life
of the Church. St. Albans Campfield Press, 1948. 171p.

1854   METHODIST CHURCH OF THE GOLD COAST. Synod discussion of the
report of the Commission on the life of the Church.
Accra, Methodist Book Depot, 1949.

1855   NATIONAL CATHOLIC SECRETARIAT. Ghana. A modern Christian
view on culture, economic and social life, prolitical
community. Accra, The author, 1966. 33p.

1856   NEEFJES, P.G. "The impact of Christianity in Ghana with
special reference to the Roman Catholic Church".
Ghana Bulletin of Theology, v.4, No.7, December 1974:
p31-47.

1857   NEEFJES, P.G. "The Knights of Marshall as a Voluntary
        association (in Ghana)". Research Review (Institute
        of African Studies, Legon). v.7. No.3, 1971: p85-109.
        Bibliog.

1858   NIMAKO, S. Gyasi. The Christian and funerals. Cape Coast,
        Methodist Book Depot, 1954. 94p.

1859   NKETSIA, Nana Kobina. "The effect of Christian missionary
        activities on some Akan social institutions from the
        Portuguese settlement on the Mina coast, 1482-1916".
        D. Phil. Thesis, Oxford University, 1959. 652p.
        bibliog.

1860   NORDY, Juel Magnar. "The role of the Methodist Class meeting
        in the growth of an African city church; a historico-
        sociological study". Ph.D. Thesis, Boston University,
        1967. 279p.

1861   OBENG, Letitia. "The faithful use of God's gifts to the
        church". In God's missions in Ghana... Accra,
        Asempa Publishers, 1974, p40-47.
        Believes that if the Church could organise the youths,
        women fellowships, Sunday schools and Bible Study groups,
        they could be taught the responsibility of helping
        the church in the judicious use of natural resources for
        the benefit of mankind.

1862   ODAMTTEN, S.K. "The role of the missionaries in the political,
        economic and social development of Ghana, c. 1820-c 1860".
        M.A. Thesis, Birmingham University, 1964.

1863   ODAMITEN, S.K. "Nationalism and religion". Insight and opinion. v.4, No.2, 1969: p66-71.

1864   OFORI ATTA I. (Nana). Memorandum to the synod of the Presbyterian Church of the Gold Coast by the State Council of Akyem Abuakwa, 1941.

1865   OLLENU, Nii Ama. "How society looks at the Churches' Ministry of healing". Ghana Bulletin of Theology, v.3, No.2, June 1967: p17-19.

1866   OPOKU, K. Asare. "A directory of spiritual churches in Ghana". Research Review. (Institute of African Studies, Legon) v.7, No.1, 1970: p85-115.

1867   OPOKU, Kofi Asare. "Kingdom: a religious community". Research Review, (Legon) v.6, no.1, 1969: p66-69.

1868   OPOKU,K. Asare. "Letters to a spiritual father". Research Review (Legon) Institute of African Studies. v7. 1970: p15-32.

1869   OPOKU, Kofi A. "Traditional religious beliefs and spiritual churches in Ghana: a preliminary statement". Research Review. (Legon) v.4. no.2, 1968: p47-60.

1870   OPOKU, K.A. "The universal prayer group "Mpaebo kuw". (Adogyiri, Nsawam): the call of the prophet". Research Review (Legon) v.5, No.1, 1968: p101-107.
    A detailed survey of sacrifice and child naming ceremonies in the Church of the Messiah.

1871   OSAFO, Ernest A. Der beitrag der Basler Mission zur
        wirtschaflichen entwicklung Ghanas von 1828 bis zum
        weltkrieg. Hansen, 1972. 164p.

1872   OTOO, S. "The actual need for Christian healing Ministry".
        Ghana Bulletin of Theology, v.3, No.2, June 1967:
        p20-23.

1873   PARSONS, Robert Thomas. Some problems in the integration
        of christianity and African culture in Ghana, 1918-1955.
        Accra, University of Ghana, 1962.

1874   PARSONS, Robert Thomas. The churches and Ghana society,
        1918-1955; a survey of the work of three Protestant
        mission societies and the African churches which they
        established in their assistance to societary develop-
        ment. Leiden, Brill, 1963. xvi, 240p. bibliog.
        This study shows the contributions made by the Presby-
        tarian Church of Ghana, the Methodist Church, and the
        Evangelical Church to the development of the country.

1875   PATERNOT, Marcel. Lumiere sur la Volta, chez les Dagari.
        Paris, Association des Missionaires d' Afrique, 1953.
        254p.

1876   POBEE, Augustine Kofi. Christology: study of Jesus Christ:
        700 proofs. Kumasi, The Author. 1968. 30p.

1877   POBEE, J.S. "Church and state in Ghana, 1949-1966".
        Universitas, v.2, No.2, New series, December 1972:
        p18-38.
        This article is intended to be a study in the relation-

ship between the church and the state in Ghana during
the Nkrumah era.

1878   PRELUDE to Ghana; the Churches part. London, Edinburgh
        House Press, 1957: 16p.

1879   PRESBYTERIAN CHURCH OF THE GOLD COAST. The church in the
        state: the reply of the Presbyterian Church of the
        Gold Coast to a memorandum presented by the State
        Council of Akim Abuakwa, Accra, Scottish Mission Book
        Depot, 1942. 42p.

1880   PRESBYTERIAN WOMEN'S FELLOWSHIP. Ghana. A historical sketch.
        Accra. The author, 1968. 39p.

1881   PROTESTANT EPISCOPAL CHURCH. Gold Coast. The Gold Coast
        annual: or the year book of the Wesleyan Methodist
        Church in the Gold Coast District, West Africa.
        Cape Coast, for years 1912, 1913, 1915.

1882   PUGH, Evelyn. "The Antigonish movement in Ghana". African
        Ecclesiastical Review, v.5, No.1, January 1963: p61-67.
        Account of Catholic Parish Credit Union organisations
        in Northern Ghana.

1883   RATTARY, R. Sutherland. "Anthropology and Christian
        missions; their mutual bearing on the problems of
        colonial administration". Africa, v.1, No.1, January
        1928: p98-106.
        The author believes that certain Ashanti religious
        rites and beliefs and certain material objects like
        stools, birth, puberty, marriage, death rites, etc.

have an intimate bearing on Ashanti customary law,
without a knowledge of which one cannot easily understand the people.

1884   RINGWALD, Walter. Die Religion der Akannstämme und das
        Problem ihrer Bekehrung; eine religions- und missions-
        geschichtliche Untersuchung. Stuttgart: Evangelischer
        Missionsverlag, 1953.

1885   RINGWALD, Walter. Stafette in Afrika. Der Weg e. jungen
        Kirche in Ghana. 3. Aufl. Stuttgart, Evangelischer
        Missionsverl., 1970. 95p. illus. (Weltweite Reihe, 7)

1886   SACKEY, Isaac. "A brief history of the A.M.E. Zion Church,
        West Gold Coast District". Ghana Bulletin of Theology,
        v.1, No.3, 1957: p16-20.
        A description of an independent Ghanaian church founded
        in the Gold Coast in 1930 under American sponsorship.

1887   SARPONG, Peter Kwasi. "African values and catechetics -
        the matrilineal father". Teaching All Nations, v.4,
        No.1, April 1967: p162-173.

1888   SARPONG, Peter Kwasi. "Christian marriage in the Ghanaian
        millieu". Insight, v.2, no.1, February 1967. p54-57.

1889   SARPONG, Peter. Ecumenical relations in Ghana. Kampala,
        Kampala, Gaba Publications, 1974. 26p. (Pastoral
        papers, no.33).

1890   SARPONG, Peter. "The worship life of the church". In
        God's mission in Ghana... Accra, Asempa Publishers,

1974: p20-30.

The main ideas of this paper are that christian religion must have a social aspect, must identify with the people, offer the best to the people, symbols of worship must be intelligible and must provide for participation by the people, and must retain the wholesome elements of African worship.

1891   SINTIM-MISA, G.K. "Healing the sick and preaching salvation". Ghana Bulletin of Theology, v.3, No.2, June 1967: p24-26.

1892   SMITH, Edwin W. Aggrey of Africa. London, Student Christian Movement Press, 1929.

1893   SMITH, Noel J. "The Presbyterian Church of Ghana, 1835-1960: a younger Church in a changing society". Ph.D. Thesis, Edinburgh University, 1964.

1894   SMITH, Noel. The Presbyterian Church of Ghana, 1935-1960: a younger church in a changing society. Accra, Ghana Universities Press, 1966. 304p.

1895   SOUTHON, Arthur Eustace. Gold Coast methodism: the first hundred years, 1835-1935. London, Cargate Press, 1934. 158p. illus.
        Account of the growth of the Methodist Church in the Gold Coast showing the development of educational institutions in the country within the period.

1896   TAWIA, E.Y. The growth of the Ewe Presbyterian Church in Peki. The Peki centenary booklet 1847-1947. Accra. Lona Printing Works. 1947. 21p.

1897   TUFUOH, I. "Relations between Christian Missions, European
        administrations, and traders in the Gold Coast, 1828-
        74". In Baeta, C.G. ed. Christianity in tropical
        Africa, studies presented and discussed at the seventh
        International African seminar, University of Ghana
        April 1965. London, Oxford University Press, 1968: p34-
        6o.

1898   TYMS, James D. "The role of the Church in the emergence of
        modern Ghana". Journal of Human Relations, v.8. Nos.
        3 & 4, 1960. p793-809.

1899   VERSTRAELEN, F.J. "Catholic missionaries, marriage and
        family in Ghana: a socio-historical study (1800-1960),
        with special reference to the Coastal Akan". M.A.
        Thesis, University of Ghana, 1969. xi, 146p.
        A study on the confrontation and impact of Catholic
        Missionary activity on the socio-cultural life of
        Ghana.

1900   VERSTRAELEN, F.J. Christians in Ghanaian life. Accra,
        National Catholic Secretariat, 1968. 119p.

1901   WALKER, F. Deaville. Thomas Birch Freeman, the son of an
        African. Cape Coast, Wesleyan Methodist Book Depot,
        1929. 221p.
        A biographical work on Freeman's missionary work in the
        Gold Coast and other parts of West Africa.

1902   WARD, Barbara E. "Some observations on religious cults
          in Ashanti". Africa, v.26, No.1, January 1956: p47-6].

1903   WARD, W.E.F. Fraser of Trinity and Achimota. Accra, Ghana
        Universities Press, 1965. 338p.
        A biographical account of a remarkable missionary and
        founder of Achimota College, Accra, Ghana.

1904   WHITE FATHERS. Vers les grands lacs; journal de la première
        caravane des Peres blancs d' Afrique, 1878-1879.
        Namur, Editions Grands Lacs, 1954. 254p. illus.

1905   WHITE Fathers of the N.Ts' (Society of Missionaries of
        Africa". West Africa Review, March 1954: p210-213.

1906   WILKIE, A.W. "An attempt to conserve the work of the Basel
        mission to the Gold Coast". International Review of
        Missions, v.9, January 1920: p86-94.

1907   WILLIAMSON, Sydney George and DICKSON, K.A. Akan religion
        and the Christian faith: a comparative study of the
        impact of two religions. Accra, Ghana Universities
        Press, 1965. 186p.
        The purpose of this book is to recognise the existence
        of an indigenous Akan religion, and to examime the
        nature and result of the impact on it of the Christian
        faith as has occurred among the Akan peoples of Ghana.

1908   WILLIAMSON, Sydney George. Christ or Muhammad? Cape Coast,
        Methodist Book Depot (1953?) 64p.

1909   WILLIAMSON, Sydney George and BARDSLEY, John. The Gold Coast:
        what of the Church? London, Edinburgh House Press, 1953.
        24p.

1910   WILLIAMSON, Sydney George. "The lyric in Fante Methodist
        Church". Africa., v.28, No.2, April 1958: p126-133.

1911   WILLIAMSON, Sydney George. "Missions and education in the
        Gold Coast". International Review of Missions, July
        1952: p364-373.

1912   WILSON, J. Michael. Christian marriage. New edition, Accra,
        Presbyterian Book Depot, 1961.

1913   WILTGEN, Ralph M. Gold Coast mission history 1471-1880.
        Techny, Illinois, Divine World Publications, 1965.
        xvi, 181p. illus.
        A scholarly history of the early years of Catholic
        missionary activity in Ghana.

1914   WOVENU, C.K.N. The third healing ceremony of barrenness.
        Accra: Presbyterian Press, 1970. 55p.

1915   WYLLIE, Robert W. "Pastors and prophets in Winneba, Ghana:
        their social background and career development". Africa,
        v.44, No.2, April 1974: p186-193.
        A study of 27 different churches in Winneba Town. The
        study is concerned with the type of leadership, the social
        characteristics of the leaders and their career development.

1916.   WYLLIE, Robert W. "Pioneers of Ghanaian pentecostalism: Peter
        Anim and James McKeown". Journal of Religion in Africa,
        v.6, No.2, 1974: p109-122.
        Examines the careers of two independent Pentecostalists
        in Ghana, Peter Anim and James McKeown, their meeting and
        the dispute which divided them, and their independent

church building activities from 1930 onwards.

GUINEA

1917 COLL, Armengol. El missionero en el Golfo de Guinea.
       Madrid, Imprenta Iberica, 1912.

1918 CRESPO PRIETO, Teodoro. Los missioneros de Guinea Ecuatorial
       Madrid, Edicolor, 1964. 48p. illus.

1919 LE COEUR, Charles. Le culte de la generation et l' evolution
       religieuse et sociale en Guinée. Paris, Leroux, 1932.
       146p.

1920 LINTINGRE, Pierre. "La mission de Guinée aux xvlle siècle".
       Afrique Documents, v.97, 1968: p77-97.
       On the role played by French Capuchins in the introduction
       of Christianity to West Africa, starting from 1634 to
       1688.

1921 OLANGUA, Augusto. "Gen Anos de historia en Las Misiones
       expanolas en Guinea". Archivos del Instituto de Estudios,
       v13, 1959.

1922 PIACENTINI, R. "Le Pere Mell C.S. Sp., apôtre de la Guinée
       Francaise 1880-1920". Paris, Dillen, 1935.

1923 TEILHARD DE CHARDIN, J. La Guinée superieure et ses missions:
       etude de geographie sociale et religieuse des contrées
       evangelisées par les missionnaires de la Societe des
       Missions Africaines de Lyon. Tours, Cattier, 1889.
       233p.

1924   AMOS-DJORO, Ernest. "Les églises harristes et le nation-
        alisme ivoirien". (The Harris churches and nationalism
        on the Ivory Coast). Mois en Afrique, v.5, May 1966:
        p26-47.
        The Harrist and neo-Harrist movements in the Ivory
        Coast contributed to the integration of the Ivoirian
        peoples by breaking down tribal and regional barriers,
        and subsequently promoting nationalism.

1925   BIANQUIS, J. Le Prophete Harris ou dix ans d' histoire
        religieuse a la Côte d' Ivoire, (1914-1924). Paris,
        Société des Missions Evangeliques. 1924.

1926   BRUCE, Ernest. " I grew up with history". African
        Challenge, April 1957,: p6-10.
        The author's personal reminiscences after his
        encounter with the Prophet Harris.

1927   BUREAU, Rene. "Le prophete Harris et le Harrisme. (Côte
        d' Ivoire, 1900-1971)." Annales de l' Université d'
        Abidjan, Series F, v.3, 1971: p30-195.

1928   CHING, Donald S. "La vie du prophete Harris". Envol
        (Abidjan). May 1955.

1929   DEAVILLE-WALKER, F. Harris le prophete noir. Paris, Privas,
        1931.

1930   DE BILLY, Edward. En Côte d' Ivoire, mission protestante
        d' A.O.F. Paris, Société des Missions Evangeliques,
        1931. 182p. illus.
        An account by a Methodist missionary who worked among

the Harris converts in the Ivory Coast.

1931   DJORO, A. Les mouvements marginaux du protestantisme africain: les Harristes en Côte d' Ivoire. Paris, Ecole pratique des hautes etudes, section des sciences religieuses, 1956. 315p.

1932   DJORO, Ernest Amos. "Les églises harristes et le nationalisme ivoirien". Le Mois en Afrique, v.5, May 1966: p26-47.

1933   GORJU, Joseph. La Côte d' Ivoire chrétienne. 2nd ed. Lyon, Librairie Catholique Emmanuel Vitte, 1915. An account of Catholic mission work in the Ivory Coast by a Priest who spent many years in that country.

1934   GORJU, Joseph. "Un prophete de la Côte d' Ivoire". Les Missions Catholiques, June 1915: p267-268. L' Echo des Missions Africaines de Lyon, v.14, No.4, September-October 1915.

1935   HALLIBURTON, Gordon M. "The development of Harrisism". International Review of Missions, v.63, No.252, October 1974: p499-506. Takes a fresh look at the sixty year development of Harrisism as a continuing movement in the light of Turner's characteristics of syncretic religious movements.

1936   HALIBURTON, Gordon M. The prophet Harris: a study of an African prophet and his mass movement in the Ivory Coast and the Gold Coast 1913-1915. London, Longman, 1971. xix, 250p. Bibliog.

A standard treatise on prophet Harris and Harrism
in Liberia, Ivory Coast and the Gold Coast.

1937   HALIBURTON, Gordon M.   "The prophet Harris and the Grebo
        rising of 1910".   Liberian Studies Journal (Newmark,
        Delawere), v.3, No.1, 1970-71.
        A portrait of Prophet William Wade Harris, a charis-
        maticreligious leader said to have precipitated
        religious and social innovation with concomitant
        political repercussions.

1938   HALIBURTON, G.   "The Prophet Harris and his work in Ivory
        Coast and Western Ghana".   Ph.D. Thesis, School of
        Oriental and African Studies.   University of London,
        1966.   357p.

1939   HALIBURTON, G.M.   The prophet Harris and the Methodist
        Church".   Paper presented at an African History
        Seminar, School of Oriental and African Studies,
        London February 1963.   8p. (mimeograph).

1940   HARTZ, J   and   VAN BULK, G.   "Le prophete Harris vu par
        lui-même Devant les sectes non-chrétien rapports et
        compte rendu de la xxxie Semaine de Missiologie,
        Louvain 1961.

1941   HAYFORD, J.E. Casley.   William Waddy Harris; the West African
        Reformer: the man and his message. London   Phillips,
        1915.
        A descriptive and interpretative work on prophet Harris.

1942   HOLAS, Bohumil.   "Bref apercu sur les principaux cultes

290

syncretiques de la basse Côte d' Ivoire." Africa,
v.24, No.1, 1954: p55-60.

1943 HOLAS, B. "Changements modernes de la pensée religieuse
baoulé (Côte d' Ivoire)". Le Monde Non-Chrétien
(Paris) No.31, Juillet-Septembre 1954: p265-275.

1944 HOLAS, Bohumil. La Côte d' Ivoire: passé-present perspectives.
Abidjan, Centre des sciences humaines, (c. 1962). 99p.
Contains a brief account of Prophet Harris and his
movement.

1945 HOLAS, B. "Mouvements proselytique en côte d' Ivoire".
West African Institute of Sociological and Economic
Research (Ibadan). 1955.

1946 HOLAS, B. "Le proselytisme en Côte d' Ivoire". Rencontres,
No.48. 1957: p155-167. Also in La Vie Intellectuelle,
v.28, No.87, December 1956: p31-41.

1947 HOLAS, Bohumil. Le separatisme religieux en Afrique
noire; l' exemple de la Côte d' Ivoire. Paris, Presses
universitaires de France. 1965. 410p. Bibliog.
illus.
A study of the Harris movement and its successors
and the cult of Prophet Boto Adai of the Ivory Coast.

1948 LAUBIER, R. "Le Harrisme se repand en Côte d' Ivoire.
Tribune des Nations, 17 June' 1956.

1949   LINTINGRE, Pierre. <u>Voyages du sieur de Glicourt a la</u>
<u>Côte occidentale d' Afrique pendant les années</u>
<u>1778 et 1779</u>. Dakar, Afrique documents, 1966. 171p.
(Dossiers africains, no.3).

1950   MEMEL-FOTE, Harris. "Un guerisseur de la basse Côte d'
Ivoire: Josue Edjro". <u>Cahiers d Etudes Africaines</u>
v.7, No.4, 1967: p547-605. bibliog.
A study of the work of a young healer from Akradjo
Adyukru area, Ivory Coast, in 1965. The study
includes psychological, economic, social and religious
aspect of his healing.

1951   MUSSON, Margaret. <u>Prophet Harris, the amazing story of</u>
<u>Old Man Union Jack</u>. Washington, Religious Education
Press, 1950. 111p.

1952   PAULME, D. "Une religion syncretique en Côte d' Ivoire".
<u>Cahiers d' Etudes Africaines</u>, v.3, No.9, 1962: p5-90.
An account of the Lalou Church founded by Marie Lalou.
It gives a biographical sketch of the Founder, the
organisation of the church, characteristics of the
priests and the faithful, texts of prayers, doctrines
and catechism.

1953   PILKINGTON, F.W. "Old Man Union Jack: William Wade Harris.
Prophet of West Africa". <u>West African Review</u>. v.23,
No.293. February 1952: p122-125.

1954   PLATT, W.J. <u>An African prophet, the Ivory Coast movement</u>
<u>and what came of it</u>. London, Students Christian
Movement Press, 1934. 157p.

1955   PRITCHARD, John. "The prophet Harris and Ivory Coast".
        Journal of Religion in Africa. v.5, No.1, 1963:
        p23-31.

1956   ROUCH, Jean. "Aspects du Harrisme en Côte d' Ivoire".
        In Syncretisme et messianisme en Afrique Noire.
        Paris, Edition du Seuil, 1963.

1957   ROUCH, Jean. "Cantiques harristes." In Textes sacrés d'
        Afrique Noire, Paris, N.R.F. 1965: p98-107.

1958   ROUX, Andre. L' Evangile dans la forêt; naissance d' une
        église en Afrique noire. Preface d' André Chamson.
        Paris, Les Editions du Cerf. 1971. 195p. (L' Evangile
        au vingtième siècle).

1959   ROUX, A. "Un prophete: Harris". Présence Africaine
        (special number) No.8/9, 1950: p133-140.
        Account of Prophet Harris and his role in bolstering
        Protestant strength in the Ivory Coast.

1960   SCHULTZ, L. "William Wade Harris und seine Massenbewegung".
        Evangelisches Missions - Magazin, v.86, No.5, May
        1942: p83-92.

1961   SIRVEN, Pierre. "Les consequences geographiques d' un
        nouveau syncretisme religieux en Côte d' Ivoire:
        le Kokambisme". Cahiers d' Outre-mer, v.20, No.78,
        April-June, 1967: p127-136. illus.

1962   "THIRTY thousand African Christians without a pastor".
        The Foreign Field. December 1924: p59-62.

IVORY COAST

1963   THOMPSON, E.W. "The Ivory Coast: a study in modern missionary
        methods". International Review of Missions, v.17, No.68,
        October 1968: p630-644.
        Account of the Methodist take over of Prophet Harris's
        churches.

1964   WALKER, F.D. "The prophet Harris found at last". The
        Foreign Field. February 1927: p107-112.

1965   "WEST African prophet found". South African Outlook, v.57,
        No.672: May 1927: p97-98.
        Account on Prophet Harris.

1966   WOOD, Paul. "How they build churches on the Ivory Coast".
        The Foreign Field. January 1927.

LIBERIA

1967   AXELSSON, Uno. Tangena - giftdrycken: ur Madagaskars
        martyrhistoria. Stockholm, Evangeliska fosterlands-
        stiftelsen, 1955. 40p.

1968   BANE, Martin J. The Catholic story of Liberia. New York,
        McMullen, 1950. 163. illus. bibliog.

1969   BARNES, Nathan. "Liberia and the church: questions and
        answers". Unpublished manuscript, Methodist Board of
        Missions Library. New York, 1929. 124p.
        Written by a Liberian Methodist teacher at the Cape
        Palmas Seminary.

1970   BROWN, Kenneth I. "Aladura baptism". Hibbert Journal,
            v.62. No.245; January 1964: p64-67.
            Account of baptismal rite in the Church of the Lord in
            Monrovia.

1971   CASON, John Walter. "The growth of christianity in the
            Liberian environment". Ph.D. Thesis, Columbia Univer-
            sity, New York, 1962, 484p. illus.

1972   CHANGING Liberia: a challenge to the Christian. Geneva,
            for the United Christian Fellowship Conference of
            Liberia, 1958. 121p.

1973   COX, Melville B. Remains of Melville Cox, late missionary
            to Liberia, with a memoir. Boston, Light & Horton,
            1835. 240p.

1974   DONOHUGH, T.S. "The Christian mission in Liberia". Inter-
            national Review of Missions, April 1945: p136-143.

1975   DREWAL, Jemru John. "Methodist education in Liberia, 1833-
            1956"   In Vincent M. Battle and Charles H. Lyons,
            (eds). Essays in the history of African Education,
            New York, Teachers College Press, 1970: p33-40.

1976   DUNBAR, Joseph Fulton. A quarter-centennial review of
            Cuttington Collegiate and Divinity School. Lagos,
            C.M.S. Press, 1914. 24p.

1977   FISHER, Henry P. "The Catholic Church in Liberia". The
            American Catholic Historical Society, Records. v.40.
            1929: p249-310.

1978   FRAENKEL, Merran. Tribe and class in Monrovia. London,
        Oxford, University Press for International African
        Institute, 1964. xii, 244p.
        P151--95 contains an account of the increasing number
        of independent churches in Monrovia.

1979   GUILCHER, Rene- F. "L' Eglise en marche dans l' Ouest-
        Africain: en Liberia". Les Missions Catholiques, v.77.
        :p37-39. 55-58, 74-75.

1980   KING, Willis J. History of the Methodist Church Mission
        in Liberia. Monrovia, Methodist Church Mission, 1953.
        77p.
        A history of the Church in Liberia from 1822 to 1944.

1981   KONKEL, Wilbur. Jungle gold: the amazing story of Sammy
        Morris, and true stories of African life. West African
        Missions, Brent Green, London, Pillar of Fire Press,
        1966. 52p.

1982   McANDREW, Anthony P. "American Missionaries return to
        Liberia". World Mission, v.7, Winter 1956: p450-465.

1983   MARTIN, Jane. "The dual legacy: government authority and
        mission influence among the Glebo of Eastern Liberia,
        1834-1910". Ph.D. Thesis, Boston University, 1968.

1984   OFFICER, Morris. A plea for a Lutheran Mission in Liberia.
        Springfield, The Nonparell Office, 1855. 24p.

1985   PARSONS, Artley B. "Missionary studies in Liberia today".
        Spirit of Missions. v.92: p81-83; 205-209; 293-294,

LIBERIA

347-348.

1986 PAYNE, John. A full description of the African field of the
Protestant Episcopal Church, 1866. Reprinted from
Spirit of Missions, v.31,:p73-79, 149-155.

1987 PROCEEDINGS of the Christian Convention held in Monrovia,
from 12th to 18th October. Monrovia, T.W. Howard, 1876.
43p.

1988 PROTESTANT EPISCOPAL CHURCH. LIBERIA. Handbooks of the
Missions of the Episcopal Church, No. IV New York,
National Council of the Protestant Episcopal Church,
1928. 122p.

1989 PROTESTANT EPISCOPAL CHURCH. LIBERIA. Journal of the First
Annual Convention of the Diocese of the Protestant
Episcopal Church in Liberia, West Africa. Monrovia,
T.W. Howard, 1877. 8p.

1990 PROTESTANT EPISCOPAL CHURCH. LIBERIA. Letter of the Liberian
Clergy. 1864. 12p.
A protest against the attitudes of John Payne, missionary
Bishop, by leading Liberian clergymen.

1991 PROTESTANT EPISCOPAL CHURCH. Journal of the proceedings of
the clergy and Laity of the Protestant Episcopal Church
in Liberia, West Africa; at a General Council for
Organization, Monrovia, T.W. Howard, 1863. 18p.

1992 SIBLEY, James L. Education and missions in Liberia. Mimeographed survey, American Advisory Committee on Education,

297

LIBERIA

1926. 120p.

1993   WEEKS, Nan F.   and   WHITE, B.S.   Liberia for Christ.
        Richmond, Virginia: Women's Missionary Union of
        Virginia, 1959. 107p.

1994   WHETSTONE, Harold Vink. Lutheran mission in Liberia. (n.p.)
        Board of Foreign Missions of United Lutheran Church in
        America, 1955. 255p. illus.

1995   WILLIAMS, Walter B. and MAUDE, Wigfried. Adventures with
        the Krus in West Africa. New York, Vantage Press,
        1955. 146p. illus.

1996   WOLD, Joseph C. God's impatience in Liberia. Grand Rapids.
        Michigan. Eeerdmans, 1968. 227p.
        Account of religious institutions in Liberia and their
        growth.

NIGERIA

1997   ABANA, G.N. Facts about cherubim and seraphim·Aba, Ideal
        Printing Press, 1956.

1998   ABIODUN EMMANUEL, Mrs. C. Celestial vision of Her Most Rev.
        Mother Capt. Mrs. C. Abiodun Emmanuel, which originated
        Cherubim and Seraphim in 1925. Yaba, Charity Press,
        1962.

1999   "A BRIEF history of the first Baptist Church, Lagos".
        Nigerian Baptist, April 1963: p5-6. illus.

2000   ADEDEJI, J.A. "The Church and the emergence of the Nigerian theatre, 1915-1945". Journal of the Historical Society of Nigeria, v.6, No.4, June 1973: p387-396.

2001   ADEDEJI, J.A. "The Church and the emergence of the Nigerian theatre, 1866-1914". Journal of the Historical Society of Nigeria, v.6, No.4, December 1971: p25-46.

2002   ADEGBOLA, Emmanuel A.A. Working with christ for church renewal in Africa today. Paper to All Africa Conference of Churches, Abidjan, Assemby, 1969. (mimeo).

2003   ADEJOBI, E.O. Adeleele. The Bible speaks on the Church of the Lord. Lagos, 1945.

2004   ADEJOBI, Emmanuel Owoade Ade. The observances and practices of the Church of the Lord (Aladura) in the light of Old and New Testament. Lagos, The Author, 1965. 14p.

2005   ADEKAHUNSI, B.A. Church catechism and religious syllabus for the Cherubim and Seraphim Missionary School, Ondo-Oudo, Orimolade Press, 1947.

2006   ADEK BIGBE, A.A.B. The expansion of the Lagos Protectorate 1861-1900. Ph.D. Thesis, University of London, 1959.

2007   ADIGUNA, Benjamin Abimbola. "Religione e istruzione nella Federazione della Nigeria". Africa (Roma) v.16, No.4, July-August, 1961: p163-167.

2008   AFIGBO, A.E. "The Calabar Mission and the Aro expedition of 1901-1902". Journal of Religion in Africa, v.5,

No.2, 1973: p94-106.

This paper attempts to examine the validity of Dr. Ayandele's thesis that the most important events in the history of Nigeria within the period of the Aro expedition was primarily missionary initiative and indigenous reaction to missionary impact.

2009   AFRICAN CHURCH ORGANIZATION. Report of proceedings of the African Church Organization for Lagos and Yorubaland, 1901-1908. Liverpool, African Church Organization, 1910. 104p.

2010   AJAYI, William Olaseinde.
        "Aspects of Protestant Missionary work in Northern Nigeria, 1887-1910". Odu, v.3, No.1, July 1966.: p40-55.
        Account of the problems encountered by missionaries in their attempt to evangelise the people of Northern Nigeria, in the "Mohamedan zone" i.e., north of Lokoja.

2011   AJAYI, William Olaseinde. "The beginnings of the African bishopric on the Niger". Bulletin of Society for African Church History, v.1, Nos 3/4, 1964: p92-99.

2012   AJAYI, Jacob F.A. "Bishop Crowther: an assessment". Odu 1970. New Series, v.4, 1970: p3-17.

2013   AJAYI, William Olaseinde. "Christian involvement in the Ijaye war". Bulletin of the Society of African Church History, v.2, No.3, 1967: p224-238.
        Account on the role of European missionaries in the war between Ijaye, Ibadan and Oyo from 1860 to 1867.

NIGERIA

2014   AJAYI, J.F.A. "Christian Missions and the making of Nigeria".
         Ph.D. Thesis, University of London, 1958.

2015   AJAYI, Jacob F.A. Christian Missions in Nigeria. 1841-1891,
         the making of a new elite. Evanston, Illinois, North-
         western University Press, 1965. xvi. 317p. illus.
         (Ibadan history series) Bibliography.
         A pioneer work in the field. This volume contributes
         to our understanding of the socio-political evoluion
         of Nigeria and the role played by christian missions
         in the evolution of new elites.

2016   AJAYI, J. F. Ade. "The development of secondary Grammar
         School education in Nigeria". Journal of the Historical
         Society of Nigeria, v.2, No.4, 1963: p517-535.

2017   AJAYI, Jacob F. Ade. "Nineteenth century origins of Nigerian
         nationalism". Journal of the Historical Society of
         Nigeria, v.2, No.2, 1961: p196-210.
         The discussion includes references to the.influence
         of christian missions and conflicts within the churches.

2018   AJAYI, William Olaseinde. "A history of the Yoruba mission,
         1843-1880". M.A. Thesis, Bristol University, 1959.

2019   AJAYI, William Olaseinde. "The Niger Delta pastorate church,
         1892-1902". Bulletin of the Society of African Church
         History, V.2, No.1, December 1965: p37-54.

2020   AINA, J. Ade. The present-day prophets and the principles
         upon which they work, with a new introduction by H.W.
         Turner. Nsukka, Crowther College of Religion, 1964.

16p. (Mimeograph) (Materials for the study of
Nigerian Church history, no.1).

2021   AKIWOWO, Akinsola. "Christian denominations in Nigeria
today". The Nigerian Christian (Ibadan) v.3, No.5,
1969: p2-3.

2022   AKIWOWO, Akinsola A. "The place of Mojola Agbebi in the
African nationalist movements, 1890-1917". Phylon.
v.26, No.2, 1965: p122-239.

2023   AMU, J.W. Omo. The rise of Christianity in Mid-Western
Nigeria. Yaba, Pacific Printers for the author. (n.d.)
177p.

2024   ANDERSON, Susan. May Perry of Africa. Nashvi, Broadman
Press, 1966. 60p. illus.

2025   ANENE, J.C. Southern Nigeria in transition, 1885-1906.
Cambridge, Cambridge University Press, 1965. xi,
359p. illus. biblicg.
A study on the pattern of British penetration into
southern Nigeria, especially among the Ibos.

2026   AUTHORITY, S.O.A. "Aiyetoro": the happy city of the Holy
Apostles' Community. Lagos, Eruobodo Memorial Press,
n.d. (1966?). 116p. illus.

2027   AWA, E.O. "The religious situation in Nigeria today".
West African Religion, No. 13/14, 1972: p4-8.

2028   AYANDELE, Emmanuel A. "The Aladura movement among the Yoruba". The Nigerian Christian (Ibadan). v.3, No.7, 1969: p15-16.; v.3, No.9, 1969: p14.
A review article of J.D. Peel's Aladura: a religious movement among the Yoruba, 1968.

2029   AYANDELE, E.A. An assessment of James Johnson (Assistant Bishop, Niger Delta, 1900-1917). In Bishops in the Niger Delta. Aba, Diocese of the Niger Delta, 1964: p102-142.

2030   AYANDELE, E.A. "An assessment of James Johnson and his place in Nigerian history". Journal of the Historical Society, v.2, No.4, 1963: p486-516. v.3, No.1, 1964: p73-101.

2031   AYANDELE, E.A. "The colonial church question in Lagos politics, 1905-1911". Odu, v.4, No.2, January 1968: p53-73.

2032   AYANDELE, E.A. "External influence on African society". In J.C. Anene and G.N. Brown, (eds) Africa in the nineteenth and twentieth centuries. Ibadan, Ibadan University Press, 1966: p133-148.
Discusses the emergence of Ethiopianism as a nationalistic consequence of missionary activity.

2033   AYANDELE, E.A. Holy Johnson: pioneer of African nationalism, 1836-1917. London, Cass, 1970: 417p. bibliog.
A definite biographical sketch of James Johnson, a clergyman of the Church Missionary Society who served in Sierra Leone, and later became the Assistant Bishop of the Niger Delta.

2034   AYANDELE, E.A. "A legitimate branch of the Church
        universal - a review article." Orita: v.4, No.1,
        June 1970: p44-61.

2035   AYANDELE, E.A. "The missionary factor in Brass 1875-1900:
        a study in advance and recession." Bulletin of the
        Society of African Church History. v.2, No.3, 1967:
        p249-258.
        Bishop Crowther first introduced mission work among
        the people of Brass in 1868. He made such good
        progress that by 1883, there were 1199 christians in
        Brass out of a total of 2,261 converts in the whole
        Niger Mission area.

2036   AYANDELE, E.A. "Missionary enterprise versus indirect rule
        among the Angass of the Bauchi plateau, 1906-14."
        Bulletin of the Society of African Church History. v.2,
        No.1, December 1965: p73-83.

2037   AYANDELE, Emmanuel Ayankami. The missionary impact on
        Western Nigeria, 1842-1914: a political and social
        analysis. London, Longmans, 1966. xx, 393p. illus.
        (Ibadan history series). Bibliog.
        A critical study on the reaction of Nigerians to
        missionary propaganda.

2038   AYANDELE, E.A. "The Nigerian church and the reformed Ogboni
        Fraternity." Nigerian Baptist; June 1966. p19-23.

2039   AYANDELE, E.A. "The relations between the Church Missionary

304

Society and the Royal Niger Company, 1886-1900".
Journal of the Historical Society of Nigeria;
v.4, No.3, December 1968: p397-419.

2040　BATUBO, A.B. The dawn of Baptist work in Eastern Nigeria.
Port Harcourt, Goodwill Press, 1964. 52p.

2041　BENIN, Oba of. The catechism of Aruosa. Benin City, Olown
Press, 1946. 2 vols.

2042　BERRY, S.S. "Christianity and the rise of cocoa growing
in Ibadan and Ondo". Journal of the Historical
Society of Nigeria; v.4, No.3, December 1968: p439-
451.

2043　BOOTH, Allan. "The Churches in the Nigerian civil war".
Round Table, April 1970: p121-127.

2044　BROWN, Kenneth. "Worshiping with the Church of the Lord
(Aladura)". Practical Anthropology v.13, No.2,
March/April 1966: p59-84.
Assigns two reasons for the proliferation of African
independent churches to be (1) dissatisfaction with
Western leadership rather than doctrinal differences,
and (2) the hunger for African cultural expression
with the experience of worship.

2045　BUCKLEY, Anthony David. "The idea of evil in Yoruba
traditional religion and its development in three
Aladura Churches". M.A. Thesis, University of
Leicester, 1969. 140p.

2046   CALABAR. Report of missionary conference November 1911.
        Calabar, Hope Waddell Training Institution, 1913.

2047   CARROLL, Kevin. "Church art and architecture in Nigeria".
        Clergy Review, v.53, No.3, March 1968: p241-248. illus.
        With the possible exception of Ibadan university Chapel,
        and the St. Paul's church in Lagos, whose architectural
        styles have been described in detail, the author feels
        that Church buildings in Nigeria have made little
        attempt to adapt the traditional architecture of Nigeria.

2048   CAROLL, Kevin. Yoruba religious carving: Pagan and Christian
        sculpture in Nigeria and Dahomey. London, Chapman, 1967.
        172p. illus.

2049   CARROLL, Kevin. "Yoruba religious music". African Music,
        v.1, No.3, 1956: p45-47.

2050   "CHERUBIM and Seraphim". Nigeria Magazine. v.53, 1957:
        p119-134. illus.

2051   CHIRCK, Jonathan. "Reformation without conversion: the
        impact of Christianity on the Bini people of West
        Africa". The Church Quarterly Review, October-December
        1967: p466-480.

2052   "The CHRIST Apostolic Church: a summary of its history and
        structure". The Nigerian Christian. (Ibadan), v.3,
        No.5, 1969: p4-5.

2053   CHRISTIAN, Carol and PLUMMER, Gladys. God and one redhead:
        Mary Slessor of Calabar. Grand Rapids, Mich.,

Zondervan Publishing House, 1971. 190p. illus.

2054   CHRISTIAN COUNCIL OF NIGERIA. INSTITUTE OF CHURCH AND
SOCIETY. Guidelines for the participation of churches
in the third national development Plan. Ibadan,
Institute of Church and society, 1974. 40p.

2055   CHRISTIAN responsibility in an independent Nigeria. Lagos,
Christian Council of Nigeria, 1962.

2056   CLARKE, P.B. "The methods and ideology of the Holy Ghost
Fathers in Eastern Nigeria, 1885-1905". Journal of
Religion in Africa, v.6, No.2, 1974: p81-108.
A study of the method of evangelization employed by
the Holy Ghost Roman Catholic Missionary Society in
the last quarter of the nineteenth century in their
mission station in Eastern Nigeria.

2057   COKER, S.A. The rights of Africans to organise and
establish indigenous churches unattached to and
uncontrolled by foreign church organizations. Lagos,
Tikatore Press, 1917. 48p.

2058   COLE, A.N. A century of Wesleyan Methodist Missions 1813-
1914. Lagos, 1915.

2059   COLEMAN, James Scott. Nigeria: background to nationalism.
Los Angeles, University of California Press, 1964.
xix, 510p. illus. bibliog.
P91-112 is an account of the role of European
Missionaries in the field of education and their
critical role in the rise of nationalism in Nigeria.

2060   COMHAIRE, Jean. "La vie religieuse à Lagos". Zaire,
        v.3, No.5, May 1949: p459-556.

2061   CROWTHER, Samuel Ajayi. African bishop and linguist,
        a second narrative of his life. Nsukka, Department
        of Religion, University of Nigeria, 6p. (mimeograph).

2062   CROWTHER, Samuel Adjai. Bishop Crowther: his life and
        work. London, Church missionary house, 1892. 55p.

2063   CROWTHER, Samuel and TAYLOR, John C. The Gospel on the
        banks of the Niger: journals and notices of the
        native massionaries accompanying the Niger expedition
        of 1857-1959. Reprint. London, Dawsons, 1968. xi,
        451p. map (Colonial history series) (First published
        in 1859).

2064   CROWTHER, Samuel Ajayi. "A second narrative of Samuel
        Ajayi Crowther's early life". Bulletin of the Society
        of African Church History, v.2, No.1, December 1965:
        p5-14.

2065   DAFFY, P.P. "Christian attitude to peace". Orita:
        v.6, No.1, June 1972: p15-26.

2066   DALLIMORE, H. "The Aladura movement in Ekiti". Western
        Equatorial Africa Church Magazine. v.36, No.443, May
        1931: p93-97.

2067   DELANO, Isaac O. One church for Nigeria. London, Lutterworth,
        1945. 48p.

2068   DIKE, K.O. Trade and politics in the Niger Delta, 1830-1885. Oxford, Clarendon Press, 1965. vl, 250p. illus. bibliog. (Oxford studies in African Affairs).
A classic study of British trade and the overtrhow of indigenous authority. Provides a framework for the understanding of missionary penetration in Igboland during the first half of the nineteenth century.

2069   DILWORTH, Joan. "Tale of two cities". Bodija Bulletin, v.15, 1973: p1-52.
A social survey of Iwere-Ile and Inisha in Western Nigeria carried out by the Ojo Catholic Diocese.

2070   DUCKWROTH, E.H. "A visit to the apostles and the town of Aiyetoro". Nigeria Magazine, v.36, 1951: p386-440. illus.
Aiyetoro ('The world is at peace) is a prosperous fishing community of over 2000 inhabitants in Nigeria. It was established by the Holy Apostoles sect, a group of the Ilaje from Benin.

2071   DUROJAIYE, J. A sixteen points message of the Lord to individuals, organizations, and societies. Ibadan O.B. & P, 1964.

2072   "EARLY Baptist Christians in the Niger Delta: Research notes". Orita, v.1, No.1, June 1967: p77-79.

2073   "ECUMENICAL Chronicle: church union in Nigeria". Eccumenical Review, v.17, No.3, July 1965: p257-264.

NIGERIA

2074   \EDO NATIONAL CHURCH OF GOD. The book of the Holy Aruosa,
            according to the ancient Binis. Benin City, Edo
            National Church of God, 1946. 2 vols.

2075   EGAH, James M. Holy message to fellow Christians in this
            dear land. Ibadan, Odudufa Printing works, 1960. 52p.

2076   EKECHI, Felix K. "Colonialism and Christianity in West
            Africa: the Igbo case, 1900-1915". Journal of African
            History, v.12. No.1, 1971: p103-115.

2077   EKECHI, Felix K. "The Holy Ghost fathers in Eastern Nigeria,
            1885-1920: observations on missionary strategy".
            African Studies Review, v.15, No.2, 1972: p217-239.
            Examines the nature of Roman Catholic missionary
            activity in Eastern Nigeria, with a brief sketch on the
            religious climate of the area prior to the advent of
            the Holy Ghost Fathers.

2078   EKECHI, Felix K. Missionary enterprise and rivalry in
            Igboland 1857-1914. London, Cass. 1972: xv, 298p. illus.
            bibliog. (Cass library of African studies: General
            Studies, no. 119).

2079   EKIT, Richmael, ed. Do you know the spirit movement of 1927
            in Ibibio land? Edem Urua Ibiono (Itu, E. Nigeria).
            The author, n.d. 1964. 54p.

2080   ENOCK, Esther Ethelind. A missionary heroine of Calabar: a
            story of Mary Slessor. London, Pickering & Inglis,
            1973. 96p. illus. (Reprint of the 1938 edition).

310

NIGERIA

2081 EPELLE, E.M. Tobiah. "Alphonso Chukwuma Onyeabo (Assistant
      Bishop, Niger Diocese, 1937-1949)" in Bishops in Niger
      Delta, Aba, Diocese of the Niger Delta 1964; p169-186.

2082 EPELLE, E.M. Tobiah. "Adolphus Williamson Howells (Assistant
      Bishop, Niger Delta). Niger Diocese, 1920-1933". In
      Bishops in the Niger Delta. Aba, Niger Delta Diocese
      1964: p143-160.

2083 EPELLE, E.M. Tobia. Bishops in the Niger Delta. Aba:
      Diocese of the Niger Delta, 1964. 196p.
      Biographical works of bishops S.A. Crowther, Herbert
      Tugwell, James Johnson, A.W. Howells, T.C. John and
      A.C. Onyeabo, including the constitutional history of
      the Delta church.

2084 EPELLE, E.M.T. "Chieftaincy titles in Igbo land and church
      membership" West African Journal of Religion, v.5,
      February 1966: p3-6.

2085 EPELLE, E.M.T. The Church in Opobo. Opobo, St. Paul's
      Church Parochial Committee, 1958. 69p.

2086 EPELLE, E.M.T. The Church in the Niger Delta: Aba, Niger
      Delta Diocese, 1955. 128p.
      Describes the evolution and growth of Christianity at
      Bonny, with special reference to the activities of the
      Niger Delta Pastorate Church.

2087 EPELLE, E.M. Tobiah. "Herbert Tugwell (Bishop of Western
      Equatorial Africa, 1894-1921)". In Bishops in the
      Niger Delta. Aba Diocese of the Niger Delta, 1964:

p68-101.

2088   EPELLE, E.M.T.   "The Sects".   West African Religion, No.
        13 & 14.   1972: p42-51.

2089   EPELLE, E.M. Tobiah.   "Thomas Charles John (Assistant
        Bishop, Niger Diocese, 1933-1936)". in Bishops in
        the Niger Delta, Aba, Discese of the Niger Delta,
        1964: p161-168.

2090   EPELLE, E.M.T.   Writing a local church history: a short
        guide.   Nsukka, Dept. of Religion, University of
        Nigeria, 1965.   10p. (mimeographed).

2091   EPPERSON, Barbara.   Out of Shang's shadow: a biography of
        James Tanimola Ayorinde.   Nashville, Convention
        Press, 1967.   83p.   (Foreign mission graded series).

2092   ERIVWO, S.U.   "The Holy Ghost devotees and Demonday's
        ministry; an evaluation".   West African Religion,
        v.15, March 1974: p19-31.

2093   ETERNAL SACRED ORDER OF CHERUBIM AND SERAPHIM.
        Explanatory notes to the "order" pamphlet, edited
        by G.I.M. Otubu.   Oshunkeye Press, 1958.

2094   EZEANYA. Stephen Nweke.   "Christian and pagan morality;
        with special reference to the Igbo of Southern
        Nigeria".   African Ecclesiastical Review v.5, No.4,
        October 1963: p318-319.

2095   EZEANYA, Stephen Nweke. "The method of adaptation in the evangelization of the Igbo-speaking people of Southern Nigeria". Rome. 1956: xx, 278p. map. D.D. Thesis, Pontifical Urban University, Rome.

2096   EZEANYA, Stephen Nweke. "A view of Christian and pagan morality". West African Religion. v.2, January 1964: p4-5.
A discussion on Ibo conception of morality, based on a study of their proverbs.

2097   FADUMA, Orieshetukeh. "Religious beliefs of the Yoruba people in West Africa". In Bowen, J.W.E. (ed). Addresses and proceedings of the Congress on Africa, Atlanta, Gammon Theological Seminary, 1896.

2098   FAJANA, A. "Missionary educational policy in Nigeria. 1842-1882". West African Journal of Education, v.14, No.2, June 1970: p100-109.

2099   FALUSI, G.K. "The Christian view of freedom". Orita, v.7, No.2, December 1973: p113-126.

2100   FERGUSON, John. "Christian byways: deviations from the Christian faith". Ibadan, Daystar Press, 1968. 60p.

2101   FLORIN, Hans W. The Southern Baptist foreign mission enterprise in Western Nigeria: an analysis. Ph.D. Thesis, Boston University, 1960.

2102   GALLOWAY, A.D. "Missionary impact on Nigeria". Nigeria Magazine, 1960: p58-65.

2103   GARRETT, Thomas Samuel. "Conservative and Unionist: background to uniting churches in Nigeria". Theology,
v.68, No.543, 1965: p417-427.

2104   GEORGE, C.T.T. "Baptist work in the Niger Delta - from
the beginning to 1950." B.A. Extended essay, University of Ibadan, 1968.

2105   GOLDIE, H. Calabar and its mission. London, 1901.

2106   GRAHAM, Sonia F. Government and mission education in
Northern Nigeria 1900-1919 with special reference
to the work of Hans Vischer. Ibadan, Ibadan
University Press, 1966. 192p.
An authoritative account of the early days of western
education in Northern Nigeria which throws an intere-
sting light on mission and government policy.

2107   GRESCHAT, Hans-Jurgen. "The National Church of Nigeria:
Beispiel des religiosen Nationalismas". Evangelische
Missionszeitscrift. v.25, No.2, 1968: p86-97.

2108   GRIMLEY, John B. and ROBINSON, Gordon E. Church growth
in Central and Southern Nigeria. Grand Rapids, Mich.
Eerdmans, 1966. 386p. illus. (Church growth series).
An optimistic and forward-looking study by Protestant
missionaries.

2109   GWAM, Lloyd Chike. "The educational work of a Christian
missions in the settlement of Lagos, 1842-1882".
Ibadan, v.12, June 1961: p18-21..

NIGERIA

Describes the activities of the Church missionary
Society, the Wesleyan Missionary Society, the Roman
Catholic Mission, and the American Baptist Mission in
Lagos during the period.

2110   GWAM, Lloyd C. "Pioneers of modern professions; no.3,
       Letters. Mujola Agbebi." Sunday Times (Lagos).
       1 November, 1964.

2111   GWAM, Lloyd C. "Pioneers of modern professions: no.7 -
       Divinity. Bishop Isaac Oluwole." Sunday Times, 6
       December 1964: p10-11.

2112   HAIR, Paul Edward Hedley. "Archdeacon Crowther and the Delta
       Pastorate 1892-1899." Sierra Leone Bulletin of Religion,
       v.5, No.1, 1963: p18-27.

2113   HAIR, Paul E.H. (ed). "The first Christian in the village:
       a case-history from Eastern Nigeria." Bulletin of the
       Society for African Church History. v.1, No.2, December
       1963: p49-61.

2114   HERSKOVITS, Jean F. Liberated Africans and the history of
       Lagos colony to 1886. D. Phil. Thesis, Oxford University,
       1960.

2115   HISTORY of Holy Trinity Anglican Church, Calabar."
       Hope Waddell Press, 1961. 16p.

2116   "The HOLY Arousa Church: research notes." Orita, v.4, No.2,
       December 1970: p149-154.

2117   HORTON, Robin. "African conversion". (Review article
        on J.D.Y. Peel's Aladura). Africa. v.41, No.2,
        April 1971: p85-108.

2118   HORTON, Robin. A hundred years of change in Kalabari
        religion. Paper prepared for the Conference on the
        High God in Africa, University of Ife, Nigeria, 1964.

2119   HOWELL, E. Milford. Nigerian Baptist leaders and their
        contribution. Th.D. Thesis, Southwestern Baptist
        Seminary, 1956.

2120   IDOWU, E. Bolaji. "Christ and African culture". Orita,
        v.2, No.1, June 1968: p45-47.
        A review article of John V. Taylor's The primal vision:
        Christian presence amid African religion. London, 1965.

2121   IDOWU, E. Bolaji. "The predicament of the church in Africa".
        In Baeta, C.G. ed. Christianity in tropical Africa,
        studies presented and discussed at the seventh inter-
        national African Seminar, University of Ghana, 1965.
        London, Oxford University Press, 1968: p.417-441.

2122   IDOWU, E. Bolaji. "Religion in Ibadan. A: Traditional
        religion and Christianity". in P.C. Lloyd(et al)
        (eds.) The city of Ibadan. Cambridge, Cambridge
        University Press, 1967: p235-247.

2123   IDOWU, E. Bolaji. "Religions on peace". Orita, v.5, No.2,
        December 1951: p83-92.

NIGERIA

An introductory lecture in a series of lectures
delivered during the Religious studies conference
which took place on 30 March - Friday 2, April 1971,
at the University of Ibadan.

2124   IDOWU, E. Bolaji. Towards an indigenous church. London,
       Oxford University Press, 1965. 60p. (Student's
       library, 3).
       Positive evaluation of the role of independent churches
       in Nigeria in the process of indeginisation of
       christianity.

2125   IDOWU, E. Bolaji. "Traditional relgion and Christianity".
       In Lloyd, P.C. (and others). The city of Ibadan,
       London, Oxford University Press, 1967: p235-247.

2126   IFEKA-MOLLER, C. "White power: socio-structural factors
       in conversion to Christianity, eastern Nigeria, 1921-
       1966". Canadian Journal of African studies, v.8, No.1,
       1974: p55-72.

2127   IFEMESIA, C.C. "The 'civilizing' mission of 1841: aspects
       of an episode in Anglo-Nigerian relations". Journal
       of the Historical Society of Nigeria, v.2, 1962:
       p291-310.

2128   IGE, Oye. "Joseph Babalota - a twentieth century prophet".
       The African Historian, v.1, No.3, March 1965: p38-42.
       Biographical account of Aladura prophet.

2129   IGWE, George Egemba. "Thomas Birch Freeman: pioneer
       Methodist missionary to Nigeria". Nigeria Magazine,

v.77, 1963: p78-89.
Biography of a Methodist missionary who is best known
for this work at Badagry, where he set up a mission
station in 1842 in response to appeals made by freed
slaves returning to Yorubaland.

2130   IKECHIUKU, Joseph. The immutable rules and conducts of St.
       Joseph's chosen Church of God selected through the
       revelation of God. Sapele, The Author, (n.d.) 55p. illus.

2131   IKIME, Obaro. "The coming of C.M.S. into Itsekiri, Urhobo
       and Isoko country." Nigeria Magazine, v.86, September
       1965: p206-215.

2132   ILOGU, Edmund. "Christianity and Ibo traditional religion."
       Nigeria Magazine, v.83, December 1964: p304-308. Also
       in International Review of Missions, v.54, 1965: p335-
       342.
       Questions the validity of teaching Christianity to non-
       Christian people by relating Christian facts to familiar
       elements in traditional Ibo religion.

2133   ILOGU, Edmund. "The contribution of the Church to national
       unity in Nigeria." International Review of Missions,
       v.53, No.211, 1964: p272-280. Also in Ghana Bulletin
       of Theology, v.2, 1962: p28-38.

2134   ILLOGU, Edmund. "Independent African churches in Nigeria."
       International Review of Missions, v.63, No.252, October
       1974: p492-498.

A short paper on the independent churches in Nigeria,
written from the perspective of an ordained minister
of one of the older orthodox churches established
by Western missions in Nigeria.

2135   ILOGU, Edmund. "Nationalism and the church in Nigeria".
        International Review of Missions, v.51, No.204, 1962:
        p439-450.

2136   ILOGU, Edmund. "The problem of indigenization in Nigeria".
        International Review of Missions, v.49, No.194,
        April 1960: p167-182.

2137   ILLOGU, Edmund C. "Religion and culture in West Africa".
        Theology Today, v.20, 1963: p53-60.

2138   INYANG, P.E.M. "The provision of education in Nigeria
        with reference to the work of the Church Missionary
        society, Catholic Mission and the Methodist Mission-
        ary Society". M.A. Thesis, University of London,
        1958.

2139   IRVING, Dr. "The Yoruba mission". Church Missionary
        Intelligence, v.4, 1853: p123-137. p185-190:
        p227-237.

2140   "IS spiritual healing a way of making money". Africa
        (Lagos) No.12, February 1962: p19-22.

2141   ISICHEI, Elizabeth. "Ibo and Christian beliefs: some
        aspects of a theological encounter". African Affairs,
        v.68, No.271. April 1969: p121-134. bibliog.

A survey of Ibo religion based on accounts,
published and archival, of observers over the past
century, and on information from individual Ibo.

2142   ISICHEI, Elizabeth. The Ibo people and the Europeans:
the genesis of a relationship - to 1906. London,
Faber & Faber, 1973. 207p. bibliog.
Chapter II of this book is an account of the impact
of missionary presence in Ibo land from 1885-1906.

2143   ISICHEI, Elizabeth. "Seven varieties of ambiguity: some
patterns of Ibo response to Christian Missions".
Journal of Religion in Africa, v.3, No.3, 1970.

2144   IWUAGWU, A.O. "The spiritual churches in the Eastern
States of Nigeria". Ph.D. Thesis, Ibadan University,
1971.

2145   JOHNSON, T.B.A. Clergy directory of the diocese of Lagos.
Lagos & Yaba, Ife-Olu Printing works, 1951. 170p.
illus.

2146   JOHNSTON, Geoffrey. "A project in local church histories".
West African Religion, v.4, July 1965: p8-13.

2147   JOHNSTON, G.D. "Ohafia 1911-40: a study in church developments in Eastern Nigeria". Bulletin of the Society
for African Church History, v.2, No.2, 1966: p139-154.

2148   JORDAN, John B. Bishop Shanahan of Southern Nigeria.
Dublin, Clonmore and Reynolds, 1949. xiv, 264p.
A graphic description of the missionary work of a

Roman Catholic bishop in Igbo and Calabar areas.

2149   JORDAN, John P. "Catholic education and Catholicism in Nigeria". African Ecclessiastical Review, v.2, No.1, January 1960: p60-62.

2150   JORGENSEN, Alfred. Skitser fra Nigeria; smaglimt og op oplevetser. Illustreret af forfatteren. Aarhus, Dansk foreset Sudanmission, 1964. 33p.

2151   JUWE, Sylve Mubundu. Why is the National Church of Nigeria and the Cameroons and the God of Africa. Port Harcourt, Goodwill Press, 1951. 41p.

2152   KALE, S.I. and HOGAN, N. Christian responsibility in independent Nigeria. Lagos, Christian council of Nigeria, 1961.

2153   KIRK-GREENE, Anthony. "Hamilton Millard..... an abiding memorial". Nigeria Magazine, v.75, December 1962: p33-46.
Biography of an early missionary to Zaria and Wusasa.

2154   KNIGHT, C.W. A study of the expansion of Evangelical Christianity in Nigeria. Th.D. Thesis, Southern Baptist Seminary, Louisville, 1959.

2155   LASBREY, B. "Problems of a church in Tropical Africa. (The Niger Diocese, Nigeria)". East and West Review, October, 1938: p312-319.

2156   LAWRENCE, A.B. A divine message entrusted to A.B.L. on Olorunkole Hill, Ibadan, on 20th February, 1932. Tikatore Press, Lagos, 1932.

2157   LAWRENCE, A.B. Observations and prophecies through the inspiration of the Holy Spirit for 1930. Lagos, Ife Olu Press, 1929.

2158   LIVINGSTONE, William P. Dr. Hitchcock of Uburu: an episode in medical missionary service in Nigeria. Edinburgh, Foreign Missionary Committee of the United free church of Scotland. 1920. 88p.

2159   LIVINGSTONE, W.P. Mary Slessor of Calabar: pioneer missionary. London, Hodder & Stoughton, n.d. A biographical sketch of an early Presbyterian Missionary to Calabar.

2160   LOCKE, A.H. "A new day in Northern Nigeria". Moslem World, January 1938: p54-60.

2161   LUCAS, J. Olumide. Lecture on the history of St. Paul's Church, Breadfruit, Lagos, 1852-1945. Lagos, St. Paul's Church, 1946? 72p. illus.

2162   MACAULAY, Herbert. The history of the development of missionary work with special reference to the United African Church. Lagos, Adedimeta Printing Works, 1942. 37p.

2163   McFARLAN, Donald M. Calabar, the Church of Scotland Mission, founded 1846. 2nd ed. Nelson.

The official centennial history of the Scotland
Mission in Calabar.

2164   MAcKAY, Ven J. Crowther: slave and Bishop. London,
C.M.S. Press, 1949. 32p.

2165   MAcKAY, Ven J. The life of Bishop Crowther, first
African Bishop of the Niger. London, Sheldon Press,
1931. 48p.

2166   McKENNA, J.C. "Church and state in contemporary Nigerian
educational legislation". World Yearbook of Education.
1966: p378-380.

2167   MAcKENZIE, R.P. "The expansion of Christianity in Nigeria -
some recurring factors". Orita: v.3, No.1, June
1969: p53-67.
A discussion on the factors which helped in the expansion
of christianity in Nigeria from 1485 to 1960.

2168   McKENZIE,R.P. "Samuel Crowther's attitude to other faiths
during the early period". Orita, v.5, No.1, June
1971: p3-17.

2169   MAcRAE, N.C. The Presbyterian Church in Eastern Nigeria
and the Cameroons. Calabar, Hope Waddell Press,
1957. 14p.

2170   MARAIS, B.J. "Northern Nigeria as a Mission field". The
Moslem World, 1937: p173-185.

2171   MARGETTS, E.L. "Traditional Yoruba healers in Nigeria".
        Man, v.65, No.182, 1965.

2172   MARIOGHAE, Michael and FERGUSON, John. Nigeria under the
        cross. London, Highway Press, 1965. 126p.

2173   MAXWELL, John Lowry. Nigeria; the land, the people and
        christian progress. London, World Dominion Press,
        1927. 164p.
        A useful book for statistical information on missions
        in Nigeria.

2174   MBACHU, Clement Arise Ekemeke. Enugwu - Ukwu in Church
        history. Enugu, The Author, 1965. 31p.

2175   MEDAIYESE, J.A. Biography of the Late Great Apostle and
        Prophet, J.A. Babalola. Okere, Alafia Tayo Press,
        (n.d.).

2176   MERRITT, Mrs. Dewey. And some believed... Ede, Nigeria,
        Women's Missionary Union, 1968. 26p.

2177   MESSENGER, John C. "The Christian concept of forgiveness
        and Anang morality". Practical Anthropology v.6, No.3,
        May - June 1959: p97-103.
        This paper discusses the common causal factors that
        give way to immorality among the Anang people of
        Nigeria, with emphasis on their acceptance of the
        Christian doctrine of a forgiving deity as being
        chiefly responsible for many infractions among the
        youth.

2178   MESSENGER, John C. "Religious acculturation among the
        Ibibio." In W.R. Bascom and M.J. Herskovits, (eds)
        Continuity and change in African cultures. Chicago,
        University of Chicago Press, 1959: p279-299.

2179   MESSENGER, John C. "Reinterpretations of Christian and
        indigenous belief in a Nigerian nativist church."
        American Anthropology v.62, No.2, April 1960: p268-278.
        Describes the reactions of the Annang people of Nigeria
        to Christian religion and the development and spread
        of indigenous christian churches which blend tradi-
        tional beliefs with reinterpreted Orthodox Christian
        doctrines.

2180   MESSENGER, John C. "Reinterpretations of Christian and
        indigenous belief in a Nigerian Nativist Church."
        In Black Africa; its peoples and their cultures today,
        edited by John Middleton. London, Macmillan, 1970:
        p212-221.

2181   MILSOME, J.R. Samuel Adjai Crowther. Ibadan; Oxford
        University Press, 1968. 60p. (Makers of Nigeria series).

2182   The MISSIONARY presence, 1885-1906. (in Ibadan). In
        Elizabeth Isichei, The Ibo people and the Europeans:
        the genesis of a relationship - to 1906. London,
        Faber & Faber, 1973: p144-156.
        Examines the pattern by which colonial rule was
        established in Iboland and the part played by

missionary influence in this expansion.

2183   MITCHELL, Robert Cameron. The Aladura Churches in Ibadan.
        Paper read to the sociology seminar, University of
        Ibadan, 1962. 11p. (mimeograph).

2184   MITCHELL, Robert C. "Religious protest and social change:
        the origins of the Aladura movement in Western Nigeria".
        In Protest and power in Black Africa, edited by R.
        Rotberg and A. Mazun. New York, Oxford University
        Press, 1970: p458-496.

2185   MITCHELL, Robert Cameron. Sickness and healing in the
        separatist churches (special seminar, the traditional
        background to medical practice in Nigeria, paper 8).
        Ibadan, University of Ibadan, Institute of African
        Studies, 1966. 15p. (mimeo).

2186   MOLLER, Caroline (Mrs. S. Ifeka). "An Aladura Church in
        Eastern Nigeria". Ph.D. Thesis, University of London,
        1968.
        Deals with Cherubim and Seraphim, Eternal Order of the
        Cherubim and Seraphim and Mount Zion Church in Onitsha.

2187   MOLLER, Caroline (Mrs. S. Ifeka). "Some aspects of belief
        in the Eternal Sacred Order of Cherubim and Seraphim
        (Onitsha Branch)". Uyo, E. Nigeria, Uyo Inter-Church
        Study Group, 1966. 4p. (mimeo).

2188   MORELL, E.D. Nigeria: its peoples and its problems. 3rd. ed.
        with a new introduction by K.D. Nworah. London, Cass,
        1968. 264p. illus.

Part IV of this book gives an account of Christianity and Islam in Southern Nigeria.

2189   MOUREN, Joseph. "Cost and conquest: foundation and first years of the Catholic Missions in Northern Nigeria 1906-1910. Extracts from the account of Fr. Joseph Mouren, S.M.A", The African Missionary, v.1, 1964: p12-15.

2190   MURRAY, A.V. "A missionary educational policy for soutthern Nigeria". International Review of Missions, v.21, October 1932, p566-574.

2191   NATIONAL CHURCH OF NIGERIA AND THE CAMEROONS. Hymn and prayers for use in the Church.... Aba, The Church, 1948. 54p.

2192   NEWTON, Kenneth and Anna. "Aiyetoro, community of co-operators". Africa Today (New York) v.11, No.4, 1964: p4-6.

2193   NIGER DELTA CHURCH BOARD (Anglican).. Reports or minutes of proceedings of the..... Church Board. Lagos, C.M.S. for the Board. 1916.

2195   NIGERIA the unknown; a missionary study textbook on Nigeria. London Church Missionary Society, 1918. 56p.

2196   NWOSU, V. ed. Prayer houses and faith healing. Onitsha, Tabansi Press, 1971.

2197   OBATERU, O.I. and FORD, B.N. "The Holy City of Aiyetoro:
        a geographic appraisal". Bulletin of Ghana Geographical
        Association, v.12, 1967: p65-79.
        Aiyetoro was founded by the Holy Apostoles' in the
        creek area of Western Nigeria as a refuge from
        religious persecution.

2198   O'BRIEN, Brian. She had a magic: the story of Mary Slessor.
        (London) Cape. 1958.
        Mary Slessor was famous for her missionary work
        amongst the women of Eastern Nigeria.

2199   O'CONNELL, James. "Catholic action and the Nigerian inte-
        llectuals". African Ecclessiastical Review, v.4,
        No.2, April 1962: p85-95.

2200   O'CONNELL, James. "Government and politics in the Yoruba
        African Churches: the claims of tradition and modernity".
        Odu, v.2, No.1, July 1965: p92-108.

2201   ODIONG, Udo. "Abasi Ibom: the supreme God in Ibibio land".
        West African Religion Nos 13/14, 1972: p59-61.

2202   ODUNAIKE, S.F. The path of a master Christian. Leeds,
        Apostolic Publications, 1945.

2203   ODUYOYE, Modupe. The planting of Christianity in Yorubaland,
        1842-1888. Ibadan, Daystar Press, 1969. 77p. illus.

2204   OJI, B.A. Originality of religion revealed. Aba, Research
        Institute of African Mission Press, 1960: 58p.

2205   OJIAKO, Johnson. "The challenge of the religious situation to parish life: analytical survey of some of the challenges". West African Religion, No.13/14, 1972: p39-50.

2206   OKAFOR-OMALI, S.D. and HAIR, P.E.W. "The first Christian in the village: a case-history from Eastern Nigeria". Bulletin of the Society for African Church History. v.1, No.2, 1963: p49-65.

2207   OKE, E.A. A short history of Christ Army Church, G.B.C and the life of Prophet Garrick Sokari Braide alias, 'Elijah' of Bakana, Eastern Nigeria. Aba, (N.p. n.d.). 15p. (mimeograph).

2208   OKE, G.A. A short history of the United Native African Church, 1891-1903. Lagos, Shalom Press, 1918.

2209   OKE, S. Adeniran. The Ethiopian National Church: a necessity. Ibadan, Lisabi Press, 1923. 32p.

2210   OKPALAOKA, C.I. ed. "A report on the Holy City of Aiyetoro". Nsukka, Sociological Association, University of Nigeria, 1962. 23p. (mimeograph).

2211   OLADUNJOYE, D.A. A short history for the Church Army of Africa. Ibadan, Privately printed, (n.d.) 5p.

2212   OLAGOKE, Olatunji. Index for history of Yoruba mission C.M.S. 1844-1914 in the National Archives at the University of Ibadan, Western Nigeria. Ibadan, Privately printed, 1965. 26p.

2213   OLAGUNJU, Bili. "The prophets of Nigeria". <u>Flamingo</u>, v.5, No.3, December 1965: p32-35.

2214   OLOWOKURE, Jacob O.K. "Christianity in Ijeshaland, 1858-1960". M.A. Thesis, University of Ibadan, 1970. 324p.

2215   OLATUNJI, Olatunde. "Religion in literature: the Christianity of J.S. Sowande (Sobo Arobiodu)". <u>Orita,</u> v.8, No.1, June 1974: p3-21.
A discussion of the religious element in the poetry of J.S. Sowande, the pioneer of written Yoruba poetry. Gives a biographical sketch of the man, followed by long passages from his poetical works, with commentary.

2216   OLUSHOLA, J.A. "The Church's loss of power". <u>African Challenge</u>, v.10, No.4, April 1960: p.5.

2217   OMO-AMU, J.W. <u>The rise of Christianity in mid-Western Nigeria</u>. Lagos, 1965.

2218   OMONIYI, Prince Bandele. <u>A defence of the Ethiopian movement</u>. Edinburgh, 1908. 124p.

2219   OMOTAYO, J. "Aladura Churches were founded by God's authority". <u>The Nigerian Christian</u> (Ibadan) v.3, No.5, 1969. p8.

2220   OMOTOYE, J.O. "The influence of Christianity in Ife District of Western Nigeria on the life of the people". (M.A. Dissertation) presented to the University of Durham, 1964.

2221   OMOYAJOWO, J.A. "The Christian view of man". Orita:
        v.6, No.2, December 1972: p119-129.

2222   OMOYAJOWA, J. Akin. "The Cherubim and Seraphim movement:
        a study in interaction". Orita: v.4, No.2,
        December 1970: p124-139.
        The Cherubim and seraphim movement is an Aladura type
        of independent church movement in Western Nigeria.

2223   ONOGE, Omafume Friday. "Aiyetoro; the successful utopia:
        a sociological study of Apostoles' community in
        Nigeria". Ph.D. Thesis, Harvard University, 1970.

2224   ONYIOHA, K.O.K. The National Church of Nigeria: its
        catechism and credo. Ebute Metta, Lagos, the
        author, 1951. 52p.

2225   OROGUN, J.B. The order of service of Christ Apostolic
        Church, Nigeria and Ghana. Akure, Nigeria: the
        author. P.O. Box 45, 1966. 70p.

2226   OSHIETELU, Josiah Olunowo. Catechism of the Church of
        the Lord..... and the holy litany... with the
        church prayer drill. Ogere, the author, 1948. 22p.

2227   OTONG, Daniel U. The development of Christ Faith Prayer
        Fellowship Ministry in Nigeria: an appeal for help.
        Port Harcourt, Goodwill Press, 1965. 10p.

2228   OTUBELU, Gideon Nweka and Nwako, J.A. St. Mary's
        Church Ukpo 1914-1964: a brief history of the
        origin and the growth of the Church. Onitsha.

Varsity Press, 1965. 16p.

2229   PADEN, John Naber. Religion and political culture in
Kano. Berkley, University of California Press, 1973.
xvii, 461p. bibliog.

2230   PAGE, Jesse. The Black Bishop: Samuel Adjai Crowther.
London, Simpkin, Marshall, Hamilton, Kent & Co.,
1910.

2231   PAGE, Jesse. Samuel Crowther: the slave boy who became
Bishop of the Niger. London, Partridge, 1892.

2232   PAGE, Jesse. Samuel Crowther: Bishop of the Niger. London,
S.W. Partridge & Co., (n.d.).
Biography of a famous Yoruba missionary.

2233   PARNIS, R.O. "A visit to Aiyetoro". Nigerian Field, v.30,
No.1, January 1965: p.37-40.

2234   PARRAT, John K. "Religious change in Yoruba society - a
test case". Journal of Religion in Africa.
A case study based on the city of Ile-Ife to find
out the impact of missionary education on traditional
religions.

2235   PARRAT, John K. and DOI, Ahmad R.I. "Some further
aspects of Yoruba syncretism". Practical Anthropology,
v.16, No.6, 1969: p252-256.

2236   PARRAT, John K. and DOI, A.R.I. "Syncretism in
        Yorubaland: a religious or sociological phenomenon?"
        Practical Anthropology, v.16, No.3, May-June 1969:
        p109-113.

2237   PARRINDER, E. Geoffrey. "Indigenous churches in Nigeria".
        West African Review, v.31, No.394, September 1960:
        p87-93.
        A description of indigenous separatist sects in Nigeria.

2238   PEEL, J.D.Y. Aladura: a religious movement among the
        Yoruba. London, Oxford University Press for the
        International African Institute, 1968. 338p. bibliog.
        A study of the Aladura movement in the religious life
        of the Yoruba people for nearly fifty years. The
        study deals with the development and growth of the
        Church and aims to relate its development to the
        course of social change in Western Nigeria over the
        last few decades.

2239   PEEL, John D.Y. The Aladura churches of Yorubaland.
        Paper read to the research seminar, Department of
        Sociology, University of Ibadan, 1965. 9p.

2240   PEEL, J.D.Y. "Religious change in Yorubaland". Africa,
        v.37, 1967: p292-

2241   PEEL, J.D.Y. "Syncretism and religious change". Comparative
        Study of Social History, v.10, 1968: p121-124.

2242   PINNOCK, S.G. The Yoruba country, its people, customs
        and missions. London, 1893.

2243   PRIOR, Kenneth H. "An African diocese adapts a rural
        programme". International Review of Missions,
        v.36, No.43, July 1947: p370-378.
        Account of the role played by the C.M.S. Church in the
        introduction of better farming methods into the rural
        areas of Eastern Nigeria.

2244   RAAFLAUB, Fritz. "Il ya 6 ans, en Nigeria du Nord, s'
        ouvrait un nouveau champ de mission". L' Actualité
        Missionnaire, v.10, No.4, August-Semptember 1964. p202-
        205p.

2245   RUBINGH, Eugene. Sons of Tiv: a study of the rise of the
        Church among the Tiv of Central Nigeria. Grand Rapids,
        Michigan, Baker Books, 1969. 263p.

2246   RYDER, Allan F.C. "The Benin Missions". Journal of the
        Historical Society of Nigeria, v.2, No.2, 1961:
        p231-259.
        Account of early Portuguese missionary attempts to
        convert the pagan peoples of the Benin between 1515
        and 1709 and the failure of such missions.

2247   RYDER, Alan F.C. "Missionary activities in the Kingdom
        of Warri to the early nineteenth century". Journal
        of the Historical Society of Nigeria, v.2, December
        1960: p1-24.

2248   SALVADORINI, Vittorio A. Le missioni a Benin e Warri nel xvii secolo. La relazione inedita di Bonaventura da Firenze. Milano, Giuffre, 1972. 314p. (Univerista di Pisa. Facolta de Science politiche. publicazioni no.2).

2249   SAWYERR, Harry. "Christian evangelistic strategy in West Africa: reflections on the centenary of the consecration of Bishop Samuel Adjayi Crowther on St. Peter's Day, 1864". International Review of Missions, v.54. No.215, July 1965: p343-352.

2250   SCHUYLER, J.B. "Church, state, and society in Nigeria". Insight and Opinion, v.6, No.3, 1971: p57-74.

2251   SCHUYLER, J.B. "Conceptions of Christianity in the context of tropical Africa: Nigeria reactions to its advent". In Baeta, C.G. ed. Christianity in tropical Africa, studies presented and discussed at the seventh International African seminar, University of Ghana, 1965. London, Oxford University Press, 1968: p200-224.

2252   SEED-TIME; the story of the Methodist Church in Idoma, 1924-1974. Oturkpo, Nigeria, Methodist Church 1974, 35p.

2253   SHELTON, A.J. The Igbo-Igala borderland: religion and social control in indigenous African Colonialism. Albany, State University of New York Press, 1971: xix, 274p.

2254   SHEPPERSON, George. "Comment on E.M. McClelland's 'The experiment of communal living at Aiyetoro'".

Comparative studies in Society and History, v.9,
No.1, 1966: p29-32.

2255   SIMPSON, George E. "Religious changes in southwestern
        Nigeria." Anthropological Quarterly, v.43, No.2,
        1970: p79-92.

2256   SMITH, Edgar H. Nigerian harvest: a reformed witness to
        Jesus Christ in Nigeria, West Africa, in the twentieth
        century, including a detailed history of the missionary
        ministry of the Christian Reformed Church in the Benue
        Province from 1940 to 1970. Grand Rapids, Michigan,
        Baker Book House, 1973. 318p.

2257   SMITH, Robert S. "Ijaiye, the western palatinate of the
        Yoruba." Journal of the Historical Society of Nigeria,
        v.2,m No.3, 1962: p329-349.

2258   STERK, Jan. "Nigerianization and the Catholic Church."
        African Ecclessiastical Review, v.14, No.1, 1972: p28-
        32.

2259   TASIE, G.O.M.. "Christianity in the Niger Delta, 1864-1918".
        Ph.D. Thesis, Aberdeen, 1969.

2260   TASIE, G.O.M. "The story of Samuel Ajayi Crowther and the
        C.M.S. Niger mission crisis of the 1880's; a re-assess-
        ment. Bulletin of Theology, v.4, No.7, December 1974:
        p47-60.

2261   TAYLOR, J.V. "Sermon texts in an independent church."
        International Review of Missions, v.55, No.217: p114-

115.

A review article of H.W. Turner's Profile through preaching; a study of the sermon texts used in a West African independent church, 1965.

2262   TIMOTY, Bankole. Missionary shepherds and African sheep. Ibadan, Ibadan University Press, 1970. 67p.

2263   TURNER, Harold W. African independent church, v.1, History of an independent church, the Church of the Lord (Aladura) v.2, the life and faith of the Church of the Lord (Aladura). Oxford, Clarendon Press, 1967.

2264   TURNER, Harold W. "The Church of the Lord: the expansion of a Nigerian independent Church in Sierra Leone and Ghana". Journal of African History, v.3, No.1, 1962: p91-110.
        History of the Church, its founder and the story of its spread throughout West Africa.

2265   TURNER, Harold W. "Dynamic religion in Africa". Learning for Living; v.12, No.5, May 1973: p3-7. bibliog.
        A discussion on the ever growing number of separatist religious movements in Africa.

2266   TURNER, Harold W. "The Late Sir Isaac Akinyele, Olubadan of Ibadan". West African Religion, v.4, July 1965: p1-4.
        Short orbituary of an outstanding leader of the Aladura Church from 1925-1964.

2267   TURNER, Harold W. "Independent religious church
        groups in Eastern Nigeria". West African Religion.
        v.5, February 1966. p281-294.
        An outline of a provisional check list of relevant
        material in the National Archives of Enugu, covering
        55 independent religious movements.

2268   TURNER, Harold W. "The litany of an independent West
        African Church". Sierra Leone Bulletin of Religion,
        v.1, No.2, December 1959: p48-55. Practical Anthro-
        pology, v.7, November-December, 1960; p254-262.
        A study based on the litany text of the Church of
        the Lord (Aladura).

2269   TURNER, Harold Walter. "Pentecostal movements in Nigeria".
        Orita, v.6, No.1, June 1972: p39-47.

2270   TURNER, H.W. "Prophets and politics; a Nigerian test
        case". Bulletin of the Society for African Church
        History, v.2, No.1, 1965: p97-118.
        A discussion on the uprising of the Braid movement
        of the Niger Delta Pastorate Church in Nigeria, and
        the attitude of Colonial administrators towards
        such revolts.

2271   TURNER, Harold W. Profile through preaching; a study
        of the sermon texts used in a West African inde-
        pendent Church. London, Edinburgh House Press, 1965.
        88p.
        Based upon thorough field research into the practices
        of the Aladura Church of Nigeria. Compares them with
        the theological ideas of the Anglican Church.

2272   TURNER, H.W.   "The relationship of churches in the
        renewed church in Nigeria".   In A renewed church in
        Nigeria, 14th report, Christian Council of Nigeria,
        Lagos.   The Council, 1964: p50-54.

2273   TURNER, Harold Walter.   "Religious groups in Eastern Nigeria:
        further lists of material in the National Archives,
        Enugu: Christian, traditional and islamic."   West
        African Religion, v.6, August 1966: p10-15.

2274   TURNER, H.W.   "Searching and syncretism: a West African
        documentation".   Practical Anthropology, v.8, May 1961:
        p106-110.   International Review of Missions, v.49,
        April 1960: p189-194.
        Analysis of the religious literature of the Church
        of the Lord (Aladura).

2275   TURNER, Harold Walter.   "A typology for modern African
        religious movements".   Journal of Religion in Africa.
        v.1, No.1, 1967: p1-34.
        Defines various categories of modern African religious
        movements with examples.   The types discussed in this
        paper include 'Neo-pagan movements, 'Hebraist'
        movements, Israelitish' movements, 'Judaistic'
        movements and the 'Ethiopian' movement.

2276   UCHENDU, Victor Chikezie.   "Missionary problems in Nigerian
        society".   Practical Anthropology., v.11, No.3, May/
        June 1964: p105-117.
        A discussion on the concepts and practices of polygamy,
        magic and sacrifice which characterise some Nigerian
        christians of today.

2277   UDO, E.A. "The missionary scramble for spheres of
        influence in south-eastern Nigeria, 1900-1952".
        Ikenga, v.1, No.2, p.22-36.

2278   USSHER, Margaret. Fifty plus flashback into H.W. Dickson's
        fifty years of vital missionary experience in Nigeria.
        Belfast, Qua Iboe Mission, 1972. 241p.

2279   VARNEY, Peter D. "Religion in a West African University".
        Journal of Religion in Africa, v.2, No.1, 1969: p1-42.
        A survey of a sample of university students at Ibadan,
        Nigeria, in 1963-64 to find out what proportion were
        regular Church goers.

2280   VERGER, P. The Yoruba supreme being: a review of the sources,
        (mimeographed paper for the seminar! "The High God
        in Africa,") at University of Ife, Institute of African
        Studies, December 1964.

2281   VOLZ, Paul M. The Evangelical Lutheran Church of Nigeria,
        1936-1961. Calabar, Hope Waddell Press, 1961. 80p.
        (Twenty-fifth anniversary publication).

2282   WALKER, F.D. A hundred years in Nigeria. The story of the
        Methodist mission... 1842-1942. London, Cargate Press,
        1943.

2283   WALKER, F. Deaville. The romance of the black river: the
        story of the C.M.S. Nigeria Mission, London, C.M.S.
        1930.

2284   WALLS, Andrew Finlay. "A second narrative of Samuel
        Ajayi Crowther's early life". Bulletin of the Society
        for African Church History, v.2, No.1, 1965. p5-14.

2285   WALSH, Michael J. "The Catholic contribution to education
        in Western Nigeria, 1861-1926". M.A. Thesis, University
        of London.

2286   WEAVER, Edwin and WEAVER, Irene. The Uuo story. Elkhart,
        Ind. Mennonite Board of Missions, 1970. 127p. illus.

2287   WEBSTER, James Bertin. "The African churches." Nigeria
        Magazine, No.79, December 1963: p254-266. illus.
        Account of the earlier independent churches in Lagos
        and Yorubaland.

2288   WEBSTER, James Bertin. The African Churches among the Yoruba,
        1883-1922. Oxford: Clarendon Press, 1964. xvii, 217p.
        bibliog.

2289   WEBSTER, J.B. "Attitudes and policies of the Yoruba African
        Churches towards polygamy". In Baeta, C.G. Christianity
        in tropical Africa. Studies presented and discussed
        at the seventh International African Seminar, University
        of Ghana, 1965. London, Oxford University Press, 1968:
        p224-248.

2290   WEBSTER, James Bertin. "Agege plantation and the African
        Church, 1901-1920." Proceedings of the Conference of
        the Nigerian Institute for Social and Economic Research,
        1962: p124-130.

2291   WEBSTER, James Bertin. "The Bible and the plough".
Journal of the Historical Society of Nigeria, v.2,
No.4, 1963: p418-434.
An appraisal of commercial schemes introduced along
the West Coast in the mid - 19th century by the
missionaries, especially the C.S.M, in Nigeria and
Ghana. It was based on the theory that commerce
could assist in the spread of Christianity.

2292   WEBSTER, Douglas. "A spiritual church". Practical Anthropology, v.11, No.5, September-October 1964: p229-232,
240.
A description of a Nigerian "nativist" church in
Lagos and the mode of worship.

2293   WELTON, Michael R. "The Holy Arousa (or Edo National
Church of God): religious conservatism in a changing
society". Practical Anthropology, v.16, No.1, January
-February 1969: p18-27.
The history, creed and mode of worship of the Edo
National Church.

2294   WOBO, M. Sam. A brief resume of the life course of Dr. J.O.
Ositelu. (Part I). Ode Remo, Western Nigeria;
Degosen Printing Works, 1955. 15p.
Biographical account of the founder of the Aladura
Church in Nigeria.

2295   "YORUBA music and the Church: conference at Abeokuta".
West African Review, No.29, No.375; December, 1958:
p1034-1035. illus.

2296   BOUCHE, P. and MAUNY, R. "Sources écrites relatives à
        1' histoire des Peuls et des Toucouleurs". Notes
        Africaines, v.31,July 1946: p7-9.

2297   DELAFOSSE, M. and GADEN, H. Chronique du Fouta senegalais
        Paris, Leroux, 1913. 328p.

2298   GRAVAND, Rev. P. "Contribution du Christianisme à 1'
        affirmation de la personalité africaine en pays Serère".
        In Colloque sur les religions, Abidjan, 5 - 12 Avril
        1961; Paris, Presence Africaine, 1962: 209-214.
        Taking examples from the Serer people of Senegal,
        the author shows the contribution of christianity
        to the affirmation of the African personality.

2299   GRAVRAND, Henri. Visage africain de 1' Eglise; une
        experience au Senegal. Paris, Editions de 1' Orante.
        1961. p237. illus. (Lumière et nations).

2300   MARTIN, V. "La chrétiente africaine de Dakar" Dakar,
        Fraternité de Saint - Dominique.

2301   MARTIN, V. "Mariage et famille dans les groupes Christri-
        anises ou en voie de Christianisation de Dakar". In
        Baeta, C.G. ed. Christianity in tropical Africa,
        studies presented and discussed at the seventh
        International African Seminar, University of Ghana,
        1965. London, Oxford University Press, 1968: p362-
        395.

2302   MARTIN, V. "Notes d' introduction à une etude socio-religieuse
        des populations de Dakar et du Senegal". Dakar,

SENEGAL

2303   MICHEL, Pierre. "Histoire de la Cathedrale de Dakar."
        Horizons Africains, v.154, October 1963: p4-10.

SIERRA LEONE

2304   BANTON, M. "An independent African Church in Sierra Leone."
        Hibbert Journal, v.55, October 1956: p57-63.

2305   BOWEN, John (bp) Memorials of John Bowen, late bishop of
        Sierra Leone. Compiled from his letters and journals
        by his sister London, 1862. 633p.

2306   CAULKER, D.H. "A short account of the origin of Kono.
        E.V.B. mission work." Sierra Leone Outlook, v.48,
        No.1, January 1961: p10-13.

2307   COX, Emmett D. The Church of the United Brethren in Christ
        in Sierra Leone. South Pasadena, Calififornia,
        William Carey Library. 1970. xi, 171p. illus.

2308   ELLIS, Ieuan Pryce. "Professor Groves and the North African
        Church." Sierra Leone Bulletin of Religion, v.5,
        No.2, 1963: p66-71.

2309   FYFE, Christopher Hamilton. "The Baptist Churches in Sierra
        Leone." Sierra Leone Bulletin of Religion, v.5, No.2,
        December 1963: p55-60.
        A brief history of the Baptist Church, founded in
        Sierra Leone in the 19th century, i.e. between 1830
        and 1840.

2310   FYFE, Christopher. H. A history of Sierra Leone. London

344

Oxford University Press, 1962, 773p.

2311   FYFE, Christopher Hamilton. "The West African Methodist
       in the nineteenth century." Sierra Leone Bulletin of
       Religion, v.3, No.1, 1963: p22-28.
       Note on the establishment of Methodism in the colony of
       Sierra Leone during the 19th century.

2312   FOSTER, R.S. The Sierra Leone Church, an independent Anglican
       Church. With a foreword by Bishop Stephen Neill. London,
       S.P.C.K., 1961.

2313   GLASSWELL, M.E. "Oecumenical advance in Freetown." Sierra
       Leone Bulletin of Religion, v.10 No.1, June 1968: p1-6.
       A discussion on new forms of church cooperation between
       different denominations in Sierra Leone since 1968.

2314   HAIR, Paul Edward Hedley. "Beating Judas in Freetown."
       Sierra Leone Bulletin of Religion, v.9, No.1, June 1967:
       p16-18.

2315   HAIR, Paul Edward Hedley. "Christianity at Freetown from
       1792 as a field for research." In Urbanisation in
       African Social Change. Edinburgh, Center of African
       Studies, 1963: p127-140.

2316   HAIR, Paul Edward Hedley. "Creole endeavour and self-criti-
       cism in the Sierra Leone Church Missions - 1900-1920."
       Sierra Leone Bulletin of Religion, v.8, No.1, June 1966:
       p6-18.

2317   HAIR, Paul Edward Hedley. "E.W. Blyden and the C.M.S:
        Freetown 1871-2." Sierra Leone Bulletin of Religion
        v.4, No.1. 1962: p22-28.

2318   HAIR, Paul Edward Hedley. "Freetown Christianity and
        Africa." Sierra Leone Bulletin of Religion, v.6, No.2,
        1964: p13-21.
        Freetown Christianity has a relevance to the study
        of religion and social evolution in other parts of
        Africa which seems to have been often ignored or even
        denied.

2319   HAIR, Paul Edward Hedley. "Niger languages and Sierra
        Leone missionary linguistics, 1840-1930." Bulletin
        of the Society of African Church History, v.2, No.2,
        1966: p127-138.

2320   HAIR, Paul Edward Hedley. "The Sierra Leone settlement -
        the earliest attempt to study African languages."
        Sierra Leone Language Review, v.2, 1963: p5-10.

2321   HAMELBERG, Rev. E. "The Jesuits in Sierra Leone 1605-17:
        a whirlwind of grace." Sierra Leone Bulletin of
        Religion, v.6, No.1, June 1964: p1-8.

2322   HARRIGAN, William N and HAIR, P.E.H. "Christian literature
        in the Yalunka language." Sierra Leone Bulletin of
        Religion, v.3, No.2, 1961: p68-72.

2323   HOLLIS, R. Lynch. "The native pastorate controversy and
        cultural ethnocentrism in Sierra Leone, 1871-74."
        Journal of African History, v.5, No.3, 1964: p395-413

2324   KUP, Alexander Peter. "Jesuit and Capuchin missions of the seventeenth century." Sierra Leone Bulletin of Religion. v.3, No.2, 1961: p68-72, v.5, 1963: p27-34. A Portuguese Jesuit Barreira came to Sierra Leone in 1605, and was followed later by Spanish Capuchins who founded a mission in Port Loko.

2325   LAW, J.R.S. "The translation of the Bible into Mende." Sierra Leone Bulletin of Religion, v.2, No.1, June 1960: p40-44.

2326   LYNCH, Hollis R. "The native pastorate controversy and cultural ethnocentrism in Sierra Leone, 1871-1874." Journal of African History v.5, No.3, 1964: p395-413.

2327   MACLURE, H.L. "Religion and disease in Sierra Leone." Sierra Leone Bulletin of Religion, v.4, No.1, June 1962: p29-34.

2328   MARKWEI, Matei. "The Rev. Charles Knight in Methodist history." Sierra Leone Bulletin of Religion, v.9, No.1, June 1967: p23-34, v.9, No.2, December 1967: p55-66.

2329   MARKWEI, Matei. "The Rev. Daniel Coker of Sierra Leone." Sierra Leone Bulletin of Religion, v.7, No.2, 1965: p41-48. Rev. Daniel Coker, an Afro-American Methodist Minister, played an active part in the early history of the Colony of Sierra Leone and of the West African Methodist Church.

2320   NDANEMA Isaac M. "The Martha Davies Confidential
        Benevolent Association." Sierra Leone Bulletin of
        Religion. v.3, No.2, 1961: p64-67.

2331   OLSON, Gilbert W. Church growth in Sierra Leone: a study
        of Church growth in Africa's oldest Protestant Mission
        Field. Grand Rapids, Michigan, Eeerdmans, 1969. 222p.

2332   PEACOCK, Mmjogollo E. "Missionary work in Sierra Leone."
        M.A. Thesis, Howard University, 1940.

2333   PORTER, Arthur T. "Religious affiliation in Freetown;
        Sierra Leone." Africa, v.23, No.1, January 1953:
        p3-14.

2334   PRATT, S.A.J. "Spiritual conflicts in a changing African
        society." Ecumenical Review, v.8, No.2, 1956: p154-
        162.
        The discussion centers around Sierra Leone.

2335   PRATT, William Elkanah Akinuwi. Autobiography. Edited by
        Gershon F.H. Anderson. Freetown, Methodist Church
        in Sierra Leone, 1973. 71p.
        Biography of the first president of the Sierra Leone
        Methodist Conference.

2336   REECK, Darrell L. "Innovators in religion and politics
        in Sierra Leone, 1875-1896." International Journal
        of African Historical Studies, v.5, No.4, 1972. p587-
        619.

2337   SEDDALL, Henry. Missionary history of Sierra Leone.
        London, Hotchards, 1874. 246p.

2338   SHOUP, Hazel and HARRIGAN, W.N. "Christian literature
        in the Kuranko language." Sierra Leone Bulletin of
        Religion, v.4, No.1, June 1962: p73-74.

2339   SIMPSON, D.H. "Bishop Vidal of Sierra Leone." Sierra
        Leone Studies, New series, No.20, January 1967:
        p211-217.

2340   WALKER, Samuel Abraham. The Church of England mission in
        Sierra Leone: including an introductory account of
        that colony, and a comprehensive sketch of the Niger
        expedition in the year 1841. London, Seeley, Burnside
        & Seeley, 1847. 589p.

2341   WALLS, Andrew Finlay. "The usefulness of school masters:
        notes on the early Sierra Leone documents of the
        Methodist Missionary Society." Sierra Leone Bulletin
        of Religion, v.3, No.1, 1961: p28-40.

2342   WILSON, H.S. "E.W. Blyden on religion in Africa."
        Sierra Leone Bulletin of Religion, v.2, No.2, December
        1960: p58-66.

2343   WOOD, Arthur S. "Sierra Leone and Bulama: a fragment of
        missionary history." Sierra Leone Bulletin of Religion,
        v.3, No.1, 1961: p16-22.

2344   DEBRUNNER, H.W. and BURTON, D.M. A church between colonial
        powers: a study of the Church in Togo. London,
        Lutterworth, 1965. 1965, xi, /68p. (World Studies
        in church mission). Bibliog.

2345   "Le PAPE Jean xxiii s' adresse au   Peuple Togolais
        celebrant son independence." Revue du Clergé Africain,
        v.15, No.4, July 1960: p377-380.

                            UPPER VOLTA

2346   BERAUD-VILLARS, J. L'empire de Gao; efat soudanais au xv^e
        siècles. Paris, Plon, 1942: 214p.

2347   LAUDRIE, Marie LeRoy. Etudes sur les vocations religieuses
        en pays Mossi. Paris, Mouton, 1964.

2348   MANDRIN, J. "Le signe de crois chez les Mossi." Mission
        Catholique, December 1942: p182.

2349   ZOUNGRANA, Etienne. "Reflexions sur la maniere de presenter
        la messe: 1' experience des Chretientes Mossies de
        Haute Volta." Lumen Vitae. v.19, No.4, October-December,
        1964: p679-700.

BOTSWANA

2350   BONHOMMO, Joseph. Noir or: Le Basutoland, mission noire,
        moisson d' or. Ottawa, Association Missionnaire de
        M.I.; 1934.

2351   BROADBENT, S. A narrative of the first introduction of
        Christianity amongst the Barolong tribe of the
        Bechuanas, South Africa; with a brief summary of the
        subsequent history of the Wesleyan mission to the same
        people. London, 1865. 204p.

2352   CASALIS, Eugne Arnaud. My life in Basutoland. Translated
        from the French by J. Brierley. Cape Town, C. Struick,
        1971. 300p. (Africana collectanea series, v.38).

2353   COATES, Austin. Basutoland. London, Her Majesty's sta-
        tionery Office, 1966. 135p. (Corona library).
        P.24-30 deals with "The coming of Christianity," and
        p.101-111 is on "the Rival Doctrine.

2354   DACHS, Anthony J. "Missionary imperialism - the case of
        Bachuanaland." Journal of African History, v.13,
        No.4, 1972: p647.658.
        Analyses the nature of missionary imperialism as a
        result of missionary motives and methods.

2355   DREYER, A. Boustowwe vir die geskiedenis van die Nederduits
        Gereformeerde Kerke in Suid-Afrika, 1804-1836. Cape
        Town, 1936. 400p.
        (Sources for the history of the Dutch Reformed Churches
        in South Africa).

BOTSWANA

2356   ELLENBERGER, V. A century of mission work in Basutoland,
        1833-1933. Translated from the French by E.M.
        Ellenberger, Morija, 1938. 380p.

2357   PRICE, Elizabeth Lees (Moffat). Journals written in
        Bechuanaland, Southern Africa, 1854-1883, with an
        epilogue: 1889 and 1900. Edited with introduction,
        annotations, etc, by Una Long for Rhodes University,
        Grahamstown, South Africa. London, E. Arnold, 1956.
        564p. illus.

2358   SCHEPERA, I. "Christianity and the Tswana." Journal of the
        Royal Anthropological Institute,v.88, No.1, January-
        June 1958: p1-9.
        Christianity which is the official Tswana religion
        was introduced by Livingstone over a century ago.
        Missionaries have played an important part in the
        transformation of Towana life. As at 1957, 27% of
        Africans in Botswana professed Christianity.

2359   SMITH, Edwin William. Great Lion of Bechuanaland: the
        life and times of Roger Price, Missionary. London
        Missionary Society by Independent Press, 1957. xvi,
        444p. illus.

2360   TLOU, T. "The Batawana of northwestern Botswana and
        Christian missionaries, 1877-1906." Transafrican
        Journal of History (Nairobi). v.3, Nos 1/2, 1973:
        p112-128.

SOUTHERN AFRICA

BOTSWANA

2361   TOBIASSEN, Svein. Kulturkollisjon. Norske misjonaerers
        mote med Madagaskars innland 1867-1883. Oslo, Pax,
        1971. 189p.

LESOTHO

2362   BERNIER, Cyrille. Plongée en Afrique. Richelieu, Quebec
        Imprimerie Notre Dame, 1969. 297p. illus.

2363   BERTHOUD, Alex. "The birth of a church: the Church of
        Basutoland." International Review of Missions v.38,
        No.150 April 1949: p156-164.

2364   BRUTSCH, M.A. "L' unite église-mission au Lessouto."
        Monde Non-Chrétien, v.68, October-December 1963: p223-
        231.

2365   COISSON, Roberto. Il popolo del fiume; breve storia della
        missione evangelica nel Barotseland. Torre Pellice,
        Liberia editrice claudiana, 1956. 144p.

2366   GOIRAN, H. Une action creatrice de la Mission Protestante
        francaise au sud de l' Afrique. Paris, Editions "Je
        sers." 1931. 280p.
        A valuable history of the mission in Basutoland, of
        particular importance for its description of the
        missions relation with European colonists and natives
        in the period of conflict.

2367   KHAKETLA, B.M. Lesotho 1970: an African coup under the
           microscope. London, Hurst, 1971, 350p.
           Chapter xvii is entitled the "Church speaks out."
           It contains an interview of prominent church leaders
           in Lesotho with Chief Lebua Jonathan as to the motive
           for the declaration of a state of emergency which led
           to the coup.

2368   PERROT, Claude H. "Un culte messianique chez les Sotho au
           milieu du xixe siècle." Archives de Sociologie des
           Religions, v.9, No.18, 1964: p147-152.

2369   PERROT, Claude H. Les Sotho et les missionnaires Européens
           au 19e siècle. Abidjan: Université, 1970: 191p. illus.
           Bibliography. (Annales de l' université d' Abidjan, F.
           Ethnosociologie, v.2. No.1.)

2370   "PETITE histoire de l' Eglise Catholique au Basutoland."
           Voix du Basutoland, v.25, 1963: p177-212; p213-248.

2371   SIORDET, J.E. Au Lessouto et au Zambeze. Paris, Société
           des missions evangeliques. 1926. 205p.

2372   WIDDICOMBE, John. Fourteen years in Basutoland: a sketch
           of African mission life. London, Church print co.,
           1891. viii, 306p.

2373   ANDRIAMANJATO, Mrs. R.R. "Confessing Christ today in
            Madagascar: a personal statement." International
            Review of Missions, v.64, No. 253, January 1975:
            p13-19.
            A statement of the author's role as Pastor's wife and a
            civil engineer in the Malagasy Republic made at a
            meeting of the Commission of World Mission and Evan-
            gelism, February 1974, in Basel, Switzerland.

2374   BOUCHAUD, J. "Les missions catholiques en Afrique noire
            et Madagascar." Cahiers Charles de Foucauld, v.43,
            No.3, 1956: p147-179.

2375   BOUDOU, Adrien. Les Jesuites à Madagascar au xixe siècle.
            Paris, Beauchesne, 1942. 2 vols.

2376   BRASIO, Antonio. Missoes portuguesas de Socotora. Lisboa,
            Argencia Geral de Colonias. 1943.

2377   CAZET, Jean Baptiste. Mission catholique des R.R. P.P.
            Jesuites à Madagascar. Tananarive, Imprimerie de la
            Mission Catholique. 1888.

2378   COLIN, Pierre. Aspects de l' âme malgache. Paris, Editions
            de l' Orante, 1959. 141p. (Lumiere et nations, 4).

2379   DELAPLACE, C.C. L' apôtre de l' Ile Maurice, ou, vie du
            serviteur de Dieu Jacques-Desiré Laval, missionnaire
            de la congregation du Saint-Esprit et du Saint-coeur de
            Marie. Paris, 1876.

2380   DELORD, Raymond. "Messianisme à Madagascar." Monde Non
                Chrétien, New Series, v.8, October-December 1948:
                p975-981.
                Account of a syncretic church founded by Prophet
                Andrianampoinimerina of Madagascar.

2381   DERVILLE, Leon, Ils sont que quarante... Les Jésuites
                chez les Betsilees. Paris, Dillen, 1931.

2382   "Les EGLISES et le mai malgache." Flambeau. No.34/35,
                1972: p172-177.

2383.   ELLIS, William. History of Madagascar comprising also the
                progress of the Christian mission established in 1818
                and an authentic account of the persecution and recent
                martyrdom of the native christians. London, Fisher,
                1838. 2 vols.

2384   ELLIS, William. Madagascar revisited, describing the events
                of a new reign and the revolution which followed;
                setting forth also the persecutions endured by the
                Christians, and their heroic sufferings, with notices
                and present state and prospects of the people. London,
                Murray, 1867. 502p.

2385   FORMAN, Charles W. "A study in self-propagating Church:
                Madagascar." In Frontiers of Christian world Mission
                since 1938. Edited by W.C. Harr. New York, Harper,
                1962.

2386   GOYAU, Georges. Les grands desseins missionnaires d' Henri
                de Solages (1786-1832) ile Pacifique, l' Ile Bourbon,

Madagascar.   Paris, Plon, 1933.

2387   HALVERSON, Alton C.O. Madagascar: footprint at the end
        of the world. Minneapolis, Minnesota, Augsburg
        Publishing House, 1973. 112p.

2388   HARDYMAN, J.T. Madagascar on the move. London,
        Livingstone Press, 1950. 224p. illus.

2389   HARDYMAN, Marjoire. "The Church and sorcery in Madagascar."
        In Barrett, David B (ed) African initiatives in religion,
        Nairobi, East African Publishing House, 1971: p208-221.

2390   HELLAND, M.A. "A conference in Madagascar. The story of
        what happened when the various missionary societies
        working in the Inland of Madagascar came together for
        an exchange of ideas." Missionary Review of the World,
        v.50, June 1927: p446-448.

2391   HENRIET, M. "The Malagasy churches under the sign of all
        things new." International Review of Missions, v.58,
        No.229, January 1969: p107-109.
        Describes the work and the missionary situation of the
        Protestant churches in Madagascar as at 1968 during
        which time was celebrated the 150th anniversary of the
        arrival of Christianity on the Island.

2392   HISTORY of Madagascar: embracing the progress of the Chris-
        tian mission and an account of the persecution of the
        native Christians. Prepared for the American Sunday
        - school union, and revised by the committee of
        publication, Philadelphia,American Sunday-School Union,

1849. 342p.

2393   HOSTACHY, Victor. Une belle mission à Madagascar.
        Lyon, Vitte, 1935.

2394   JORDAN, Bee. Splintered crucifix: early pioneers for
        Christendom on Madagascar and the Cape of Good Hope.
        Cape Town, Struick, 1969. 276p. illus., bibliog.

2395   KROENER, Francis. "L' echec de l' ethiopianisme dans les
        églises protestantes malgaches." Revue francaise d'
        Histoire outre-mer, v.58, No.211, 1971: p215-238.

2396   LA VAISSIERE, Camille de. Histoire de Madagascar, ses
        habitants et ses missionnaires. Paris, Lecoffre,
        1884. 2 vols.

2397   LA VAISSIERE, Camille de. Vingt ans à Madagascar:
        Colonisation, traditions historiques, moeurs et
        croyances, d' apres les notes du P. Abinal et du
        plusieurs autre missionnaires de la Compagnie de
        Jesus. Paris, Lecoffre, 1885.

2398   LEDOUX, Marc-Andre. "Les eglises separatistes d'Afrique
        et de Madagascar." Revue Francaise d' Etudes Politiques
        Africaines, v.32,August 1968: p30-36.
        Separatist churches in Africa and Madagascar.

2399   LHANDE, Pierre. Notre epopée missionnaires: Madagascar
        1832-1932. Paris, Plon, 1932.

2400   MONDAIN, Gustave. Un siècle de mission protestante à Madagascar. Paris, Société des missions evangeliques, 1920. 128p.

2401   MOSS, Charles Frederick A. A pioneer in Madagascar, Joseph Pearse of the L.M.S. New York, Negro Universities Press, 1969. xvi, 261p.

2402   MUNTHE, Ludvig. La Bible à Madagascar. Les deux premieres traductions du Nouveau Testament Malgache. Oslo, Egede Instituttet, 1969: 244p.

2403   NESDAL, Sivert. Em misjonaeurs erindringer. Leon, Gullborg Nesdal, 1965: 519p. illus.

2404   RENNES, J. "Eglises et pasteurs à Madagascar." Monde non chrétien, v.43-44, July-December 1957: p207-217.

2405   RUSILLON, H. "The gospel in Madagascar." International Review of Mission, v.23, No.92: p530-538.

2406   SIBREE, James. Madagascar before the conquest; the island, the country and the people, with chapters on travel and topography folklore strange customs and superstitions, and animal life of the island, and mission work and progress among the inhabitants. New York, Macmillan, London, Fisher Unwin, xii, 382p.

2407   SIBREE, James. The Madagascar mission: its history and present position briefly sketched. London, London Missionary Society, 1907. 104p.

2408   SUAU, Pierre. La France a` Madagascar: histoire, politique,
        et religieuse d' une colonisation. Paris, Perrin, 1909.

2409   SYRDAL, Rolf A. Mission in Madagascar; studies of our
        mission in Madagascar and the beginnings and develop-
        ment of the Malagasy Lutheran Church. Minneapolis.
        Augsburg Pub. House, 1947. 48p.

2410   VIDAL, Henri. La separation des églises et de l' état a
        Madagascar (1861-1968). Paris,Pichon et Durand-
        Auzias, 1970. 304p. Bibliog. (Bibliotheque africaine
        et malgache. Droit sociologie politique, 6).
        A detailed study of the legal relationship between the
        State and the Churches in Madagascar.

2411   VILKAZI, Absalom. "Isonto Lamanazaretha: the Zulu Church
        of the Nazarites in South Africa." M.A. Thesis,
        Kennedy School of Missions, Hartford, Conn. (U.S.A.)
        1954.

MOCAMBIQUE

2412   ALVES CORREIA, Manuel. Missoes Franciscanas portuguesas
        de Mocambique et da Guinea. Braga, Tip, das Missoes
        Franciscanas, 1934.

2413   CLAPHAM, J.W. John Olley: pioneer missionary to the Chad.
        Revised by N.J. Taylor. Pickering & Inglis, 1966:
        139p.

2414   CLEMENTE DA TORZORIO, O.M. Le missioni dei Minori Cappuccini:

sunto storico. vol. 10. Africa. Roma, Curia Genera-
lizia, 1938.

2415   DOS SANTOS, Edoard. L' état Portugais et le probleme
missionaire. Lisbon, J.I.U. 1964. 162p.

2416   GARCIA, Antonio. Historia de Mocambique cristao. Lourenco
Marques, Diario Grafica, 1969.

2417   KEYS, Clara Evans. We pioneered in Portuguese East Africa;
a Methodist missionary memoirs of planting Christian
civilization in Mozambique. Foreword by Bishop Glenn
R. Phillips. Tribute by Julian S. Rea. New York,
Exposition Press, 1959. 89p. illus.

2418   MARGARDIDO, Alfredo. "L' église catholique en Afrique
portugaise." Revue Francaise d' Etudes Politiques
Africaines, v.61, January 1971: p87-112.

2419   MENDES, Pedro, A. "Attitudes persante o maometismo na Africa
Portuguesa." Estudos ultramarinos, 1961, No.1, p43-56.

2420   MOREIRA, Eduardo. General report of the Reve Eduardo
Moreira's journey in the Portuguese African Colonies.
London, World Dominion Press, 1935. 31p.

2421   MOREIRA, Eduardo. Portuguese East Africa: a study of its
religious needs. London, World Dominion Press, 1936.
104p. (World Dominion survey series).

2422   REGO, Antonio da Silva. Atlas missionario portugues. 2 ed.
Lisboa, Junta de Investigacoes do Ultramar, 1964:

vii, 198p.

2423   SCHEBESTA, Paul. Portugals Konquistamission in Sudost-
        Afrika; Missionsgeschichte Sambesiens und Monomo-
        tapareiches (1560-1920). St. Augustin, Steyler, 1966.
        xiv, 487p. illus. (Studia Instituti Missiologici
        Societatis Verbi Divini, N.7).

2424   SERAPIO, Luis B. "The influence of the Catholic Church on
        Portuguese colonial policy." A Current Bibliography
        on African Affairs, v.7, No.2, Spring 1974: p138-155.

2425   SILVA, Antonio da. "A familia Mocambicana vista pelos
        missionarios Jesuitas anteriores a 1759." Arquivo
        Historico de Portugal, v.2a No.1, 1964: p394-428.

2426   SILVA, Antonio da. Mentalidade missiologica dos Jesuitas
        em Mocambique antes de 1759; esboco ideologico a
        partir do nucleo documental. Lisboa, 1967-
        (Estudos missionarios, no.2).

2427   SILVA, Maria da Conceicao. As missoes catolicas femininas.
        Lisboa, Junta de Investigacoes do Ultramar, Centro de
        Estudos Politicos e sociais, 1960. 91p. illus.
        (Etudos de ciencias politicas e sociais, no.37).

2428   SILVA, Manuel Ferreira da. Triptico mocambicano: Sofala,
        Saba, e Ofir; ensaio historico-religioso das cristand-   s
        ades de Sofala e da localizaco de ofir em Mocambique.
        Braga, Grafica de S. Vicente, 1967. 213p. illus.

2429   ADVENTURES of a missionary: or, Rivers of water in a dry
place; being an account of the introduction of the
Gospel of Jesus into South Africa and of Mr. Moffat's
missionary travels and labors. New York, Carlton
Porter, Miami, Mnemosyne Publishing Co., 1969.
295p. illus.

2430   AFRICAN GOSPEL CHURCH. South Africa. Amended constitution
of the African Gospel Church. Durban, The Church, 1958.

2431   AGAR-HAMILTON, J.A.I. A Transvaal Jubilee; being a history
of the Church of the Province of South Africa in the
Transvaal. London, 1928. ix, 165p.

2432   ALDERSON, C.W. and others. Christianity and separate
development, by C.W. Alderson, H.G. Towsend and K. Mew.
Gwelo, Rhodesia, Mambo Press, 1967. 55p.

2433   APPLEYARD, Gladys. The war of the axe and the Xosa Bible;
the journal of the Rev. J.W. Appleyard. Edited by John
Frye. Cape Town, C. Struick, 1971. 157p.

2434   AXENFELD, Karl. "Die allegemeine sudafrikanische
Missionskonferenz zu Johannesburg vom 13 bis 20 Juli
1904." (The General Missionary Conference of South
Africa at Johannesburg....) Allegemeine Missions-
zeitschrift (Berlin). v.32, No.1, 1905: p13-29.

2435   AXENFELD, Karl. "Nachwirkungen der Johannesburger
missionskonferenz." (Aftermath of the Johannesburgh
Missionary Conference). Allegemeine Missions-Zwitschrift
(Berlin) v.32, No.7, 1905: p332-342.

2436   BAARTMAN, Ernest. "The black man and the Church." Pro
        Veritate, v.13, No.12, April 1973: p2-5.

2437   BADENHORTST, W.J. "Die geskiedenis van die Nededuits
        Gereformeerde kerk in die Transvaal, 1842-1885."
        D. Litt. Thesis, Potchefstroon University, 1951.   226p.
        bibliog.
        (The history of the Dutch Reformed Church (N.G.K.) in
        the Transvaal, 1842-1885).

2438   BADENHORST, W.J. (and others). Wonderdade van God,
        jubileumgedenkboed, 1842-1942; hoofstukke uit die
        geskiedenis van die onstaan, groei en werksaamhede
        van die Nederduits Hervormde of Gereformeerde kerk
        van Suid-Afrika. Johannesburg, 1942. 323p. illus.
        (Wonders of God; jubilee commemorative issue, 1842-
        1942; chapters from the history of the origin, growth
        and activities of the Dutch Reformed Church of South
        Africa).

2439   BAER, G.F.A. "Missionary endeavour in Pondoland."
        International Review of Missions, v.42, No.168.
        October 1953: p413-420.

2440   BANTU-EUROPEAN STUDENT CHRISTIAN CONFERENCE. Christian
        students and modern South Africa; a report, Fort
        Hare, June 27 - July 3 1930. Alice, Cape Province,
        Student Christian Association, 1930.

2441   BARDEN, John Glenn. A suggested program of teacher
        training for mission schools among the Batetela.
        New York, Bureau of Publications, Teachers' College,

Columbia University, 1941.

2442   BARNES, J.A. "African separatist churches." Rhodes-
        Livingstone Journal, v.9, 1950: p26-30.
        A review article on Sudkler's Bantu prophets in South
        Africa. London, 1948.

2443   BASIL, Brother. "The dilemma of Bantu Church music."
        African Music, v.1, No.4, 1957: p36-39.
        Views African music as not generally suitable for
        adaptation to religious use because African instruments
        tend to be boisterous and disturbing in the church.

2444   BATTS, H.J. The story of a hundred years, 1820-1920; being
        the history of the Baptist Church in South Africa, Cape
        Town, n.d. x, 211p. illus.

2445   BECHLER, Theodor. "Unabhangigkeitsbewegungen der Farbigen
        in Sudafrika." (Independence movements among native
        peoples of S. Africa.) Evangelishes Missions Magazine
        (Basel) v.4. 1903: p265-280; 324-341.

2446   BECKEN, Hans-Jurgen. "Patterns of organizational structures
        in the African independent Churches movement in South
        Africa." Africana Marburgensia, v.1. No.2, 1968: p17-
        24.

2447   BECKEN, Hans-Jurgen (ed.) Relevant theology for Africa:
        report on a Consultation of the Missiological Institute
        at Lutheran Theological College, Mapumulo, Natal,
        September 12-21. 1973. Durban, Lutheran Publishing

House for the Missiological Institute at Lutheran
Theological College, 1973. 198p.

2448   BECKEN, Hans-Jurgen. ed. Our approach to the independent
        church movement in South Africa. Lectures of the
        first Missiological Institute at the Lutheran
        Theological College, Mapumulo... 1965. Mapumolo,
        Natal, The Institute, 1966. 162p. (mimeo).

2449   BECKEN, Hans-Jurgen. "On the holy mountain: a visit to
        the new year's festival of the Nazaretha Church on
        Mount Nhlangakazi, 14 January, 1967." Journal of
        Religion in Africa, v.1, No.2, 1967: p138-149. illus.
        Description of an annual festival of a Zionist church
        in South Africa which considered as an interesting
        attempt to present the Gospel in the form of animistic
        religion.

2450   BECKEN, Hans-Jurgen. "Liturgisches verhalten in sudafrikani-
        schen Bantukirchen." Evangelische Missions Zeitscrift.
        (Stuttgart), v.26, No.3, 1969: p163-169.

2451   BECKEN, Hans-Jurgen. "A healing church in zululand: the
        new church step to Jesus Christ Zion in South Africa."
        Journal of Religion in Africa, v.4, 1971/72: p213-221.

2452   BECKEN, Hans-Jurgen. "The constitution of the Lutheran
        Bapedi Church of 1892." Bulletin of the Society for
        African Church History, v.2, No.2, 1966: p180-189.
        A study of the written constitution of an African
        independent church in Sekukuniland, Northern Transvaal,
        which was founded in 1889.

366

2453   BECKERS, Gerhard. Religiose Faktoren in der Entwicklung
        der sudafrikanischen Rassenfrage. Ein Beitrag zur
        Rolle des Kalvinismus in Kolonialen Situationen.
        Munchen, W. Fink, 1969. 169p.

2454   BENNET, H.M. "Ciskeian Missionary Council. Regional
        survey - Medical, 1945." South African Outlook,
        v.76, No.897, January, 1946: p7-8.

2455   BERGLUND, Axel-Ivar. "Concepts of water and baptism
        amongst African Zionist movements." Credo: Lutheran
        Theological Journal for Southern Africa. (Durban).
        v.16, No.1, 1969: p4-11.

2456   BERGLUND, Axel-Ivar. Rituals of an African Zionist Church.
        Johannesburg, University of Witwatersrand, 1967. 13p.
        (African Studies Programme. Occasional paper 3).

2457   BERRY, Llewellyn L. A century of missions of the African
        Methodist Episcopal Church, 1840-1940. New York,
        Guttenberg Printing Co., 1942, 336p.

2458   BERTHOUD, Alex L. "The missionary situation in South Africa."
        International Review of Missions, v.49, No.193, January
        1960: p83-90.

2459   BETHGE, Eberhard. "A confessing church in South Africa?
        conclusions from a visit." Study Encounter, v.9, No.3,
        1973.

2460   BIRTWHISTLE, Norman Allen. William Threlfall; a study in
        missionary vocation. London, Oliphants, 1966. 168p.
        illus.

2461   "BISCHOFF Turner und die athiopische kirche." (Bishop
        Turner and the Ethiopian Church). Die Evangelischen
        Missionen (Guterslosh), v.4, 1894: p214.

2462   "BLACK religion in South Africa." African Studies, v.33,
        No.2, 1974, Special number.
        Contains five articles on various aspects of religious
        life among the Black peoples of South Africa. Includes
        bibliographical references.

2463   BOAS, Jack. "The activities of the London Missionary
        Society in South Africa, 1806-1836: an assessment."
        African Studies Review, v.16, No.3, December, 1973:
        p417-435.
        This essay attempts to examine the specific role played
        by the missionaries of the society in the formulation
        cf the apartheid policy of South Africa, with the
        object of determining whether their influence in fact
        was as great as has been alleged both by supporters
        and opponents of their activities.

2464   BOCKERLMAN, Wilfred and Eleanor. An exercise in compassion;
        the Lutheran Church in South Africa. Minneapolis,
        Augsburg Publishing House, 1972. 112p.

2465   BOOTH, Newell Snow. "The ministry in Bantu religion."
        International Review of Mission, v.26, No.103, 1937:
        p334-344.

2466   BOOYENS, B. "Kerk en staat, 1795-1843." Activities
        Yearbook for South African History, v.28, No.2, 1965:
        p1-176. bibliog.

History of Church and State in South Africa, 1795-
1843.

2467   BOSCH, J.A. "Die geskiedenis van die Nededuits Gereformeerde
kerk gemeente van Philippolis en die invloed daarvan
op die vrystaatse kerk tot 1907." M.A. Thesis, University of the Orange Free State, 1957. 139p. illus.
(The history of the Dutch Reformed Congregation of
Phillipolis and its influence on the Free State Church
to 1907).

2468   BOSCH, David J. "Currents and crosscurrents in South African
black theology." Journal of Religion in Africa. v.6,
No.1, 1974: p1-22.
Traces the evolution of black theology in South Africa,
showing to what extent it has been influenced by Black
American theology.

2469   BOSMAN, H.S. Een terugblik op kerkelijke en godsdienstige
toestanden in de Transvaal. Cape Town, 1923. 154p.
illus.
(Church and religious conditions in the Transvaal
in retrospect).

2470   BOTHA, L.W.N. Die maatskaplike sorg van die Nederduits
Gereformeerde kerk in Suid - Afrika, 1928-1953.
Pretoria, 1956. xv, 426. bibliog.
(The welfare work of the Dutch Reformed Church in
South Africa, 1928-1953).

2471   BRADY, J.F. Trekking for souls: the epic story of the
pioneer days of the Missionary Oblates of Mary
Immaculate in Natal, Basutoland, the Free State,
Diamond Fields, Traansvaal and South West Africa;
centenary year 1852-1952. Cedara, 1952. 271p. illus.

2472   BRANDEL-SYRIER, Mia. Black woman in search of God. London,
Butterworth,.1962. v. 251p. illus. bibliog.
Exposes some of the weaknesses of Christianity in
African life and shows its appeal to women in South
Africa.

2473   BRIDGMAN, Frederick B. "The Ethiopian movements in South
Africa." The Missionary Review of the World,
(Princeton, N.J.) v.17, No.6, June 1904: p434-445.

2474   BRIDGMAN, Frederick B. "The Ethiopian movement and other
independent factors characterised by a national spirit."
Report of proceedings of the First General Missionary
Conference for South Africa. Johannesburg, 1904: p162-
177.

2475   BRENNECKE, Gerhard. Bruder in Schatten. Das bild einer
Missionsreise durch Sudafrika gesehen bedacht und
aufgezeichnet. Berlin, Evangelische Verlagsantalt,
1974. 359p. illus.

2476   BROOKE, Audrey. Robert Gray: a biography of the first
Bishop of Cape Town. Cape Town, Oxford University
Press, 1947. 158p.

2477   BROOKES, Edgar Harry. "A century of missions in Natal and
Zululand." Durban, n.p. n.d. (1927). 60p.

2478   BROOKES, Edgar H   and WEBB, Colin de B. A history of
Natal. Pietermaritzburg, University of Natal Press,
1967. 371p.
Chapter x contains a biographical account of Bishop
Colenso, and his missionary activities.

2479   BROWN, Evelyn M. Edel Quinn, beneath the Southern Cross.
Illustrated by Harold Lang. New York, Vision Books,
1967. xv, 175p.

2480   BROWN, Edward. A historical profile of the Nederduitse
Gereformeerde Kerk (Dutch Reformed Church) in South
Africa. Kwa Dlangezwa, South Africa, University of
Zululand, 1973. 48p.

2481   BROWN, W.H. On the South African frontier: the adventures
and observations of an American in Marshonaland and
Matabeleland. London, Sampson Low, Martson & Co., 1899.

2482   BROWN, William Eric. The Catholic Church in South Africa,
from its origins to the present day, edited by Michael
Derrick. London, Burns, 1960. xiv, 384p. illus.
A factual account of the Roman Catholic Church's
missionary activity in South Africa.

2483   BRUCE, James. "The Ethiopian Church." In. Foreman, Charles
W. Christianity in the non-western world. Englewood
Cliffs, New Jersey, Prentice-Hall, 1967: p2-7.

2484   BRULS, J. "Prophetes bantous en Afrique du sud." <u>Eglise</u>
<u>Vivante</u>, v.1, No.3, 194(: p341-353.

2485   BUCHER, Hubert. "Pfingstereignis fur die sudafrikanischen
kirchen? Internationaler Kongress uber. "Mission and
Evangelism" in Durban." <u>Zeitschrift fur Missionswissen-</u>
<u>chaft,</u> v.29, No.4, 1973: p297-299.

2486   BUCHER, Hubert. <u>Youth work in South Africa: a challenge for</u>
<u>the Church.</u> Schoneck-Beckenried, NZM, 1973, 221p.

2487   BUCHER, Hubert. "Black theology in South Africa." <u>African</u>
<u>Ecclesiastical Review</u>, v.15, No.4, 1973: p329-339.

2248   BUDAZA, G.S. "The native separatist church movement."
M.A. Thesis, University of South Africa, 1948.

2489   BURCKHARDT, G. "Die tembukirche des Kaffernhaiiptlings
Dalindyebo" (The Tembu Church of the Kaffir leader
Dalindyebo). <u>Die Evangelischen Missionen</u>, v.2, 1896:
p235-237.

2490   BURNETT, B.B. "The missionary work of the first Anglican
Bishop of Natal, the Rt. Reverend John William Colenso,
D.D. between the years 1852-1873." M.A. Thesis, Rhodes
University College, 1947. v.i, 92p. illus. bibliog.

2491   BURNETT, B.B. <u>Anglicans in Natal.</u> Durban, 1955. xii, 180p.
illus. bibliog.

2492   BUTHELEZI, Manas. "Christianity in South Africa." <u>Pro</u>
<u>Veritate</u>, v.12, No.2, 1973: p4-6.

2493   CACHET, J.L. Gedenkboek van het 50-jarig bestaan der
        Gereformeerde kerk van Zuid-Afrika, A.D. 1859-1909.
        Potchefstroom, 1909. 239p. illus.
        (Commemorative issue of the 50th anniversary of the
        Reformed Church in South Africa, 1859-1909).

2494   CALKINS, Thomas. Umfundundisi, missioner to the Zulus.
        Milwaukee, Bruce Pub. Co., 1959. 173p. illus.

2495   CAMERON, J. and FLETCHER, G.C. "The Ethiopian movement
        in South Africa." The Mission Field, v.48, No.579,
        October 1903: p309-313.

2496   CAMERON, W.M. "The Ethiopian movement and the order of
        Ethiopia." The East and the West, v.2, No.8, October
        1904: p375-397.

2497   CAMPBELL, Dugald. In the heart of Bantuland: a record
        of twenty nine years' pioneering in Central Africa
        among the Bantu peoples, with a description of their
        habits, customs, secret societies and languages. New
        York, Negro Universities Press, 1969. 313p. illus.

2498   CAMPBELL, John. Travels in South Africa, undertaken at the
        request of the London Missionary Society; being a
        narrative of a second journey in the interior of that
        country. London, Westley, 1822. 2v.

2499   CARLYLE, J.E. South Africa and its mission fields. London,
        Nisbet, 1878. viii, 325p.
        An early survey of the whole of the South African
        mission field.

2500   CAWOOD, Leslie. The churches and race relations in South
         Africa. Johannesburg, African Institute of Race
         Relations, 1964. 140p.

2501   CEGIELKA, Francis A. Life on rocks among the natives of the
         Union of South Africa. North Tonawanda, N.Y. Pollott-
         inum, 1957. 187p. illus.

2502   CHAMPION, George. Journal of the Rev. George Champion,
         American missionary in Zululand, 1835-9. Edited and
         annotated by Alan R. Booth. Cape Town, Struik, 1967.
         xv, 149p. illus.

2503   CHAMPION, George. The journal of an American missionary in
         the Cape Colony, 1835. Edited by Alan R. Booth.
         Cape Town, South African Library.

2504   CHAMPION, George. Rev. George Champion, pioneer missionary
         to the Zulus; sketch of his life by Mrs. Sarah E.
         Campbell and extracts from his journal, 1834-38.
         New Haven, 1896. 51p.

2505   "CHRISTIANITY and revolution in Southern Africa." Africa
         Today, June-July 1968: p12-21.

2506   CHRISTOFERSEN, Arthur Fridjof. Adventuring with God; the
         story of American Board Mission in South Africa.
         Edited by Richard Sales. Durban, Julia Rau Christofersen,
         1967. 183p.

2507   CLAYTON, Geoffrey Hare. Where we stand: Archishop Clayton's
charges 1948-57 chiefly relating to church and state
in South Africa, edited by C.T. Wood. Cape Town, Oxford
University Press, 1960. vii, 55p.

2508   CLINTON, D.K. The South African melting pot; a vindication
of missionary policy, 1799-1836. London, Longmans, xvi,
158p. Bibliog.
An account of the formation of the London Missionary
Society, the entrance of its missionaries into South
Africa, their policy and relations with the colonists
and Government.

2509   CLINTON, D.K. "The London Missionary Society in South Africa
during the years 1798-1836." B. Litt, Oxford University,
1935.

2510   COAN, Josephus Roosevelt. "The expansion of missions of the
African Methodist Episcopal Church in South Africa,
1896-1908." Ph.D. Thesis, Hartford Seminary Foundation, 1957. 522p.

2511   COLENSO, John William. The life of John William Colenso,
D.D. Bishop of Natal, by Sir George William Cox. 1888.
2 vols.

2512   COOK, Calvin. "From break water to open sea." Pro Veritate,
September 1967: p9-11.
The background, task, structure and possible future
of the University Christian Movement in South Africa.

2513   COWIE, Margaret J. The London Missionary Society in
              South Africa. Cape Town. University, 1969, 11, 81p.
              (School of Librarianship Bibliographical series, 44a).

2514   CROSS, Sholto. "A prophet not without honour: Jeremiah
              Gondwe." In African perspectives, edited by C. Allen
              and R.W. Johnson. New York, Cambridge University
              Press, 1970: p171-184.
              A case study of the leader of the Watch Tower
              (Kitawala), one of the most popular millenarian
              religious movements in South Central Africa.

2515   The CROSS in Africa: the forty-fifth annual report of the
              Missionary Society of the Wesleyan Methodist Church
              of South Africa, East London, The Society, 1927. 256p.

2516   DAVIES, H.   and SHEPHERD, R.H.W. South African missions;
              1800-1950, an anthology, compiled by Horton Davies
              and R.H. W. Shepherd London, New York, Nelson 1954.
              A collection of passages drawn from the extensive
              literature of missionary activity in South Africa
              from the end of the eighteenth century to 1950.

2517   DAVIES, Horton. Great South African Christians. Westport,
              Conn., Greenwood Press, 1970. vii, 190p.

2518   DALZIEL, J. "The origin and growth of Presbyterian
              ordinances of worship among English-speaking European
              South Africans prior to the formation of the Presby-
              terian Church of South Africa in 1897." Ph.D. Thesis,
              Edinburgh University, 1956-57.

SOUTH AFRICA

2519   DARBYSHIRE, J.R. and others. The centenary of the Church
        of the Province of South Africa, 1847-1947.
        (Johannesburg), The Church. 1947. 108p. illus.

2520   "DER Aethiopismus in sud-Africa. (Ethiopianism in South
        Africa). Koloniale Abhandlungen (Berlin) v.6, 1906.
        3p.

2521   DE BLANK, Joost Abp. Out of Africa. London, Hodder and
        Stoughton, 1964. 160p.

2522   DE KLERK, P.J.S. Kerk en sending in Suid-Afrika. Amsterdam,
        1923. xii, 190p. bibliog.
        (Church and mission in South Africa).

2523   DELAYED action: an ecumenical witness from the Afrikaans
        speaking church by Prof. A.S. Geyser, B.J. Marais,
        Hugo Du Plessis, B.B. Keet. A Van Selms and others.
        Pretoria, The authors, (1960).

2524   DE VILLIERS, D.W. Reisbeskrywinge as bronne vir die
        kerkgeskiedskrywing van die Nederduiste Gereformeerde
        Kerk in suid-Afrika tot 1853. Kampen, 1959. 178p.
        illus. bibliog.
        (Narratives of travels as sources for the historiography
        of the Dutch Reformed Church in South Africa.)

2525   DICKSON, Mora. Beloved partner: Mary Moffat at Kuruman.
        London, Gollancz, 1974. 238p.

2526   DLEPU, B.S. "Native separatist church movements." Report
        of the Sixth General Missionary Conference of South

377

Africa, 1925. Cape Town, Nasionale Pers, 1925: p110-118.

2527   DODGE, Ralph Edward. "Missions and anthropology; a program of working among the Bantu speaking people of Central and Southern Africa." Ph.D. Thesis, The Hartford Seminary Foundation, 1944. 482p.

2528   DREYER, A. Die kaapse kerk en die Groot trek. Cape Town, 1929. xv, 217p.
(The Cape Church and the Great Trek).

2529   DREYER, A. Eeuwfeest - album van de Nederduits Gereformeerde kerk in Zuid-Afrika: 1824-1924. Cape Town, 1924. 200p. illus.
(Centenary album of the Dutch Reformed Church in South Africa).

2530   DREYFUS, Francine. "Nationalisme noir et separatisme religieux en Afrique du sud." Mois en Afrique, v.19, July 1967: p12-32.

2531   DUBB, A.A. "The role of the Church in an urban African society." M.A. Thesis, Grahamstown, Rhodes University, 1961.

2532   DUGMORE, D.P. "The beginning of Methodist missionary policy in the Transvaal." M.A. Thesis, University of Pretoria, 1939. 80p. bibliog.

2533   DUNCAN, Hall. "Interview with a sect leader." African Christian Advocate (Salisbury) v.23, No.3, 1964: p13.

An interview with R.G. Sibande, Swazi founder of
New Salem Apostolic Church in Zion of South Africa.

2534   DU PLESSIS, Johannes. "Die oorsake can separatisme in die
        sendingvelde van suid-Africa." Op die Horison
        (Stellenbosch). v.1, No.1, January 1939: p39-42.
        No.2, April 1939: p56-60.
        The causes of separatism in the South African mission
        field."

2535   DU PLESSIS, Johannes. "Die oorsprong van die Ethiopiesse
        Kerkeweiging in suid-Afrika." Het Zoeklicht, v.2,
        1924, p196-201. p232-238, p274-279.
        The origin and growth of the Ethiopian church move-
        ment in South Africa.

2536   DU PLESSIS, Johannes. A history of Christian Missions in
        South Africa. London, Longmans, 1911. xx, 494p.
        Bibliog.
        This is a standard work, giving an account of the
        origin and progress of the various missions, with a
        survey of principles and problems.

2537   DU PLESSIS, J. The Evangel in South Africa. Cape Town,
        Cape Times Ltd., iv, 80p. bibliog.
        An outline of missionary activities and policy in
        South Africa.

2538   DU TOIT, Stefanus. Holy scripture and race relations,
        with special application to South African conditions.
        Potchefstroom, Pro Rege-Press, 1960. 23p.

2539   DU TOIT, H.D.A. "Pre dikers en hul prediking in die
Nederduits Gereformeerde kark van suid-Afrika, 1652-
1860." 3 vols. D.D. Thesis, University of Pretoria,
1947. bibliog.
(Preachers and their reaching in the Dutch Reformed
Church of South Africa).

2540   DU PLESSIS, Johannes. "Hoe die Ethiopische beweging in
Suid-Africa begin het." Die Sending Institut
Jaarblad, (Wellington, S. Africa) 1937: p14-17.
How the Ethiopian movement began in South Africa.

2541   DU PLESSIS, Johannes. "The missionary situation in South
Africa." International Review of Missions, v.1, 1912:
p573-586.
A summary of achievements and responsibilities in the
mission field in South Africa.

2542   DU PLESSIS, Johannes. "Missions as a sociological factor."
South African Journal of Science, v.29, 1932: p84-97.

2543   EBERHARDT, Jacqueline. "Christianity and African separatist
churches in South Africa." Occasional Papers: International Missionary Council (London), v.1, No.4, 1960.
9p. (mimeograph).

2544   EBERHARDT, J. "Messianisme en Afrique du sud." Archives
de sociologie des Religions, no.4, July-December 1957:
p31-56.

2545   EDMUNDS, A. A great adventure: the story of the founding
of Methodism in Southern Africa. Palmerston, 1936. 144p.

2546   EISELEN, W.M. "Christianity and the religious life of
       the Bantu." In Western civilization and the nati s
       of South Africa, edited by I. Schapera. London,
       Routledge, 1934: p65-82.

2547   EVELEIGH, W. The settlers and Methodism, 1820-1920. Cape
       Town, 1920, 198p. illus.

2548   FERNANDEZ, James W. "The precincts of the prophet: a
       day with Johannes Galilee Shembe." Journal of
       Religion in Africa, v.5, No.1, 1973: p32-53.

2549   FERNANDEZ, James W. "Zulu zionism." Natural History
       (New York) v.80, No.6, 1971: p44-51. illus.

2550   FLORIN, Hans W. Lutherans in South Africa: report on a
       survey 1964-1965. Durban, Evangelical Lutheran Church,
       1965.

2551   GARDINER, G.B.A. Recent developments in the South African
       Mission field. London, Marshall, Morgan & Scott. 1958.

2552   GENERAL MISSIONARY CONFERENCE OF SOUTH AFRICA. Evangelism:
       the message and the methods. A report of the proceedings
       of the 8th General Missionary Conference of South Africa.
       Pretoria, June 27th to 30th June, 1932. Lovedale Press,
       1932.

2553   GERDENER, G.B.A. Studies in evangelisation of South Africa.
       London, Longmans, 1911. xvii, 212p.
       A discussion of the missionary's attitude to segregation
       and native conditions.

2554   GERDENER, G.B.A. The training of missionaries for Africa.
        Pretoria, Carnegie Visitors' Grants Committee, 1935.
        40p.
        A short review of the facilities for training mission-
        aries in South Africa and other countries, with a
        discussion of the personal qualities and type of
        training required.

2555   GERDENER, G.B.A. Reguit koers gehou: die wording, wese en
        werking van die Nederduits Gereformeerde kerk se
        sendingbeleeid. Cape Town, 1951. 142. bibliog.
        (Kept a straight course: the origin, nature and
        operation of the mission policy of the Dutch Reformed
        Church).

2556   GERDENER, G.B.A. "The Dutch Reformed Church and the racial
        situation in South Africa." Race Relations, v.17, Nos
        1/2, 1950: p1-9.

2557   GERDENER, Gustav Bernhard August. Recent developments in the
        South African mission field. Foreword by Rev. R.W.H.
        Shepherd. Cape Town, Kerk-Uitgewers, 1958. 286p. tabs.

2558   GIBSON, Alan G.S. "Christianity among the Bantu." The East
        and the West, v.11, 1913: p383-396.

2559   LORAM, C.T. "The separatist church movement." International
        Review of Missions, v.15, 1926: p476-482.
        Review of the Report of the South African Government
        Commission on the 1921 disturbances.

2560   "GOVERNMENT recognition of Bantu churches and allocation
        of sites in Bantu areas and Bantu urban townships."
        Bantu, (Pretoria), v.9, September 1959: p101-108.

2561   GRANT, A.C. "South African Missionary Institutions. St.
        Matthews." South African Outlook, v.62, 1932: p220-221.

2561   GRANT, S. "Church and chief in the colonial era." Botswana
        Notes, v.3, 1971: p59-63.
        Account of the struggle between Chief Molefi Kgafela of
        Mochundi and the Dutch Reformed Mission which ended in
        the suspension of the chief before the second world war,
        and the continued opposition of the chief and his line-
        age after reinstatement.

2563   GREBAULT, Sylvain. "Quelques nomenclatures pour l' inte-
        lligence de l' hymnologie de l' église ethiopienne."
        Journal de la Société des Africanistes, v.12, Nos. 1/2,
        1942: p123-132.

2564   GREEN, Bertrand W. "The impact of Christianity on the
        position of the Bantu Chief in the Union of South Africa,
        1887-1961." M.A. Thesis, Howard University, 1960.

2565   GREYING, P.F. Die Nederduits Gereformeerde Kerk en armesorg.
        Cape Town, 1939, 401p. (The Dutch Reformed Church and
        poor relief).

2566   GROTH, Siegfried. "The Church's responsibility in South-West
        Africa." Race Today. October, 1970: 176p. illus.

2567   GRUBB, Kenneth S. The christian handbook of South Africa.

383

Lovedale, Lovedale Press on behalf of the Christian
Council of South Africa, 1938: viii, 290p.

2568   GUENTHER, M. "The effect of Christianity on Bushmen."
        Botswana Notes and Records; v.2, 1969: p125-126.

2569   HAMMERSCHMIDT, Ernst. "Jewish elements in the cult of the
        Ethiopian Church." Journal of Ethiopian Studies, v.3,
        No.2, July 1965: p1-12.

2570   HANS-JURGEN, Becken. "Patterns of organizational structures
        in the African independent churches movement in South
        Africa." Africana Marburgensia, v.1, No.2, 1968: p17-
        29.

2571   HANCE, Gertrude R. The Zulu yesterday and today: twenty nine
        years in South Africa. New York, Negro Universities
        Press, 1969. 247p. illus. Reprint of 1916 ed.
        Missionary activities among the Zulus.

2572   HANEKOM, T.N. "Die gemeente Namakwaland: n' eeufeesgedenkboek,
        1850-1950. Woodstock, 1950, xi, 195p. illus. map.
        (The congregation Namaqualand: centenary commemorative
        issue, 1850-1950).

2573   HARRINGTON, F.P. "An interview with the Black Prophet."
        In The African Missionary. Dublin, 1917. p13-16.

2574   HASELBARTH, H. Die auferstehung der toten in Afrika. Eine
        theologische Deutung der Todesriten der Mamabolo in
        Nordtransvaal. (Diss. Munchen 1970/71) Gutersloh, 1972.
        275p. (Missionswissenschaftliche Forschungen, 8).

2574   HAULE, Cosmas. Bantu witchraft and Christian morality;
            the encounter of Bantu uchawi with christian morality:
            an anthropological and theological study. Beckenried,
            Schoneck, 1969. 187p.

2576   HELGESSON, Alf. Gud och guld i Afrika: en skildring av
            methodistkyrkans arbete 1 Sydost-Afrika. Stockholm,
            Nya bokforlag, 1955. 38p. illus.

2577   HELLBERG, W.H.C. "Die Deutschen Evangelische - Lutherischen
            kirchengemeinde in Western des Kaplandes." D. Litt.
            Thesis, University of Stellenbosch, 1957.
            (The German Evangelical Lutheran congregation in the
            Western Cape).

2578   HERRMAN, L. The Cape Town Hebrew congregation, 1841-1941: a
            centenary history. Cape Town, 1941, v.1, 146p. illus.

2579   HEWITT, J.A. Sketches of English church history in South
            Africa, from 1795 to 1848. Cape Town, 1941. vi, 146p.
            illus.

2580   HEPBURN, James Davidson. Twenty years in Khama's country;
            and, pioneering among the Batauna of Lake Ngami, told in
            the letters of J.D. Hepburn, Edited by C.H. Lyall. 3rd.
            ed. with a new introduction by Cecil Northcott, London,
            Cass, 1970. xvi, 397p. (Cass library of African studies,
            no.7).

2581   HEWSON, L.A. An introduction to South African Methodists.
            Cape Town, 1950. vii, 114p.

2582   HEYER, Friedrich. <u>Die kirche Athiopiens. Eine Bestan-</u>
<u>dsaufname</u>. Berlin, W. de Gruyter, 1971. 360p.
The author's purpose in writing this work was to provide
a survey of the contemporary life of the Ethiopian
Orthodox Church.

2583   HINCHLIFF, Peter. <u>The Church in South Africa</u>. London,
S.P.C.K. for the Church Historical Society, 1968. 116p.
(Church History outlines).

2584   HINCHLIFFE, Peter Bingham. <u>ed.</u> <u>The journal of John Ayliff</u>,
<u>1821-1830</u>. Rotterdam and Cape Town, Balkema, 1971.
136p.
Ayliff was one of the early missionary settlers in the
Eastern Cape in 1820.

2585   HINCHLIFF, Peter. <u>John William Colenso, Bishop of Natal</u>.
London, Nelson, 1964. 199p.

2586   HINCHLIFF, Peter. "Revising Christian initiation rites:
practical problems in South Africa." <u>Studia Liturgica</u>,
v.2, No.4, 1963: p273-284.

2587   HILL, F. "Native separatist movements and their relation
to the problem of evangelization." <u>Report of the Sixth</u>
<u>Missionary Conference of South Africa</u> 1925. Cape Town,
Nasionale Pers, 1925. p110-118.

2588   HINCHLIFF, Peter. "Comment on P.O.G. White; the Colenso
controversy." <u>Theology</u>, v.66, No.511; p21-22.

2589   HINCHLIFF, Peter Bingham. <u>The Anglican church in South</u>

Africa: an account of the history and development of
the Church of the province of South Africa. London,
Darton, 1963. ix, 266p. bibliog.

2590   HOCKLY, Harold Edward. The story of the British settlers
of 1820 in South Africa. With illustrations, maps and
appendixes. 2nd enlarged and revised ed. Cape Town,
Juta, 1957. 284p. illus.
Chapter xv, is on religion and education, Ministers,
churches, missionaries etc.

2591   HOEKENDIJK, Johannes C. "Enkele opmerkingen over 'Kerk
en Ras' in het bijzonder met het oog op Zuid-
Afrika." De Heerbaan (Amsterdam) v.4, 1951: p253-256.

2592   HOFFMEYER, J.H. Christian principles and race problems.
Johannesburg, South African Institute of Race Relations,
945.

2593   HOLDEN, W.C. A brief history of Methodism and of Methodist
missions in South Africa. London, Wesleyan Conference
Office, 1877. viii, 519p.
An outline of the growth of Wesleyan missionary work in
Southern Africa, based upon personal experiences and
published records.

2594   HOLT, B. Joseph Williams and the pioneer mission to the
South-Eastern Bantu. Lovedale, 1954, viii, 186p. illus.

2595   HUDSON, Norman. Evangelism and migrant labour. Pro Veritate
v.12, No.1, 1973: p8-10.

2596   HURLEY, Denis. "The need for reform: apathy in the church."
Pro Veritate, v.13, No.12, April 1973: p7-13.

2597   HURT, N.K. "Wesleyan missions on the eastern frontier of
Cape Colony, 1820-1840, with special reference to the
Kaffir war of 1834-1835." M.A. Thesis, University of
London, 1957-58.

2598   HUTCHINSON, Bertram. "Some social consequences of nineteenth
century missionary activity among the South African
Bantu." Africa, v.27, 1957: p160-177.

2599   "INDEPENDENT churches in South Africa offered aid by
Christian Institute." Ministry, v.5, No.4, July 1965.
p200.

2600   INTER-RACIAL CONFERENCE OF CHURCH LEADERS. Johannesburg, 1954.
God's kingdom in multi-racial South Africa; a report on
the Inter-racial Conference of Church Leaders, Johannesburg, 7 to 10 December 1954. Johannesburg, Printed
by Voortrekkerpers Beperk, 1955. 141p.

2601   JABAVU, Davidson D.T. "Lessons from the Israelite episode."
South African Outlook, July 1921, p105-106.

2602   JABAVU, Davidson D.T. An African indigenous church: a plea
for its establishment in South Africa. Lovedale,
Lovedale Press, 1942. 15p.

2603   JACOTTET, E. "Native churches and their organization."
Report of proceedings of the First General Missionary

SOUTH AFRICA

Conference for South Africa, 1904: p108-133.

2604   JACOTTET, E. The Ethiopian church and the missionary
conference of Johannesburg: an open letter to the...
special conference of the African Methodist Episcopal
Church held at Pretoria in August, 1904. Morija,
Basutoland, Morija Printing Office, 1904. 30p.

2605   JONES, J.H.R. "Missionary work among the Bantu in South
Africa." International Review of Missions; v.17, 1928:
p175-185.
An outline of native needs and problems in relation to
evangelization.

2606   JANSEN, G.J. "Some observations about ritual mutilation in
a Transkei mission hospital, with special refernce to
the 'Ingqithi' custom." African Studies, v.25, No.2,
1966: p73-79.
The 'ingqithi' custom is a ritual mutilation found
among several xhos-speaking tribes, which is performed
on children of pre-school age.

2607   JOUSSE, T. La mission francaise evangelique au sud de
l' Afrique: son origine et developpement jusqu' à nos
jours. Paris, 1889. 2 vols.
(The French Evangelical Mission in Southern Africa; its
origin and development to the present day.)

2608   JUNOD, Henri P. "Bantu marriage and Christian society."
Bantu studies, v.11, 1941: p26-29.

2609   KAGAME, A. "La place de dieu et de l' homme dans la religion
             des Bantu." Cahiers des Religions Africaines, v.2, No.4,
             July 1968: p213-222.

2610   KELLERMANN, Abraham Gerhadus. "Profectiome in Suid Africa in
             akkulturasie perspektief. Vrieburg, Zanoni-Offset, 1964.
             Prophetism in South Africa in the perspective of accul-
             turation.

2611   KIERNAN, J.A.P. "The changing role of (independent) African
             churches with particular reference to South Africa."
             M.A. Thesis, University of Manchester, 1967.

2612   KIERAN, J.A.P. "Where Zionists draw the line; a study of
             religious exclusiveness in an African township."
             African Studies, v.33, No.2, 1974: p79-90.

2613   KILGER, Laurenz. Die erste mission unter den Bantustammen
             ostafrikas. Munster, Aschendorff, 1917.

2614   KNAK, Siegfried. Zwischen nil und tafelbai: eine studie
             uber evangelium, volkstum und zivilisation am Beispiel
             der missionsprobleme unter den Bantu. Berlin, Berliner
             Evangelischen Missionsgesellschaft, 1931.

2615   KRUGER, Bernhard. The pear tree blossoms: a history of the
             Moravian Mission Stations in South Africa, 1737-1869.
             Genadenal, Moravian Book Depot, 1966. 335p. illus.

2616   LEWIS, C and EDWARDS, G.E. Historical records of the
             Church of the Province of South Africa. London, 1934,
             xviii, 821p. illus.

2617   LENNOX, J. "The relation of European and native Churches."
        Report of the proceedings of the Third General Missionary
        Conference for South Africa 1909. Cape Town, Townshend,
        Taylor & Snashall, 1909: p82-90.

2618   LEA, A. The native separatist church movement in South Africa.
        Cape Town, Juta, 1927. 84p.

2619   LEA, Allen. "Native separatist Churches." In Christianity and
        the natives of South Africa; edited by J.D. Taylor.
        Lovedale Institution Press, 1928: p73-85.

2620   LATROBE, Christian Ignatius. Journal of a visit to South Africa
        in 1815 and 1816 with some account of missionary settlement
        of the United Brethren near the Cape of Good Hope, with a
        new introduction by Frank R. Bradlow. Cape Town, Struick,
        1969. 406p.

2621   LAUTENSCHLAGER, Georg. "The Church in South Africa since the
        Council: impression of a two-years'stay in the country."
        Teaching All Nations, 1968: p100-114.

2622   LEENHARDT, Maurice. Le mouvement ethiopien au sud d' Afrique
        de 1896 à 1899. Cahors Couesland, 1902. 128p.

2623   LIVINGSTONE, David. Missionary travels and researches in
        South Africa; including a sketch of sixteen years'
        residence in the interior of Africa. Maps by Arrowsmith.
        New York, Harper, 1858. xxiv, 732p. illus.

2624   LODNON MISSIONARY SOCIETY. Transactions of the Missionary
        society, containing the Rev. Mr. Kicherer's narrative

of his mission to the Hottentots and Bushmen; with
a general account of the South African mission... London,
Printed by Bye & Law for T. Williams, 1804. vii, 408p.

2625 LONG, Norman. "Bandawe mission station and local politics
1878-86" Human Problems in British Central Africa.
v.32, December 1962: p1-22.
Describes the Bandawe Observation (Mission) post and
its role in the Bandawe area of Tongoland.

2626 LUFULU ABO, Francois-Marie. "Pour une crhistianisation en
profondeur de l' âme bantoke." Revue du Clergé Africain,
v.17, No.3, May 1962: p245-251.

2627 MABASO, L. "Can the traditional churches learn something
from the Bantu sects in South Africa?." Credo (Durban)
v.11, No.4, 1964: p20-24.

2628 M'CARTER, John. The Dutch Reformed Church in South Africa,
with notices of the other denominations; an historical
sketch. Edinburgh, Inglis, 1869. 152p.

2629 MALAN, C.H. La mission francaise du sud de l' Afrique. Paris,
1878.
Mostly about Basutoland, with a discussion of Coillard's
plans for Barotseland, by an important supporter of the
missions.

2630 MAPLES, Ellen .ed. The journals and papers of Chauncy Maples,
Bishop of Likoma, London, Longmans, 1899.

2631 MARKS, Shula. 'Ethiopianism' and the 1906 Natal disturbances

paper presented to the Society for African Church
History. London, 1964. 9p. (mimeograph).

2632 MARKS, Shula. "Christian African participation in the 1906
Zulu rebellion." Bulletin of the Society for African
Church History. v.2, No.1, 1965: p55-72.
This article describes the part played by Christian
Africans - the Amakolwa - in the 1906 Poll tax
rebellion.

2633 MARTIN, Marie-Louise. The biblical concept of messianism and
messianism in Southern Africa. Morija (Basutoland).
Sesuto Book Depot, 1964. 207p.

2634 MAWBY, A.A. "The Right Reverened Dr. Henry Brougham Bousfield,
first (Anglican) Bishop of Pretoria." Historia, v.8, No.2,
p81.

2635 MAYCOCK, E.A. "The Church's duty to separatist religious sects."
Daystar 24 April 1955: p617.

2636 MAYER, Philip. Religion and social control in a South African
township. In Adam, H. ed. South Africa: social perspectives, 1971. p177-196.

2637 MAYER, Philip. "Some forms of religious organization among
Africans in a South African City." In Urbanization in
African social change. Edinburgh, University Centre of
African Studies, 1963: p113-126.

2638 MEARS, Walter George Amos. Government contributions to the
salaries of clergymen at the Cape, 1806-1875. Rondenbosch,

The Author, 1967. 21p.

2639   MEARS, W. Gordon. Mission to Clarkebury. Cape Town,
        Methodist Publishing House, 1973. 78p.
        Clarkebury is a District of the Methodist Church of
        South Africa.

2640   MEARS, W. Gordon. Methodism in the Cape ..... an outline.
        Cape Town, Methodist Publishing House, 1973. 194p.

2641   MERSENSKY, Alexander. "Die Athopische bewegung unter den
        eingeborenen Christian sud-Afrikas." Allegemeine
        Missions-Zeitschrift, June 1903: p261-274; p334-345.

2642   MERWE, William J. Van der. The development of missionary
        attitudes in the Dutch reformed Church in South Africa.
        Cape Town, Nasionale Pers, 1936: x, 279p. illus. bibliog.

2643   METHODIST CHURCH OF SOUTH AFRICA. "Christian convictions about
        multi-racial society." Cape Town, Methodist Publishing
        House, 1958. 27p. bibliog.

2644   MEYER, Roelf. Poverty in abundance or abundance in poverty?
        Braamfontein, Christian Institute of Southern Africa,
        1973: 65p.

2645   MITCHELL, Constance I. "History and development of the Seventh
        Day Adventist Church in the Union of South Africa, 1887-
        1958." M.A. Thesis, Howard University, 1959.

2646   MOFFAT, Robert and MOFFAT, Mary. Apprenticeship at Karuman:
        being the journals and letters of Robert and Mary Moffat,

<u>1820-1828</u>. Edited by I. Schapera. London, Chatto and
Windus. 1951. (Central African Archives, Oppenheimer
series, no.5).

2647   MOFFAT, Robert. <u>The Matabele journals of Robert Moffat</u>.
Vol.1, 1829-1854. Vol.2, 1829-1860. Edited by J.P.R.
Wallis. London, Chatto and Windus, 1945. (Central
African Archives, Oppenheimer series, no.2).

2648   MPUMLWANA, P.M. "Indegenisation of Christianity." <u>Ministry</u>,
v.4, No.1, October 1963: p14-17.

2649   MQOTSI, L. <u>and</u> MKELE, N. "A separatist Church: Ibandla lika-
Kretu." <u>African Studies</u>, v.5, No.2, June 1946: p106-125.
Description of the Church of Christ founded at Cape Town
in 1910, in revolt against the so-called apostasy of the
European churches.

2650   MSOMI, Vivian V. "The healing practices of the African
independent churches." in <u>The Report of the Umpumulo
Consultation on the healing ministry of the church</u>.
Mapumulo, Missiological Institute, Lutheran Theological
College, 1967: p65-74. (mimeo).

2651   MULAGO, Vincent. <u>Un visage africain du christianisme: l' union
vitale bantu face à l' unité vitale ecclesiale</u>. Paris,
Edition Presence Africaine, 1965. 263p.

2652   MULAGO, Vincent. "Le dieu de Bantu." <u>Cahiers des Religions
Africaines</u>. No.3, 1968: p23-64.
Analytical study of the religious views held by the Bantu.

2653   MULAGO, Vincent. "Quelques jalons pour catechese bantoue."
       Oreintations Pastorales, v.13, 1961: p1-10.

2654   MURRAY, A. The kingdom of God in South Africa: a survey of
       missions to the heathen, south of the Zambesi. Cape
       Town, Christian Literature Depot, 1906. 40p.
       Brief historical notes on the missions with statistical
       data on the workers and members of the church.

2655   MULTI-RACIAL CONFERENCE. UNIVERSITY OF THE WITWATERSRAND.
       1959.
       Christian responsibility toward areas of rapid social
       change; report. Johannesburg, Printed by Voortrekerpers
       Beperk, 1961. 159p.

2656   MZIMBA, L.M. "The African Church." in J.D. Taylor (ed)
       Christianity and the natives of South Africa; a yearbook
       of South African missions. Lovedale, Lovedale Press,
       1927: p86-95.

2657   NEAME, L. Elwin. "Ethiopianism: the danger of a black church."
       Empire Review, v.10, No.57, October 1905: p256-265.

2658   NEL, B.F. "The Church and education in the Republic of South
       Africa." World Yearbook of Education, 1966: p381-384.

2659   NGEMA, F. "The significance of Manyano." in The missionary
       outreach in an urban society. Lectures of the Second
       Missiological Course of the Missiological Institute of
       Lutheran Theological College, September 1960: Mapumulo:
       the Institute, 1967: p211-215.
       Description and evalualtion of the Manyano and Udodona

movements.

2660   NORTHCOTT, William Cecil. Robert Moffat; Pioneer in Africa,
        1817-1870: London, Lutterworth Press, 1961: 357p.

2661   NORTHCOTT, W.C. "Life and work of Robert Moffat, with
        particular reference to the expansion of missions and
        white settlement north of the Orange River, 1817-1870."
        Ph.D. Thesis, London, 1960-61.

2662   NORTON, G.R. "The emergence of new religious organizations
        in South Africa: a discussion of causes, part II."
        Journal of the Royal African Society, v.40, No.58, 1941:
        p48-67.

2663   OMER-COOPER, J.D. The Zulu aftermath: a nineteenth-century
        revolution in Bantu Africa. London, Longmans, 1966.
        208p.

2664   OOSTHUIZEN, Gerald Cornelis. "Wie Christlich ist die kirche
        shembes?" Evangelische Missionszeitschrift, v.31, No.3,
        1974: p129-132.

2665   OOSTHUIZEN, G.C. "Isiah Shembe and the Zulu world view."
        History of Religions, v.8, No.1, 1968: p1-30.

2666   PATON, A. Apartheid and the archbishop. The life and times
        of Geoffrey Clayton, archbishop of Cape Town. London,
        Cape, 1974. 311p.

2667   PATON, David Macdonald, ed. Church and race in South Africa:
        papers from South Africa, 1952-57, illustrating the

Churches search for the will of God. London, S.C.M.
Press, 1958. iv, 128p.

2668   PAUW, B.A. "African christians and their ancestors." In
E.W. Hayward. African independent church movements.
London, Edinburgh House Press, 1963: p33-46.

2669   PAUW, B.A. Bantu christians and their churches. Cape Town,
Oxford University Press, 1966.

2670   PAUW, B.A. "Patterns of Christianization among the Tswena
and xhosa-speaking peoples." In African systems of
thought, edited by M. Fortes and G. Dieterlen. London,
Oxford University Press, 1965. p240-257.

2671   PAWLIKOWSKI, John T. "The judaic spirit of the Ethiopian
Orthodox Church: a case study in religious acculturation."
Journal of Religion in Africa, v.4, 1971/72: p178-199.

2672   PAYNE, Adam. "A prophet among the Zulus: Shembe. A power for
peace and a restraining influence." The Illustrated London
News, v.176, 8 February 1930: p203.

2673   PEART-BINNS, John S. Ambrose Reeves. London, Victor Gollancz,
1973. 303p.
A biography of the former Bishop of Johannesburg.

2674   PAGE, B.T. The harvest of Good Hope: an account of the
expansion of the Church of the province of South Africa.
London, S.P.C.K. 1947. 1947.

2675   PELEMAN, M. "De Ethiopische beweging in zuid-Afrika"
           (The Ethiopian movement in South Africa) Dendermonde,
           (N. Transvaal). St. Peter en Paulus Abdij, 1937.

2676   PHILIP, John. Researches in South Africa; illustrating the
           civil, moral, and religious condition of the native
           tribes, including journals of the author's travels
           in the interior, together with detailed accounts of
           the progress of the Christian missions, exhibiting
           the influence of Christianity in promoting civili-
           zation. New York, Negro Universities Press, 1969. 2v.

2677   PRETORIUS, Hendrick L. "The future of missions in the
           Transkei." Missionalia, v.2, No.1, 1974: p17-29.

2678   REES, John. "The Church at the crossroads." Pro Veritate,
           v.13, No.5, 1974: p5-8.

2679   REYNOLDS, K.M. "The beginnings of missionary enterprise
           in South Africa, 1795-1812." M.A. Thesis, University
           of London, 1928.

2680   ROSETTENVILLE CONFERENCE. The Christian citizen in a ulti-
           racial society: a report, July 1949. The Christian
           Council of South Africa, Strand, Cape Province, 1949.

2681   TAYLOR, James Dexter. "The Rand as a mission field."
           International Review of Missions,v.15, No. 60,
           October 1926: p647-661.

2682   TAYLOR, James Dexter. One hundred years of the American
           Board Mission in South Africa, 1835-1935. 1935, 45p. illus.

2683 TAYLOR, James Dexter. Christianity and the natives of South Africa, Lovedale, 1928, xii, 503p.

2684 TAYLOR, John Vernon. Christianity and the natives of South Africa; a yearbook of South African missions. (London), Lovedale Press, 1928. xii, 503p.
Surveys by various writers of missions who worked in South Africa. Contains a directory of European missionaries and native clergy and descriptions of educational institutions.

2685 TAYLOR, James Dexter. The American Board Mission in South Africa, a sketch of seventy five years. Durban, J. Singleton & sons, 1911. 99p.

2686 TEMPELS, R.P. "L' homme bantou et le Christ." In Colloque sur les religions, Abidjan, 5-12 Avril, 1961. Paris, Presence Africaine 1962: p225-228.

2687 TEMPELS, P. Catechese bantou. Bruges, Abbaye de Saint-Andre, 1948?

2688 TEMPLIN, John Alton. "Permutations of the idea of elect people in South Africa." Ph.D. Thesis, Harvard University, 1966: 197p.

2689 THOMAS, Thomas Morgan, Eleven years in Central South Africa. 2nd ed. with a new introduction by Richard Brown. London, Cass, 1971. (Missionary researches and travels, no.23).
Chapters xix to xxii contain the history of the Amandebele Mission from 1859 to 1970 and the history of

Makololo and Zambezi missions.

2690   THOMPSON, Doris. Priest and pioneer: a memoir of Father
           Osmund Victor, C.R. of South Africa. With a preface
           by Sir John Kennedy and a foreword by Lord Malvern.
           London, Faith Press, 1958. 134p.

2691   The CATHOLIC church and southern Africa: a series of essays
           published to commemorate the establishment of the
           hierachy in South Africa. Cape Town, 1951, xxii, 180p.
           illus.

2692   The CHRISTIAN handbook of South Africa. Lovedale, Cape,
           Lovedale Press, 1938. 289p.

2693   "The CHURCH'S place in native education." South African
           Outlook, v.69, No.815, 1939: p62-64.

2694   "The WORK of the Holy Ghost Fathers in Africa." Interracial
           Review, v.34, January 1961: p22-23.

2695   SALES, Jane M. "The mission station as a agency of
           civilisation: the development of a Christian coloured
           community in the Eastern Cape, South Africa, 1800-1859."
           Ph.D. Thesis, University of Chicago, 1972.

2696   SALES, J.M. The planting of the Churches in South Africa.
           Grand Rapids, Michigan, Eerdmans, 1971. 170p.

2697   SALES, Richard ,ed. Adventuring with God: the story of
           the American Board Mission in South Africa. Durban,
           Lutheran Publishing House, 1967. 183p.

2698   SASS, F.W. "The influence of the Church of Scotland on
        the Dutch Reformed Church of South Africa." Ph.D.
        Thesis, University of Edinburgh, 1955-56.

2699   SAUBERZWEIGH-SCHMIDT, P. Der Athiopismus: die kirchliche
        selbstandigkeitsbewegungen unter den eingeborenen
        sudafrikas, Berlin, Evangelische Missionsgellschaft,
        1904: 32p.
        (Ethiopianism - the independent church movement among
        the natives of South Africa).

2700   SAUBERZWEIG-SCHMIDT, P. "Die kirchliche selbstandigkeits-
        beweg unter den eingeborenen sudafrikas." Die Reforma-
        tion, v.3, No.43, 1904: p679-682. No.44, 1904: p698-
        700.
        The independent church movement among South African
        natives.

2701   SAUNDERS, C.C. "Tile and the Thembu: politics and inde-
        pendency on the Cape eastern frontier in the late
        nineteenth century." Journal of African History, v.11
        No.4, 1970: p553-570. map.

2702   SCHIMLEK, I. ed. Marianhill; a study in Bantu life and
        missionary effort. Marianhill, 1953. 351p. illus.

2703   SCHNEIDER, Theo. "Sauvegardier la verite de l' evangile:
        inventaire de quelques obstacles a l' evangelisation
        en Afrique du sud." Monde Non-Chretien, v.41, January-
        March, 1957: p18-37.

2704   SCHNEIDER, Theo. "Les églises independantes africaines
        en Afrique du sud." Verbum Caro (Basel) v.6, No.23,
        1952: p116-126.

2705   SCHOLZ, Hans George. "Die selbststandigkeitbewegung unter
        den Herero-Christen. Eine reise durch das Watersberg-
        Reservat." Berichte der Rheinischen Mission. (Wupper-
        tal-Bremen). v.106, November 1956: p418.
        The independence movement among Herero Christians: a
        journey through the Watersberg Reserve.

2706   SCHUTTE, A.G. "Dual religious oreintation in an urban
        African church." African Studies. v.33, No.2,: p113-
        120.
        Attempts to interprete the social implications of the
        fusion of two beliefs - ancestor beliefs and christian
        worship - into the concept of spirit, (moya) among the
        Africans in the Dutch Reformed Church in Soweto.

2707   SCHUTTE, A.G. "Thapelo ya sephir: a study of secret prayer
        groups in Soweto" African Studies, v.31, No.4, 1972:
        p245-260.
        A research study based on interviews among some African
        congregations of the Dutch Reformed Church who belong to
        secret prayer groups believed to be practicing witchcraft
        and adultery. The study covers group structure, mythical
        character, membership and recruitment, beliefs and ritual
        practices.

2708   SCULLY, Robert T. "The 'Bantu prophets' of Mount Elgon."
        Ethnos, v.35, No.1/4, 1970: p96-102. biblig. illus.
        An account, derived mostly from oral tradition, of the

role of Bukusu prophets in war leadership against major
Teso invasions in the 1880s.

2709   SEMPLE, Duncan Wilkieson. A Scots missionary in the Transkei;
recollections of fieldwork. Lovedale, Lovedale Press,
1965. xi, 74p. illus.

2710   SETILOANE, Gabriel M.W. "The separatist movement in South
Africa: its origins, danger to the church and comparison
with American negro cults." Unpublished S.T.M. Thesis,
Union Theological Seminary, New York, 1955.

2711   STEAD, W.Y. "The order of Ethiopia and its relation to the
Church." The African Monthly (Grahamstown). v.3, No.15,
February 1908: p311-331.

2712   SHAW, Paul. Never a young man: extracts from the letters
and journals of the Rev. William Shaw; compiled by
Celia Sadler. Cape Town, H.A.U.M. 1967. 189p.

2713   SHAW, William. "Correspondence between William Shaw, Metho-
dist missionary, and the colonial government of the
Cape of Good Hope." Journal of the Methodist Historical
Society of South Africa. v.3, No.5, 1961: p171-201.

2714   SHAW, W. The story of my mission in South-Eastern Africa;
comprising some account of the European colonists, with
extended notices of the Kaffir and other native tribes.
London, 1860. ix, 576p. illus.

2715   SHEPPERSON, George. "Ethiopianism: past and present." In
Christianity in tropical Africa, edited by C.G. Baeta.

London, Oxford University Press for the International
African Institute, 1968: p249-268.   Includes bibliography.

2716   SHEPPERSON, George. "Ethiopianism and African nationalism."
        Phylon, v.14, No.1, 1953: p9-18. bibliog.

2717   SHEPHERD, R.H.W. "The separatist churches of South Africa."
        International Review of Missions, v.26, 1937: p453-463.
        Shows the causes of the separatist movement.

2718   SHROPSHIRE, D.W.T. The church and primitive peoples; the
        religious institutions of the Southern Bantu and their
        bearing on the problems of the Christian missionary.
        London, S.P.C.K., 1938. xxxiii, 466p.
        Interpretes Bantu religious conceptions, and discusses
        the problem of adjusting christian teaching to Bantu
        culture.

2719   SMITH, Edwin William. The life and times of Daniel Lindley
        (1801-80) missionary of the Zulus, pastor of Voorstre-
        kkers, Ubebe Omhlope. London, Epworth Press, 1949. xxx,
        456p. illus.

2720   STANDAERT, Eugene H.G. A Belgian mission to the Boers.
        London, New York, Hodder & Stoughton, 1917. xi, 268p.

2721   SUNDKLER, Bengt Gustaf. "Bantu messiah and white Christ."
        Practical Anthropology, v.7, No.4, July-August, 1960:
        p170-176. Also in Frontier, (London) v.3, No.1, 1960:
        p15-32.

2722   SUNDKLER, Bengt Gustaf Malcolm. Bantu prophets in South
        Africa. 2nd ed. London, New York, Published for
        the International African Institute by the Oxford
        University Press, 1961. 381p. illus., bibliog.
        A definitive work on the proliferation of syncretic
        religious movement in South Africa.

2723   SUNDKLER, Bengt Gustaof. "Response and resistance to the
        gospel in a Zulu congregation." In J. Hermelink and
        H.J. Margull, (eds), Basileia, Stuggart, Evangelisher
        Missiosverlag, 1959: p128-145.

2724   SUTER, F. "The Ethiopian movement." Report of the Second
        General Missionary Conference for South Africa,
        Johannesburg, 1906. Morija, Morija Printing Office,
        1907: p107-113.

2725   STRASSBERGER, Elfriede. The Rhenish Mission Society in South
        Africa, 1830-1950. Cape Town, C. Struick, 1969. xv,
        109p.

2726   STUDY PROJECT ON CHRISTIANITY IN APARTHEID SOCIETY. SOCIAL
        COMMISSION. Towards social change; report of the Social
        Commission of the Study Project on Christianity in
        Apartheid Society. General editor, Peter Randall.
        Johannesburg, 1971. 197p. (SPRO-CAS publication no.6).

2727   TAYLOR, William. (bp.). Christian adventures in South Africa.
        New York, Nelson, 1877. 557p.

2728   TOUT, Kenneth J. Mary of Vendaland (Mary Styles) London,
        Salvationist Publishing & Supplies, 1967. 16p.

(Victory books, no.33).

2729   VAN DER MERWE, William J. "The development of missionary attitudes in the Dutch reformed church in South Africa." Ph.D. Hartford Seminary Foundation, 1934.

2730   VAN DER MERWE, W.J. The development of missionary attitudes in the Dutch Reformed Church in South Africa. Cape Town, Nasionale, 1936: xi, 279p. maps. bibliog.
A history of the missionary activities of the church in South Africa.

2731   VAN ANTWERP, Cornelius Markinus. Die separatistiese kerklike beweging onder die Bantu van Suid-Afrika. (The separatist church movement among the South Africa Bantu) Ph.D. Thesis, University of Cape Town, 1938.

2732   VAN ZYL, Danie. "Spies out in the cold: the challenge of the African independent church movement." Pro Veritate (Johannesburg) v.7, No.1, May 1968: p415.

2733   VAN ZYL, Danie. "2500 churches in South Africa." The African Christian Advocate (Florida, Transvaal) v.27, No.1, 1968: p4-7.

2734   VAN ROOY, J.A. "Sinkretisme in Vendaland: sinkretisme onder die separatistiese in Vendaland." M.Th. Dissertation, Potchefstrom University for Christian Higher Education, 1964.

2735   VERRYN, Trevor David. A history of the Order of Ethiopia. 3rd ed. Cleveland, Transvaal, Central Mission Press, 1972.

2736   WAGNER, (Pere). "Les sectes en Afrique du sud."
        In Museum Lessianum. Devant les sectes non-chrétiennes.
        Louvain, Desclée de Brouwer, 1962. p144-163.

2737   WALKER, Reginald F. The Holy Ghost fathers in Africa:
        a century of mission effort. Blackrock, College,
        1933.

2738   WHITESIDE, J. History of the Wesleyan Methodist Church
        of South Africa. London, Elliot Stock, 1906. viii,
        479p. illus.
        Describes the religions and educational work of the
        Church amongst non-Europeans.

2739   WEST, M.E. "Independence and unity: problems of co-operation
        between African independent Church leaders in Soweto."
        African Studies, v.33, No.2, 1974: p121-129. bibliog.
        A two year study, based on African Independent Churches,
        mainly in Soweto, to find out the level of cooperation
        in the form of combining in associations, with parti-
        cular reference to the African Independent Churches
        Association.

2740   WHITE, P.O.G. "The Colenso controversy." Theology, v.65,
        No.508: 1962: p402-408.

2741   WILLIAMS, D. "The missionaries on the eastern frontier of
        the Cape Colony, 1799-1853." Ph.D. Thesis, University
        of Witwaterssand, 1959. 553p. illus.

2742   WILSON, Monica and THOMPSON, Leonard. The Oxford history
        of South Africa, Oxford, Clarendon Press, 1971. vol.2,

Pages 72-84 cover church and school activities in South Africa from 1870-1966.

2743   WIRGMAN, Augustus Theodore. The history of the English church and people in South Africa. London and New York, Longmans, Green, 1895. xi, 276p.

2744   WORLD COUNCIL OF CHURCHES. Report on the World Council of Churches mission in South Africa, April-December, 1960. Prepared by the W.C.C. Delegation to the Consultation in December, 1960. Franklin Clark Fry, Chairman (and others). Geneva, 1961. 36p.

2745   WOOD, A.V. The British reaction to Christianity. London, Prism, 1961. 61p.

2746   WOOD, Cecil Thomas. "A Crowther manuscript in Cape Town." Bulletin of the Society for African Church History, v.2, No.1, 1965: p5-14.

2747   WOOD, Michael. A father in God: the episcopate of William West Jones, D.D. Archbishop of Cape Town and Metropolitan of South Africa, 1874-1908. London, Macmillan, 1913, xxviii, 500p. illus.

2748   WRIGHT, Charlotte. Beneath the Southern Cross: the story of an American bishop's wife in South Africa. New York, Exposition Press, 1955. 184p.

2749   "ZION Christian Church." Drum (Johannesburg). v.4, No.7, July 1954. p719. illus.

2750   BAUMANN, Julius. Mission und Okumene in Sudwestafrika, dargestellt am Lebenswerk von Herman
Heinrich Vedder. Leiden, E.J. Brill, 1965. xiii,
168p. (Oekumenish studies, 7).

2751   ENGEL, Lothar. "Rasse und Mission in Namibia."
Evangelishe Missions-Zeitschrift, v.30, No.3, 1973:
p121-133.

2752   GESCHICTE der Katholische Mission in Sudwestafrika 1896-
1946: fests-chrift zum funfzigjahrigen Bestehen
der Katholischen Mission in Sudwest-afrika. Heraus-
gegeben vom Apostolischen Vikariat in Windhoek.
Windhosk, John Meinert, 1946.

2753   KLEINE, Hans de. Um Einhet und Auftrag. 125 Jahre
Kirche und Mission in Sudwestafrika. Eine Aufsatz-
sammlung. In verbindung mit s. Groth hrs. von
H de Kleine. Wuppertal, Verlag der Rheinischen
Mission, 1967. 71p.

2754   LOTH, Heinrich. Die christliche Mission in Sudwestafrika; zur destruktiven Rolle der Rheinischen
Missionsgesellschaft beim Prozess der Staatsbildung
in Sudwest afrika (1842-1893). Berlin, Akademie-
Verlag, 1963. 180p. illus. (Studien zur Kolonial-
geschichte, bd. 9).
The aim of this book is "to demonstrate the destructive
influence of Christian missionary activity upon the
formation of states in South West Africa."

2755   LOTH, H. "Zur bedeutung sektenkirchlicher fruhformen im
        sogenannten Witbooi-aufstand im Sudwestafrika." In
        Kongressmaterialen der Delegation der D.D.R. des
        xxv Internationalen Orientalistenkongresses...
        section xx: Afrikanistik. Berlin, Nationalen vorbereit-
        ungskomitee in der D.D.R., 1960.
        The significance of the early sect-church forms in the
        so-called Witbooi rebellion in South-West Africa.

2756   LOYTTY, Seppo. The Ovambo sermon: a study of the preaching
        of the Evangelical Lutheran Ovambo-Kavango Church in
        South West Africa. Tampere, Finland, Luther Agricola
        Society, 1971: 173p.
        A useful study which gives insight not only into the
        method, performance and content of Ovambo preaching,
        but in passing, gives also much insight into the
        problems of the daily life of the Church.

2757   MENZEL, Gustav. "Eine neue sekte in Sudwest."? (A new
        sect in South-West Africa?). Berichte der Rheischen
        Mission (Wuppertal-Barmen) v.105, February 1955:p33-35.
        Report on the secession of the Herero African Church
        of Evangelists from the Rhenish Mission.

2758   MIRBT, Carl. Mission und kolonialpolitic in den Deutschen
        Schutzgebeiten. Tubingen, Mohr, 1910. xii, 287p.
        Mission and colonial politics in the German colonies.

2759   ONGERKI, Y. Ambo-Kavangon kirkko. The Ovambo-Kavango
        church. Aalongekidhi - Toim. Helsinki, Suomen,
        Lahetysseura, 1970. 32p.

2760 SCHLOSSER, Katesa. "Die sekten der eigeborenen in
sud-und sidwestafrika als manifestationen des
gegensatzes Zwischen Weissen und nichtweissen."
(The sects of South and South-West African natives
as manifestations of conflict between whites and non-
whites). Africanisher Heimatkalender (Windnock)
1962: p101-107.

2761 SCHLOSSER, Katesa. Eingeborenenkirchen in Sud-und
Sudwestafrika: Geschichte und social struktur
(Native churches in South and South West Africa
and their social stucture). Kiel, W.G. Muhlau, 1958.
355p. illus. bibliog.

2762 SCHLOSSER, Katesa. "Profane ursachen des anschlusses
an separististenkirchen in sud-und Sudwestafrika."
(Non-religious reasons for joining separatist churches
in South and South-West Africa) In E. Benz, Messianishe
kirchen, sekten und bewegungen in heutigen Afrika.
Leiden, Brill, 1965: p24-45.

2763 SCHOLZ, Hans Georg. "Junge kirche und separatistische
bewegungen in Sudwestafrika." Kirche in der Zeit
(Dusseldorf). v.16, 1961: p197-201.
Young churches and separatist movements in South West
Africa.

2764 SIMOJOKI, V. "Courses for deacons in the Ovambokavango
Church in Southwest Africa." African Theological
Journal, No.3, March 1970: p59-68.

2765   KUPER, Hilda. "The Swanzi reaction to Missions." African
               Studies, v.5, No.3, 1946: p176-188.
               Brief introductory history of the introduction and
               growth of Christian Missions in Swaziland, and the
               response of the people to the new religion.

2766   MATABESE, D.T. "Missionary enterprise and influence in
               Swaziland." Swaziland Teachers Journal, v.66, No.2,
               1974: p36-39.

2767   SCUTT, Joan F. The drums are beating: missionary life in
               Swaziland. London, African Evangelical Fellowship.
               1966. 132p. illus.
               A fictional biography, depicting the conversion of an
               African woman in Swaziland by the name of Food-of-earth.

2768   SUNDKLER, Bengt Gustaf.Malcolm. "Chief and prophet in
               Zululand and Swaziland." In M. Fortes and G. Dieterlin,
               (eds). African systems of thought. London, Oxford
               University Press for the International African Institute,
               1965: p276-290.

2769   ADEGBOLA, Adeolu. "A Christian interpretation of the African revolution." in Christ and the younger churches theological contributions from Asia, Africa and Latin America, London, S.P.C.K, 1972: p32-41.
Attempts to give a Christian interpretation to the African revolution and to relate it to the parallel revolution which is going on within the life of the Churches in Africa.

2770   ALLIOT, Michel. "Christianisme etdroit traditional." In Etudes a Gabriel Le Bras. Paris, Sirey, 1965. v.2.

2771   ASSIMENG, Max. "Religious values and social change: paradigms in theory and research." Research Review (Legon) v.9, No.1, 1973: p7-19.

2772   ASSUON, B.K. "Religion and social change among the Ahanta of Ghana." Thesis, M.A. Legon, University of Ghana, 1970. 161p.

2773   BECKMANN, David M. Eden revival: spiritual churches in Ghana. St. Louis, London, Concordia Publishing House, 1975. 144p. bibliog.

2774   DELAVIGNETTE, Robert. Christianisme et colonialisme. Paris, Edition Fayard, 1974? (Collection Je sais Je crois).

2775   FERNANDEX, James W. "The ethnic communion: inter-ethnic recruitment in African religious movements." Journal of African Studies, v.2, No.2, Summer 1975: p131-147.

1276   GROH, Dennis Edward. "Christian community in the writings
        of Tertullian, an inquiry into the nature and problems
        of community in North African Christianity." Ph.D.
        Thesis, Hartford Seminary Foundation, 1971. 188p.

2777   GROHS, G. and NEYER, H. eds. Die kirchen und die
        portugiesische Prasenz in Afrika. Munchen, Kaiser,
        1975. 176p.

2778   LIVINGSTON, Thomas W. "Paradox in early mission education
        in Buganda." Journal of African Studies, v.2, No.2,
        Summer 1975: p161-176.

2779   MBITI, John S. "Some African concepts of Christology."
        in Christ and the African revolution: theological
        contributions from Asia, Africa and Latin America.
        London, S.P.C.K. 1972: p51-62.

2780   MENSAH, Ronald. The gospel minister. Accra, Ghana Bible
        Research Centre, 1971? 34p.

2781   MUGAMBI, J.N.K. "The African experience of God." Thought
        and Practice (Nairobi) v.1, No.1, 1974: p49-58.

2782   NICQ, Chanoine. Vie du R.P. Simeon Lourdel, de la Congre-
        gation des Peres Blancs de Notre-Dame d' Afrique,
        premier missionnaire catholique de 1' Ouganda (Afrique
        Equatoriale). Paris, Poussielgue. 1895.

2783   NIEDERBERGER, O. The African clergy in the Catholic Church
        of Rhodesia: reflections of a survey. Gwelo, Rhodesia,
        Mambo Press, 1973. 45p. (Mambo occasional papers:

missio-pastoral, 2).

2784   ODJIDJA, E.M.L. Mustard seed: the growth of the Church
in Kroboland. Accra, Waterville Publishing House,
1973. 162p. illus.

2785   ODUYOYE, M. "The role of Christian publishing house in
Africa today." In Oluwasenmi, E. (and others)
Publishing in Africa in the seventies. Ile-Ife, 1975:
p209-232.

2786   PRESBYTERIAN CHURCH OF GHANA. Minutes of the 42nd Synod,
held at the University of Science and Technology 28th
August - 1st September, 1971. 89p.

2787   PRESBYTERIAN CHURCH OF GHANA. Report for 1973 presented
to the 45th synold held at Agona Nsaba from 24th
August to 29th August 1974. (n.p.) 1975? 106p.

2788   PRESBYTERIAN CHURCH OF GHANA. Central Finance Committee.
Report and statement of accounts: Presbyterian Church
of Ghana, Central Finance Committee. Accra, Presbyterian Church, 1974. 28p.

2789   QUARCOOPOME, T.N.O. The Acts of Apostles. Accra,
Afram Publications, 1975. 114p. (Comprehensive
studies series).
Notes and model examination questions and answers
intended for the G.C.E. and School Certificate exa-
minations.

ADDENDA

2790   QUARCOOPME, T.N.O. The gospel according to St. Mark.
        Accra, Afram Publications, 1975. 63p. (Comprehensive
        studies series).

2791   QUARCOOPOME, T.N.O. History and religion of Israel from
        Samuel to the fall of the Northern Kingdom: "O" Level
        Bible Knowledge questions and answers. Accra, Afram
        Publications, 1975: 204p. (Afram "O" level success
        series).

2792   SIDDIQUE, M.M. "A complimentary and missionary letter to
        the Archbishop of Canterbury on his visit to Sierra
        Leone." Freetown, Ahmaddiya Movement, 1951. 7p.

2793   TUBOKU-METZGER, C.E. "Sectarianism and divided Christendom:
        the African Situation." Report of proceedings, Anglican
        Congress, 1963. London, S.P.C.K. 1963. p38-40.

2794   TUCKER, John T. "Fifty years in Angola." International
        Review of Missions, v.19, 1930: p256-265.

2795   YEBOA-DANKWA, J. History of the Presbyterian Training
        College, Akropong-Akwapim: 125 years anniversary
        1848-1973. Accra, Waterville Publishing House, 1973.
        95p. illus., bibliog.

2796   VICEDOM, Georg F. ed. Christ and the younger churches:
        theological contributions from Asia, Africa, and
        Latin America. London, S.P.C.K., 1972. 112p.
        (S.P.C.K. theological collections, 15).
        A collection of seven essays on Christian theology
        from the point of view of Theologians from Asia,

417

Africa and Latin America.

2797   WILLIS, J.J. "Christianity and the native government of
        Uganda." Church Missionary Review, v.67. 1921: p294-
        301.

LIST OF JOURNALS AND PERIODICALS ON CHRISTIANITY
IN AFRICA

2798   AACC bulletin. Nairobi, All Africa Conference of Churches,
        P.O. Box 20301) 2 nos. a year.
        Includes articles on church and mission activities in
        Africa.

2799   ACTUALIDAD africana, v.1 - 1951-   Madrid, Blancos y Hermans
        Blancas, monthly.
        Includes articles on African religions and missionary
        activities.

2800   ACTUALITE missionnaire, v1- 1956- Lausanne.
        Issued by the Mission suisse dans 1' Afrique du sud,
        Mission de Paris, Mission de Bale, Mission morave, and
        Action chrétienne en Orient.

2801   AEQUATORIA, mission catholique, v1- 1937- Coquilhatville
        (Congo, Kinshasa.) Mission catholique de Coquihatville,
        quarterly.

2802   AFRICA. v.1- 1931- (Piscataway, N.J. 08854) Missionary
        sisters of Our Lady of Africa, quarterly.

2803   AFRICA Christian advocate, v1+ 1943+ Transvaal
        (South Africa) quarterly.

2804   The AFRICAN angelus, v.1+ -947- (Taanafly, N.J), Society of
        African Missions in U.S.A.

2805   AFRICAN challenge, 1951- Jos, Nigeria, Sudan Interior
        Mission,

2806   AFRICAN ecclesiastical review. Masaka, Uganda, (P.O. Box
232) quarterly.

2807   AFRICAN features, vl- 1958. London, Christian Literature
Council, monthly.

2808   The AFRICAN missionary. v.1- Cork, (Blackrock Rd), monthly.
Official organ of the Society of African Missions in
Ireland.

2809   AFRICAN tidings, 1889- Westminster, (England), Universities
Mission to Central Africa. monthly.

2810   AFRIQUE Chrétienne, v.1- 1961- Kinshasa (B.P. 7653).
weekly.

2811   L' AFRIQUE urbaine, No.1- Younde, Centre de litterature
evangelique (B.P. 4048). quarterly.

2812   L' AMI du clergé malgache, vl- 1955- Tananarive, Institut
superieur de theologie, bimonthly.

2813   ARCHIVES de sociologie de religions. Vl- 1956- Paris,
Editions du Centre national de la recherche scientifique.
Includes occasional contributions on indigenous religions,
Islam and Christian missions in Africa.

2814   BASUTOLAND witness. Morija, Paris Evangelical Missionary
society (B.P.12). irregular.

2815   BOLETIM eclesiastico de Angola e S. Tome. Luanda, Missoes
Catholicas Portuguesas.

2816   BURAKEYE, Kitega, Burundi, Centre evangelique, (B.P. 76)
          monthly.
          Organ of the Protestant Churches of Burundi.

2817   BURUNDI Chretien, v1- 1962- Usumbura, Archeveque de
          Kitega, (B.P. 232.) biweekly.

2818   A CATHOLIC directory of East Africa, 1950- Mombasa,
          Apostolic Delegation.

2819   The CATHOLIC directory of Southern Africa. Cape Town,
          Selesian Press.

2820   CATHOLIC mirror. v1- 1966- Nairobi, Holy Ghost Fathers,
          monthly. Text in English and Swahili.

2821   CATHOLIC voice. Accra, (P.O. Box 54) monthly.

2822   The CHRISTIAN messenger, 1960- Accra, Presbyterian Book
          Depot, (Box 3075) monthly.

2823   CONGO mission news, No.1- 1219- Kinshasa-Kalina, Conseil
          Protestant du Congo (B.P. 3094) quarterly.

2824   CONGO missionary messenger, v.1- 1930- Chicago, Congo
          Inland Mission Board.

2825   CONTEXT, v1- 1965- Stellenbosch, South Africa, Published
          by the Dominican Students for the Executive of the
          Interseminary Seminar, 5 no. a year.

2826   La CROIX au Dahomey, No. 1- 1964- Cotonou, (B.P.32).
Semi-monthly.

2827   La CROIX du Congo, No.1- 1933- Leopoldville, Secretariat de
1' Action catholique et sociale, weekly.

2828   CULTURE chretienne, no.1- 1962- Kabayi, Rwanda, Seminaire,
monthly.

2829   DRUM call. 1922-   Elat, Ebolowa, Cameroon, quarterly.
Journal of the Fraternal Workers of the United Presbyterian Church, U.S.A; serving in West Africa.

2830   ETHIO-ECHO, 1960- Addis Ababa, Ethiopian Mission of the
United Presbyterian Church in the U.S.A. quarterly.

2831   EVANGILE en Afrique, no.1- 146. 1933-1958. (Journal bimes-
triel du Conseil protestant du Congo.) ceased
publication.

2832   Le FLAMBEAU! Revue trimestrielle de theologie pour 1' engagement des 1' eglises dans le monde Africain (Protestant)".
Douala, Association des ecoles de theologie de 1' Afrique
occidentale et centrale (B.P. 22).

2833   GRANDS lacs; revue generale des missions d' Afrique, 1884-
1954. Namur, Peres blancs d' Afrique. superseded by
Vivante Afrique.

2834   HORIZONS africain; journal de la vie catholique au Senegal,
1947- Dakar, (B.P. 3213) monthly.

2835   INSIGHT and opinion, v.1- 1966-   Cape Coast, Ghana,
          irregular.
          A general review of current events for the Christian
          Ghanaian intellectual.

2836   INTERNATIONAL review of missions. v.1- 1912- Geneva,
          World Council of Churches Publications Office, quar-
          terly.

2837   MAINTENIR, 1937-   Dakar, Mission evangelique, monthly.

2838   MISSION suisse dans l' Afrique du sud, Bulletin, 1872-
          Lausanne, Switzerland, Swiss Reformed Church Mission
          in South Africa, bimonthly.

2839   MISSION en Afrique. Lyon, France, La Pastorale missionaire,
          bimonthly. Each issue is usually devoted to a particular
          topic.

2840   NIGERIAN Christian, v.1- April 1967- Ibadan, (Box 1261),
          monthly.

2841   NUMEN; international review for the history of religions.
          v.1- 1954- Leiden, Netherland, E.J. Brill. 3 nos.
          a year.
          Text in English, French, German and Italian.

2842   The OFFICIAL Nigerian Catholic directory. Lagos, African
          Universities Press, annual.

2843   PORTUGAL em Africa; revista de cultura missionaria, v.1-

423

1894- Lisbon, Instituto Superior Missionario do
Esprito Santa. bimonthly.

2844 PRESENCE chrétienne; bimensuel togolais catholique d'
information, 1960- Lome, (B.P. 1205) illus.

2845 REPONSE tiers - monde et catholicité - 1945- Louvain,
Association universitaire catholique d' amitie
mondiale. quarterly.

2846 REVUE du clerge africain, v.1, 1964- Mayidi (Congo Kinshasa)
bimonthly.

2847 RYTHMES du monde, 1946- Paris, quarterly.
Roman Catholic missionary journal with occasional issues
devoted to Africa.

2848 SIERRA LEONE freeman, v.1- 1958- Catholic Mission, Freetown,
(P.O. Box 250) monthly.

2849 SIERRA LEONE messenger. Truro, Eng. (Barrack Lane) quarterly,
Journal of Anglican Churches in Sierra Leone.

2850 SOUTH AFRICAN missionary advocate, v.1- 1922- Cleveland,
Transvaal (South Africa).

2851 The SOUTH AFRICAN outlook, v.1- 1870- Lovedale, Lovedale
Press, monthly.

2852 SOUTH AFRICAN pioneer, v.1- 1888- Cape Town, bimonthly.
An interdenominational mission journal.

2853   SUDAN diocesan review. Croydon, Surrey, England, 3 nos.
        a year.
        Journal of the Anglican Churches in the Sudan.

2854   THE SUN, v.1- 1961- Lusaka, Sisters of St. Peter Claver,
        (P.O. Box 8067) monthly.

2855   THEOLOGIE et pastorale au Rwanda et au Burundi, v.1- 1961-
        Bujumbura, (B.P. 1390) bimonthly.
        Roman Catholic journal containing theological articles
        and news items on religion in Africa.

2856   UGANDA church review, No.1- 1960-   Kampala, Uganda
        Diocesan Association, (P.O. Box 56) semiannual.

2857   UNIVERSITIES' Mission to Central Africa: Report. London,
        S.W.1 Annual.
        Includes financial and other information on the
        dioceses of Tanzania, Malawi and Zambia.

2858   VIVANTE Afrique. Namur, Editions Grands Lacs (14 chaussee
        de Charleroi) illus., bimonthly.
        Reviews missionary activities of the Peres blancs d'
        Afrique and the soeurs blanches.

2859   ZEITSCHARIFT fur Missionswissenschaft und Religionwissen-
        schaft. v.1- 1911- Munster, Verlag Aschandorff.

Cambier, J., 850

Cameron, J, 2495

Cameron, W.M., 2496

Campbell, Dugald, 2497

Campbell, John, 2498

Campor, Alexander Priestley, 298

Camps, Arnulf, 851

Capon, M.G., 1412

Capovilla, Agostino, 1459

Caprasse, P, 835

Caquot, Andre, 133711338

Cardenso, Julio Porro
    see
        Porro Cardenso, Julio

Cardew, C.A., 1086

Cardoso, Carlos Lopes, 789

Carlson, Lois, 853

Carlyle, J.E., 2499

Carpenter, George W., 299, 725, 852

Carrington, John F., 300

Caroll, Kevin, 301, 2047-2049

Carouge, Alfred de
    see
        De Carouge, Alfred

Carter, Fay, 1497

Casalis, Eugene Arnaud, 2352

Case, S.J., 11

Cason, John Walter, 1971

Casteele, J.J. Van de,
    see
        Van De Casteele, J.J.

Catholic directory of East Africa, 2818

Catholic directory of Southern Africa, 2819

Catholic morror, 2820

Catholic voice, 2821

Catrice, Paul, 726

Caulk, R.A., 1339

Caulker, D.H., 2306

Cave, Sigrid, 1207

Cawood, Leslie, 2500

Cazet, Jean Baptiste, 2377

Cereti, Giovanni, 1702

Cerulli, Enrico, 1340

Champagne, Gabriel, 1786

Champion, George, 2502-2504

Charsley, Simon, 1498

Chauleur, Pierre, 61

Chery, H.C., 1208

Chesterman, C.C., 854

Chicago, 12

Chick, Jonathan, 2051

Childs, Gladwyn, M. 790

Childs, S.H., 304

Ching, Donald, S. 305

Chirenje, J. Mutero, 1144

Chirgwin, A.M., 306

Chirnside, A., 1087

De Waal Nakefijt, Annemarie, 76.

De Waele, Frank, 887

De Wilson, George, 1786

De Witte, Jehan, 888

Diangenga, J., 889

Dickson, Kwesi A., 1651,1787,1901

Dickson, Mora, 2525

Dieu, Leon, 890

Dickson Kwesi, 336-337

Dike, K.O., 2068

Dilworth, Joan, 2069

Di Martino, A., 1571

Djoro, Ernest Amos, 1931-1932

Dlen, B.S., 2526

Dodge, Ralph Edward, 2527

Dodson, James R., 891

Doens, Irene, 1263

Doerr, L., 1503

Doï, A.R.I., 2235-2236

Doig, Andrew B., 338

Dominion Sister, 1152

Donovan, V.J., 343-344,1415

Donohugh, T.S., 1974

Doornbos, Martin R., 1501

Dos Santos, Edoard, 2415

Dougall, James W.C., 77-78, 339-342,1416

Douglas, Arthur Jeffreys, 1089

Doutreloux, Albert, 892-894

Dovlo, E.K. Yevuga, 1788-1791

Drake, St. Clair, 345

Drewal, Henry John, 1975

Dreyer, A., 2355,2528-2529

Dreyfus, Francine, 2530

Drum call., 2829

D' Souza, Jerome, 346

Dubb, A.A., 347-2531

Duckworth, E.H., 2070

Duff, H.L., 1090

Duffy, T. Gavan
see
Gavan Duffy, T.

Dugmore, D.P., 2532

Duignan, Peter, 13, 15

Dunbar, Joseph Fulton, 1976

Douncan, Hall, 348, 2533

Dunstone, A.S., 79

Du Plessis, J., 733,1210,2534-2542

Durojaiye, J., 2071

Du Toit, H.D.A., 2538-2539

Dzobo, N.K., 1792

Earthy, E. Dora, 349

Eberhardt, Jacqueline, 2543-2544

Eby, Omar, 80

Eca, Filipe Gastao de Moura, 16

Edmondson, L., 351

Edmunds, A., 2545

Edo National Church of God., 2074

Edwards, G.E., 2616

Egah, James M., 2075

Ehret, C., 1264

Eiselen, W.M., 2546

Ekechi, Felix K., 2076-2078

Ekit, Richmael, 2079

Ekollo, Pasteur, 352

Ekwa, M., 81

Ifemesia, C.C., 2127

Ige, Oye, 2128

Iglesias Ortega, Luis Maria, 914

Igwe, George Egemba, 2129

Ikechiuku, Joseph, 2130

Ikime, Obaro, 2131

Iliffe, J., 1587

Illogu, Edmund C., 2132-2137

Imray, Elizabeth, 102

Ingvarsson, B., 1589

Insight and opinion, 2835

International African Institute, 23

International Missionary Council, 425, 742, 1824

International review of missions, 2836

Inter-Racial Conference of Church Leaders, 2600

Inyang, P.E.M., 2138

Irvine, Cecilia, 916, 1421

Irving, Dr., 2139

Isenberg, Karl Wilhelm, 1363

Isichei, Elizabeth, 2141-2143

Iwuagwu, A.O., 2144

Iyala, N.B., 1668

Jabavu, Davidson D.T., 2601-2601

Jack, James W., 1101

Jackson, Rex, 1825-1826

Jacobsson, Per-Olof, 917

Jacobson, Stiv, 1669

Jacottet, E., 2603-2604

Jadin, Louis, 918-921

James, E.O., 105

Jamieson, Gladys, 1245

Jansen, G.J., 2606

Janssen, T.M., 922

Jasper, Gerhard, 106, 1276

Jassy, Marie-France Perrin see Perrin-Jassy, Marie-France

Jeanroy, Vincent, 923

Jehu-Appiah, Metapoly Moses, 1827

Jenkins, D., 744

Jenkins, Paul, 1828

Johanssen, Ernst, 1277

Johnson, A.F., 24

Johnson, Hildegard Binder, 426-427

Johnson, Howard A., 107

Johnson, Joseph A., 108

Johnson, T.B.A., 2145

Johnson, Walton, R., 1246

Johnson, William Pervical, 428

Johnston, G.D., 2147

Johnston, Geoffrey, 2146

Johnston, J.W., 1473

Joinet, B.A., 1586

Jones, A.M., 658

Jones, Elizabeth Brown, 109

Jones, F.M., 429

Jones, J.H.R., 2605

Jones, Thomas Jesse, 430, 1278

Jones, William R., 110

INDEX

Shaw, Trevor, 1681

Sheen, Fulton, J., 174

Shejavali, Abisai, 624

Shelton, A.J., 2253

Shenk, Wilbert T., 625

Shepherd, R.H.W., 2516

Sheppard, W.H., 1035

Sherrod, Jane, 1082

Shaw, Paul, 2712

Shaw, W., 2713-2714

Shepherd, R.H.W., 2516, 2717

Shepperson, George, 2715-2716

Shewmaker, Stan, 1249

Shinnie, P.L., 1480

Shorter, A., 628-634, 1617-1619

Shoup, Hazel, 2338

Shropshire, D.W.T., 2718

Sibley, James L., 1992

Sibree, James, 2406-2407

Sicard, S. Von
  see
  Von Sicard, S.,
Sierra Leone Freeman, 2848

Sierra Leone Messenger, 2849

Siddique, M.M., 2792

Silva, Antonio da, 2425-2426

Silva, Maria da Conceicao, 2427

Silva, Manuel Ferreira da, 2428

Simpson, I.H., 2339

Simpson, George E., 2255

Sinda, Martial, 1036-1037

Singer, Kurt D., 1082

Sintim-Misa, G.K., 1891

Siordet, J.E., 2371

Sirven, Pierre, 1961

Sithole, Ndabaningi, 635-636

Skolaster, Hermann, 1714-1715

Slade, R., 1038-1041

Slageren,J. Van
  see
  Van Slageren, J.

Slater, Eleanor C., 1682

Slevin, Thomas B., 637

Sloan, W.W., 1548

Smalley, Stephen, 175

Smart, John, 396

Smart, John Karefa-
  see
  Karefa-Smart, John

Smedjebacka, Henrik, 1621

Smith, A.C.S., 1202-1203

Smith, Anthony, 1622-1623

Smith, Charles Spencer, 176

Smith, E.W., 177, 638-640, 1178, 1892

Smith, Edgar H., 2256

Smith, Edwin William, 2359, 2719

Smith, Judson, 178, 641

Smith, N. Langford, 1311

Smith, Noel J., 1893-1894

Smith, Robert S., 2257

Smoker, E.W., 1312

Smyke, Raymond, 642

Society of African Missions, 179

Sodepax Conference on the Churches in Development, Planning and Action, Limuru, Kenya, 1971, 1313

456

Willis, J.J., 705, 1448, 2797

Willis, R.G., 1631

Wills, A.J., 782

Wilmore, Gayraud S., 203

Wilson, Bryan R., 1449

Wilson, George de
  see
    De Wilson, George

Wilson, Frank T., 706

Wilson, H.S., 2342

Wilson, J. Michael, 1912

Wilson, Monica, 2742

Wilson, William J., 707-709

Wilson, Thomas Ernest, 802

Wilson, George Herbert, 783

Wiltgen, Ralph M., 1913

Wing, J. Van, 1070

Wingert, Norman A., 1204

Winspear, Canon Frank, 1135

Wirgman, Augustus Theodore, 2743

Wishdale, Robert Leonard, 1136

Witte, Baron Jehan de, 1069

Wobo, M. Sam, 2294

Wood, Arthur S., 2343

Wold, Joseph C., 1996

Wood, A.V., 2745

Wood, Cecil Thomas, 2746

Wood, Michael, 2747

Wood, Paul, 1966

Woodstock Conference, March
  1967, 204

Work, Monroe N., 42

World Council of Churches, 2744

World Student Christian
  Federation, 710

Worsley, Peter M., 784

Wovenu, C.K.N., 1914

Wright, Marcia, 711, 1632-1633

Wright, S., 1398

Wrigley, C.C., 1564

Wright, Charlotte, 2748

Wrong, Margaret, 464, 712

Wyllie, Robert W., 1915-1916

Yannoulatos, Anastasios, 1450

Yates, Walter Ladell, 1691

Ydewalle, Charles d' 205

Yeboa-Dankwa, J., 2795

Youell, George, 1692

Young, T. Cullen, 714

Zeitz, Leonard, 713

Zola, E., 1071

Zoungrana, Etienne,

Zoungrana, Etienne, 2349

REF
AAC

A C BILBREW 323

FOR LIBRARY USE ONLY